MW00774405

REORGANIZING GOVERNMENT

Reorganizing Government

A Functional and Dimensional Framework

Alejandro E. Camacho *and* Robert L. Glicksman

NEW YORK UNIVERSITY PRESS
New York

NEW YORK UNIVERSITY PRESS
New York
www.nyupress.org

References to Internet websites (URLs) were accurate at the time of writing. Neither the author nor New York University Press is responsible for URLs that may have expired or changed since the manuscript was prepared.

Library of Congress Cataloging-in-Publication Data
Names: Camacho, Alejandro E., author. | Glicksman, Robert L., author.
Title: Reorganizing government : a functional and dimensional framework /
Alejandro E. Camacho and Robert L. Glicksman.
Description: New York : New York University Press, 2019. | Also available as an ebook. |
Includes bibliographical references and index.
Identifiers: LCCN 2018043745| ISBN 9781479829675 (cl ; alk. paper) |
ISBN 1479829676 (cl ; alk. paper)
Subjects: LCSH: Administrative agencies—United States—Reorganization. |
Decentralization in government—Law and legislation—United States. |
Interagency coordination—United States. | Delegated legislation—United States. |
Federal government—United States. | Authority. | United States—Politics and
government—2017–
Classification: LCC KF5407 .C36 2019 | DDC 352.3/670973—dc23
LC record available at https://lccn.loc.gov/2018043745

New York University Press books are printed on acid-free paper, and their binding materials are chosen for strength and durability. We strive to use environmentally responsible suppliers and materials to the greatest extent possible in publishing our books.

Manufactured in the United States of America

10 9 8 7 6 5 4 3 2 1

Also available as an ebook

To Kathleen, Santiago, Nicolas, and Elisa

A.E.C.

To Emily, Jaclyn, Zack, and Bertie

R.L.G.

CONTENTS

ABBREVIATIONS USED IN THE TEXT

ACES American Clean Energy and Security Act of 2009

AMS Agricultural Marketing Service

APA Administrative Procedure Act

APHIS Animal and Plant Health Inspection Service

ARS Agricultural Research Service

BACT best available control technology

CAA Clean Air Act

CDC Centers for Disease Control and Prevention

CDR Carbon dioxide removal

CEA Commodity Exchange Act

CEQ Council on Environmental Quality

CFMA Commodity Futures Modernization Act

CFPB Consumer Financial Protection Bureau

CFTC Commodity Futures Trading Commission

CFTC Act Commodity Futures Trading Commission Act of 1974

CIA Central Intelligence Agency

CPP Clean Power Plan

CRS Congressional Research Service

CWA Clean Water Act

DCI Director of Central Intelligence

DCO derivatives clearing organization

DEA Drug Enforcement Administration

DHS Department of Homeland Security

DIA Defense Intelligence Agency

DNI Director of National Intelligence

DoD Department of Defense

DOE Department of Energy

DOJ US Department of Justice

EA environmental assessment

EIS environmental impact statement

EPA Environmental Protection Agency

ERS Economic Research Service

ESA Endangered Species Act of 1973

FAA Federal Aviation Administration

FBI Federal Bureau of Investigation

FDA Food and Drug Administration

FDIC Federal Deposit Insurance Corporation

FEMA Federal Emergency Management Agency

FFSMA FDA Food Safety Modernization Act

FIP federal implementation plan

FRB Federal Reserve Board

FRS Federal Reserve System

FSA Financial Services Authority (UK)

FSIS Food Safety and Inspection Service

FSOC Financial Stability Oversight Council

FTC   Federal Trade Commission

FWS   US Fish and Wildlife Service

GAO   Government Accountability Office

GHG   greenhouse gas

GIPSA   Grain Inspection, Packers, and Stockyards Administration

HHS   Department of Health and Human Services

HSA   Homeland Security Act of 2002

IMF   International Monetary Fund

IRTPA   Intelligence Reform and Terrorism Prevention Act

ITS   incidental take statement

NAAQS   National Ambient Air Quality Standards

NAS   National Academy of Sciences

NASS   National Agricultural Statistics Service

NCTC   National Counterterrorism Center

NEPA   National Environmental Policy Act of 1969

NHTSA   National Highway Traffic Safety Administration

NMFS   National Marine Fisheries Service

NOAA   National Oceanic and Atmospheric Administration

NSA   National Security Agency

NSPS   New Source Performance Standards

OCC   Office of the Comptroller of the Currency

ODNI   Office of the Director of National Intelligence

OFR   Office of Financial Research

OIRA   Office of Information and Regulatory Affairs

OMB   Office of Management and Budget

ONDI Office of the Director of National Intelligence

OTC over-the-counter

OTS Office of Thrift Supervision

RCRA Resource Conservation and Recovery Act

RPA reasonable and prudent alternative

SEC Securities and Exchange Commission

SIFI "systemically important" financial institution

SIP state implementation plan

SMCRA Surface Mining Control and Reclamation Act

SRM solar radiation management

SRO self-regulatory organization

TBEL technology-based effluent limitation

TMDL total maximum daily load

UNFCCC United Nations Framework Convention on Climate Change

USDA US Department of Agriculture

USGS US Geological Survey

WMD weapons of mass destruction

WQS water quality standards

LIST OF FIGURES

Introduction

Midway through its second year, the Trump administration, with great fanfare, rolled out a plan recommending a reorganization of the federal government.[1] The administration touted the reform plan as "a cornerstone" for making "the Federal Government more responsive and accountable to the American people."[2] An official at the Office of Management and Budget (OMB), who helped draft the plan, called it an audacious rallying cry for small government.[3] The President pronounced that it was the latest step in his administration's efforts to "improve and streamline the Federal Government," which included reducing its footprint and "repealing a historic number of regulations."[4]

The Trump reorganization plan is just the latest in a long line of similar efforts to urge alterations in the structure of administrative governance. As the plan notes, beginning with President Harding, "Nearly every new administration has sought to enhance and streamline the Government bureaucracy to better align with policy and efficiency priorities."[5] Some of these efforts, like Trump's plan, have been fueled by a desire to reduce the scope of regulation and the bureaucracy needed to implement it. The post–World War II Hoover Commission, for example, aimed to constrain the post–New Deal expanded administrative state through a series of proposed organization changes.[6] Ronald Reagan's creation of the Office of Information and Regulatory Affairs within the OMB to provide centralized oversight of the issuance of regulations by other agencies[7] also had a deregulatory tenor.[8] The Clinton administration's National Partnership for Reinventing Government, while not driven by a desire to deregulate, nevertheless sought to reorganize the federal bureaucracy to achieve greater regulatory efficiency and effectiveness by reducing the number and size of agencies.[9]

A common thread in these and many other restructuring initiatives appears to be a fundamental absence of a thorough and accurate understanding of the various different components and dimensions of intergovernmental relationships. Modern regulatory problems, in particular, transcend conventional jurisdictional boundaries and raise unprecedented levels of complexity. The Government Accountability Office (GAO), in the wake of the Trump reorganization plan, deemed governmental reform and reorganization "a major endeavor" and "an immensely complex activity."[10] Governments and agencies routinely manage problems that intersect with those of other institutions, requiring them to regularly interact with each other. While a robust literature has developed examining government agencies and various aspects of their organization, few have comprehensively analyzed the structures and relationships among government institutions.[11] To be sure, for centuries observers have explored important aspects of government institutional relationships, especially in the context of federalism.[12] We suggest, however, that these discussions have focused on particular elements of the problem, such as whether authority should be centralized or overlapping, without providing a systematic framework for characterizing, understanding, and assessing the full array of intergovernmental relations.

A. A Novel Framework

We proceed on the premise that institutional structures can significantly influence the fate of regulatory programs. As James Q. Wilson has put it, "Organization matters, even in government agencies."[13] And organizational systems are key determinants of bureaucratic success or failure.[14] Many governance challenges arise from the way government institutions exercising regulatory or management authority relate to one another. Our book advances a novel framework for assessing how governmental authority may be structured and restructured that can generate critical insights in characterizing, assessing and formulating proposals like the Trump reorganization initiative.

We believe that our approach to incorporating analysis of government organization into reform of policy-making institutions and structures is unique. Others, of course, have explored government institutional relationships. We suggest, however, that most of the efforts of those who have addressed such relationships, including the legal process school of the 1950s,[15] proponents of the "structure and process thesis,"[16] and scholars of public administration,[17] have largely focused on particular elements of the problem without providing a systematic framework for characterizing, understanding, and assessing intergovernmental relations.

Our framework offers two fundamental insights. First, it asserts that differentiating among three dimensions of authority—centralization, overlap, and coordination—is key to identifying the tradeoffs of organizational alternatives. Second, it posits that allocations of authority could and often should account for the different functions that government performs (e.g., information distribution, standard setting, planning, and enforcement). Reliance on this two-pronged framework has the potential to clarify previously obscured tradeoffs and configurations and ultimately improve the performance of government.

The kind of analytical infrastructure that our book provides is sorely needed. In its absence, inadequately understood relationships among regulatory institutions have prompted, and are likely to continue to produce, poorly designed attempts to create new regulatory programs or restructure existing ones that underperform. Past approaches to designing and assessing intergovernmental relationships have failed to appreciate, in particular, the full array of alternatives for organizing government to address human problems. These failures have contributed to mismatches between the perceived defects of existing structures and the allocations of authority chosen to replace them. We identify recurring flaws in how regulatory authority is understood and therefore distributed. We also recommend ways of thinking about government organization that should enable policymakers to structure authority to better promote public values such as effectiveness,[18] efficiency,[19] a fair distribution of the benefits and burdens of regulation,[20] and accountability.[21]

B. Illustrative Examples

To demonstrate the need for our analytical framework, we have selected an emergent proposal and a multi-decade organizational reshuffling as introductory examples. The first is the Trump administration's 2018 reorganization plan, written in response to an executive order whose goal is to "improve the efficiency, effectiveness, and accountability of the executive branch" through a government reorganization that eliminates unnecessary agencies, components, and programs.[22] The plan purports to be the outcome of a carefully conceived "Reorganization Alignment Framework" that draws on public and private sector "organizational change and strategic transformation thought leaders."[23] It states that achieving greater efficiency, effectiveness, and accountability "requires a range of transformational approaches to support reorganization" and purports to outline "a range of additional priorities and tools."[24]

Like many of the federal reorganization plans that preceded it, the Trump plan belies these claims in several ways. First, it provides no citations, evidence, or even careful analysis to support its specific reorganization recommendations.[25] Some legislators criticized the administration for failing to explain the analysis that shaped the plan, with one senator calling it "woefully short on details."[26] Second, the plan largely ignores certain dimensions of authority (such as independence)[27] and conflates them, ignoring that choices about the extent of centralization, overlap, and coordination each present a variety of different policy advantages and disadvantages.[28] Third, it does not consider in any depth whether restructuring would benefit from varying the allocation of authority by function. The Trump plan thus represents yet another reorganization proposal that ignores, confuses, and conflates the different justifications, dimensions, and functions of authority.

The plan offers what essentially amounts to a default, unsubstantiated response to virtually all restructuring challenges instead of carefully assessing reorganization options both for different functions and along each of the three dimensions we identify.[29] Even Republican legislators reacted adversely to some of the recommendations for centralization, expressing fears that they would create "bloated" and "unwieldy" bureaucracies.[30] Proposals such as those that would merge the Departments of Education and Labor were met with bipartisan opposition.[31] Indeed, in anticipation of the Trump plan, Congress, with bipartisan support, included explicit prohibitions in appropriations legislation on the expenditure of any funds to implement reorganizations like those proposed in the plan.[32]

Some of the potential adverse consequences of the kind of misguided or incomplete analysis that characterizes the Trump plan are reflected in our second introductory example, which involves a litany of reform efforts relating to the federal government's disaster response authority.

Until 1971, emergency management authority was centralized in the Office of Emergency Planning.[33] In that year, President Nixon decentralized that Office's authority by dividing it among multiple federal agencies.[34] In 1979, however, in response to critiques about inadequate coordination,[35] President Carter centralized disaster management authorities in the newly established Federal Emergency Management Agency (FEMA).[36] Ensuing critiques asserting poor coordination and mismanaged responses to high-profile disasters[37] prompted a reorganization of FEMA in 1993 that divided authority into three directorates, one each for preparedness, damage mitigation, and response and recovery.[38] Prompted by the terrorist attacks of 9/11 and criticisms that only a single agency could "connect all the dots" implicated in major disasters,[39] a fourth reorganization in 2003 consolidated FEMA into the new Department of Homeland Security (DHS).[40] Incident response authority, however, was separated and centralized in a new Preparedness Directorate within DHS.[41] In 2005, critiques of this bifurcation of disaster planning and response,[42] as well as of FEMA's abysmal performance during Hurricane Katrina,[43] prompted a fifth reorganization back toward decentralization.[44]

What is striking in this pattern of action and reaction is that most or all of the analyses involved seemed to profess concern about inadequate coordination. But instead of enhancing agency coordination authority and responsibility, policymakers generally embarked on a restructuring that moved in the opposite direction from the last one, along the centralization–decentralization dimension. Criticism of the centralization of disaster response authority in DHS,[45] coupled with FEMA's miserable performance following Katrina and other disasters,[46] suggests that decentralized but coordinated authority may hold more promise than an indirect effort to spur coordination through recalibration of the degree of centralization. Policymakers should at least have considered the tradeoffs involved in decreasing centralization but increasing coordination, as well as what forms of coordination might be more appropriate, neither of which they did in any systematic way.[47]

Moreover, in each of these reorganizations, little effort was spent considering the tradeoffs of adjusting authority over separate governmental functions (such as planning or implementation) implicated in disaster response. Few have appreciated that centralization or coordination may be more beneficial for some regulatory functions than others. It might be preferable, for example, to centralize functions for which economies of scale are most likely to be achieved (such as scientific research) or in which uniform treatment of participants in disaster management is important (such as planning the allocation of federal funding or facilities for disaster response), while retaining decentralized authority for functions (such as information analysis) for which these advantages are likely to be less important than assuring diverse regulatory approaches or the application of local or particularized expertise. Similarly, although coordinated disaster response planning and implementation generally is desirable for achieving efficient resource allocation and minimizing conflicting responses by different governmental actors, there may be instances in which the transactions costs of coordination outweigh the advantages.[48] In the rare instances when policymakers have differentiated structures according to function, they appear to have made curious choices (such as separating disaster management planning and implementation authority) and have made little effort to think through their implications.

As further illustrated through the six detailed case studies in this book, plan recommendations based on weak evidence and conflated dimensions often produce reorganizations—such as the efforts to redefine the relationships between FEMA and other components of the executive branch—that do not address identified structural problems or that otherwise miss more effective alternatives. Experience in the wake of the Homeland Security Act provides a cautionary tale, suggesting that policymakers who give short shrift to institutional design do so at their (and the public's) peril. As legislators consider whether to endorse the Trump reorganization plan or move forward with other reorganization initiatives, it is critical that they devote careful attention to the appropriate allocation of authority along multiple dimensions and consider whether functional differentiation provides the best opportunity to promote policy objectives.

C. Purposes

This book urges reliance on a transformational framework for facilitating the adoption of structural changes that mitigate rather than contribute to problematic allocations of authority. More specifically, the book has at least five purposes.

1. A Unifying Taxonomy

The book's first goal is taxonomic, or semantic. We believe that a significant source of difficulty for designing regulatory structures that are well suited to addressing social problems effectively (and for understanding why existing programs are not working effectively) is the lack of a common taxonomy. To mitigate the tendency to talk past others when debating regulatory structural reforms, chapters 1 and 2 provide a lexicon for thinking about the design of government that is clearer and more comprehensive than the terminology used in most academics' and policymakers' discussions. We distinguish between two ways to allocate authority to government institutions: by substance and by function. We also identify three dimensions of authority that establish the manner in which government institutions relate to one another. This terminology is meant to provide a common vocabulary for describing, critiquing, and, if appropriate, reforming allocations of regulatory or management authority. If people use the term *functional jurisdiction* to mean different things, for example, efforts to understand and discuss allocations of authority are likely to generate misunderstandings and crossed signals. Similarly, assessments of whether allocations reflect too much or not enough overlapping authority are not likely to be helpful if policymakers understand *overlap* to mean different things. Our typology can help foster meaningful discussion of the value of allocations of authority. In other contexts, the introduction of new vocabularies has contributed to legal and policy development. Legal realism, for example, has "influenced legal doctrine enormously," as Nourse and Shaffer have written, by shifting from common law–based to sociologically based vocabularies.[49]

2. Descriptive Insights

A second, related goal might be characterized as descriptive. The book explores the application of our allocation framework in various contexts, particularly through six case studies, three of which explore the value of differentiating allocations of authority along functional lines, and three of which consider the implications of conflating two or more dimensions. By so doing, we develop explanatory insights about the nature of interjurisdictional relations that we think demonstrate the value of the book's taxonomy.

3. Some Normative Postulates

The third goal, which follows from the first two, is more normative. In the absence of a common framework for evaluating available structural options, those who create and evaluate regulatory programs may miss the options that have the best chance of succeeding. It is likely that some institutional arrangements will be better suited to achieving identified regulatory or management goals than others. Although we offer a few generalized postulates about circumstances in which particular distributions of authority are likely to be attractive, we have neither the capacity for nor the interest in "essentializing" interjurisdictional relations—to develop a singular, universal set of rules that detail optimal, fixed allocations of authority.[50] Allocational and structural choices will largely be context-specific. At the same time, by looking generically and comparatively at interagency relationships, we believe we are able to draw insights about the effects of such relationships on agency performance that may have been missed by narrower agency, program, or case-specific evaluations conducted by policymakers and scholars.[51] A critical question that our framework seeks to illuminate is whether a proposed reallocation is reasonably designed to address the problem or problems that spurred the reorganization initiative—that is, whether there is an appropriate ends-means fit.

Although we are convinced that our approach to analyzing interagency relationships is valuable regardless of one's perspective on the value of regulation, we openly acknowledge that we are not free of our own substantive precommitments, developed in the course of our individual and joint work on environmental and natural resource management issues. These precommitments, which lean in a progressive direction, include maximizing market cost internalization to promote the equitable distribution of social benefits and burdens, as well as a greater emphasis on addressing the risks resulting from under-regulation than from over-regulation. Accordingly, our preliminary judgments about appropriate allocations will often tend to favor precautionary and proactive regulatory approaches[52] and approaches that seek to minimize regulatory capture (that is, improper influence or control by regulated entities over agencies tasked with overseeing them).[53] We also place a high value on participatory governance, though which way that preference cuts is likely to be context-driven. Decentralized decision making, for example, may provide greater opportunities for public participation, especially if authority is exercised at lower levels of government, but policymakers at that level may be more prone to capture.[54] That risk of capture may in turn support overlapping authority, especially for functions such as standard setting and enforcement, despite the duplication and inefficiencies it may create. Finally, given our concerns about capture and the risk of under-regulation that may arise from agency shirking and free-riding, we are inclined to put greater stock in coordination mechanisms than to foster independence as a means of promoting interagency competition.[55]

These precommitments certainly will not be shared by all of this book's readers, and even if they are, they will not always point to the same structural arrangements. By appreciating the potential relationships among agencies and the tradeoffs of particular allocation choices, scholars in political science, public administration, legislation, and administrative law, as well as—perhaps more importantly—legislative and executive policymakers, can compare and contrast the full range of available options, regardless of any normative preferences they may have. That kind of analysis, which at present we regard as often incomplete, can improve government programs.

4. Cultivating Empiricism

A fourth purpose of the book is to set the stage for the future accumulation of empirical evidence about which institutional arrangements work and why others fail. Naturally, we do not write on a clean slate. The legal realists' attacks in the 1920s and 1930s on legal formalism sought to, as Calabresi has written, "reshap[e] legal decision making in accordance with the emerging empirical sciences" and to afford "keener attention to actual institutional and social practices."[56] These efforts were hampered, however, by the realists' "inability to develop any kind of theoretical framework for making their empirical findings relevant to normative legal scholarship."[57]

Our book takes a page from the realists by urging greater reliance on empirical analysis in institutional design. We seek to fill some of the gaps in previous scholarship by focusing on regulatory reorganization and by offering the kind of comprehensive theoretical framework the critics have found missing in the early realist scholarship. Perhaps because a comprehensive taxonomy of government functions and dimensions of the kind we introduce has been lacking, assessments of past regulatory performance typically have not fully characterized or understood the full extent of agency structures and relationships. In chapters 3 through 8, we provide case studies in which we apply the framework introduced in chapters 1 and 2 to illustrate how an appreciation of the dynamics of intergovernmental relationships using our mode of analysis might have averted problems or improved outcomes. Our hope is that scholars and policy analysts will assess regulatory institutions using this new taxonomy and thus develop useful evidence based on practical experience about the tradeoffs of organizational alternatives in a range of contexts.

5. Promoting Adaptive Governance

A fifth and final goal is experimentalist: to advocate that policymakers integrate such analyses systematically into the design, assessment, and periodic redesign of regulatory institutions through more widespread use of adaptive governance.[58] As we explore more fully in the conclusion, we hope that scholars will rely on what we believe is a novel method of analyzing agency relationships to assess regulatory allocations. Furthermore, policy analysts and policymakers should not only use our framework in crafting allocations but also systematically integrate the assessment of allocations into the regulatory process itself. Instituting such an infrastructure would allow policymakers to learn from both successful and unsuccessful ventures and use the resulting insights to engender further reforms.[59]

Our focus on adaptive governance builds, and aims to improve on, past calls for periodic review of the operation of government. The philosophical pragmatism of the early twentieth century was grounded in "an ongoing experimental search for a durable conception of the public order."[60] Charles Lindblom's version of policy making, based on "muddling through," envisioned government reliance on "incremental steps that permit administrators to adjust decisions over time."[61] Lindblom's critics, however, bemoaned the lack of analytical rigor in this approach, warning that proponents would miss the "big picture," engage in counterproductive strategies, and miss opportunities to promote desired policies most effectively.[62] More recently, new governance scholars have embraced a form of "democratic experimentalism."[63] But that effort also differs from ours in that it has focused in part on replacing traditional regulatory methods with a more dynamic approach informed by enhanced stakeholder participation, rather than on the interagency relationships that are our concern here.[64]

The approach we recommend builds on these appeals for iterative policy making based on empirical evaluation of the ways to improve regulatory programs but does so by urging its application to resolve questions about the best ways to structure administrative government. As Nourse and Shaffer have noted, "empiricism requires experimentalism [. . .] to ground itself in the experience of how law works, and to upend assumptions that turn out to be wrong [. . .]. Experimental methods inform other empirical approaches, help test theory, and provide new, more reliable information that builds from ground level experience to reevaluate theory."[65]

We think it is critically important that policymakers engage in ongoing evaluation of agency performance and provide opportunities to adjust allocations of authority in response to changed circumstances or new information. For one thing, reorganized agencies may fail in ways that differ from those that prompted reorganization. In the wake of 9/11, for example, the federal government's capacity to respond to natural disasters appears to have been impaired when FEMA was folded into DHS, a larger entity whose priority was terrorism prevention, not disaster response.[66] A well-designed administrative regime should be capable of identifying and responding to such pathologies. Our functional and dimensional approach can assist in understanding why previous reforms created unintended consequences and in identifying appropriate solutions. The learning infrastructure that we propose in the conclusion is a critical step for embedding adaptive governance into the administrative state.

D. Audience

The primary intended audience for this book is policymakers—in particular, legislators and their policy staff, the institutional actors with the most direct influence over the choice of regulatory allocation. Yet any policymaker, including executive officials, could use this framework for assessing organizational choices, as could scholars or entities (such as GAO or the Congressional Research Service) whose responsibilities include evaluating governmental performance or organization. Even courts might find this framework useful. A court might use it in determining how a legislature intended to allocate authority based on an evaluation of which allocation choice best promotes identified statutory goals. It might be more likely to recognize authority as overlapping (such as through floor but not field preemption, for example) if evidence of legislative intent identifies the need for a redundant regulatory safety net as a core purpose of an allocation.

We understand that policymakers may not approach decisions about allocations of authority with a primary focus on which design would best achieve particular normative goals. We are not naïve enough to believe that such decisions are driven wholly, or even principally, by rational debate over the advantages and disadvantages of alternative design options. We also do not assume that policymakers are well intentioned at promoting effective regulation or that politics is irrelevant or unimportant. Political realities often pose significant obstacles to regulatory reform, even if there is a consensus that existing regimes are not working well. For one thing, congressional committee members may oppose efforts to eliminate or reduce the power of an agency over which they have jurisdiction.[67] Political partisanship may also prevent reform.[68] Although political economy is not our focus, we do acknowledge the existence of political and other practical obstacles to institutional reform and refer to them in several of the book's case studies.

We nonetheless believe that organizational choices matter, that structural choices can dictate the effectiveness of regulatory allocations of authority and that if policymakers seriously consider the impact of these choices, using a framework like the one we advance here, the performance of regulatory programs is likely to benefit. The legitimacy of US administrative law is fundamentally linked to the legislative delegation of authority to administrative agencies to advance effective governance,[69] as well as to the requirement that regulators provide reasons for policy choices or decisions related to that delegation.[70] The framework for understanding the allocations of authority we introduce seeks to build on this premise to catalyze the democratic process by fostering debate, reason giving, and deliberation as a basis for allocations of authority by policymakers. It thereby endeavors to shift the emphasis for making decisions about agency organization and relationships, at least incrementally, away from political considerations and toward policy justifications.

This book's purposes are ultimately directed at mitigating the political difficulties of achieving sensible regulatory reform, in several ways. First, a common taxonomy can help policymakers and other analysts appreciate what is at stake in reform efforts and, by helping to structure the debate, guide more attention to allocation considerations. Second, the analytical framework we provide may help policymakers identify structural options that spur fewer political roadblocks, while at the same time creating the prospects for successful reform. Third, the empirical evidence that this book may help generate could contribute to convincing policymakers that even reforms that some entrenched interests object to are worthwhile pursuits in light of evaluations of past reform efforts. Fourth, if the practice of analyzing regulatory design options in the systematic way we recommend is institutionalized as its advantages become clear, the upshot may make political considerations that pay little heed to the comparative substantive merits of available options less salient.

We also recognize that this kind of institutionalization will not be accomplished without pushback from those who stand to lose politically from particular reforms suggested by our analysis. Yet, in spite of political pressures to entrench the status quo, reforms—sometimes dramatic ones—do occur, and with considerable frequency. The creation of the Environmental Protection Agency (EPA) and the Department of Energy in the 1970s, the creation of DHS after 9/11, and the adoption of the Dodd-Frank Wall Street Reform and Consumer Protection Act (known as the Dodd-Frank Act or simply Dodd-Frank) in 2010 are all examples of reallocations of authority that proceeded in the face of pressures to retain the status quo, even if the reforms ultimately adopted were not unaffected by those pressures.

E. A Few Caveats

We should make clear that we are not arguing that institutional design choices of the kind we promote here are sufficient to guarantee regulatory success. First, admittedly limited empirical evidence exists at this time to assess the value of our approach. Structural changes that work well in some contexts may be less helpful in others. Second, as we emphasize throughout the book, organizational choices affect regulatory values, and relevant values may conflict. A structural design solution that promotes efficiency, for example, may appear to be unfair. A move to enhance effectiveness may impair accountability. Alternative allocations may advance fairness at the expense of efficiency, or advance accountability at the expense of effectiveness. Our analytical framework can clarify the manner in which allocation choices will affect regulatory values, but policymakers will have to prioritize values in the event of conflict.

Third, how authority is allocated among regulatory institutions is likely only one factor that shapes the efficacy of government programs. Even a well-structured allocation may not succeed if the scope or tools of authority that are allocated to the implementing institutions are deficient, if government personnel are hostile or indifferent to the programs they implement, or if legislators fail to provide sufficient resources to allow effective administration. Although some configurations of authority may be capable of combating shirking by regulators or minimizing inefficient use of limited resources, we do not attempt to comprehensively address those sources of regulatory failure, which are covered well elsewhere.[71] Nevertheless, we believe that poorly designed programs are likely to create significant barriers to success. Our aim here is to provide a framework for minimizing those barriers.

Two additional provisos are appropriate. To begin with, this book does not purport to be a comprehensive study of all aspects of regulatory design. We have chosen to focus on the capacity of changes in the structure of intra- and interagency relationships to improve government performance. As such, we do not engage the debate over whether policymakers should rely on private rather than public law to address social problems[72] or should rely more heavily on market-based mechanisms when implementing regulatory problems.[73] Moreover, as we have written elsewhere, we are aware that institutional design choices will be significantly shaped by the adaptive capacity of the background legal system in which they operate.[74] For example, constitutional provisions relating to separation of powers and federalism may constrain realistic organizational options in the United States.[75] The thrust of this book, however, is to help policymakers choose, from among the constitutionally permissible options, those that are best suited to promoting substantive policy goals. We have directed our attention to the relationship between regulatory institutions, which we regard as vital to the success of government but also as, to date, insufficiently explored.

In addition, it is worth acknowledging that the focus of the book is primarily on administrative structures within the federal government of the United States, and on the relationship of federal to state-level structures. Nonetheless, we believe that our framework is useful for evaluating regulatory structures in other jurisdictions or at other scales of government. Indeed, we touch on the relevance of international law to organizational choices (for example, the discussion of climate change geoengineering in chapter 9) and hope that our framework will spur comparative evaluation of government organization in other nations.

F. Road Map

The book proceeds in nine chapters. Chapter 1 distinguishes between substantive and functional allocations of decision-making authority. The former involves defining an agency's jurisdiction on the basis of the subject matter it is authorized to regulate or manage. The latter entails defining an agency's responsibilities, or tasks, in functional terms. Different agencies, for example, may be in charge of planning, standard setting, or enforcement, even if their authorities relate to a common subject matter. We believe that the possibility of adjusting authority along functional lines is underappreciated. Our book points out how doing so—for example, by creating overlapping authority for some functions but not others—may provide the advantages of that (or some other) dimension of authority while minimizing its disadvantages.

Chapter 2 describes the three dimensions along which policymakers may allocate substantive or functional regulatory authority. Authority may be centralized or decentralized, it may be distinct or overlapping, and it may be coordinated or independent. Although we describe these dimensions in terms of their polar opposites, each represents a spectrum of possibilities. Notwithstanding the well-trodden nature of at least one of these dimensions (centralization–decentralization, around which longstanding federalism debates revolve), policymakers and scholars routinely ignore one or more of these dimensions when considering how to allocate authority. Even those who explore more than one dimension habitually confuse and conflate them. That kind of misstep is highly problematic because it can result in the identification of a structural problem along one dimension but the adoption of a solution along an entirely different dimension, thereby thwarting effective regulation. It can also prevent accurate assessment of how the three dimensions interact with one another in a particular context. Chapter 2 therefore seeks to provide a common lexicon to facilitate informed organizational choices that reduce the risk of program failure.

The remainder of the book demonstrates the value of thinking about government organization in terms of the substantive–functional divide and along three different but interrelated dimensions of regulatory authority. Chapters 3 through 8 present detailed case studies drawn from disparate areas of government regulation or management that include food safety, pollution control, natural resource management, financial regulation, and protection of national security. The first three of those chapters explore how differentiating government authority based on function may enhance regulatory effectiveness. Chapter 3 addresses functional differentiation along the centralization–decentralization dimension, using food safety regulation as an example of policymakers' failure to appreciate the value of centralizing certain functions but not others. Chapter 4 focuses on the overlap–distinctness dimension, using EPA's regulation of polluting activities to illustrate the value of providing greater overlap for some regulatory functions than for others. Chapter 5 compares Congress's more effective use of certain functional distinctions along the coordination–independence dimension under the Endangered Species Act with those under the National Environmental Policy Act. Each case study illustrates how attending to functional jurisdiction more accurately characterizes the relationship among governmental institutions and reveals opportunities for harnessing the advantages of each pole of a dimension while minimizing its disadvantages.

The second group of case studies illustrates how dimensional conflation can lead to suboptimal regulatory programs. Chapter 6 explains how conflation of the overlap–distinctness and centralization–decentralization dimensions has contributed to an ineffective regulation of securities and futures that has never been adequately addressed, including most recently in the Dodd-Frank Act. Chapter 7 evaluates the ill effects of conflating the coordination–independence and centralization-decentralization dimensions, using changes in the allocation of the authority to gather and assess intelligence information in the wake of 9/11 to highlight the value of a crisp delineation of these dimensions of authority. Finally, chapter 8 deals with conflation of the coordination–independence and overlap–distinctness dimensions. It relies on regulation of the safety and soundness of depository institutions to suggest that if Congress had appreciated the differences between those two dimensions, it may have produced more effective regulatory structures than it adopted in Dodd-Frank.

In each case study, we show how the failure of policymakers to appreciate the impact of situating authority along each dimension, or of differentiating allocations on a functional rather than substantive basis, may undermine structural reform efforts. These chapters explain how an evaluation conforming to our analytical framework could have identified alternative allocations of authority with greater promise for achieving prescribed policy goals, avoided the adoption of unresponsive solutions, or reduced political resistance to allocational reforms. Application of this framework would also have allowed policymakers to weigh more clearly the policy tradeoffs of alternative allocation choices. Although the optimal allocations of authority will inevitably be contextual, we are able to draw on the case studies to develop at least a tentative set of postulates that may assist in future reorganizational initiatives. We emphasize, however, that while the book is meant to provide a working road map to guide such efforts, it does not purport to provide a grand equation capable of calculating a prescribed solution for each and every puzzle of reorganization.

Chapter 9 provides an opportunity to apply our analytical framework in a more integrated fashion. Whereas the six case study chapters all (necessarily but somewhat artificially) focus on exploring a particular aspect of functional or dimensional allocations of authority, this chapter more holistically illustrates the advantages of a dimensional and functional analysis. We use global climate change—an area in which both the need for and shape of government intervention remain contested—as a capstone analysis of our approach to thinking about the distribution of government power. The chapter considers how allocations of authority may influence the effectiveness of regulation in three discrete but related areas of climate change governance: mitigation (greenhouse gas emission reduction), adaptation (managing climate change effects), and geoengineering (large-scale climate manipulation). Because each governance area presents different challenges, disparate allocations of authority, both in relation to function and along the three dimensions, are likely to be appropriate. Chapter 9 also explores more fully a point noted in earlier chapters: that situating authority along a single dimension may alleviate or exacerbate the ill effects of structural choices along another dimension. Thus, the best solution may be to situate authority at a point along one dimension that in isolation fails to maximize its advantages, but that allows positioning along another dimension to compensate for any adverse consequences of failing to push further toward one end of the first dimension.

Government is not perfect and never will be. But by structuring government institutions carefully, policymakers can create mechanisms for addressing social problems that are positioned to work well in ways that are consistent with important social values. We wrote this book to provide a framework that relies on past experience to evaluate regulatory problems, and to suggest solutions that have the potential to alleviate regulatory failures, even if it is impossible to eliminate them. Scholars and policy analysts can use this framework to evaluate which approaches have worked and which have not. And policymakers can and should integrate a more adaptive governance framework to craft, evaluate, and adjust policies over time to better achieve regulatory or management goals. This book explains how to do so.

PART I

An Analytical Framework

Chapter 1

Substantive and Functional Jurisdiction

Scholars and policymakers have devoted considerable attention to the ways governmental authority can or should be allocated within and among governmental bodies. Rarely, however, do such discussions involve a detailed and complete examination of the scope of authority for each regulatory actor. In this chapter, we identify the different types of regulatory or management authority vested in agencies by legislatures or executive branch officials, such as the President or heads of government departments. In so doing, the chapter highlights a key but underappreciated distinction between the subject matter authority of regulators and the locus of control over different governmental tasks.

In each allocation of regulatory authority, there is not only a substantive allocation but also a functional one. First, an agency's jurisdiction can be determined on the basis of the subject matter it is authorized to regulate or manage (such as activities that result in air pollution or mineral extraction on public lands). As we describe in detail in section A, we call this *substantive jurisdiction*. Second, and perhaps less obviously, jurisdiction can be defined in terms of the functions an agency performs (such as planning or enforcement). We label this *functional jurisdiction* and explore it more fully in section B.

Figure 1.1 provides a straightforward, if simplistic, illustration of the difference between functional and substantive authority by looking at a single administrative agency. It shows how that agency might be primarily organized internally along substantive or functional lines. Assume an agency has regulatory authority to monitor, set standards for, license, and enforce compliance over the trading of financial securities by issuers, exchanges, and investment advisors. That regulator might be organized into separate substantive divisions—each respectively regulating issuers, exchanges, investment companies, and investment advisors through monitoring, standard setting, licensing, and enforcement functions. Alternatively, departments might be divided according to the

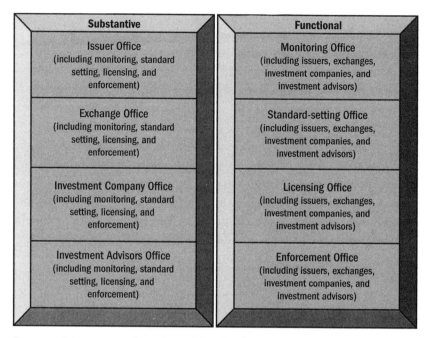

Figure 1.1. Intra-agency substantive and functional organization.

governmental functions they undertake, such as monitoring, standard setting, licensing, and enforcement, without regard to the identity of the regulated entity. In both circumstances, the agency has been allocated the same substantive and functional jurisdiction, but in the former case its subdivisions are divided based on substantive jurisdiction while in the latter case they are divided according to functional jurisdiction.

To take another example, national pollution control authority might be (and, in the United States, often is) apportioned into substantive silos according to the particular type of resource (e.g., air, water, or solid waste) targeted for protection. Such authority, however, might also be divided into functional categories according to the governmental activity at issue (e.g., standard setting, permitting, and enforcement).

Of course, most configurations of governmental authority are more complex than these simple examples, and the functional–substantive framework helps reveal these intricacies and their implications. Most government organizations have authority over a segment of many, though often not all, of the possible functions for a particular substantive area. And government organizations are quite commonly composed of both substantive and functional divisions. More significantly, a government organization's particular mix of substantive jurisdiction and suite of functions will inevitably coincide with, and/or relate to, those of other government organizations. Different agencies may be responsible for performing discrete tasks within the same substantive area. Multiple agencies with the same substantive jurisdiction may also be assigned some of the same tasks as others within that area.

Precisely because of these complexities, affording attention to functional jurisdiction in addition to substantive jurisdiction provides insights about the policy and value tradeoffs among available options for allocating government authority that may otherwise be obscured. In characterizing governmental jurisdiction, primary attention tends to be given to evaluating the scope of an agency's responsibilities based on the scope of the substantive authority of the governmental entity. However, regulatory authority is also consistently (though often only implicitly) apportioned based on the function or functions that a particular governmental institution may exercise. As illustrated in chapters 3, 4, and 5, policymakers' neglect, either of the functional component of delegated authority or of the ways in which an agency's substantive and functional jurisdictions interact with one another and with the jurisdictions of other relevant actors, can easily thwart those policymakers' regulatory or management goals. The following two sections describe the parameters of substantive and functional jurisdiction in greater detail.

A. Substantive Jurisdiction

Substantive jurisdiction is perhaps the most elementary component for understanding allocations of agency authority to manage social problems addressed by regulatory programs. Congress grants to administrative agencies limited substantive authority to regulate or manage specific social issues or problems. The protection of federal workplace health and safety, for example, falls within the purview of the Occupational Safety and Health Administration. The US Department of Agriculture oversees the agriculture industry. Transportation infrastructure is covered by the Federal Highway Administration and the Department of Transportation. Immigration is supervised by US Citizenship and

Immigration Services. The Centers for Disease Control and Prevention conduct research and coordinate prevention measures for disease. The Federal Emergency Management Agency is charged with disaster planning and management.

In environmental regulation, administrative authority is typically restricted to regulation or management of a particular environmental resource (such as clean air or clean water). Indeed, substantive authority may be further divided based on particular features or components of a protected resource or "medium." Surface water quality, for example, is regulated by the US Environmental Protection Agency (EPA) and designated state water quality agencies (such as California's State Water Resources Control Board), while the allocation of water supply falls within the domains of various federal, state, and local water resources agencies (such as the federal Bureau of Reclamation, the California Department of Water Resources, and the Metropolitan Water District of Southern California). Similarly, the Interior Department's US Fish and Wildlife Service (FWS) has jurisdiction over management of terrestrial or fresh water (including endangered or threatened) species, while the Commerce Department's National Marine Fisheries Service manages marine species. Public land management is divided based on particular land management goals: the National Park Service and the FWS being charged primarily with the duty to preserve natural resources and provide recreational opportunities, while the US Forest Service and the Bureau of Land Management are required to promote a broader range of multiple uses of the lands under their jurisdiction.[1]

Division of authority on the basis of subject matter is not unique to pollution control or natural resources law. The Food and Drug Administration generally regulates some food products, while the United States Department of Agriculture's Food Safety and Inspection Service has jurisdiction over other foods (meat, poultry, and processed egg products).[2] The Dodd-Frank Act[3] vested in one agency the authority to regulate providers of consumer financial products and services, including insured banks, savings and loans, and large credit unions. But it delegated to a different agency regulatory control over smaller depository institutions, and it retained authority in still other agencies to regulate transactions in securities and commodities futures.[4] Meanwhile, informational privacy, as Bamberger and Mulligan have described it, "is governed by a variety of different laws, administered by different agencies [...] setting forth divergent requirements governing the treatment of information by type and business sector."[5]

Substantive authority may be delegated to a particular agency in recognition of the technical expertise that it may bring to bear on the regulatory problem. Expertise in atmospheric chemistry, for example, is useful for understanding and regulating air quality; an ecology background is useful for managing biological resources; a public health or medical background for disease prevention; and forestry expertise for forest management.[6] California has vested multiple agencies with the authority to regulate different aspects of the electric utility industry in order to reflect the expertise of each agency.[7] Similarly, scholars have urged an expansion of the Copyright Office's authority over the complex and dynamic issues in which it has expertise.[8]

B. Functional Jurisdiction

The academic literature often focuses on agencies' substantive jurisdiction, but the manner in which Congress and other policymakers allocate authority along functional lines may also influence the extent to which a regulatory program achieves statutory goals. Governmental authority may be allocated or analyzed according to the particular regulatory activities or tasks in which the agency is authorized to engage. Thus, although a statute may delegate to several agencies the authority to regulate a particular set of private activities (so that the agencies share substantive jurisdiction in that regulatory area), each agency may be in charge of a particular aspect of the regulatory program. One agency, for example, may be responsible for collecting information needed to make regulatory decisions, while another may be charged with using that information to adopt regulatory standards that constrain private conduct. Still another agency may be in charge of enforcing standards through litigation against regulated parties.

We use the word *function* to refer to the nature of the authority vested in, or the role assigned to, a government organization, as opposed to the substantive subject matter of that organization's delegated authority. As listed in Figure 1.2, we categorize agency functions to include funding; research, data generation, and ambient monitoring; information

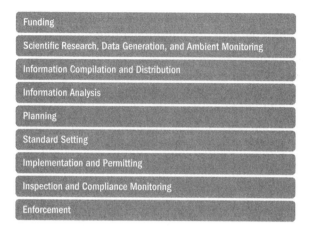

Figure 1.2. Categories of functional jurisdiction.

compilation and distribution; information analysis; planning; standard setting; implementation and permitting; inspection and compliance monitoring; and enforcement. We define these categories as follows:

- *Funding.* This term refers to the provision of financial resources (toward an activity, social need, program, or project) by the same or another organization or government.[9] Clear examples include the funding of private and public research and education activities by the National Science Foundation and the National Institutes of Health[10] and the many federal grant programs to states and local governments.[11]

- *Scientific research, data generation, and ambient monitoring.* This function refers to a range of governmental activities involving the systematic investigation into and production of materials and sources to establish facts and reach new conclusions relevant to a particular issue. For example, the United States Geological Survey is the sole bureau of the Department of the Interior charged with engaging in scientific research "about natural resource conditions, issues, and problems,"[12] while the National Oceanic and Atmospheric Administration (NOAA) includes research laboratories, the Office of Weather and Air Quality, and the Office of Ocean Exploration and Research.[13] This function may include both baseline[14] and ambient monitoring.[15] The National Aeronautics and Space Administration[16] and NOAA[17] both routinely engage in ambient monitoring, for instance.

- *Information compilation and distribution.* This function refers to the collection and dissemination of information to be made available and possibly used by the same or other private or public actors. The Secretary of Transportation, for example, is required by statute to establish, operate, and maintain a national clearinghouse for records relating to the testing of commercial motor vehicle operators for alcohol and controlled substances.[18] Similarly, the Department of Transportation's Research and Innovative Technology Administration maintains the Transportation and Climate Change Clearinghouse whose role is, among other things, to share information.[19] This function might also include activities such as the power to convene interested stakeholders to gather information, ensuring the security (i.e., non-dissemination) of information, or media or congressional relations.[20]
- *Information analysis.* This term refers to governmental examination and/or assessment of information or research, whether or not it is generated, compiled, or disseminated by the particular governmental unit. For example, federal agencies proposing significant new regulations must analyze and compare their costs and benefits; the Office of Information and Regulatory Affairs must then review that analysis and return the regulation to the agency for revision if it is inadequate.[21] Other executive orders require analysis of the impacts of regulation on matters such as federalism, private property rights, environmental justice, and national energy security.[22] Similarly, EPA is required to analyze every draft environmental impact analysis prepared by other federal agencies.[23] Information analysis might also include legal analysis.[24]
- *Planning.* This function refers to a suite of early-stage governmental activities intended to consider, develop a framework for, and/or guide decisions for later governmental action.[25] Examples include mechanisms for land use planning by the federal land management agencies.[26] Program evaluation and reform can be understood as a subset of planning or even a separate governmental function.[27]
- *Standard setting.* This function includes a variety of government activities in developing, promulgating, and revising general benchmarks that are to be applicable to a group of private or public actors.[28] For our purposes, standard setting will often track the quasi-legislative activities of administrative agencies, that is, the promulgation of generally applicable rules and regulations. The paradigmatic case of standard setting is any activity that

qualifies as administrative rulemaking under the Administrative Procedure Act (APA).[29]

- *Implementation and permitting.* This term refers to governmental activities involving the interpretation and application of identified standards in a particular circumstance or set of circumstances, such as the permitting or licensing of activities.[30] For our purposes, implementation and permitting functions will often track the quasi-judicial activities of administrative agencies as articulated under the APA.[31]
- *Inspection and compliance monitoring.* This term refers to governmental observation and/or review of the performance of an entity or activity that is being managed or regulated.[32] This includes compliance monitoring[33] or effect and effectiveness monitoring.[34]
- *Enforcement.* This function refers to activities meant to induce compliance with and enforce statutes, regulations, licenses, permits, and other sources of legal duties through civil administrative proceedings or judicial civil and/or criminal proceedings.[35] The Securities and Exchange Commission's Division of Enforcement, for instance, is charged with conducting investigations into possible violations of federal securities laws and litigating the Commission's civil enforcement proceedings in administrative proceedings and federal court.[36]

The distinction between these functional jurisdiction categories may undoubtedly often be blurred in any particular case, as is the case with categories of substantive jurisdiction. Certain monitoring activities will often include the generation of data. Information collection will frequently be paired with information dissemination. Planning activities may include the setting of standards. Standard setting may occur in a cascade of nationwide and more subsidiary levels. As is evident from reams of judicial cases and scholarship on administrative law, the precise distinction between quasi-legislative standard setting and quasi-judicial implementation can be vexing.[37] Enforcement activities, moreover, often coincide with compliance monitoring. Nonetheless, we maintain that in general these categories are sufficiently discrete to make them useful in describing the scope of an agency's jurisdiction, and, as we detail in chapters 3, 4, and 5, they ultimately raise significantly different tradeoffs for allocations of authority.

Policymakers and scholars continue to insufficiently appreciate this distinction. Some scholars have noted the existence of divisions of authority along functional lines. Yet scholars investigating government organization who do refer to agency functions frequently do so in a different sense than we are using that term. Rather than focusing on the various kinds of tasks agencies perform, these scholars use the term *function* to describe the scope of an agency's substantive jurisdiction (such as the authority to regulate air pollution, but not water pollution), which elides the distinction between substantive and functional jurisdiction.[38] The scholarly literature, in particular, largely lacks policy-based analyses of the potential consequences of functional jurisdiction in developing or assessing the relationship between government organizations.

Substantive authority remains the primary organizing principle for determining the bounds of an administrative agency's authority. An agency's jurisdiction may also be based on function, but, for many allocations of authority, function is largely a subordinate form of regulatory division. Typically, an agency is provided substantive authority over particular resources, issues, or problems for which it creates offices or divisions that focus on subtopics of that substantive authority.[39] These divisions often have authority over a range of functions, including monitoring, standard setting, and implementation/permitting, with authority further subdivided by substantive subcategory and/or by functional activity.[40]

However, agencies also often contain divisions or offices dedicated to particular regulatory functions, regardless of their substantive focus.[41] The Internal Revenue Service has separate offices to handle tax issues concerning small businesses and tax-exempt organizations. This is a substantive division of authority, but it also reflects functional divisions, with separate offices for privacy and disclosure, whistleblowers, and criminal investigations, all of which cut across substantive lines.[42] Agencies routinely have separate offices to deal with congressional relations, media and communications, and legal matters, regardless of the substantive nature of the issue for which negotiations with the legislature, outreach to the media, or legal advice is required.[43]

Function is, however, the principal basis for the authority of a few agencies. Congress has delegated to the US Government Accountability

Office, for instance, responsibility for the auditing, investigation, reporting, and evaluation of federal agencies, regardless of their substantive area of regulation.[44] Another example is the US Geological Survey (USGS). It is a research-only agency that generates biological, geographical, geological, and hydrological information to help inform the policy making of regulatory authorities, but it has no regulatory functions of its own.[45] The mission of the US Department of Justice (DOJ) is to "enforce the law" through both preventive measures and sanctions against those who violate it; its responsibilities extend across the entire spectrum of federal law.[46] More broadly, of course, the separation of legislative, executive, and adjudicative power among the branches of government could be considered a form of functional jurisdiction.[47]

Although the distinction between functional and substantive jurisdiction is relevant for understanding and assessing the distribution of authority within a particular agency, this book focuses primarily on the distribution of power *between* government organizations. Chapters 3, 4 and 5 illustrate how policymakers and scholars have neglected to consider how functional allocation affects characterizations of agency authority and how the effectiveness of allocations of regulatory authority is likely to depend on the particular type of governmental function being exercised. These oversights may lead to missed opportunities or regulatory failures. As chapter 9 and the conclusion explore more fully, one of the book's principal aims is to encourage policymakers and scholars to focus more attention on whether evaluating and allocating agency authority along functional rather than substantive lines holds greater promise of achieving the policy goals of particular government programs at less cost to competing policy objectives.

Chapter 2

The Dimensions of Allocations of Authority

For any substantive area of regulation and governmental function, regulatory authority can be further evaluated along three key dimensions. As illustrated in Figure 2.1, these include (1) how centralized the authority is; (2) how much overlap in governmental authority there is among multiple government bodies with concurrent jurisdiction over a particular regulatory problem; and (3) the extent to which such authority is exercised independently or in coordination with other governmental entities with authority over a particular substantive area or function. As the Figure depicts, the choices along each dimension are not antipodal. Rather, each dimension represents a spectrum of choices with authority located closer to one end of the spectrum or the other.[1]

As demonstrated in chapters 6, 7, and 8, scholars of governance have not sufficiently explored the distinctions among these dimensions. Each measures a particular component of regulatory authority, representing largely different sets of policies and ultimately values tradeoffs over the appropriate design for managing social problems. Moreover, the manner in which policymakers choose to define the relationships among government actors along one dimension will often affect the relationships along the other two dimensions. Most obviously, if authority is fully centralized in one entity, by definition there can be no overlap and there is no need to consider whether to coordinate authority with other entities. If, however, authority involves more than one entity, policymakers must make choices concerning both the extent to which that allocation of authority should be overlapping or distinct, on the one hand, and the extent to which it should be coordinated or independent, on the other.

Accordingly, a complete understanding of the implications of the structure of a government program requires evaluation of the impacts of situating authority among multiple government institutions along each of the three dimensions, and of the manner in which choices along each dimension affect moves along the other two dimensions. This chapter

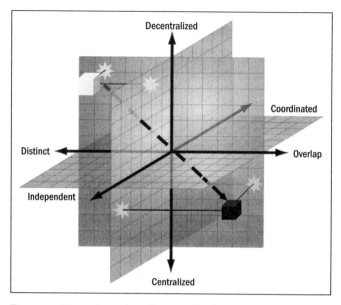

Figure 2.1. Dimensions of regulatory authority.

analyzes the three dimensions, identifying the values implicated in choosing to locate agency authority at each end of the spectrum represented by each dimension. Subsequent chapters include case studies that reveal the implications of structural choices along each dimension and the consequences of conflating the dimensions for the success of governmental programs.

A. The Centralization–Decentralization Dimension

Perhaps the most frequently analyzed dimension for characterizing the allocation of regulatory authority—in the legal academic literature, at least—is the scale or level of government that is granted jurisdiction to address a social problem or need. As illustrated in Figure 2.2, governmental authority could be allocated anywhere in a range between highly centralized and highly decentralized. The dimension operates both among different levels of government and within a single level.

A key question for this dimension is the extent to which authority to address a social problem is primarily decentralized to a local or state jurisdiction or is primarily centralized at the federal level. On one end of the spectrum, a preemptively federal regime (e.g., in general, the regulation of immigration[2] or space exploration) is centralized at one governmental level. In other regulatory contexts, authority is shared among multiple governmental levels. Some regimes split authority among multiple federal agencies and a state regulator;[3] others consist of a single federal regulator and a single state regulator whose standards other states can opt to follow;[4] still others allocate authority to federal and state agencies, each of whom may take a different approach from other state regulators.[5]

Another question is whether regulatory authority within a certain level is delegated to one entity or divided among two or more entities. Within a single level of government such as the federal government, regulatory authority may be fully centralized in one agency or decentralized by dividing authority among multiple agencies or among local offices of a single agency.[6] The Nuclear Regulatory Commission has exclusive authority within the federal government to address the radiation hazards associated with nuclear power. Authority to enforce antitrust laws is shared between the Federal Trade Commission and DOJ.[7] As chapter 3 demonstrates, federal authority to prevent foodborne illnesses is divided up among at least a dozen agencies. We regard this horizontal decentralization, or the degree of fragmentation of authority

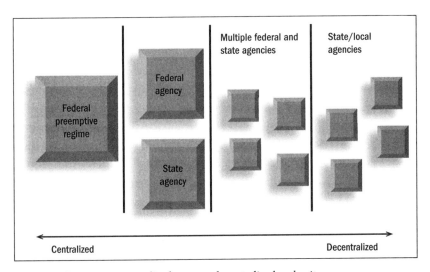

Figure 2.2. From more centralized to more decentralized authority.

among multiple regulators at the same level or scale, as a second aspect of characterizing a regulatory regime as centralized or decentralized.[8]

1. Decentralized Authority

For centuries—at least as far back as the origination of the concept of subsidiarity[9]—scholars have promoted the idea that authority is best allocated at the local level.[10] One popular rationale for decentralized regulation is its ability to leverage local knowledge and expertise,[11] while another, related justification is to ensure regulation is better tailored to local conditions, preferences, and economic conditions.[12] Many also argue that government that is decentralized along vertical lines allows opportunities for regulatory experimentation that can encourage innovation.[13] We refer to these justifications respectively as the expertise, diversity, and experimentation rationales for decentralized decision-making authority. These three justifications for localizing regulation are primarily (although not exclusively) based on the pursuit of more effective regulation.

A fourth related and commonly purported advantage of decentralized governance is that interlocal competition maximizes social utility by allowing each local community to shape its interests and goals.[14] As further explained in section C.2 of this chapter, however, even though some level of decentralization may be a necessary condition for competition to occur, we think that competition of this kind flows more precisely from what we define as independently structured government authority (our third dimension) than from decentralization. A fifth and final argument for decentralization is that localized allocation of authority makes decision-makers more accessible and therefore promotes more accountable and democratic governance.[15] A related claim postulates that local regulators tend to be more accountable than regulators at higher government levels.[16]

These rationales may help explain, at least in part, the historical predominance of state or local regulation of certain social problems. Pre-1960 environmental law is a good example. Before 1960, state and local laws were the only significant governmental constraints on pollution in the United States, with a few exceptions.[17] These included state common law tort causes of action such as nuisance or trespass as well as local land use regulations designed to segregate industrial, polluting uses from residential uses.[18] Into the 1970s, proponents of such state and local authority emphasized its diversity, expertise, or democratic accountability advantages.[19] Other examples of traditional state and local regulation that the Supreme Court has identified include matters of health care and protection of public safety,[20] such as regulation of vaccines,[21] advertising,[22] family and probate law,[23] employee welfare benefit plans,[24] protection of the security of real estate titles,[25] insurance contracts,[26] education,[27] and enforcement of criminal laws.[28]

Although decentralized authority is most likely to be associated with local or state regulatory control, federal regulatory authority could be modified to be more or less horizontally decentralized (or fragmented) as well. Some of the same justifications for local or state regulatory authority may be similarly levied for delegating jurisdiction over particular substantive areas or regulatory functions to a variety of disparate federal agencies or to local offices within a single agency. Particularized expertise[29] and regulatory experimentation to promote innovation[30] may lead to the allocation of federal authority away from a heavily consolidated model toward one with more decentralized federal jurisdiction.[31] These expertise and experimentation rationales tout the effectiveness advantages of decentralized regulation. The diversity and accountability rationales for decentralizing regulation to state or local authorities, however, are less relevant to this second aspect of decentralization because decentralization among multiple federal agencies is not especially likely to result in either government action that is more tailored to local conditions or greater accessibility to decision makers.

2. Centralized Authority

Despite critiques of centralized government based on factors of expertise, experimentation, diversity, and accountability,[32] many legislatures and scholars accept that, at least for some regulatory problems, centralization makes sense. Centralization might take advantage of economies of scale that are forfeited if regulatory authority is dispersed.[33] Some have argued, for example, that research or standard-setting functions should be centralized at the federal level because of the economies of scale of a single authority administering the function.[34] This argument is premised on the comparatively greater administrative efficiency of centralized regulation.

In addition, some suggest that centralization at the federal level may be appropriate because of the national character of the issues involved or because of collective action concerns (which stem from the dynamics of individual behavior in group settings)[35] that may be best addressed by a federal authority.[36] These might include immigration policy,[37] pension plan administration,[38] protection of intellectual property rights,[39] protection of union-related advocacy,[40] or control of activities on the high seas,[41] such as maritime commerce.[42] In environmental law and other contexts, some harms may cross jurisdictional lines, necessitating more centralized regulation to manage interstate spillovers.[43] State product labeling requirements have been characterized as laws that generate interstate spillovers that justify centralized federal regulation.[44] In addition, states may export economic burdens to other jurisdictions if they regulate the sale of products that produce local harms but that are manufactured (and produce employment and economic benefits) in other states.[45] Finally, some suggest that centralized federal regulation may be an appropriate response to state efforts to regulate socially important but externality-producing activities so stringently that they are driven to states with weaker regulation, allowing states with strong regulation to reap the economic benefits of the activities while shielding their residents from adverse environmental effects. Federal regulation of the siting of radioactive waste disposal sites is an example.[46] In these contexts, centralized regulatory structures may be more effective than decentralized regulation.[47]

A desire to address collective-action problems to enhance regulatory effectiveness underlies much of modern federal environmental law. Much of that law is premised on averting a "race to the bottom" from decentralized governance, in which local jurisdictions compete with each other by progressively lowering environmental standards.[48] Under this dynamic, individual states have incentives to lower standards to compete for industry whether or not other states do the same, even though the states as a collective would be better off if none did so.[49] Congress raised the undesirable specter of a race to the bottom when, in 1977, it amended the Clean Air Act (CAA).[50] A House report warned that "if there is no Federal policy, States may find themselves forced into a bidding war to attract new industry by reducing pollution standards."[51]

Such a dynamic has been noted in various regulatory areas.[52] Though typically considered a feature associated with decentralized authority, such interjurisdictional competition is largely influenced by the extent of interjurisdictional independence or coordination, as we detail later.[53]

Congress has also resorted to horizontal centralization to promote regulatory effectiveness or to achieve other important national goals. It chose to vest exclusive federal authority over the health, safety, and environmental aspects of nuclear power plant operation in the Nuclear Regulatory Commission because, among other things, it wanted to minimize access to information whose distribution would adversely affect national security.[54]

In some instances, Congress has chosen to centralize authority for only a particular governmental function, or to centralize authority incrementally over time on a function-by-function basis, as it did in adopting air and water pollution control laws. Before Congress centralized other functions, it imposed greater centralization of information gathering and dissemination through the passage of laws that funded research into the causes and effects of pollution.[55] It did so based on its judgment that states and localities lacked the resources to engage in or fund the research needed to support the adoption of effective pollution control laws.[56] Federally assisted research could then be disseminated to the states and localities, allowing them to avoid the adverse health effects of pollution more effectively.[57] In the 1960s, Congress provided technical and financial assistance to the states, such as by subsidizing the construction of municipal sewage treatment works.[58] By the end of the decade, the federal government had increased its role in standard setting in a limited range of situations in which state and local regulation had been ineffective—namely, the control of interstate pollution.[59] Congress subsequently gave the Environmental Protection Agency (EPA) and other federal agencies broad standard-setting authority over a range of environmental media, activities, and substances.[60]

Finally, James Madison and others have argued that centralized regulation has comparative fairness and democratic legitimacy advantages because of its ability to promote uniform treatment of similarly situated entities regardless of location, and to temper the ability of self-interested "factions" to control the levers of power to the disadvantage of less powerful groups or interests.[61]

B. The Overlap–Distinctness Dimension

Another important dimension takes the form of a spectrum ranging from overlapping to distinct regulatory authority. As represented in Figure 2.3, at one end, governmental authority over a substantive issue or governmental function may be separate from any other governmental authority. For the purposes of our analysis, two governmental entities have overlapping jurisdiction only to the extent that both their substantive and their functional authority is concurrent. As such, overlapping authority involves the power to regulate the same activities.[62]

The Occupational Health and Safety Administration and the Occupational Safety and Health Review Commission share federal authority to regulate workplace safety, but their authorities do not materially overlap because the former is responsible for standard setting, investigation, and prosecution of regulatory violations, while the latter has exclusive adjudicatory enforcement authority.[63] In other instances, multiple federal agencies perform similar functions in managing federal lands, but their authority is nevertheless substantively distinct. For example, authority to enforce the 1972 International Regulations for Preventing Collisions at Sea is shared, but distinct. The Coast Guard enforces the regulations against pilots operating US-flagged vessels, the Navy enforces the regulations against Naval officers, and state maritime commissions have exclusive authority to enforce against pilots of foreign-flagged vessels.[64] To take another example, three federal agencies now dominate bank regulation and resolution authority, but their authority is likewise distinct. The Office of the Comptroller of the Currency is primarily responsible for regulating nationally chartered banks, the Federal Reserve regulates state-chartered Federal Reserve member banks and bank holding companies, and the Federal Deposit Insurance Corporation has authority over non–Federal Reserve member state banks.[65]

At the other end of the spectrum are regimes in which there are many governmental institutions with considerable overlapping authority. For instance, the Council on Environmental Quality, the federal land management agencies, and state wildlife and land agencies share authority over wildlife management on federal lands.[66] Similarly, both EPA and state permit issuing agencies may enforce alleged violations of the same Clean Water Act permit provisions.[67] If regulatory power is fully central-

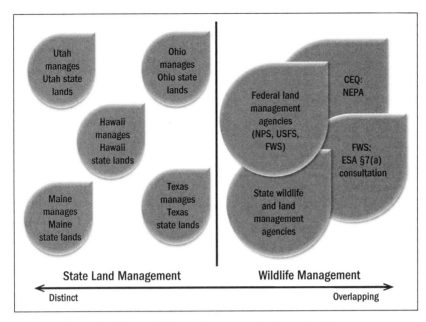

Figure 2.3. Examples of more distinct and more overlapping authority.

ized in one regulator, that power necessarily falls at the distinctness end of this dimension because by definition overlap requires the existence of at least two regulators. If, however, policymakers decide to divide authority among more than one entity, this dimension implicates two key questions. One is the extent to which subject matter authority over a particular resource or regulatory problem (e.g., water pollution) should be divided up so that, even though there are multiple regulators, each is solely or primarily responsible for addressing a distinct component of the larger problem (e.g., one controls industrial sources and another controls diffuse runoff from agricultural or construction activity, or one controls pollution by non-nuclear materials while another has sole authority over nuclear materials).[68] The second is the extent to which regulatory functions should overlap (e.g., if one agency is authorized to review and, if appropriate, veto, the issuance of permits by another) or instead comprise distinct mandates (e.g., if one agency sets standards, while another applies those standards in the context of resolving individual permit applications).[69] We do not treat authority as overlapping unless two or more agencies perform the same function within the same substantive area (e.g., shared enforcement authority between federal and state regulators for state requirements adopted under delegated federal authority).

1. Distinct Authority

Legislatures have long adopted and scholars have promoted the idea that authority over a particular regulatory problem is best allocated to a single or few regulators. Such a perspective is primarily based on an explicit or implicit "matching principle"—that legislatures should match each regulatory problem (or aspect of a regulatory problem) to the single authority that can best address that problem.[70] Advocates of this principle urge, for example, that environmental regulatory authority generally should be vested in "the political jurisdiction that comes closest to matching the geographic area affected by a particular externality."[71]

Scholars have also identified various weaknesses of a regulatory system with overlapping regulatory authority. One of the more common criticisms is that overlapping jurisdiction is wasteful and inefficient, for both regulators and regulated entities. The government's "transaction costs" of regulating increase if multiple agencies perform tasks that could have been handled by a single agency.[72] Thus, whereas decentralized authority may create administrative inefficiency due to the absence of economies of scale,[73] overlapping authority may create inefficient duplication of regulatory effort. Efforts to coordinate among multiple regulators can address the duplicative inefficiencies resulting from redundant authority, but can themselves be costly.[74] While consolidation of authority can enhance the ability to enjoy economies of scale, a reduction in overlap through creation of more distinct authority can minimize redundancy and duplication of effort, thereby promoting administrative efficiency.[75]

Overlap may also create inefficiency for regulated entities. Multiple bodies of regulation require tracking and complying with disparate and potentially conflicting sets of obligations.[76] Overlapping regulation can also reduce certainty and thus effectiveness if the relationships among the mandates of different regulators are unclear.[77] Some also claim that overlapping authority can lead to inefficient over-regulation[78] "through the introduction of regulatory goals other than externality elimination, and through interference with the free movement of firms through government over-appropriation of fixed capital assets."[79]

Others, however, have asserted that overlapping jurisdiction can lead to under-regulation, an unintended result of what Professor William Buzbee has dubbed the creation of a "regulatory commons,"[80] especially when the regulated problem or harm is large-scale and broadly dispersed.[81] Buzbee attributes this to the high information costs of developing a regulatory response, limited credit for regulators, bias toward the regulatory status quo, and regulator risk aversion.[82] The result may be that although multiple regulators have authority to address a particular problem, regulatory gaps develop as each assumes or hopes that others will deal with the matter.[83] Buzbee suggests that reducing the number of potential regulators and/or combining the regulatory authority of particular regulators could lessen the incentives for such regulatory inaction in some contexts.[84]

Relatedly, some contend that regulator accountability may be diminished in a regulatory system where authority is shared.[85] Agencies may shirk their responsibilities, blaming co-regulators for program failures.[86] Others have posited that overlapping jurisdiction can lead to a lack of finality in the regulatory process.[87] Thus, some argue that distinct regulation may be more effective than overlapping regulation.

2. Overlapping Authority

Overlapping authority has its proponents. A large and growing literature identifies a variety of effectiveness and accountability advantages associated with concurrent regulatory authority. In addition to pointing to the implausibility of eliminating already extensive regulatory segmentation,[88] many scholars have detailed the undesirability of minimizing overlap and consolidating decision making in a single or a few authorities.[89]

Some scholars favor the redundancy that overlapping jurisdiction creates.[90] Although much of this literature relates to allocation of authority between the federal government and the states and localities,[91] the same dynamic applies to overlap within a particular level of government. To begin with, although overlap can create inefficiencies, as described above,[92] it can also enhance the prospects for effective regulation. The key idea is that concurrent jurisdiction increases the likelihood of regulatory action because there are more authorized actors.[93] Should one regulatory entity backslide or fail to regulate, others are available to fill the gap.[94] Concurrent jurisdiction may thus be particularly valuable for regulatory contexts[95] where the costs of under-regulation are high, such as those that seek to address high-cost or irreversible effects. Examples of such contexts include the risk of a terrorist attack or systemic market failure or the management of nonrenewable resources.[96] Concurrent jurisdiction may also enhance regulatory effectiveness by allowing authorities with a range of different competencies to be brought to bear on a problem.[97]

The regulatory safety net resulting from overlap can also foster accountability by indirectly combating interest-group capture.[98] As Anne Joseph O'Connell has noted, "One interest group generally will find it more difficult to capture several agencies than a single agency; to wield power over multiple agencies, interest groups may have to work together, which is a costly enterprise for the groups."[99] Agencies with overlapping subject matter and functional jurisdiction may also be more reluctant to respond favorably to interest-group pressure because other agencies sharing regulatory authority may detect and cast adverse light on that behavior.[100]

Finally, overlapping authority can combat the phenomenon of regulatory arbitrage, which can occur when a regulated entity has the option of structuring its activities in ways that trigger one regulator's authority while disabling another's. If an entity is subject to overlapping regulation, the fact that one regulator's jurisdiction is triggered does not allow it to evade the jurisdiction of another regulator.[101] Likewise, a regime in which a regulated entity's conduct dictates which regulator will have exclusive jurisdiction may induce regulators to compete with one another in a race to the bottom in an effort to expand their influence.[102] As chapter 7 explains, some scholars and policymakers appear to miss this point, attributing arbitrage opportunities to overlap rather than to its absence.[103]

Both distinct and overlapping authority, therefore, have the potential to enhance accountability, depending on the circumstances and incentives of regulators. Distinct authority is better situated to promote accountability if the primary problem is the tendency of co-regulators to shirk their responsibilities and blame co-regulators for program failures.[104] On the other hand, overlapping authority is better designed to promote accountability if one co-regulator's likely response to another's lack of regulation is not to assign blame, but instead to step into the regulatory breach, or if capture is a prominent concern. Determining which account is more compelling to policymakers may depend on assessments of the history of the particular regulatory program and social problem in question as well as on policymakers' philosophies about institutional incentives and behavior.[105]

Some also argue that overlapping authority may provide space for initial regulatory strategies by one entity that can serve as a proving ground.[106] These commenters contend that a dispersed and overlapping regulatory system may allow for a diversity of tailored approaches and advance innovative management experimentation.[107] As detailed in chapter 6, however, in our view, these arguments touting the diversity and experimentation advantages of overlapping jurisdiction appear to be erroneously conflating it with decentralized authority.

C. The Coordination–Independence Dimension

A final dimension for characterizing the allocation of authority focuses on the extent of formal or informal coordination among authorities that share jurisdiction over a particular regulatory problem or government function. In contrast to the centralization–decentralization dimension, which is about scale, and the overlap–distinctness dimension, which is about the extent to which authority coexists, coordination is about the extent and type of interactions between agencies. In fact, because it is about intergovernmental relations, unlike for the overlap and centralization dimensions, coordination can occur between functions (e.g., an agency in charge of standard setting can coordinate with another in charge of implementation).

For this dimension, the key question is how much multiple regulatory authorities communicate, coordinate, and collaborate in addressing any particular substantive problem or performing a delegated governmental function. As illustrated in Figure 2.4, on one end of the spectrum[108] is a regulatory framework in which governmental entities are highly independent and isolated in their regulatory activities. For example,

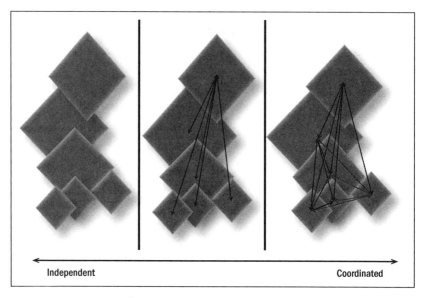

Figure 2.4. From more independent to more coordinated authority.

numerous federal, state, and local agencies have authority to investigate and prosecute the sale of illegal drugs such as crack cocaine, and
there is no requirement that they coordinate with each other in deciding
whether to do so.[109] At the other end is a regulatory relationship characterized by close agency collaboration and regulatory coordination.

1. Coordinated Authority

In response to the considerable incentives and effects of regulatory fragmentation, some scholars and regulatory actors have called for more
coordination among regulatory authorities. Coordination exists or has
been proposed over a wide range of substantive jurisdictions, such as
natural resources,[110] food safety,[111] and bioterrorism.[112] Although eliminating overlap may be implausible or even undesirable, scholars have
emphasized the value of agency dialogue and collaboration to reduce its
adverse effects.[113] Coordination can increase the effectiveness of government action by promoting the exchange of ideas and the pooling
of expertise among different agencies.[114] Although efforts to coordinate
require investments of time and resources that are unnecessary when

agencies act independently, this disadvantage may be offset by reductions in duplication of effort and inconsistent action, potentially even resulting in a net administrative efficiency gain.[115]

Scholars also argue that coordination can promote accountability by combating drift,[116] shirking,[117] and free-riding through facilitation of interagency monitoring.[118] Coordination can also promote accountability by providing governmental authorities the opportunity or even imposing the duty to review and serve as a check on other authorities in the performance of delegated functions, thereby reducing capture risks.[119] Each regulatory authority can essentially serve as an accountability check on the others.[120] Finally, the coordinated exercise of multi-jurisdictional authority can promote effectiveness and fairness by minimizing inconsistent or redundant demands on regulated entities.[121]

Although scholars and government officials have examined the various characteristics of interagency coordination,[122] its definition is unsettled. Different schools of organizational theory seek to explain institutional coordination, and their definitions differ.[123] In addition, coordination can take any number of forms. Coordination can be formal or informal.[124] It can be long- or short-term[125] and frequent or occasional.[126] Coordination can be voluntary and cooperative[127] or mandated by legislative or executive action.[128]

And though coordination may be cooperative, it can also be adversarial. Indeed, Farber and O'Connell contend that adversarial or conflict-driven interagency relationships[129] can be particularly constructive "when they bring differing expertise, information bases, constituencies, and values into policy decisions, [. . .] enhancing expertise and ensuring that all points of view are heard."[130] The National Environmental Policy Act,[131] discussed in depth in chapter 5, is a prominent example of mandated, formal federal interagency coordination over agency planning and information-gathering functions, which in some circumstances is cooperative and in others adversarial.

Coordination can also be understood as a spectrum that ranges from less synchronized interjurisdictional relationships to those requiring significant harmonization.[132] The range of coordination activities includes (1) mere communication of adopted agency actions;[133] (2) creation of formal or informal fora for interjurisdictional discussion;[134] (3) discretionary[135] or mandatory[136] opportunities for agencies to comment on or respond to potential or proposed agency actions by other agencies; (4) required consideration of or response to the comments or recommendations of other governmental authorities;[137] (5) the harmonization of agency activities through voting arrangements or mutual/consensus agreement;[138] and (6) providing a governmental authority a de facto or express veto power over the activity of another authority.[139] This last alternative would be a more hierarchical form of coordination. Of course, each of these types of coordination can itself vary considerably. For example, interjurisdictional agreements can range in scope, strength, and duration.[140]

Because of this multiplicity of factors, it may at times be challenging to characterize one regulatory program as more or less coordinated than another. To be sure, infrequent and short-term communication typically would be less coordinated than continued and enduring interaction; cooperation on a few issues ordinarily involves less coordination than cooperation on many issues. And voluntary discussion between agencies usually would be less coordinated than mandatory consultation. However, in some circumstances these factors may point in different directions. For example, voluntary weekly meetings between agencies to discuss issues of common concern may be considered more or less coordinated than a program that requires an agency to solicit and integrate comments from another agency annually. Similarly, a short-term interjurisdictional agreement involving a wide range of problems may be more or less coordinated than a long-term one on a narrow issue.

We do not offer a formula for calculating where a government program rests along the coordination–independence dimension. Instead, our point is that policymakers should consider whether the goals of a regime, be they distinct or overlapping, would best be promoted by requiring coordination or allowing independent exercise of authority. Part of that assessment, of course, will entail consideration of various forms of coordination, each of which will have its own set of advantages and disadvantages.

2. Independent Authority

Although coordination of regulatory efforts has theoretical effectiveness and administrative efficiency advantages, calls for collaboration and the formation of coordinating regimes can be reflexive, without regard to the costs of such regimes.[141] Adding layers of consultation and collaboration requirements to an overlapping regulatory landscape will undoubtedly divert agency resources, and it is worth considering whether the advantages of particular communications or collaborations are worth these disadvantages.[142]

Moreover, close agency coordination may impair regulatory effectiveness, particularly in the management of complex and uncertain regulatory problems. In discussing divided authority's advantages, scholars have often focused on the value of interjurisdictional competition in promoting socially optimal environmental regulation. Richard Revesz has argued, in an influential article, that interstate competition for industry should produce "an efficient allocation of industrial activity among the states."[143] Jonathan Adler argues that interjurisdictional competition "can encourage policy innovation as policymakers seek to meet the economic, environmental, and other demands of their constituents."[144] Competition among authorities may be a contest for political credit, resources, or additional regulatory responsibilities.

Such competition, however, is premised on regulatory autonomy and independence. Highly coordinated decentralized authority is not likely to generate competition, and a set of fairly centralized agencies (e.g., several federal agencies) can be induced to be competitive if independent. Although competition benefits are often ascribed as a feature of decentralization,[145] it is the authority to act independently rather than in a coordinated fashion that yields the competitive dynamic.

There are also, of course, adverse effects from agency competition. Competition may discourage one agency from assisting another and promote strategies that reduce overall welfare, such as the race to the bottom that, as described earlier,[146] some have advocated should be addressed through increased centralization of authority. Nonetheless, as further explored in chapter 7, such interjurisdictional competition might also be addressed through efforts to promote greater coordination among authorities.

Beyond the efficiency and competition justifications of independence, some forms of coordination may lead to an "anti-commons" problem.[147] The most acute forms of coordination include requiring all governmental authorities with jurisdiction over a particular problem to agree to a particular regulatory strategy.[148] Some scholars have argued that a consensus decision rule can encourage holdouts and mutual vetoes that can result in the underutilization of resources when regulatory action viewed as beneficial by most co-regulators is blocked by a lone holdout.[149]

Finally, independence may promote accountability. Regulators may have substantial incentives to vigilantly review and challenge the actions of other intersecting authorities,[150] particularly when there are interjurisdictional spillovers or attempts by an authority to obtain a competitive advantage. Independence can also reduce the risk of collusion between regulators and combat agency "groupthink"[151] by increasing the diversity of viewpoints.[152]

Consequently, as in the case of the overlap–distinctness dimension, proponents of both coordination and independence have identified accountability advantages. Both accounts note the potential for one agency armed with information about what others are doing to serve as a check on the failures of its co-regulators. Which account one finds more convincing in a specific context may turn on factors that include the particular governmental function at issue.[153] It may also depend on whether this checking function is best promoted by relatively greater access to information about the activities of co-regulators among coordinating agencies or by the potentially greater willingness of independent agencies to call other agencies to account for regulatory failures. Such tradeoffs will also likely vary by the particular type of coordination, as some forms (such as mandatory consultation and approval) may be more burdensome than others (such as mere communication)—but also more likely to provide interagency accountability.

Proponents of independence often pair it with decentralized authority to advance interstate competition.[154] However, it is worth noting that independence might be valuable even among more centralized (such as federal) agencies. In analyzing the possible reorganization of the authority to provide national security intelligence, for instance, Professor O'Connell has argued that competition among autonomous federal authorities may provide advantages that include preventing "pernicious" collusion, encouraging a creative "race to the top," motivating correction of other agencies' mistakes, facilitating adaptation to changing conditions, and combatting "groupthink."[155] Accordingly, whether between levels of government or within a single level, in some circumstances maintaining agency independence may promote better management than a heavily collaborative model. Most prominently, depending on the governmental function at issue, the advantages of regulator independence, including beneficial competition and avoidance of groupthink, may outweigh the desirable byproducts of coordination, such as enhanced accountability resulting from reduction of shirking, drift, and free-riding behavior. This outcome might particularly be the case when interjurisdictional competition is more consistent with—and may better promote—advantages associated with the other dimensions of authority, such as the redundancy advantages of overlapping jurisdiction. Such a circumstance might exist during periods of change,[156] when there is considerable uncertainty, harm may be catastrophic, and prevention or mitigation of such harm by one of the independent authorities is possible.[157]

D. The Relationship between the Dimensions of Authority

In this chapter and the preceding one, we have distinguished between the substantive and functional components of jurisdiction, identified three dimensions for organizing regulatory and management authority, and described potential advantages and disadvantages of situating or shifting agency authority along the spectrum of each dimension. Figure 2.5 summarizes these various justifications. Note that though the polar ends of dimensions largely differ in their justifications, certain rationales may be used to move along more than one dimension. For instance, certain diametric points of dimensions may manage uniformity concerns differently (i.e., coordination fosters uniformity through harmonization of the efforts of multiple agencies, distinctness does so by reducing overlap, and centralization may achieve this goal by reducing the number of potentially conflicting authorities). Although our focus in this chapter has been to identify each dimension of authority and explore the values that may drive policymakers to allocate authority closer toward one end of the spectrum or the other of that dimension, policymakers also need to consider how the dimensions may relate to and interact with each other. Those interactions can influence the effects of allocating authority along each of the relevant dimensions.

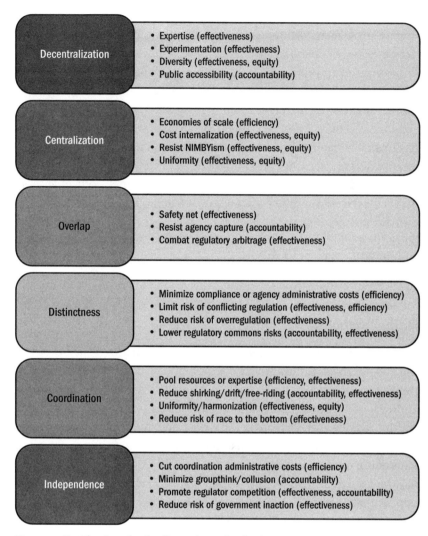

Figure 2.5. Justifications for the dimensions of authority.

For example, though obviously related, in many cases the centralization and overlap dimensions do not present the same choices to policymakers, and moves along the two dimensions may often have different effects on regulatory authority. Depending on the baseline distribution and how authority is restructured, increases in the centralization of substantive regulatory power may result in a decrease or an increase in overlap. On the one hand, federal deregulation that provides for unitary state regulation would decrease overlap in authority, just as complete federal preemption of state law[158] typically would. Thus, in addition to being a shift toward centralization, the creation of federal authority over automobile tailpipe emission standards,[159] pesticides,[160] and nuclear waste[161] in each case represented movement away from overlap by preempting supplemental state standards, even if those standards were more stringent than the federal standards. On the other hand, a federal law establishing a new federal agency with floor preemption authority— under which state authorities may adopt more but not less stringent regulation than their federal counterpart—would increase centralization but also increase overlap.[162] Moreover, decreases or increases in overlap may occur over one or numerous regulatory functions. For example, increasing limitations on or barring the authority of federal agencies to commence enforcement action against permit holders in addition to state agency enforcement would decrease overlap only in enforcement functions. Thus, fully characterizing a reallocation of authority will often require an understanding of the baseline allocation.

Similarly, the coordination dimension necessarily assumes at least some level of decentralization because when there is only one regulator there is no need to consider whether it should coordinate its actions with another entity or act independently of such an entity.[163] However, the extent of coordination may come into play whether or not there is jurisdictional overlap among authorities. To be sure, coordination among agencies with overlapping authorities is common. The Toxic Substances Control Act, for example, precludes EPA from exercising its authority to regulate certain chemicals if another federal agency with jurisdiction over a chemical either determines that no such risk exists or takes action to address that risk.[164] Sometimes, however, such coordination is lacking, even if not necessarily by design. As chapter 3 explains, for example, more than one federal agency may have authority to inspect the same food production facility, but there is often little if any coordination among them, resulting in inefficient multiple inspections of the same facility.

Coordination among agencies with distinct jurisdictional charges is also possible. For example, two agencies might seek to coordinate efforts to address the risks posed by asbestos exposure, even if one is responsible for controlling asbestos emissions from factory smokestacks and another regulates the use of asbestos in brake linings. The two agencies could agree that their regulations should limit human exposure to a certain level of acceptable health risk. Alternatively, they could coordinate by doing joint research on the degree of health risks posed at different levels of exposure, and then make independent decisions as to what degree of risk to regulate. Another example is the issuance by EPA and the National Highway Traffic Safety Administration (NHTSA) of joint regulations establishing fuel efficiency standards for new cars and trucks emitting greenhouse gases,[165] even though EPA's authority under the CAA authorizes regulation to prevent pollution[166] and NHTSA's authority under the Energy Policy and Conservation Act seeks to conserve energy.[167] As one might expect, agencies with distinct substantive or functional authority can also operate independently of one another.

A failure to appreciate the existence of the three dimensions and the differences among them can mask both these interactions and the policy advantages and disadvantages of allocating authority along them. Chapters 6–8 explore situations in which scholars or policymakers have failed to appreciate the full array of organizational choices by conflating two or more of the dimensions of governmental authority. The result may be organizational structures that fail to promote regulatory or management goals such as effectiveness, efficiency, equity, or legitimacy.

PART II

The Importance of Functional Jurisdiction

Chapter 3

Decentralization and the Functions of Food Regulation

The Trump administration's 2018 "Reform Plan and Reorganization Recommendations" criticize federal oversight of the safety of the nation's food supply as illogical, fragmented, and duplicative. It provides the following examples:

> While FSIS [the Food Safety and Inspection Service] has regulatory responsibility for the safety of liquid eggs, FDA [the Food and Drug Administration] has regulatory responsibility for the safety of eggs while they are inside of their shells; FDA regulates cheese pizza, but if there is pepperoni on top, it falls under the jurisdiction of FSIS; FDA regulates closed-face meat sandwiches, while FSIS regulates open-faced meat sandwiches.[1]

The Plan recommended consolidation of the food safety functions into a single agency within the Department of Agriculture to be called the Federal Food Safety Agency. The recommendation is the latest in a long line of proposals that envision across-the-board centralization of all aspects of food safety regulation.[2] Like the vast majority of such proposals, it does not consider whether a preferable approach would be to differentiate the degree of centralization based on the allocation that best promotes regulatory goals for different regulatory functions. This chapter summarizes the current structure of federal food safety regulation, explores repeated calls for greater centralization that by and large neglect the possibility of functional differentiation in the desired degree of centralization, and preliminarily suggests the structural configurations that are likely to best accommodate the policy tradeoffs implicated in centralizing or decentralizing food safety regulation for the various functions whose exercise is critical to the provision of a safe and healthy food supply.

As with each of the three dimensions of authority highlighted in this book, allocation at one or another point along the centralization–decentralization dimension implicates tradeoffs among the values that government programs seek to promote.[3] Policymakers selecting governance frameworks should determine contextually whether the advantages of decentralized (or centralized) governance outweigh the disadvantages.[4] One of the most important contextual factors for assessing the tradeoffs of centralization and decentralization is governmental function. The optimal balance will often differ depending on the function being performed. The efficiency and effectiveness advantages of centralized governance, for example, may outweigh any countervailing effectiveness and accountability advantages resulting from decentralization of functions, such as scientific research, data generation, and ambient monitoring, but not for other functions, such as information analysis, permitting, or enforcement.

This chapter uses regulation of food safety in the United States to illustrate the value of differentiating by function when deciding on the appropriate degree of regulatory centralization. Section A summarizes the existing decentralized federal food safety regulatory regime. Policymakers and academics have consistently called for greater centralization of food safety regulatory authority. Too often, however, the critics have approached the question of the appropriate degree of centralization in an across-the-board fashion, failing to consider whether regulatory authority is more appropriately centralized for some functions than others. Section B describes recurring criticisms of the existing regime and associated legislative and administrative proposals for greater centralization, emphasizing their failure to differentiate by regulatory function in considering the desired degree of centralization. We believe that this kind of incomplete analysis may fail to achieve greater net regulatory advantages than a function-specific approach would.

Section C urges policymakers to consider the advantages and disadvantages of centralization and decentralization on a function-by-function basis and offers a preliminary framework for systematic assessment of the relevant tradeoffs, which might be adjusted based on future empirical research and practical experience. Both in the food safety arena and more generally, we conclude that, although analysis of the optimal allocation of authority is necessarily context-specific and the optimal balance of tradeoffs may shift over time, centralizing some but not other regulatory functions will usually be appropriate. The arguments for centralization will often be strongest for scientific research, data generation, ambient monitoring, and financing. Particularly in the food safety context, a strong case can also be made for centralized inspection authority. Decentralized authority is more often likely to be a better fit for planning, permitting, and enforcement, and standard setting may often best be accomplished through a mix of centralized and decentralized authority. The chapter also notes the importance of recognizing that the choice between centralization and decentralization is not binary but rather provides a spectrum of possibilities. Finally, we suggest that policymakers' consideration of the interactions of all of the dimensions in connection with each function will further improve organizational choices by leveraging the advantages of decentralization (or centralization) while minimizing its costs.

A. Decentralization in Food Safety Regulation

At least fifteen federal agencies are responsible for ensuring the safety of the food supply in the United States: FSIS, the Animal and Plant Health Inspection Service (APHIS), the Grain Inspection, Packers, and Stockyards Administration (GIPSA), the Agricultural Marketing Service (AMS), the Agricultural Research Service (ARS), the Economic Research Service (ERS), the National Agricultural Statistics Service (NASS), the National Institute of Food and Agriculture, all of which are housed within the Department of Agriculture (USDA); FDA and the Centers for Disease Control and Prevention (CDC), both of which are part of the Department of Health and Human Services (HHS); the National Marine Fisheries Service (NMFS) within the Department of Commerce; the Environmental Protection Agency (EPA); the Department of Transportation; the Bureau of Alcohol, Tobacco, Firearms, and Explosives within the Department of the Treasury; US Customs and Border Protection, which is a part of the Department of Homeland Security; and the Federal Trade Commission (FTC), an independent agency.[5] A similar array of actors is likely to exist at the state and local levels, ranging from state agriculture departments to local restaurant inspectors responsible for enforcing health codes.[6]

Food safety regulatory authority is carved up based on both substantive and functional grounds.[7] Some substantive jurisdictional dividing lines are clear. FSIS, for example, has authority over meat, poultry, and eggs, but not grains. NMFS's authority is confined to seafood. FDA has no authority over meat and poultry. FTC is charged with rooting out false advertising of food products. Authority is sometimes limited to a particular governmental function. ARS is tasked exclusively with research functions, while the NASS supplies statistical data relating to the safety of the food supply.[8] Thus, the jurisdiction of some agencies covers a broader array of food-related activities (e.g., FDA and FSIS have a broader range of authority than GIPSA) or governmental functions (e.g., EPA is responsible for performing more tasks than ARS or ERS) than others.

This decentralized system emerged piecemeal, typically in response to particular health threats or economic crises.[9] The resulting allocation of authority often appears to be irrational. The description of regulatory authority over eggs at the beginning of the chapter is only one example of splintered (and sometimes overlapping) federal regulatory authority. Facilities that produce processed foods may be subject to inspections by both USDA and FDA. A canning facility that produces soup containing meat or poultry, for example, is subject to inspections by USDA, but also by FDA if it also produces soup containing seafood.[10] Figure 3.1 illustrates the configuration of regulatory authority noted at the beginning of this chapter; the federal agencies responsible for regulating a packaged ham and cheese sandwich and the manner of such regulation depends on whether it is closed-faced (daily FSIS inspections of manufacturers who sell in interstate commerce) or open-faced (FDA inspections, on average, once every five years), even though the risks posed by the two kinds of sandwich are the same.[11] Figure 3.2, again echoing the 2018 Reform Plan, shows that frozen pizza production may be subject to regulation by six different federal agencies, with different agency configurations for regulation of inputs, on-farm activities, and processing.[12]

B. Ignoring Function in Assessing and Proposing Structural Reforms

Critics of this regulatory patchwork have long called for greater centralization,[13] but they have rarely differentiated among governmental

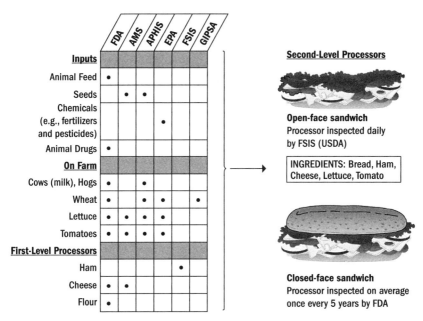

	FDA	AMS	APHIS	EPA	FSIS	GIPSA
Inputs						
Animal Feed	•					
Seeds		•	•			
Chemicals (e.g., fertilizers and pesticides)				•		
Animal Drugs	•					
On Farm						
Cows (milk), Hogs	•		•			
Wheat	•		•	•		•
Lettuce	•	•	•	•		
Tomatoes	•	•	•	•		
First-Level Processors						
Ham					•	
Cheese	•	•				
Flour	•					

Second-Level Processors

Open-face sandwich
Processor inspected daily
by FSIS (USDA)

INGREDIENTS: Bread, Ham,
Cheese, Lettuce, Tomato

Closed-face sandwich
Processor inspected on average
once every 5 years by FDA

Figure 3.1. Federal agencies responsible for safety of packaged ham and cheese sandwiches. Source: US Government Accountability Office, GAO-02-47T, Fundamental Changes Needed to Ensure Safe Food 4 (2011).

functions in doing so. Nor, generally, have reform proposals offered by food safety or regulatory experts, legislators, or administrative bodies, almost all of which have echoed that call for consolidated authority. The US Government Accountability Office (GAO), a persistent advocate for centralization, has repeatedly urged the creation of a new federal food safety agency on the model of EPA to combat inconsistent oversight and enforcement authorities and inefficient resource use that interagency coordination agreements had failed to address effectively.[14] The National Academy of Sciences (NAS), responding to a congressional directive to examine the organizational needs for an effective food safety system, reached similar conclusions in a 1998 report.[15] In place of the existing decentralized, overlapping, and uncoordinated structure, it urged vesting a single official with authority over "all federal activities related to food safety,"[16] including "outbreak management, standard-setting, inspection, monitoring, surveillance, risk assessment, enforcement, research, and education,"[17] without endorsing any particular structure.[18] More than two decades later, NAS supported centralization to increase

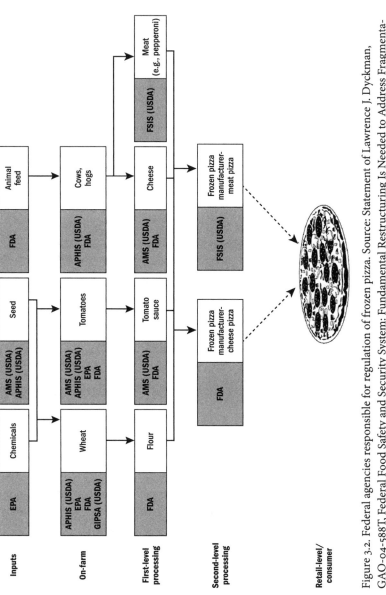

Figure 3.2. Federal agencies responsible for regulation of frozen pizza. Source: Statement of Lawrence J. Dyckman, GAO-04-588T, Federal Food Safety and Security System: Fundamental Restructuring Is Needed to Address Fragmentation and Overlap, Figure 3.1: Federal Agencies Responsible for Ensuring Safe Pizza (Mar. 30, 2004).

efficiency and effectiveness by establishing a single federal food safety agency with responsibility for "all aspects" of regulation, "from planning and data collection to policy and regulatory development, including oversight of all food safety inspections."[19] An interagency Council on Food Safety, established by President Clinton,[20] also recommended that Congress make a single official responsible for controlling "all federal food safety activities" in an effort to ensure consistency, accountability, and enhanced consumer protection.[21]

Critics' recommendations have sometimes focused on a single or limited number of agency functions, though even then they have rarely considered or assessed the extent of centralization for each function. On multiple occasions, GAO has recommended consolidation in a single agency of inspection and/or enforcement authority to decrease inefficiency and inconsistency,[22] improve communications between government and industry,[23] and reduce arbitrary differences in inspection frequency among agencies, such as those reflected in Figure 3.3.[24] It has also urged centralized planning to help achieve "a comprehensive perspective on federal food safety performance."[25] On one occasion, GAO did explicitly conclude that "it may make sense to maintain some functions separately," while consolidating others.[26] But it did not pursue this insight by assessing systematically why centralization of some functions was more desirable than others, and in other reports it has continued to recommend wholesale centralization without regard to function.[27] Similarly, GAO has also noted that although seven other developed countries had embarked on food safety structural reforms involving consolidation to enhance effective, efficient, clear, consistent, and timely regulation,[28] the nature and extent of those reforms varied.[29] Denmark, for example, "consolidated almost all the food safety functions and activities,"[30] while countries like Germany and Ireland engaged in more selective centralization of functions.[31] Ultimately, GAO drew no overarching lessons from these experiences on which functions might best be consolidated, stating only that they might illuminate US efforts to improve regulation. Thus, for the most part, the existing regulatory system's critics recommended greater centralization of federal food safety regulation while either missing the possibility of functional differentiation[32] or recommending greater centralization of limited functions without explaining why their consolidation is more advisable than for others.

Appendix II: Differences in Inspection Frequency of Manufacturers of Similar Products

Manufacturing plant inspected daily by FSIS	Manufacturing plant inspected on average about once every 5 years by FDA
Open-face meat and poultry sandwiches	Closed-face (traditional) meat and poultry sandwiches
Hot dog in pastry dough	Hot dog in roll
Corn dog	Bagel dog
Dehydrated chicken soup	Dehydrated beef soup
Beef broth	Chicken broth
Spaghetti sauce with meat stock	Spaghetti sauce without meat stock
Beans with bacon (2 percent or more bacon)	Pork and beans (no limit on amount of pork)
Pizza with meat topping	Pizza without meat topping
Soups with more than 2 percent meat or poultry	Soups with less than 2 percent meat or poultry

Source: Food Safety and Quality: Uniform, Risk-Based Inspection System Needed to Ensure Safe Food Supply (GAO/RCED-92-152, June 26, 1992).

Figure 3.3. Differences in inspection frequency of manufacturers of similar products. Source: US Government Accountability Office, GAO-02-47T, Fundamental Changes Needed to Ensure Safe Food 20 (2011).

Legislative and administrative reform proposals have likewise sought restructuring of food safety regulation through greater centralization.[33] A Senate committee, for example, recommended in 1977 that all food safety regulatory functions be consolidated in FDA, although nothing came of that or subsequent proposals until 2011.[34] In that year, Congress enacted the FDA Food Safety Modernization Act (FFSMA),[35] which provides FDA with enhanced authority to prevent, detect, and respond to food safety problems.[36] Instead of greater centralization of regulatory authority, the FFSMA focuses mostly on increased coordination.[37] It requires horizontal or vertical interagency coordination for research, data analysis, education, financing, planning, standard setting, inspections, surveillance, and enforcement. It did not, however, restructure existing agencies or consolidate shared authority in a smaller number of agencies,[38] notably retaining separate responsibilities for USDA and FDA.[39] Remarkably, given the decades-long attention to reform, GAO concluded in 2011 that a detailed analysis of the options for reorganization through greater centralization "has yet to be conducted."[40] Indeed, GAO itself failed to analyze whether differing the degree of centralization by regulatory function would most effectively redress the deficiencies of decentralization it had been complaining about for years.

Similarly, Senator Richard Durbin, a consistent proponent of reorganization, professed concern that the FFSMA did "nothing to address" the persistence of overlapping authority and lack of coordination.[41] He urged greater centralization in bills such as the Safe Food Act of 2015[42] to replace "fragmented" regulatory authority with a more effective and efficient "systemwide" approach."[43] Durbin's proposal also sought to minimize regulatory gaps[44] and increase transparency.[45] The bill proposed centralization in a new Food Safety Administration of virtually "all functions"[46] relating to food safety administration or enforcement currently being exercised by a host of federal agencies, thereby repeating past failures to assess whether the tradeoffs of centralized authority may vary by regulatory function.[47] Indeed, the bill would also have vested in the proposed Food Safety Administration's administrator the power to establish internal bureaus and divisions, thereby potentially replicating within the new agency some of the same decentralized structure and associated problems the bill was meant to address.[48]

President Obama's fiscal year 2016 budget proposal took a similar tack, proposing to consolidate food safety regulation in a new agency within HHS[49] to be vested with "primary responsibility for food safety inspections, enforcement, applied research, and outbreak response and mitigation."[50] The proposal's emphasis appears to have been primarily on creating efficiency gains, though secondarily it sought to promote effectiveness and accountability.[51] Obama's plan added emergency response responsibility to the list of functions that would have been centralized under Durbin's proposal, but for a narrower range of agencies. The new agency also would have had "a primary" but apparently not exclusive role in standard setting and enforcement.

Most recently, as noted at the beginning of this chapter, the Trump administration recommended merging the food safety regulatory authorities of FSIS and FDA into a new Federal Food Safety Agency to be housed within USDA. The new configuration would strive to eliminate fragmented and duplicative regulation, "rationalizing and simplifying the Federal food safety regulatory regime [. . .] while ensuring robust and coordinated food safety oversight."[52] The Trump proposal includes, among its goals, reducing duplication of inspection authority, better allocation of resources, better communication during illness outbreaks, and improved policy through development of a single strategic plan, reflecting recognition that food safety regulators perform a variety of functions. But the proposal does not suggest that the configuration of regulatory authority should differ based on function, or that the plan's drafters even considered the possibility that the tradeoffs of centralized and decentralized regulation may differ based on function. The plan is thus of a piece with most previous reform proposals, which have seemed oblivious to the value of functional differentiation.

In raising concerns about these legislative and administrative proposals, critics have similarly ignored functional jurisdiction. Among other things, they have asserted that the proposals would not increase regulatory effectiveness[53] (because, for example, they would sacrifice expertise and experience[54]), subordinate important missions of some of the merged components,[55] or be thwarted by long-standing turf battles or differences in agency cultures and practices among formerly separate agencies now housed under one roof.[56] Finally, some have feared that concentration of power in a single agency would create a problematic monopoly of regulatory power.[57] None of these evaluations seriously considered whether any of these problems could be mitigated by confining centralization to certain functions. Most obviously, centralizing only selected functions would directly address the concerns about the creation of excessive power in a single agency. Policymakers' consistent failure to consider varying the degree of centralization based on regulatory function has precluded them from identifying structural options that may have best accommodated the tradeoffs of situating authority along this dimension.

C. Differentiating Centralization and Decentralization by Function

Notwithstanding decades of dissatisfaction with the existing regime and a host of proposals to amend it by centralizing regulatory authority, analysis of whether it is advisable to differentiate the degree of centralization by governmental function has, by and large, been sorely missing from the debate over how to restructure the nation's food safety regulatory apparatus. According to GAO, no agency (including GAO itself) has engaged in a careful function-by-function analysis of the policy advantages and disadvantages of centralized food safety regulation.[58] That kind of analysis is likely to yield several advantages, including: (1) more accurate characterizations of the extent to which a regulatory program or component is centralized or decentralized; (2) mitigation of the political obstacles to regulatory restructuring that promises to produce more efficient and effective regulation; (3) clarification of the tradeoffs of centralized and decentralized organizational structures; (4) insight into the range of allocation options, as well as assistance in determining the appropriate point along the centralization–decentralization dimension for a particular problem; and (5) the opportunity for policymakers to improve the net advantages of functional choices along the centralization–decentralization dimension by making organizational choices along the other two dimensions.

1. Functional Jurisdiction Affects How Centralization Is Characterized

By failing to distinguish among regulatory functions, policymakers may be mischaracterizing the degree to which a program is centralized or decentralized. In one program, only one or two functions may be centralized, while in another all or most functions may be centralized. Some federal regulatory functions are already considerably centralized. For instance, CDC has a predominant role in foodborne illness surveillance (which entails both research and information compilation and distribution). CDC collaborates with FSIS and FDA but does not involve the full range of fifteen federal agencies that participate in food safety regulation in those efforts.[59] GAO has noted the potential benefits of CDC's retention of foodborne illness surveillance authority.[60]

A proper understanding of the degree of a program's centralization can assist assessments of whether its failure to achieve regulatory goals is either organizational or substantive in nature. If the former, it also provides the opportunity to analyze how restructuring can eliminate those problems. If foodborne illness surveillance has worked well, it might suggest the desirability of greater centralization of other aspects of research, information compilation, and information distribution than currently exists.

2. Functional Allocation of Authority Can Enhance the Feasibility of Regulatory Reform

Structural reform of longstanding allocations of regulatory authority tends to provoke political resistance, if for no other reason than the inclination of stakeholders to develop vested interests in maintenance of the status quo.[61] Restructuring efforts, for example, often stoke resistance from congressional committees whose jurisdictions would be narrowed or eliminated as agencies they supervise lose authority to other agencies.[62] For this reason, among others, the FDA's late chief counsel expressed skepticism about the political feasibility of consolidation.[63] Congress's failure to make significant efforts to impose consolidation despite decades of expert support for it seem to bear out that pessimistic view.

Political obstacles to consolidation of food safety regulatory authority might decrease if reallocation of authority did not involve wholesale elimination of existing agencies with legislative allies. One way to minimize political resistance to centralization might be to address the desirability of consolidation on a function-by-function basis, thus allowing all or most existing agencies to continue to participate in food safety regulation while avoiding the irrationality of splintered regulation.

3. Functional Analysis Can Highlight Values Tradeoffs

Functional analysis can also highlight the possibility that tradeoffs among conflicting regulatory goals or values will vary by function.[64] Absent such analysis, policymakers may miss opportunities to maximize the net advantages of available organizational options. For some functions, the efficiency and uniformity advantages of centralization are likely to outweigh the advantages of decentralization, such as enhancing opportunities for experimentation. As described above, GAO and others have repeatedly called for centralization of food safety inspection authority, in part because of the efficiency gains of such restructuring.[65] For other functions, such as permitting, and perhaps other aspects of enforcement, the balance might cut in the other direction.

This section provides illustrations of functions that might be more appropriately centralized or decentralized in the food safety context. Nonetheless, in light of the dearth of attention to governmental function by policymakers and researchers, these propositions are inevitably provisional and would benefit from future empirical study. Moreover, alternative allocations of authority inevitably implicate values tradeoffs. Whether one finds the structural configurations suggested here convincing is likely to depend on how one prioritizes the relevant conflicting values. A more efficient system, for example, may not necessarily be the most accountable one.

At least for food safety, there are three reasons why federal inspection authority is a candidate for centralization. First, centralization may increase the efficacy of inspections in protecting public health. The recall in 2010 of more than half a billion eggs after regulators traced a salmonella outbreak (which sickened more than 2,000 people) to two egg producers is revealing. Both APHIS and AMS inspectors detected salmonella at the farms before the recall, but neither was responsible for regulating the responsible activities. Instead of passing along the information to other agencies with relevant jurisdiction, they kept silent.[66] Had one agency been in charge of all inspections, it is more likely that the aggregated information on inspections would have highlighted the problem and ensured that it was supplied to regulators in charge of regulatory implementation and enforcement in time to minimize contamination.

Second, centralization may enhance efficiency by permitting a reduction in the size of the workforce if a single inspection were to displace sequential inspections by different agencies of different food products at the same facility. Both FDA and USDA may have inspectors working at the same ports of entry without sharing duties or information used to select which shipments to inspect.[67] All three agencies that share authority for regulation of the on-farm stage of frozen pizza production depicted in Figure 3.2 could conceivably inspect the same farm.

Third, centralization of inspection authority in a single body may promote fairness by reducing cross-agency inconsistencies. Inspections conducted with uniform frequency and content might also reduce misallocations of inspection resources that occur if agencies with more frequent or rigorous inspections address risks less serious than those subject to less comprehensive inspections. Centralized inspections would facilitate comparative risk assessments that allow resources to be targeted where they are most needed.[68]

Of course, these advantages need to be weighed against the potential advantages of decentralized inspections. Although a significant advantage of decentralization is often the ability of multiple decisionmakers to experiment with different approaches, this advantage may not be as great for inspections as for functions such as standard setting. The range of available policy options is likely to be greater for standard setting than for inspections, at least in the food safety context, providing a greater likelihood that novel approaches will generate improved regulatory results.

Scientific research and data generation about food safety risks also seems like a potential candidate for centralization. At least eight federal agencies are engaged in food safety research. NAS and others have called for centralization in CDC of research relating to foodborne illnesses.[69] Data collection by numerous agencies makes it difficult to integrate information that facilitates tracing food-borne illnesses.[70] Centralization may also mitigate problems resulting from the lack of data standardization and sharing among agencies as well as the persistence of data gaps.[71] Centralization can generate economies of scale and facilitate the transfer of insights learned in conducting research on one kind of food safety problem to another kind. That type of cross-synergy is more likely to occur if the same entity is conducting both kinds of research. Finally, accountability may improve if one entity is responsible for all research successes and failures, especially if the jurisdictional boundaries of multiple entities is unclear. Centralization of research duties in a single entity with existing expertise that expands over time may generate greater confidence than research conducted by disparate entities.

These effectiveness, efficiency, and accountability advantages of centralization may justify sacrificing the potential for experimentation in research methodology that a more decentralized allocation would provide. This tradeoff is perhaps most likely to be desirable if the problem being addressed is a familiar one (such as the effects of exposure to *E. coli* bacteria) rather than a novel problem for which innovative research breakthroughs are more likely (such as the impacts of exposure to genetically modified foods or a newly manufactured pesticide). Moreover, as noted below, to the extent that preservation of an agency's expertise is desirable (such as EPA's expertise in assessing the consequences of exposure to pesticides applied to fruits and vegetables), that agency's authority can be exempted from any broader centralization effort.

The discussion of the 2010 egg salmonella outbreak and CDC's role in foodborne illness surveillance illustrate that information compilation and distribution is another function that may usefully be centralized. Had APHIS and AMS inspectors shared information about the contamination of eggs with salmonella they had detected, the 2010 outbreak may have been mitigated. The chance of thwarting terrorist attacks may similarly improve if multiple entities share analyses of vulnerabilities and suspicious activities and of past policy successes or failures.[72] Although interagency coordination of information might help, connecting the dots may require aggregation in one entity of information complied by many.

Relatedly, centralized funding of scientific research and data generation allows regulators to take advantage of economies of scale and may overcome collective-action problems. Centralization is often a response to such collective-action problems as resource inadequacy.[73] Allowing one federal agency to disburse research funds would enhance efficiency by allowing it to allocate funds based on a comprehensive set of comparative risk assessments so that minor problems are not funded at the expense of more significant ones.[74]

For other functions, the values tradeoffs may often cut in the opposite direction. We see greater downsides, for example, to centralization of the responsibility for information analysis. The expertise advantage that often accompanies decentralized authority may be more salient in analyzing than collecting or distributing information. Decentralization also gives rise to experimentation advantages. Multiple agencies may draw different insights from interpretations of the same data, generating novel policy approaches. Many of the repeated calls by GAO, NAS, and others for centralization of all food safety regulatory functions seem to ignore these advantages of decentralized information analysis, thus painting with too broad a brush.

The arguments in favor of decentralized planning and implementation might be stronger still. Planning, as we use the term, involves establishing a framework for achieving regulatory objectives that is implemented through subsequent decisions that conform to the plan. Both functions have a large policy component. Allowing agencies to fashion and pursue their own policy preferences engenders experimentation that may redound to the benefit of other agencies that address similar problems relating to a different industry or set of products.

On the other side of the coin, the efficiency advantages of centralized planning and implementation are more likely to be relatively small, except for matters that are common to all or most aspects of a regulatory program. Economies of scale are not likely to emerge from centralizing the responsibility to formulate and implement policy frameworks for addressing risks that may differ based on the nature of the contaminants (e.g., endocrine-disrupting pesticides versus microbial exposures), the capacities of the industries that create those risks, or other context-specific factors. Perhaps for these reasons, decentralization is the norm in contexts such as land use planning by local rather than state governments, and the development of unit plans by regional rather than national offices of the federal land management agencies.

Planning sometimes occurs at multiple levels, however, and centralization of some aspects may be appropriate. Planning for management of the national forests, for example, is tiered, with systemwide planning conducted by the national office of the US Forest Service and unit-level planning decentralized among the agency's regional or ranger district–level offices.[75] Among other things, centralized national planning facilitates the ability to address resource impacts that affect multiple landscapes spread over multiple forest units. Similarly, centralized macro-level planning that involves integrating aspects of food safety (such as allocating federal funding to the most serious threats or establishing uniform standards for inspection frequency) might enhance the efficiency, effectiveness, and fairness of regulatory efforts. If policymakers were to pursue the kind of across-the-board centralization that GAO and others have recommended, they would miss opportunities to craft planning (and other) responsibilities to best promote the goals that ought to drive food safety regulation.

Permitting or licensing activities is another function for which allocating authority to the decentralized end of the spectrum may provide a better fit than for other functions. Because these activities involve assessments of the circumstances of individual applicants, centralization is not likely to generate significant economies of scale. Decentralization is also not likely to impair accountability through shirking by regulators,[76] as long as the responsibility of each licensing official for facilities and activities within its jurisdiction is clear. Decentralization may generate equitable concerns, however, if licensing officials apply standards differently, affording some licensees competitive advantages over licenses issued to firms regulated by disparate federal agencies. That problem can be addressed through centralized planning of the sort described above.

In contrast with inspections, enforcement in food safety might more often be a better candidate for more decentralized authority. GAO and President Obama's 2016 budget both recommended centralization of both inspection and enforcement (referring, presumably, to efforts to impose liability for past violations and to prevent future violations).[77] Establishing identical regulatory structures for inspections and other aspects of enforcement is not inevitable, however. Ireland, for example, consolidated enforcement functions, but not inspections.[78]

On the one hand, decentralized control over administrative and judicial actions against alleged violators risks creating inefficiencies if multiple agencies investigate and assess whether to pursue potential regulatory violations based on the same set of facts. It also risks creating disparate treatment of regulated entities if one agency pursues more onerous remedies than another for like violations.

On the other hand, centralization is not likely to create economies of scale, as each enforcement action requires attention to the circumstances of the alleged violator. Perhaps more importantly, decentralization provides opportunities for regulatory experimentation. Scholars have touted the value of innovative enforcement in many contexts.[79] In the environmental context, for example, EPA during the Obama administration sought to rely on new monitoring and communications technology to improve compliance and maintain a vigorous enforcement presence despite declining resources.[80]

For some functions, such as food safety standard setting, the selection of centralized or decentralized authority is likely to be especially contextual. There is a rationale for centralization of federal regulation. Regulation of frozen pizza, discussed in section A above, provides an example. Although regulation of on-farm activities and processing by different agencies may be justified because the nature of the threats posed at those two stages of food production may differ, regulation of inputs by four different agencies, of on-farm activities by four agencies, and of processing by three agencies seems to invite inefficiency, confusion, and conflicting mandates. Centralized federal standard setting may also generate economies of scale.[81] It may also mitigate accountability concerns that may arise if multiple agencies with standard-setting authority over the same product do little and seek to blame inadequate regulation on others.

But retention of decentralized federal standard setting may be appropriate if the products pose different kinds of threats, implicating different kinds of expertise. Thus, division of authority between EPA for toxic chemical contamination of food and FDA or USDA for microbial contamination may be more justifiable than division of authority for microbial contamination among multiple agencies for beef, poultry, pork, and eggs. In addition, centralization may sacrifice the expertise and experimentation advantages of decentralized authority. For products that present novel risks or for which regulatory experience is lacking, the advantages of experimentation that result from decentralized standard setting may be worth sacrificing the uniformity and efficiency advantages of centralization. Policymakers should prioritize these potentially conflicting goals in deciding how much centralization of standard-setting authority is desirable.

Most of the reform proposals discussed in this chapter called for centralization of standard setting. GAO did so, for example, even when it acknowledged that retention of a decentralized structure might work best for other functions.[82] There is little evidence, however, that these positions were based on a careful evaluation of the advantages and disadvantages of centralized standard setting, either generally or in the context-specific fashion addressed here. More broadly, the failure of most analysts and policymakers to engage in functional analysis of the appropriate structure of food safety regulation risks forfeiting significant policy advantages that a more finely grained analysis is capable of providing.

4. Functional Analysis Helps Identify the Appropriate Degree of Centralization

The value of functional analysis is likely to be enhanced through recognition that a structure that is neither completely centralized nor decentralized may provide the best opportunity to balance competing regulatory goals or values. The choice between centralized and decentralized authority is rarely binary. Rather, the options along each dimension typically reflect a spectrum of possibilities. It may be advisable to move further to one end of the spectrum for one function than another, even if both functions would be well served by moving in the same general direction.

The research function, for example, need not be completely centralized to achieve some of the advantages associated with its centralization. NAS has suggested the possibility of separating authority based on the nature of the activities to which the research relates (e.g., education, production, and processing).[83] Having multiple entities researching the risks posed by a single food product just because the research results may need to be framed differently for different user groups hardly seems efficient, however. Retention of separate research responsibilities on the basis of the nature of the risk may be more justifiable.[84] Chemical and microbial contamination, for example, present risks that arise from different activities and that affect the body in different ways. Allowing EPA and either CDC, USDA, or FDA to conduct separate research agendas for chemical and microbial contaminants, respectively, may make sense. Although splitting research authority in that way may sacrifice efficiency and uniformity in approach, those losses may be relatively small if knowledge about one set of risks is unlikely to shed light on how to identify or address a different set.[85] Decentralized and coordinated authority may be preferable if centralization risks the loss of desired expertise, the ability to tailor approaches to local condition, or the greater accessibility that decentralized authority is capable of providing.[86] The appropriate degree of centralization is likely to be different for other functions, such as functions for which the achievement of economies of scale are deemed particularly important. Focusing on the appropriate regulatory structure for each function enhances opportunities to identify the suitable degree of centralization instead of making determinations along that dimension on a binary, all-or-nothing basis.

5. Integration of Functional Analysis Along All Three Dimensions

The focus in this chapter and the next two (perhaps somewhat artificially) is on recognizing that assessments of organizational options should be function-specific. Differentiating the degree of centralization or decentralization by function may allow policymakers to maximize the net advantages of choices along that dimension. Ideally, however, policymakers' consideration of the interactions of all of the dimensions in connection with each function will further improve organizational choices. Even when one focuses on a single governmental function, the choice between centralization and decentralization is only one piece in the allocation puzzle. Policymakers should also assess the extent to which authority over this particular function should overlap with others, or be coordinated.

Focusing on the relationship between the centralization and coordination dimensions may prompt the adoption of regulatory allocations that create synergies that a focus on a single dimension in isolation would not likely reveal. Decentralization, for example, may be desirable for functions whose exercise implicates policy experimentation (such as implementation, standard setting, and enforcement) or for functions that would benefit from location or activity-specific expertise (such as permitting or liability-seeking enforcement). But decentralized authority must also necessarily be either coordinated or independent, and the tradeoffs along this dimension likely will vary from function to function as well.

Allowing decentralized authority to be exercised independently may spur competition among agencies engaged in information analysis, for example, and reduce the risk of groupthink that may otherwise squelch willingness to think outside the box.[87] On the other hand, decentralized but coordinated planning may promote the experimentation and diversity advantages of decentralization while enhancing communication, collaboration, and trust. This contrasts with GAO's recommendations urging increased centralized planning on food safety to promote better coordination, collaboration, communication, trust, and information sharing among agencies, which in our view conflate the centralization and coordination dimensions.[88] Similarly, decentralized and coordinated information compilation and distribution between FDA and USDA may be a good way to promote efficient food safety protective responses.[89]

Movement along the overlap–distinctness dimension may also allow policymakers to leverage the advantages of decentralization (or centralization) while minimizing its costs. For example, policymakers may be able to retain the expertise and experimentation advantages of decentralized standard setting while avoiding regulatory inconsistency by reducing functional or substantive overlap among federal agencies. Different federal agencies might be responsible for setting standards that govern different kinds of food-related risk (e.g., exposure to chemical or microbial contamination). Experimentation by multiple regulators may generate insights that are valuable to agencies responsible for a different set of products or activities. Likewise, policymakers may be able to secure the advantages of decentralized enforcement, including policy experimentation, while avoiding duplication, inefficiency, and inequities stemming from differences in enforcement strategy, by creating minimal overlap but requiring at least some coordination of effort. Considering the appropriate configuration of each regulatory function along all three dimensions is likely to reveal structural options and opportunities that a more cloistered focus on a single dimension in isolation would not.

Because the basic structure of federal food safety regulation has not changed much in decades, limited empirical data exists to assess the extent to which the prescriptions identified here would improve regulatory performance. There is more experience with regulatory reform in states and other countries.[90] Stakeholders affected by these reorganizations have opined that consolidation has enhanced regulatory programs through improved service delivery, more consistent or timely enforcement, reduced overlap in inspections, and clearer responsibilities.[91] They have also suggested that it has reduced gaps in oversight, streamlined communications, increased coordination, adjusted the frequency of inspections to the degree or nature of the risk, improved accountability and transparency, improved information systems, and geared expenditures to the risk of foodborne illness.[92] Yet analysis of the results of even those reforms is, to date, incomplete. None of the countries studied by GAO that consolidated their food safety regulatory systems had formally analyzed the effects of greater centralization at the time of the report,[93] and GAO did not systematically assess the degree of centralization on a function-by-function basis.[94] The report does identify the effects of consolidation on some functions, however, providing potential insights into whether a particular version of each country's centralization reforms had contributed to improvements in the implementation of those functions. The results seem to confirm our intuition that, for example, food safety inspections and information distribution may particularly benefit from centralization.[95] Further systematic evaluation of these experiences by policymakers in the United States or implementing countries may fill some of the existing information gaps and provide guidance to those contemplating the redesign of federal regulatory structures.

Chapter 4

The Functions of Overlapping Pollution
Control Federalism

How many locks should a homeowner install on her front door? Although homeowners incur additional time and expense from installing and using an extra lock, the safety advantages from this redundant system may often be worth it.[1] Installation of more and more locks, however, would likely yield diminishing returns. A home security alarm would tackle related concerns, and might (or might not) be worth the additional cost.

Homeowners face similar choices for other aspects of homeownership. For fire protection, a homeowner might install smoke detectors, carbon monoxide detectors, fire extinguishers, and/or a smoke-activated sprinkler system. In a region prone to electrical storms and flooding, she might find it efficient and effective to install a backup power generation system for sump pump operation in the event of electric failure. But would duplicate HVAC systems or even internet service providers be worth it, in case one fails? Homeowners should typically assess the advantages and disadvantages of employing multiple systems on a case-by-case basis. The tradeoffs of installing multiple safeguards will differ, of course, depending on whether one is considering door locks, air conditioning, or internet access. Most would counsel against a wholesale approach to these different decisions.

Unlike prudent homeowners, policymakers and scholars regularly fail to appropriately consider the advantages and disadvantages of overlapping authority in government. As we suggest in chapter 2, authority is only overlapping if two or more agencies perform the same governmental function within the same substantive area.[2] Although this may be a straightforward axiom, commenters too often mistakenly assume more or less overlap in existing allocations of authority because they fail to analyze the extent to which respective agencies' functional and substantive jurisdictions overlap. In his 2011 State of the

Union address, for example, President Obama took the time to criticize duplication in government, using salmon resource management as his "favorite example" even though the two agencies regulating such activities have minimal overlap in jurisdiction.[3]

Moreover, as others have pointed out, critics of overlap often overlook the many illustrations of how overlap provides redundancy advantages, such as serving as a failsafe when one level of government or institution within a level is unable or unwilling to take the actions needed to promote statutory goals.[4] Just as importantly, critics also routinely ignore the value of distinguishing among different regulatory functions in assessing the extent to which jurisdiction should overlap or be distinct. On the other hand, the growing number of scholars who spotlight the significant advantages of overlapping jurisdiction often make the mistake of defending it as a wholesale proposition.[5]

Using the federal pollution control laws as examples, this chapter explores the significance of governmental function in overlapping authority, with two purposes. Its first goal is to make the case that proponents and detractors have typically neglected and/or misunderstood the role of functional jurisdiction in the context of overlapping authority. Several leading environmental laws adopted during the 1970s, including the Clean Air Act (CAA),[6] Clean Water Act (CWA),[7] and Resource Conservation and Recovery Act (RCRA),[8] are frequently described as exercises in cooperative federalism, in which Congress sought to encourage a federal–state partnership for protecting health and the environment. Typically, the Environmental Protection Agency (EPA) is the federal authority responsible for administering these laws, but Congress carved out significant roles for the states. In this sense, these laws are rare efforts by policymakers to differentiate, at least implicitly, among functions in allocating overlapping or distinct authority.

A common narrative among policymakers and scholars for describing these and other "cooperative federalism" laws is that the federal government is distinctly charged with setting standards and the states with implementing them.[9] In section A of this chapter, we show that these laws actually create a complex assortment of distinct and overlapping authority involving EPA and state environmental agencies. The environmental laws situate EPA and the states in different places along the overlap–distinctness dimension for different functions.

Moreover, as explained in section B, most characterizations by Congress and scholars of these regimes have focused on the relative advantages of centralizing authority at the federal level versus more decentralized state authority, conflating or neglecting to explore the possible merits or demerits of shared (or distinct) authority. More recently, some policymakers and scholars have begun to identify advantages and disadvantages from the implicitly overlapping authority to regulate pollution. Nonetheless, even these assessments of, and prescriptions to improve, the effectiveness of existing levels of overlapping authority generally do not differentiate among functions in their evaluations of the tradeoffs of greater or lesser overlap.

This omission leads to the second purpose of this chapter. In section C, we argue that policymakers should systematically and explicitly distinguish among functions in deciding the extent to which authority should overlap. Focusing on functional jurisdiction not only helps observers parse out the extent of overlap. It also provides opportunities to tailor the extent of overlap for each function to correspond to the concerns and opportunities that relate to the performance of that function. For overlapping authority, the advantages may include enhanced effectiveness stemming from the creation of a regulatory safety net, resistance to capture, and minimization of opportunities for regulatory arbitrage. Distinct authority may provide the efficiency gains associated with reductions in agency administrative and private sector compliance costs, the accountability advantages of avoiding a regulatory commons, and the fairness benefits resulting from reductions in inconsistent regulatory approaches. The chapter thus provides preliminary observations about the functions for which overlapping authority may generally be more or less valuable.

Furthermore, using the federal pollution control laws as an illustration, section C asserts that differentiating among governmental functions opens up the possibility of advancing the effectiveness goals of overlapping authority while concurrently promoting the efficiency and accountability advantages of distinct authority. These laws demonstrate that creating overlap for certain functions—particularly in planning, implementation, and enforcement—may create valuable safety net benefits, for example. However, making authority overlap for every function has diminishing returns in safety-net benefits (just as a dozen locks on a door might). Similarly, concerns regarding inconsistency from overlapping authority may be less acute for certain functions (such as research or ambient monitoring) than for others (such as standard setting). Finally, by distinguishing among functions, policymakers have the opportunity to simultaneously reduce functional overlap while maintaining joint substantive jurisdiction. Even a modest level of overlap, potentially combined with a strict coordination requirement, has the potential to achieve many of the advantages of shared authority with fewer disadvantages.

We should note that, unlike the other case study chapters that primarily explore allocations of authority among federal agencies, this chapter focuses on the extent of overlapping authority between the federal government and the states. These classic statutory examples of federalism inevitably involve significant policy tradeoffs appropriately associated with the centralization–decentralization dimension. As explored in the extensive literature on federalism and detailed in greater detail in chapter 2, these may include a range of purported advantages attributed to decentralization (such as expertise, diversity, experimentation, and democratic accountability) and centralization (such as economies of scale and the capacity to address a range of collective-action problems).[10] Nevertheless, although the chapter may at times reference the relative tradeoffs along the centralization–decentralization dimension, the aim here is to consider how these statutory regimes serve to explore the tradeoffs of the overlap–distinctness dimension, and how these may interact with functional jurisdiction.

A. Pollution Control Federalism and Functional Differences in Overlap

Although the federal regimes first established in the 1970s to address pollution are customarily regarded as examples of divided authority between state and federal governments, they actually serve as vivid illustrations of congressional allocations that inadvertently vary the extent of distinct and overlapping authority by governmental function. Before 1960, a few federal laws restricted pollution-generating activities,[11] but state and local statutory and common law were the only significant constraints on pollution.[12] The federal government incrementally increased

Exclusively federal	• CAA ambient standard-setting • Hazardous waste packaging and transportation regulation • Pesticide product labeling and packaging regulation
Primarily federal	• CAA new mobile-source standard-setting, implementation, and enforcement
Generally co-equal	• CAA, CWA, and RCRA research, data generation, and ambient monitoring • CAA and CWA information compilation/distribution • CAA and CWA stationary-source standard setting
Primarily state	• CAA planning and implementation • CWA planning • CAA and CWA permitting • CAA, CWA, and RCRA enforcement • CAA and CWA financing
Exclusively state	• CAA indirect source control • CWA non-point source control implementation

Figure 4.1. Examples of overlapping authority in US pollution control.

its responsibility, starting with funding research into the causes and effects of pollution[13] and technical and financial assistance to the states.[14]

By the 1970s, various concerns led Congress to adopt more comprehensive federal regulatory approaches to curtail pollution. For some problems, such as hazardous waste transportation, nuclear waste disposal facility siting, nuclear material transportation and disposal, and biomedical waste management, Congress allocated exclusive authority to the federal government.[15] However, Congress was unwilling to do so to address most pollution problems such as water, air, and solid waste. Although the expansion of federal authority in these pollution control regimes inevitably increased the centralization of authority, in most such contexts it did not displace the power of the states or localities to adopt more stringent controls.[16]

A conventional narrative describes these "cooperative federalism" regimes as largely bifurcating authority. In this description, the federal government is charged with certain functions (such as standard setting) and the states with others (such as implementation). Yet, as summarized in Figure 4.1 and further detailed below, these regimes actually provide exclusive federal or state authority for only a few government functions and programs. Instead, they typically provide a spectrum of overlapping federal and state authority over most functions.

1. Exclusively Federal Authority

In a few regulatory regimes, Congress granted the federal government virtually exclusive authority for certain government functions. For example, only EPA engages in ambient standard setting under the CAA, determining the nationwide level of air quality for a particular pollutant that is "requisite" to protect the public health and welfare through the adoption of National Ambient Air Quality Standards (NAAQS).[17] There also are various federal environmental law regimes that preempt all state regulatory action over particular issues, such as certain activities relating to the management of nuclear waste,[18] hazardous waste packaging and transportation,[19] and the packaging and labeling of pesticide products.[20]

2. Primarily Federal

For most functions and programs, however, the federal pollution-control statutes provide for overlapping authority between the federal government and states. As with the other dimensions of authority, the overlap–distinctness dimension reflects a continuum; it is often the case that a statute creates neither completely overlapping nor completely distinct authority. These regimes illustrate that overlapping authority for any given governmental function may range from primarily federal authority to relatively co-equal authority to state primacy.

Title II of the CAA provides the federal government almost exclusive authority to engage in standard setting for new mobile sources that cause or contribute to air pollution that may be reasonably anticipated to endanger public health.[21] The statute generally prohibits the adoption or enforcement of state tailpipe emission standards, with the single exception of allowing EPA to waive the prohibition by granting a waiver to California.[22] Other states are allowed to adopt California's more stringent vehicle emissions standards if EPA approves them, and at least ten states have already adopted them or are in the process of doing so.[23] But by generally preempting supplemental state standards even if they are more stringent than EPA's standards, the CAA's delegation to EPA of near-exclusive authority to set standards to control tailpipe emissions represented a movement not only toward centralization, but also toward more distinct authority.

3. Generally Co-equal Authority

Under some federal pollution control statutes, government functions such as data gathering and some forms of standard setting involve closely overlapping federal and state authority. Initially, for various pollution control programs, Congress vested in the federal government the principal role in research and compiling and distributing information needed to make regulatory decisions because of purportedly greater resources and economies of scale.[24] Under most federal pollution control regimes today, federal authorities continue to engage in data gathering and dissemination.[25] However, states play an important role in information collection and distribution (particularly in the context of compliance monitoring). Under the CAA, for example, states are expected to engage in air quality monitoring to determine compliance with federal NAAQS and other standards,[26] and are not otherwise prohibited from engaging in their own monitoring and research activities. However, EPA is required to establish a national research program for the prevention and control of air pollution, including research related to the causes, effects and prevention of air pollution[27] and the measurement, monitoring, and modeling of air pollutants.[28]

Emissions standards for stationary sources under the CAA are an example of closely overlapping federal–state authority. Certain federal stationary source control standards preempt less stringent state standards, thus acting as regulatory floors. For example, EPA sets baseline New Source Performance Standards (NSPS), which are nationally uniform technology-based standards for categories of new industrial facilities.[29] The CAA also establishes federal standards for new and existing stationary sources in any nonattainment area (that is, one not meeting any of the NAAQS)[30] and for new major emitting facilities in areas already in attainment (that is, in compliance with the NAAQS) to prevent the significant deterioration of clean air quality (which are called Prevention of Significant Deterioration or clean air areas).[31] Yet Congress allowed the states, in most instances, to adopt more stringent control standards for new stationary sources[32] and to define the emission standards applicable in nonattainment and clean air areas (provided they are at least as stringent as EPA's NSPS).[33]

The CWA delegates standard-setting authority to both levels of government, though it places primary responsibility at different levels for different kinds of standards. Like the CAA, the CWA charges EPA with establishing technology-based effluent limitations (TBELs) for industrial and municipal point sources based on the cost and technological feasibility of available pollution control technologies.[34] Yet it preserves state authority to adopt more stringent source standards.[35]

To protect against the possibility that compliance with TBELs will not produce levels of water quality that meet the Act's goals,[36] the CWA also requires states to establish water quality standards (WQS) for each water body subject to the statute.[37] EPA is responsible for developing the scientific criteria for those standards,[38] from which a state may deviate only if it provides EPA an adequate justification, and EPA may reject a state standard that is not consistent with statutory requirements and replace it with a federal standard.[39] In addition, states with water bodies not in compliance with applicable WQSs must establish total maximum daily loads (TMDLs) that specify aggregate maximum pollutant loadings designed to achieve the standards.[40] EPA may adopt a TMDL for a state if it fails to do so,[41] though it lacks the authority to implement such a TMDL by imposing enforceable effluent limits on sources.[42] The CWA puts the onus of developing TBELs on EPA and of adopting WQSs on the states, though it carves out a role for the other authority in both instances.

4. Primarily State Authority

Federal pollution-control statutes retain significant roles for the states in planning, implementation, enforcement, and even standard setting in certain contexts. The CAA primarily vests the states with planning and implementation authority.[43] Each state has "the primary responsibility for assuring air quality" within its geographic area by developing a state implementation plan (SIP) capable of achieving and maintaining the NAAQS.[44] In developing the SIP, each state has considerable discretion to make policy choices about how best to allocate emission reduction requirements based on its knowledge of local conditions and consistent with its own economic, social, and environmental goals.[45] However, EPA may reject a SIP it deems incomplete or inadequate[46] and, in certain instances, it may replace a defective state plan with a federal implementation plan (FIP).[47] Thus, EPA's relatively limited role in implementation of the NAAQS it has adopted is to review state plans to ensure that they comply with statutory requirements and to take over planning and implementation responsibility only if a state persists in failing to meet its responsibilities.

The CWA also carves out a predominant planning role for the states. The statute obligates the states to develop and implement a nonpoint pollution management program[48] that identifies best management practices and measures to reduce pollution discharged not only from all point sources (such as pipes or ditches) but also nonpoint sources (such as runoff).[49] Each state must submit its plan for EPA review, but EPA lacks the power to implement a state plan if a state fails to do so.[50] The CWA also requires states to adopt a "continuing planning process" that must include effluent limitations sufficient to satisfy TBELs, TMDLs, and adequate implementation of WQSs.[51]

Both the CAA[52] and the CWA[53] afford states the opportunity to administer permitting programs that are integral to the regulatory programs those statutes create, provided the state permit programs comply with minimum federal requirements. Under the CWA, states may administer their own permit programs (subject to EPA veto of individual permits),[54] with all but four states having elected to do so.[55] The CAA likewise empowers states to develop comprehensive permit programs for the operation of sources emitting air pollutants and to tender these programs for EPA approval.[56] States must submit permits for EPA review, and EPA may veto those that do not comply with CAA provisions, including SIP requirements.[57] Under both the CAA and the CWA, EPA may suspend or terminate permit programs and take over their administration if a state consistently violates the statute.[58]

A review of the permit enforcement function in federal pollution-control statutes serves as a particularly useful illustration of how the extent of overlap may vary even among regimes that allocate authority primarily to one entity or level of government. Although states generally serve as the primary permit enforcement authority in most federal pollution-control regimes, federal involvement in this governmental function varies considerably.[59] Under certain judicial interpretations of RCRA, federal enforcement authority is relatively limited. EPA may bring suit if waste disposal practices for either nonhazardous or hazardous solid waste are found to pose an imminent endangerment to human health or the environment.[60] EPA also retains the power to issue a compliance order[61] or commence a civil action based on an alleged violation.[62] However, EPA does not have the authority to enforce RCRA's prohibition against "open dumping" of nonhazardous solid waste directly; only states and citizens may enforce this prohibition.[63] Moreover, some federal appellate court interpretations of RCRA allow EPA to pursue permit enforcement of hazardous waste–related duties only if the state has not begun enforcement at all; otherwise, EPA's only alternative is to withdraw the state's authorization to operate the RCRA program.[64] Other federal appellate courts disagree and allow EPA to institute enforcement proceedings even if the state has taken some action, provided it has not engaged in diligent prosecution.[65]

EPA is given greater enforcement authority under the CAA and CWA to "over-file" or commence enforcement action against permit holders regardless of what state regulators have chosen to do (or not do).[66] This authority differs depending on the nature of the regulatory requirement allegedly violated and the identity of the government that adopted it. State governments issue most permits, monitor compliance, and conduct the majority of inspections.[67] For federally adopted CAA requirements, however, EPA is the sole enforcer.[68] For obligations derived from SIPs and related permits, EPA and the states enjoy concurrent enforcement authority.[69]

Of course, the extent of overlap will depend on more than just the extent of legal authority. Among other factors, the allocation of resources undoubtedly influences how overlap operates. The Trump administration's 2017 budget proposal for EPA provides an extreme example. By seeking to largely defund EPA enforcement,[70] this proposal would have made enforcement virtually a distinct function of the states.

Finally, under several federal pollution control regimes, Congress initially relied on the federal government's superior resource capacity in vesting in EPA a significant role in financing the development of pollution control infrastructure, such as the construction of municipal sewage treatment plants.[71] Over time, states have increasingly been expected to take on a more significant role in financing.[72] Though declining, federal financing continues to supplement certain state activities.[73]

5. Exclusively State Authority

Under federal pollution control laws, there are few instances of exclusively state governmental functions. However, states routinely retain police power authority to regulate in order to promote public health, safety, and the general welfare, and Congress has precluded federal interference with some exercises of this authority. Most prominently, Congress has by and large blocked EPA from engaging in land use regulation. EPA cannot, for example, require states to include in their CAA SIPs indirect source controls that restrict land uses likely to attract automobiles (such as shopping malls or parking lots),[74] or even impose them in a FIP,[75] despite the continuing contribution of such sources to air pollution. Similarly, Congress's decision not to adopt (or require states to adopt) enforceable requirements for nonpoint sources under the CWA is typically attributed to a reluctance to vest in EPA regulatory authority in the nature of land use regulation.[76] Relatedly, EPA has no authority to implement a TMDL under the CWA, even if it has adopted one for a state. Under both the CAA and the CWA, then, Congress chose to exclude the federal government from routine land use regulation that traditionally has been the prerogative of state and local governments.[77]

B. Assessments of Pollution Control Federalism Neglect Functional Jurisdiction

Federal pollution control regimes thus exemplify how regulatory authority may vary according to the governmental function at issue—not only the extent to which this authority is centralized, but also the extent to which it is overlapping or distinct. Moreover, authority for each function typically is overlapping under these laws, though the degree of overlap varies considerably from function to function. Historically, however, the congressional justifications for these programs, and even much of the commentary, have missed the existence of overlapping authority. More recent scholarship does recognize that overlapping authority has its advantages and disadvantages, but has only begun to explore the implications of this dimension of authority and how the tradeoffs of overlap may vary by governmental function.

1. Overlooking Overlap

Federal pollution statutes serve as a rare example of policymakers distinguishing among functions in varying the extent of overlap in authority, but Congress appears to have engaged in this functional differentiation inadvertently. The sparse legislative history for provisions of these laws that allocate regulatory authority suggests that Congress focused principally on the relative advantages and disadvantages of centralizing authority in the federal government versus devolving authority to states, often missing or at least neglecting the role of the overlap–distinctness dimension. One of the most prominently identified problems was the extent of interstate pollution, and the lack of capacity,[78] incentives,[79] and legal authority[80] for individual states to effectively address it. Some policymakers also expressed concerns about states engaging in a race to the bottom, that is, adopting weak pollution controls to attract industry.[81] In some pollution control contexts, Congress has raised fears of NIMBYism, in which state governments would seek to exclude activities policymakers deemed socially beneficial (such as low-level nuclear waste disposal sites) in an effort to force them to locate elsewhere. That strategy seeks to shield the enacting state's residents from exposure risks while allowing them to reap the benefits of out-of-state disposal facilities subject to less stringent laws.[82] Congress and agencies thus have relied largely on conventional critiques of decentralization in instituting these arrangements, rarely discussing the advantages and disadvantages of allowing federal and state governments to have concurrent authority.[83]

Similarly, many analysts of the design of these regimes predominantly focus on the relative merits of federal versus state authority. Some emphasize the potential advantages of devolving implementation of pollution controls to the states—including tailored decision making, localized knowledge, experimentation potential, and increased political accountability[84]—without directly discussing the possibility of shared federal and state authority.[85] In summarizing the arguments in favor of federal authority, other scholars likewise illustrate how these assertions largely concentrate on the advantages of centralization without exploring the advantages and disadvantages of overlap.[86] Some may simply presume centralized environmental regulation necessarily involves overlapping authority, for example through floor but not field preemption.[87]

2. Recent Attention to Overlapping Authority

More recently, however, a number of observers of these federal regimes have recognized the existence and significance of overlapping authority and explored its merits and demerits.[88] Proponents of adaptive, polyphonic, or interactive federalism offer a range of advantages to relying on overlapping federal and state pollution control authority. They usually focus particularly on the effectiveness advantages of redundant institutions,[89] with the duplicative authority serving as a safety net against regulatory inaction or insufficient protection.[90] This redundancy might be of particular value in the protection of irreplaceable resources or to address situations in which massive costs are anticipated if regulatory failure occurs.[91] Proponents also identify the accountability advantages of overlapping authority, with multiple authorities serving as checks on each other and reducing opportunities for agency capture.[92] Relatedly, some critics of ceiling preemption, that is, distinct federal control, emphasize the advantages of shared federal and state authority rather than complete devolution and distinct state control.[93] Professors Adelman and Engel, for example, upon identifying concerns with exclusive federal control that include increased risk of capture and governmental unresponsiveness, embrace reliance on state and federal overlap rather than complete devolution of power to the states.[94]

Others identify disadvantages of overlapping authority in these pollution control regimes. They typically emphasize the inefficiencies of excessive, scattered, or duplicative authority from overlapping federal and state authority,[95] both for regulators[96] and regulated entities.[97] However, some argue that overlap can diminish the effectiveness of these regimes due to conflicting, competing, or inefficient regulation,[98] as well as impair accountability to the public due to the diffusion of responsibility.[99] Some proponents of the matching principle—which emphasizes that jurisdiction should be assigned to the authority that can best address that problem[100]—would ostensibly reject reliance on overlapping authority in pollution control. These scholars consider overlapping federal and state authority to be inefficient because it may introduce regulatory goals other than externality elimination and interfere "with the free movement of firms through government over-appropriation of fixed capital assets."[101] Professors Butler and Macey would limit federal authority "in most instances [. . .] to the assignment of property rights and the facilitation of bargaining," stating that "the federal response should be matched with particularized environmental and federalism concerns."[102]

3. Discounting Functional Jurisdiction in Assessing Overlap

Yet, with a few exceptions, even this growing literature exploring the value of overlapping authority has largely missed how functional jurisdiction may affect the analysis. Proponents and opponents of overlapping federal and state authority largely discuss the advantages and disadvantages as a wholesale proposition.[103] As such, they appear to not appreciate the actual amount of overlap in these regimes or to fully explore the range of possible allocation alternatives.

Importantly, some commenters implicitly appreciate that the choice of overlapping and distinct authority is not binary. Though not directly considering how functional jurisdiction may affect an assessment of the advantages and disadvantages of overlap, any proponent of "dual federalism"—which emphasizes that federal and state governments should operate in distinct and mutually exclusive areas—at least tacitly recognizes the possibility of assigning different functions (or at least programs) to different government entities. Rather than contending that jurisdiction over a problem should be fully under federal control or fully under state control, dual federalism seeks to entirely divide jurisdiction between federal and state authorities.[104] Similarly, some proponents of adaptive federalism acknowledge that federal and state jurisdiction can vary by function when championing distinct federal authority over certain functions (such as standard setting or funding) and distinct state authority over others (such as implementation and enforcement).[105] Some of these commenters thus recognize the possibility that the extent of overlapping authority can vary by governmental function.

Moreover, a few scholars have expressly assessed the advantages of overlapping authority in pollution control laws in connection with particular functions. This analysis has primarily occurred in the context of the enforcement function and debates over the value of federal over-filing beyond state permit enforcement.[106]

Encouragingly, some commenters thus have observed that poli-cymakers can distribute different functions to different government authorities, while others have analyzed the tradeoffs of overlap for par-ticular functions, such as enforcement. But scholars do not appear to have considered that overlap is a continuum, that adjustments in over-lap may range from exclusive or primary federal authority, to co-equal authority, to state primacy. They also do not appear to have considered the possibility of adjusting the extent of overlap differently for each gov-ernmental function, and the ways that the tradeoffs of doing so might vary.[107]

C. Appreciating Functional Jurisdiction in Overlapping Authority

So why does function matter? By neglecting the existence of different structural alignments based on regulatory function, policymakers and observers of federal pollution control legislation and in other contexts miss important possibilities in understanding, assessing, and improving allocations of authority.

1. Functional Jurisdiction Affects How Overlap Is Characterized

One way functional jurisdiction matters is that by failing to examine it closely, a policymaker or observer may simply misunderstand the character and amount of overlap. In characterizing pollution control authority as overlapping simply because both federal and state author-ity exists, some appear to assume more overlap than is actually there. Put simply, an allocation of the same substantive jurisdiction to two government agencies would not result in overlap (and thus implicate its advantages and disadvantages) if the agencies were given discrete functions.

Conversely, others appear to understand state and federal agencies to exercise distinct authority under the pollution control laws when a close review reveals that most such regimes embrace some level of overlapping federal and state authority for various functions. As such, proponents and opponents of overlapping authority may assume either more or less overlap than actually exists if they do not distinguish among functions in characterizing authority. Relatedly, our review of the CAA, CWA, and RCRA in section A of this chapter illustrates that even when one focuses on a particular governmental function, quite a variation in overlap—ranging from primarily federal to predominantly state authority—can exist even in "cooperative federalism" regimes. In both of these ways, failure to explore functional jurisdiction can mask the nature and extent of overlapping authority.

2. Overlap Can Vary by Function

A second way functional jurisdiction matters is that at least some policymakers and observers appear to miss the fact that prescriptions responding to concerns about excessive or insufficient overlap do not need to be absolute. As suggested by advocates of dual federalism,[108] responses to assessments of unwarranted overlap do not necessarily require an allocation of all governmental authority to one agency or another (e.g., in the federalism context, federal field preemption or full devolution to the states). Rather, by allocating certain governmental functions to one agency and other functions to another, policymakers can actually curtail overlap while continuing to rely on shared authority.

However, proponents of dual federalism only appear to consider the possibility of distinct federal or distinct state authority for any given governmental task or function. In our view, evaluations of the value of overlap, taken on a function-by-function basis, may reveal circumstances under which the redundancy advantages of overlapping authority may outweigh its risks. Although some functions may be appropriately allocated to only one level of government, overlap for a particular function may be valuable as well.

A prominent dissenting opinion by Justice Kennedy, joined by Justices Rehnquist, Scalia, and Thomas, is illustrative of how even eminent jurists may not appreciate how attention to functional jurisdiction can provide clarity about the nature and extent of overlapping authority. In *Alaska Department of Environmental Conservation v. E.P.A.*, Justice Kennedy disagreed with the majority's interpretation of the CAA that EPA has the authority to overrule state determinations of certain stationary source standards that are based on the best available control technology (BACT) when EPA concludes they are unreasonable.[109] The majority effectively concluded in this instance that the states and EPA have overlapping standard-setting authority.

In contrast, Justice Kennedy asserted that states should have "the exclusive role in making BACT determinations,"[110] that is, distinct authority over stationary-source standard setting (at least for the sources at issue in that case). In making this assertion, he focused only on the tradeoffs associated with the (de)centralization dimension; he rejected EPA's concerns regarding a race to the bottom among states by referencing Congress' "overriding judgment that States are more responsive to local conditions and can strike the right balance between preserving environmental quality and advancing competing objectives."[111]

In doing so, however, Justice Kennedy appears to have fallen into the dual-federalism trap of ignoring the possibility of overlapping jurisdiction for a particular function. Indeed, without exploring evidence of congressional intent or the policy tradeoffs of having both federal and state involvement in source standard setting, Justice Kennedy assumed that Congress designed the CAA to assign "certain functions to the States"—presumably including stationary-source standard setting—and "charged EPA with setting ambient standards and enforcing emission limits [...] to ensure that the Nation takes the necessary steps to reduce air pollution."[112] Additionally, he assumed that the only way to ensure a robust state role in a federalism regime is to provide states exclusive authority over a particular function—here, standard setting for stationary sources. He thus concluded that the majority's reasoning allowed federal agencies to "consign States to the ministerial tasks of information gathering and making initial recommendations, while reserving to themselves the authority to make final judgments under the guise of surveillance and oversight."[113]

Close attention to function and overlapping authority makes evident, however, that contrary to Justice Kennedy's analysis, under the majority's ruling states can continue to have a significant role in standard setting, and more generally, under the CAA. One reason is that allowing EPA to reject a state BACT determination as unreasonable still allows states a role in standard setting for stationary sources. Federal review is not tantamount to selection of the proper standard by EPA,[114] and states, moreover, retain significant authority over other aspects of stationary-source standard setting. Another reason is that states can and do also have a robust role under the CAA through their authority over other governmental functions. As the close analysis of the CAA in section A of this chapter makes clear, states retain primary authority over other major functions, including planning and implementation, permitting, and permit enforcement. Justice Kennedy's failure to closely review functional jurisdiction led him to overlook the fact that state authority under the CAA is hardly "ministerial" when one takes all governmental functions into account.

3. Overlap Should Often Vary by Function

This leads to a third implication of attending to governmental function in assessing the appropriate type and level of overlap. The extent and orientation of overlapping authority likely will—and should—vary not only from one regulatory regime to another, but more precisely from function to function within a regime. Accordingly, any attempt to assess the tradeoffs of overlapping authority in a regulatory regime should differentiate among functions in making such an assessment.

More specifically, the assessment of whether the advantages of overlapping authority are worth the disadvantages may differ from function to function. Policymakers might structure authority differently, for example, because the relative value of efficiency and redundancy likely differs according to the function at issue. For instance, duplicative collection of health data by federal and state regulators on the risks of exposure to pollutants may result in significant administrative costs without considerably improving the quality of the output. Yet the efficiency gains of vesting exclusive implementation or enforcement authority in state (or federal) regulators may not justify the loss of the safety net that results from having multiple authorities to protect against ineffective or absent regulation by one authority. Unfortunately, federal pollution control laws illustrate how policymakers and scholars largely miss the opportunity to differentiate among functions in assessing the relative advantages and disadvantages of overlap.[115]

Assessments of this kind will inevitably be most appropriately context-specific and, optimally, grounded in empirical evidence. Even more so than for the centralization and coordination dimensions assessed in chapters 3 and 5, one can make only limited generalizations in the abstract about which governmental functions might be particularly likely to benefit from more overlapping authority. And of course, assessments of the value of overlap will vary depending on the priority the observer gives to competing regulatory goals and values (such as promoting regulatory effectiveness through the creation of safety nets and the erection of safeguards against capture, even if achieving those goals comes at the expense of administrative efficiency and regulatory consistency). Nevertheless, preliminary postulates may have some value even here. For those most concerned about promoting effective regulation, for example, arguments in favor of jurisdictional overlap are likely to be strongest for those governmental functions where the safety net benefits and concerns regarding regulatory failure and agency capture are greatest. For other functions, such as information gathering, these concerns may be subsidiary to a desire to avoid wasteful duplication of effort.

Accordingly, at least in the pollution control context, the planning, implementation and enforcement functions are more often going to be the strongest candidates for overlapping authority if one identifies the primary goal as creating a precautionary regulatory regime. Indeed, under federal pollution control laws such as the CAA and CWA, many of the persistent concerns about regulatory failure and agency capture have focused on state resistance to implementation of federally adopted standards and "sweetheart deals" by state enforcement officials with permittees.[116] On the other hand, state involvement can help advance planning, implementation, and enforcement in the face of federal inaction. Moreover, distinct, centralized federal authority would jettison the decentralization advantages of empowering state expertise and promoting diversity and experimentation in regulatory approaches. And some state officials have explained that overlapping enforcement authority helps promote compliance by providing states with a valuable federal "bad cop" foil, as well as federal resources for particularly weighty or complex enforcement actions.[117] Thus, for those particularly concerned about the health and environmental consequences of regulatory failure, the case for overlap is particularly strong in planning, implementation, and enforcement—though likely accompanied by redundant costs for administration and compliance for regulated entities, and increased risk of a regulatory commons. Of course, for those with other concerns, such as administrative or market inefficiencies from duplicative regimes, even responsibility to implement these functions may be more appropriately assigned exclusively (or at least primarily) to the federal or state level.

Standard setting, whether through ambient or source controls, is likely the function for which the tradeoffs of overlapping authority is most contextual. It may often be the case that authorizing overlapping standards will offer such significant advantages as creating a safety net, protecting against capture, and minimizing arbitrage opportunities. With respect to the safety-net advantages of overlap, although federal pollution control standards have served as a floor for promoting a minimum level of health and environmental protection nationwide, states have often filled important regulatory gaps left by federal inaction. Prominently, state renewable performance standards and other programs for minimizing climate change–inducing greenhouse gases have helped reduce emissions, increase energy efficiency, promote a "green" economy, reduce dependence on foreign oil, and prompt broader federal action.[118] For those convinced that regulation to mitigate climate change is desirable, these actions illustrate the value of the safety net created by overlapping authority.

In some circumstances, however, policymakers may reasonably decide that, on balance, a unitary federal standard is justified. A more distinct allocation may be warranted if the disadvantages of overlap (including redundant administration and compliance costs and the risk of regulatory commons) are deemed to outweigh the safety net and capture alleviation advantages. In addition, a more centralized allocation may be deemed advisable if the identified advantages of centralization (such as the potential to achieve economies of scale, promote uniformity, and address externalities) outweigh the perceived diversity, experimentation, expertise, and democratic accountability values of decentralization.[119] Such might be the case if, for example, supplemental state regulation of nationally marketed products is judged to impose enormous costs on manufacturers faced with the choice of not selling at all in highly regulated markets or differentiating product lines to conform to varying state standards. Lastly, in certain situations the disadvantages of redundancy (when considered in conjunction with the diversity, expertise, and/or experimentation advantages of decentralization) may suggest exclusively local or state control. Such exclusive control might be particularly attractive in circumstances deemed to involve particularly localized conservation problems with limited interjurisdictional externalities, and/or for which economies of scale in regulatory decision making are considered to be low. Although we would consider such circumstances to be rare in the pollution control context, it nonetheless would not be illogical for a policymaker to allocate exclusive standard-setting authority to states for regulating what it deemed to be entirely intrastate pollution, for example, or for managing public lands with almost exclusively local significance.[120]

As further detailed in the next subsection, however, it is important to note that a delegation of overlapping authority for a particular function need not be entirely duplicative. As it has done under some provisions of RCRA, for example, Congress may authorize EPA to regulate only as a backstop, with overlapping authority limited to circumstances of persistent state recalcitrance in implementation.[121] Doing so can reduce concerns about capture and accommodate the advantages of decentralized authority while curtailing the disadvantages of redundancy. Moreover, concerns regarding inefficiencies caused by such overlap could potentially be managed through adjustments along the coordination dimension.

Some functions are more likely to experience limited benefits from reliance on significant overlapping authority. For instance, though there may still be other advantages from redundancy, the need for a safety net may be comparatively smaller for government research, data generation, and ambient monitoring activities, and state capacity and resources in pollution control have historically been relatively weak for these functions. Moreover, the consequences of regulatory failure are likely to be less substantial for these functions than in the context of implementation or enforcement. Accordingly, a policymaker might be more likely to find that the duplicative costs of overlapping regimes for these functions outweigh the advantages.[122]

Information compilation and distribution may be an even stronger general candidate for fairly distinct authority. There are likely to be fewer redundancy advantages for duplicative information dissemination than for other functions, as the concern of ineffectiveness from a single information infrastructure or the potential for regulatory capture and arbitrage will generally be more limited than for other functions. In contrast, the disadvantages of overlap may be considerable. These include the expected administrative inefficiencies of having duplicative portals for data distribution, but there is also the potential for decreased effectiveness due to the existence of multiple portals that may potentially hinder the accessibility and spread of information. Nonetheless, even if the tradeoffs in information compilation may point to less rather than more overlap compared to other functions, there may still be instances in which the absence of redundancy is problematic or even dangerous— when federal agencies took down information portals on climate change at the onset of the Trump administration, for example.[123] Such an assessment might prompt policymakers to reassess whether the effectiveness advantages of overlap outweigh the efficiency costs.

4. Blending Overlap with Distinct Authority

Perhaps most importantly, attention to functional jurisdiction allows policymakers to focus on whether there are good reasons to decrease overlap for one function but maintain or increase it for another. As suggested by the adaptive federalism literature, the pollution control laws provide ample evidence of the significant advantages of shared jurisdiction in filling regulatory gaps.[124] Nonetheless, these advantages do not mean that more redundancy—like more locks on a door—is an unequivocal good. Making each governmental function subject to overlap, making overlap between agencies fully duplicative, or increasing the number of overlapping entities will not always yield advantages, or at least not marginal advantages that outweigh marginal disadvantages. For instance, some scholars suggest that providing California a special prerogative to set more stringent standards for mobile sources may be successful because it pairs some (but not excessive) redundancy with the virtually exclusive federal authority to regulate automobiles.[125]

Similarly, we suggest that instituting overlapping authority between regulators for every governmental function would rarely be optimal. Although this might seem like a modest insight, proponents of overlapping authority run the risk of advocating such a position—and miss an opportunity to address concerns about unnecessary duplication—when they fail to explore the appropriateness of overlap for each function. In fact, it may often be valuable to reduce overlap in functional jurisdiction, even as shared substantive jurisdiction is maintained or increased. Differentiating among functions in this fashion can provide the potential for minimizing some of the potential disadvantages of overlapping authority while harnessing the advantages.

Reducing overlap in functional jurisdiction even as shared substantive jurisdiction is maintained would substantially reduce the inefficiencies from duplication of effort commonly associated with overlap. Meanwhile, because more than one regulatory entity would remain involved in (albeit different parts of) the regulatory process, such an allocation might still maintain some of the safety-net and anti-capture effectiveness and accountability advantages of shared governance.[126] This might particularly be the case if the relatively distinct allocations include a limited but robust requirement of agency coordination.

The variation in overlapping enforcement authority under existing US pollution control laws serves as an illustration of this potential opportunity. The CWA and CAA in particular allow for significant duplication of enforcement effort.[127] EPA and states are concurrently involved in many aspects of the enforcement process, incurring duplicative costs and potentially sending conflicting signals to permittees. This duplication includes allowing EPA to enforce plan and permit requirements regardless of what state regulators do.[128] Meanwhile, under at least some interpretations of RCRA and other laws such as the Surface Mining Control and Reclamation Act,[129] federal options in the event of lax state enforcement are limited to taking the draconian and rarely used[130] option of de-authorizing the entire permit program.[131]

But different configurations of federal and state authority are possible. For example, when EPA certifies a state permit program, policymakers could authorize states to assume virtually all direct permit enforcement activity. However, EPA could still retain a limited oversight role, accompanied by a strong coordination requirement, such as compulsory but deferential federal enforcement review of state enforcement actions, and/or perhaps required consultation during enforcement. For those statutory restrictions for which direct federal enforcement is deemed vital, EPA could retain sole authority. The proposed reduction in overlap would likely reduce duplicative administrative costs of permit enforcement without the crudeness and inefficacy of limiting federal authority to de-certifying the state program. Because limited overlap (combined with the check of formal coordination) would remain, however, the allocation of authority could retain much of the effectiveness and accountability advantages that typically accompany overlapping authority.

Similar parsing of authority could occur for other governmental functions. For instance, EPA might be allocated more distinct control of standard setting, funding, ambient monitoring, and information generation and dissemination, although states might still play a range of roles in these functions. At the same time, in addition to enforcement, the states might hold more distinct control over implementation, planning, and compliance monitoring, with again a narrow but vigorous backstop role for EPA.

Charging agencies with relatively distinct functions over the same substantive problem area can offer many of the safety-net benefits and ability to combat capture of overlap while minimizing administrative costs. By not considering whether distinct or overlapping authority is preferable for each function, policymakers miss other configuration alternatives, including those that might better accommodate the efficiency and effectiveness tradeoffs of duplicative authority. In short, their choice of locks may be more varied than they realize.

Chapter 5

NEPA, the ESA, and the Tradeoffs
of Interagency Coordination

Since the enactment of the National Environmental Policy Act of 1969 (NEPA),[1] each year federal agencies have engaged in hundreds of detailed studies of the effects of their proposed actions through abridged environmental assessments (EAs) or detailed environmental impact statements (EISs).[2] Though typically developed with input from stakeholders and in communication with other federal, state, and local authorities,[3] coordination usually ceases and the studies are buried once a decision about a proposed action is made. Agencies are required neither to distribute information about these analyses, nor to work with others to monitor whether the actual effects match what was anticipated or that adopted measures were appropriately calibrated.[4] Without such coordination, long-term learning within and between authorities is very difficult, and reinventing the wheel inevitable.

NEPA has been the subject of much praise and criticism by policy-makers and scholars. Yet only a limited segment of this commentary has focused on this statute as a mechanism for coordinating the activities of federal agencies,[5] with most such analyses pitting the efficiency costs of interagency coordination against their effectiveness gains without consideration of functional jurisdiction. However, a careful exploration of the similarities and differences between NEPA and the Endangered Species Act of 1973 (ESA)[6] illuminates many of the varying tradeoffs for situating different governmental functions along the coordination–independence dimension of authority. As detailed in chapter 2, many policymakers and scholars have recognized that in some circumstances interjurisdictional coordination can help promote effectiveness,[7] efficiency,[8] fairness,[9] and accountability[10] in the provision of regulatory services. However, some suggest that, at least in certain circumstances, maintaining agency independence and limiting cooperation would be less administratively costly, and perhaps even more effective, than a heavily collaborative model.

An analysis of NEPA and a comparison to analogous provisions in the ESA plainly illustrates the value of a careful exploration of interagency coordination—not only the choices that exist for policymakers in deciding the extent to which regulatory authority should be coordinated, but also how policymakers should assess such allocations on a function-by-function basis. NEPA requires any agency proposing "major Federal actions significantly affecting the quality of the human environment" to consult with and solicit the comments of other federal agencies with jurisdiction or special expertise during the process of preparing EISs.[11] The proposing agency must incorporate or respond to any comments in the final EIS. In addition, NEPA created an agency, the Council on Environmental Quality (CEQ), to observe compliance by other agencies with their NEPA responsibilities, and it has issued binding regulations that govern NEPA implementation by other agencies. NEPA thus provides for formal coordination across the federal government of data generation, information analysis, and planning responsibilities concerning agency actions that may affect the environment.

Unfortunately, many analyses of NEPA effectiveness have focused on improving planning or information generation coordination while neglecting the possibility of coordinating other regulatory functions. In this chapter, we argue that NEPA would likely have been more effective at actually minimizing adverse environmental consequences if it extended coordination obligations to at least two other functions: (1) information distribution and (2) compliance monitoring of the effects of project activities and adopted mitigation measures. This expansion of coordination duties would allow agencies to have the benefit of information and input from the CEQ and other affected agencies in deciding whether to alter ongoing projects to reduce unanticipated adverse environmental effects.

In addition, although the disadvantages of interagency coordination and advantages of independent agency action appear to be greater for project implementation under NEPA than for other functions, a case could also be made for some form of interagency coordination during project implementation. The ESA illustrates one form that formal interagency coordination of implementation and monitoring might take. In requiring federal agencies to consult with the National Marine Fisheries Service (NMFS) or the US Fish and Wildlife Service (FWS) on any agency action likely to jeopardize a listed species, the ESA mandates coordination in adopting and implementing alternatives as well as in post-decision monitoring.

This chapter ultimately argues that policymakers should consider the advantages and disadvantages of interagency coordination and independence on a function-by-function basis. They may conclude in a particular context that a formal and strict coordination requirement of one function will provide efficiency and policy effectiveness gains that justify the administrative disadvantages of coordination and the risk of groupthink that stifles innovation. For a different function and in other regulatory contexts, however, the balance may point to less formal or less strict forms of coordination (i.e., communication or required response to comments), or even independent authority.

A. NEPA: Coordinating Information Generation, Analysis, and Planning

Through NEPA, Congress has mandated formal federal interagency coordination over data generation, planning, and information analysis. NEPA is most commonly known and assessed by policymakers and scholars for its instruction to all federal agencies to develop "a detailed statement" on the environmental consequences of any "major Federal actions significantly affecting the quality of the human environment."[12] Much of the analysis and evaluation of NEPA by policymakers and scholars has focused on the efficacy and efficiency of this procedural mandate.[13]

However, a core feature of NEPA is its mandate for coordination of planning and information generation and analysis. NEPA created CEQ to observe the compliance of other agencies with their NEPA evaluation and disclosure responsibilities.[14] NEPA also instructs federal agencies, prior to preparation of an EIS, to "consult with and obtain the comments of any Federal agency which has jurisdiction by law or special expertise with respect to any environmental impact involved."[15] The "lead agency"[16] must request the participation of each "cooperating agency"[17] at the earliest time and use the environmental analysis and proposals of cooperating agencies "to the maximum extent possible consistent with its responsibility as lead agency."[18] Correspondingly, CEQ regulations require each federal agency with jurisdiction or special expertise to comment, even if the agency replies that it has no comment.[19] Such co-operating agencies must participate in the NEPA process at the earliest possible time, participate in the process for determining the scope of an EIS,[20] and may take over responsibility for developing portions of the EIS for which they have special expertise.[21] NEPA also requires the proposing agency to make the EIS and the comments and views of the appropriate federal, state, and local agencies available to the President, CEQ, and the public.[22]

NEPA and its implementing regulations thus mandate formal inter-agency coordination in agency planning as well as information genera-tion and analysis. CEQ itself has stated: "During the debate preceding the passage of NEPA, many members of Congress expressed concern that federal agencies were not working collaboratively and in some cases were working at cross purposes. As a result, one of the underlying pur-poses of NEPA was to provide a framework for a coordinated approach to environmental problem-solving across agencies."[23]

Mandatory coordination extends even into certain procedural standard-setting activities. CEQ regulations require federal agencies to adopt their own supplemental implementing procedures and to consult with CEQ in doing so.[24] Agencies are also encouraged to coordinate with other agencies in the development and adoption of these imple-menting procedures.[25]

B. Assessments and Criticisms of NEPA Coordination

1. Coordination of Planning, Information Generation, and Analysis

Many have lauded NEPA's establishment of a framework for coordi-nating information sharing. Observers have identified how NEPA's mandates of interagency coordination improved agency planning and decision making. For example, the Department of Energy and others have recognized many instances when NEPA's coordination mandate helped the agency's preparation and planning.[26]

Because of this interagency coordination of planning, information generation, and analysis, commenters often state that NEPA has thus laid out "the central architecture for agency collaboration, cooperation, and public participation in evaluating federal actions."[27] Indeed, in its

1997 report reviewing NEPA's effectiveness, CEQ opined that NEPA's "most enduring legacy is as a framework for collaboration between federal agencies and those who will bear the environmental, social, and economic impacts of agency decisions."[28] The report identified "five elements of the NEPA process critical to its effective and efficient implementation": (1) strategic planning; (2) public information and input; (3) interagency coordination; (4) interdisciplinary place-based approaches to decision making; and (5) science-based and flexible management approaches.[29]

However, policymakers and scholars have often levied criticisms and suggested avenues for improvement. One of the most frequent critiques centers on inefficiencies and/or ineffectiveness resulting from trying to harmonize disparate agency planning processes. CEQ has previously acknowledged that although "an efficient NEPA process requires that all interested agencies become involved in proposals early on and remain involved until solutions are found, many agencies have failed to use NEPA in this way."[30] It explains that "interagency coordination is hampered because agencies often have different timetables," modes of public participation, and conflicting requirements that arise from different statutory missions.[31]

Some experienced observers have recently pointed out that a number of congressional actions to reform NEPA on an agency-by-agency basis have actually hampered agency coordination. In response to perceived inefficiencies, Congress "has taken a surgical approach to NEPA by enacting legislation that amends specific federal agencies' NEPA procedures or exempts certain federal actions from NEPA review."[32] As a result, agency processes vary considerably, and changes intended to increase efficiencies in one agency may be negated by another agency's NEPA procedures.[33] These attempts to streamline NEPA processes might actually increase compliance costs due to requirements that differ by agency.[34] Indeed, the changes have arguably diminished NEPA's effectiveness by making it difficult for interested stakeholders to determine when and how they can most effectively participate.[35]

CEQ has also engaged in a number of initiatives seeking in part to enhance NEPA interagency coordination and facilitate resolution of interagency conflict.[36] One major step was a 2002 CEQ guidance memorandum issued to heads of all federal agencies striving to promote

cooperation among federal and non-federal agencies in the preparation of NEPA analyses.[37] The memorandum required federal agencies
responsible for a NEPA analysis to identify other potentially responsible
agencies that appear either (1) capable of assuming the responsibilities
of becoming a formal cooperating agency, or (2) appropriate for inclu-
sion in interdisciplinary teams and on distribution lists for review and
comment on the NEPA documents.[38] It has also required federal agencies declining to accept cooperating agency status to do so formally, in
writing, and urged lead agencies "to set time limits, identify milestones,
assign responsibilities for analysis and documentation, specify the scope
and detail of the cooperating agency's contribution, and establish other
appropriate ground-rules [sic] addressing issues such as availability of
pre-decisional information."[39]

In the same year, CEQ convened a NEPA Task Force that made intergovernmental collaboration a significant part of its focus.[40] It issued
a report suggesting that lead agencies actively "identify other agencies
that might have an interest in the new or revised proposal or project."[41]
The report also "set forth various concepts, including use of training, fa-
cilitators, interagency work groups, and cooperative agreements to foster
collaboration through all phases of NEPA processes."[42] In 2012, CEQ's
Chair, Nancy Sutley, issued the guidance memorandum referred to above
in an effort to promote timely and efficient NEPA reviews.[43] Other initiatives similarly focused on early interagency coordination, negotiating
timelines to review critical documents and decisions, expediting issue
resolution, and utilizing new information technology to create efficiencies in information generation and NEPA tracking.[44] As such, there has
been some improvement in planning coordination, particularly by those
federal agencies most frequently called on to engage in NEPA analyses.

Observers still find, however, that existing NEPA processes often
continue to lack "early and continued coordination between agencies,"
resulting in "unnecessary sequential reviews and delays in the decision-
making process."[45] Some conclude that these processes are still inefficient and ineffective at fostering quality outcomes, particularly for large
projects with multiple federal approvals.[46] An Obama executive order
sought to address these concerns in part by offering best practices for
interagency permit synchronization.[47] However, critics argue that its
failure to require agencies to implement these changes makes it unlikely

to lead to systemic, long-term improvement in multiple-agency large infrastructure project-permitting approval.[48] And more recent actions by Congress[49] and President Trump[50] seeking to modify how NEPA applies to infrastructure planning and perhaps more broadly[51] have similarly emphasized reducing, streamlining, and harmonizing front-end planning by agencies. Notably, these governmental initiatives and scholarly proposals never sought to alter NEPA's limited focus on interagency coordination in the information generation, analysis, and planning stages of project development.

2. Failure to Coordinate Information Distribution

A less common critique centers on the failure to promote agency coordination for other governmental functions beyond information generation, analysis, and planning. Some have focused on the lack of any coordination or centralization in information dissemination.[52] Professor Bradley Karkkainen has decried the difficulty of even obtaining copies of the core assessment documents for most proposals, especially for less impactful projects for which there are no requirements of publication in the Federal Register, transmittal to CEQ or other compiler, or even coordinated tracking by lead agencies.[53] Karkkainen called for enhanced coordination not only of information assessment but also its dissemination through the development of a repository to collect and compile these elementary documents, pointing to Canada's incorporation of such an information distribution hub for its analogue to NEPA as a successful example.[54]

In general, access to NEPA documentation has substantially improved since Karkkainen's critique, yet it very much remains deficient. It has become fairly easy to obtain a previously adopted final EIS through the EIS Database of the Environmental Protection Agency (EPA),[55] and access to other environmental clearance documents such as EAs or Findings of No Significant Impact has also improved. Yet this basic and long-overdue upgrade in information dissemination does not come close to addressing the limited coordination in information distribution. It remains exceedingly difficult to track information relevant to NEPA analyses, especially for analyses short of a full EIS. Drafts of EISs, which are particularly relevant for assessing interagency or intergovernmental coordination, continue to be difficult to obtain. It is also hard to secure monitoring information that tracks compliance with mitigation programs adopted pursuant to NEPA. In short, there is no coordinated framework for the distribution of NEPA-related information.

3. Failure to Coordinate Post-approval Monitoring

Similarly, a few observers have stated that NEPA would likely have been more effective at actually minimizing adverse environmental consequences if it had extended coordination obligations to another function: post-approval monitoring. Although interagency coordination is encouraged and even required for information gathering and planning, there is no requirement under NEPA for agencies to coordinate either the monitoring of the effects of an action after it has been approved or how effective adopted measures are in minimizing harm.

NEPA has generally been interpreted as not requiring agencies to undertake or coordinate post-decision monitoring of an action's actual environmental effects.[56] NEPA also does not require coordination of any monitoring of the effectiveness of strategies adopted by the agency to mitigate or minimize the adverse environmental effects of agency actions. CEQ regulations do mandate that a "monitoring and enforcement program shall be adopted and summarized where applicable for any mitigation."[57] The regulations also mention that agencies may "provide for monitoring to assure that their decisions are carried out and should do so in important cases," and that monitoring results shall be made available to other agencies and the public upon request.[58] Beyond the well-documented neglect of such mitigation monitoring by agencies under NEPA,[59] NEPA generally does not require any interagency coordination of project monitoring (other than CEQ's regulations stating that lead agencies shall make available to cooperating agencies monitoring results when they choose to conduct it).[60]

Various commenters have identified the advantages of requiring coordination of post-decision monitoring under NEPA.[61] Coordination of monitoring can improve monitoring efficiency by leveraging resources and expertise.[62] It can also help promote learning among authorities, which in turn can lead to better informed management and thus improve outcomes over time, not only for particular projects but also for

NEPA analyses and resource management more generally.[63] Leveraging multiple authorities might improve accountability as well.[64] These advantages are in addition to the often-asserted general benefit of post-approval monitoring, such as promoting the effectiveness of decisions, agency learning, and accountability.[65]

Accordingly, if NEPA monitoring activities were better coordinated, agencies might have access to information and input from CEQ and other affected agencies in deciding whether to alter ongoing projects to reduce unanticipated adverse environmental effects. CEQ's regulations require the preparation of a supplemental EIS if substantial changes occur that are relevant to environmental concerns or if there are significant new circumstances or information relevant to those concerns.[66] Nonetheless, there is no requirement to coordinate any monitoring of project effects that might give rise to a supplemental EIS.[67]

4. Failure to Coordinate Implementation

Finally, a few critics of NEPA have suggested that the law should extend formal coordination activities to the implementation function as well. Scholars and policymakers have urged that NEPA be amended or reinterpreted to require agency coordination in implementation by compelling agencies to adopt or comply with environmental mitigation measures proposed by CEQ or other federal agencies.[68] Such proposals could be understood as similar to a common criticism of NEPA for failing to require substantive changes to a proposed action in response to effects anticipated in an EIS.[69]

Although the Supreme Court has clearly ruled that NEPA's mandates are procedural in nature, not substantive,[70] some have urged that NEPA be amended (or reinterpreted by courts) to infuse substantive content into its environmental protection mandates. One possibility is to require agencies to adopt or comply with mitigation measures proposed by a designated agency, such as CEQ. This would be a particularly rigorous form of coordination. A less robust coordination alternative might be to mandate that lead agencies justify departures from the designated agency's recommendations,[71] and/or to vest in that designated agency the authority to remand projects on the basis of their adverse environmental effects and halt projects until they do so. Such modifications would not make

NEPA "substantive" in the sense that a lead agency would be required to adopt any mitigation or alternatives that would reduce environmental effects; rather, the focus would be on ensuring adequate consideration of measures or alternatives identified as appropriate by the designated agency. The resulting system would provide a more robust form of agency coordination—and perhaps a more effective process for avoiding federal actions that harm the environment—than NEPA now provides.

Although this expanded coordination role might be lodged in CEQ, it might make more sense to allocate it to EPA. Though initially envisioned by NEPA's drafters as a strong oversight authority,[72] CEQ has evolved to be substantially less influential than that in its legal and political authority.[73] Meanwhile, through the Clean Air Act (CAA), Congress conferred special authority on EPA to review and publicly comment on draft EISs prepared by other federal agencies.[74] EPA has developed detailed criteria for rating the quality of draft EISs; it rates each EIS and makes recommendations to the lead agency for improving it.[75] If a rating is sufficiently low, the project is frequently substantially modified or abandoned.[76] Regardless of which agency is authorized to extend interagency coordination into implementation and monitoring, requiring such coordination potentially gives other agencies, not just CEQ or EPA, the ability to affect the actions of other agencies.

C. Coordinating Additional Functions: Section 7 of the ESA

1. Interagency Coordination of Implementation

Although an expansion of NEPA's coordination mechanisms to other functions is unlikely to occur any time soon, the ESA provides a model for what that form of coordination might look like. Unlike NEPA, the ESA mandates federal interagency coordination not only in planning and information gathering but also in project implementation and monitoring. The ESA's core coordination provision is in Section 7, which requires federal agencies to avoid actions that will "jeopardize the continued existence" of listed endangered or threatened species or "result in the destruction or adverse modification of" their critical habitats.[77] Section 7 mandates that such an action agency must consult with NMFS (for marine species) or the FWS (for freshwater and wildlife species) before proceeding with the proposed action.[78]

The consultation process typically occurs in two phases: (1) informal consultation and (2) formal consultation.[79] In informal consultation, a federal agency, in the early stages of project planning, approaches the Service with jurisdiction and requests informal consultation.[80] The agency and Service are to discuss whether any types of listed species may occur in the proposed area, and what effect, if any, the proposed action may have on those species.[81] If the action agency, after informal consultation with the Service, determines that the project is not likely to affect any listed species in the project area, and the Service concurs, the informal consultation process is complete and the proposed project may move ahead.[82] If the Service determines that a listed species may be present in the project area, the action agency may prepare a biological assessment "for the purpose of identifying any endangered species or threatened species which is likely to be affected by such action."[83] If the agency determines, through a biological assessment or other review, that its action may adversely affect a listed species, the agency must submit to the Service a request for formal consultation.[84]

During formal consultation, the Service and action agency share information about the proposed project and likely affected species.[85] Formal consultation ends when the Service issues one of two types of biological opinions.[86] If the Service determines that the action is neither likely to jeopardize the listed species nor likely to adversely modify critical habitat, it issues a "no jeopardy" biological opinion and an incidental take statement (ITS) detailing the amount and extent of any anticipated incidental take.[87] Importantly, the ITS must include terms and conditions that the action agency and any applicant must implement to minimize the impact of the incidental take.[88] An agency that does not comply with the recommendations in the biological opinion and the ITS opens itself up to civil and criminal penalties.[89] On the other hand, if the action is implemented in accordance with the ITS, both the action agency and applicant are exempt from the ESA's prohibition on the taking of listed species.[90]

Conversely, if the Service concludes that the proposed action is likely to jeopardize the listed species or destroy or adversely modify its critical habitat, it must issue a "jeopardy" biological opinion.[91] Such an opinion must propose reasonable and prudent alternatives (RPAs) to the action which, if implemented, would avoid such harms.[92] The RPAs may be accompanied by an ITS conditionally authorizing the take of individual species members, provided the agency complies with the specified RPAs.[93] RPAs must be consistent with the purpose of the proposed project, consistent with the federal agency's legal authority and jurisdiction, economically and technically feasible, and (in the Service's opinion) avoid jeopardy.[94]

The US Supreme Court has recognized that the Service's biological opinion has a powerful coercive effect.[95] Critically, if the Service determines it is unable to develop RPAs to avoid jeopardy, the action cannot move forward. If the action agency ignores RPAs that the Service has identified, it must articulate its reasons for disagreement. If those reasons are adjudged to be wrong, the agency runs a substantial risk[96] of violating the statutory prohibition on the taking of listed species.[97] The action agency's or applicant's only other recourse is to apply to the Endangered Species Committee for a rarely granted exemption from Section 7.[98] In contrast, an agency that complies with the terms of an incidental take statement is shielded from a finding that it has violated that prohibition.[99]

Thus, unlike NEPA, in which a federal agency's interagency coordination obligations are generally satisfied after soliciting and responding to input from other agencies that have expertise in the area, federal interagency coordination plays a large role in project implementation under the ESA in the form of the consultation process, the biological opinion, the ITS, and RPAs. Freeman and Rossi note that this provision represents "one of the strongest mandatory consultation provisions," in contrast to NEPA's more "generic analytic or disclosure requirements" model.[100]

Some critics have challenged the efficiency of Section 7's extensive consultation requirements, contending that the process is lengthy and expensive.[101] Others have raised effectiveness concerns, asserting that Section 7 overly hinders economic development.[102] Perhaps in response, the FWS has instituted a number of initiatives to increase the efficiency and effectiveness of interagency coordination under Section 7.[103]

However, a 2015 empirical study of past Section 7 consultations has found "that median consultation duration is far lower than the maximum allowed by the Act" and that between January 2008 and April 2015 "no project was stopped or extensively altered as a result of FWS finding jeopardy or adverse modification."[104] As such, the authors note that their results "discredit many of the claims about the onerous nature of Section 7."[105] In addition, the number of jeopardy findings during that period was drastically lower than the number cited in earlier studies.[106] Although the researchers raise concerns that these results might suggest that current resources for or applications of Section 7 consultation are inadequate for protecting species, they also recognize that this trend is at least in part due to federal agencies becoming better at designing projects so as not to adversely affect listed species or critical habitat.[107] Although there is room for improving efficiency, there also is substantial evidence that the current design is not inefficient.[108]

Ultimately, current data is inconclusive regarding the effectiveness of Section 7's implementation coordination requirements.[109] There is reason to believe, however, that those requirements have improved species conservation. Although Section 7 does require agencies to spend more upfront to coordinate implementation, these initial costs are arguably offset by the long-term efficiency advantages of avoiding duplicative or even contradictory implementation processes.[110] In addition, allowing the FWS and other federal agencies, each with expertise relevant to a particular Section 7 decision, to be directly involved in the implementation process could increase trust among agencies[111] and make the ultimate decision more effective at promoting ecological and other regulatory goals. Perhaps this is why US Government Accountability Office (GAO) reviews of collaboration under Section 7 have recommended ways to further facilitate interagency coordination rather than decrease it. These recommendations include memoranda of understanding, comprehensive training, integrated data collection, and the development and implementation of an interagency strategy.[112]

2. Interagency Coordination of Monitoring

The ESA mandates federal interagency coordination not only in information generation, planning, and implementation, but also in post-approval monitoring. Federal agencies must (1) monitor the effects of implemented actions to determine whether the project is having unanticipated effects on endangered species and critical habitat, (2) the effectiveness of any mitigation measures (including RPAs) to determine whether the mitigation measures are actually working, and (3) the overall health of the listed species and its critical habitat to determine whether additional measures may be necessary. The ESA and its interpretive regulations require compliance, effects, and effectiveness monitoring.[113] While compliance monitoring is limited to verifying permittee compliance with permit terms, the bulk of post-decision monitoring activities takes the form of effect or effectiveness monitoring.[114] "Effects" monitoring is designed to determine the actual effects of the approved action; "effectiveness monitoring" measures how effective the adopted measures are in minimizing harm; and "ambient monitoring" gauges the long-term health and vitality of listed species and their critical habitat.[115]

ESA regulations require an action agency or the relevant Service to re-initiate formal consultation if the scope of the take increases, there is new information that may reveal new effects, the action is modified in a way that causes a new effect, or "a new species is listed or critical habitat designated that may be affected."[116] In such cases, the action agency or Service must reinstate formal consultation to analyze the new effects and assess mitigation measures.[117] Similarly, formal consultation must be reinstated if the amount or extent of taking specified in the ITS is exceeded, or if a new species is listed or habitat designated that may be affected by the action.[118] Moreover, an action agency may not modify the action if it would cause an effect on a listed species or critical habitat not considered in the biological opinion without reopening formal consultation.[119] In effect, these requirements impose upon action agencies and the Services an obligation to monitor the long-term health and vitality of listed species and critical habitat within project areas to ensure that the project is not having unforeseen deleterious consequences on the species and habitat. Should the project have such unforeseen effects, or should new species or habitats be listed that may be affected by the action, the agency and Service must go back to the drawing board.

This set of duties distinguishes the ESA from NEPA and its implementing regulations, which fail to require action agencies to reopen their EAs or EISs if unintended consequences arise. Moreover, because NEPA does not require follow-up monitoring, actual impacts often remain undisclosed and there is no assurance that mitigated impacts will remain below EIS-triggering thresholds[120] for mitigated findings of no significant impact.[121] Because the agency conducting the EA or EIS ordinarily has no obligation to follow up on its predictions to determine their accuracy, and agencies rarely do so in practice, there is very little data concerning the accuracy of such statements.[122] In contrast, California's analogous state environmental assessment law promotes interagency coordination of post-decision monitoring and reporting.[123]

D. Tradeoffs of Coordination Vary for Different Functions

As suggested in chapter 2, there are tradeoffs to encouraging or requiring agencies to coordinate with each other in the exercise of their authority. In the context of NEPA, policymakers and proponents[124] of interagency coordination have emphasized minimizing the administrative inefficiencies from duplication and delay by harmonizing otherwise disparate regulatory processes.[125] CEQ also promotes interagency coordination to help minimize conflict and litigation costs,[126] increase trust among agencies as well as with the broader public,[127] and foster fairer regulatory processes by increasing the likelihood that important interests are represented.[128] CEQ and others also contend that interagency coordination under NEPA will lead to more effective decisions by bringing a wide range of agency experience and expertise to governmental planning.[129] One national survey of environmental professionals emphasized the importance of regulatory integration and the coordination of actions with agencies having subject-matter expertise for the development of adequate information under NEPA.[130] Yet policymakers and scholars rarely differentiate among government functions in offering these assessments.

Similarly, there may often be advantages to agency independence. There undoubtedly are administrative costs to instituting interagency coordination through NEPA and other processes.[131] In fact, courts have declined to require NEPA analyses for certain decisions in part because of additional regulatory costs[132] or due to concerns that it might induce agencies to consider effects not allowed by other statutory authorizations.[133] In addition, regulatory initiatives for promoting coordination have at times functioned essentially as a perfunctory layer of bureaucracy that hinders rather than advances regulatory action.[134] Moreover, some scholars, at least, have suggested that dividing authority by function could lead to a desirable lack of coordination. Professors Weisbach and Nussim, for instance, suggest allocating control of federal financing (i.e., investment subsidies) for agriculture to the Internal Revenue Service and not coordinating such authority with general regulation by the Department of Agriculture because the advantages from independent exercise of expertise might outweigh the disadvantages.[135] Similarly, Professor O'Connell has asserted that dividing but not coordinating authority can promote accountability and effectiveness by minimizing agency collusion and groupthink.[136] In fact, in certain circumstances, there may be advantages from competition among agencies, rather than collaboration.[137] Interjurisdictional competition in standard setting, for example, might encourage authorities to develop more efficient regulatory standards. Similarly, regulatory competition in information gathering might help address uncertainty by creating incentives for data generation and analysis.

Yet these assessments are inevitably contextual. The growing literature on interagency coordination and competition has detailed many of the advantages and disadvantages of coordination and independence, but the possibility that the tradeoffs of coordination may differ by government function within a regulatory program is hardly ever considered.

This chapter's review of NEPA and the ESA supplies a range of insights in this regard. First, it reveals how agency coordination may exist for a single agency function but be non-existent for others. Second, by neglecting this core feature of authority, some critics seeking to improve NEPA's effectiveness have focused exclusively on improving or increasing existing coordination of the statute's planning functions, while ignoring the possibly more effective approach of fostering coordination of other regulatory functions, such as monitoring and/or implementation. The ESA's Section 7 illustrates the potential value of such an approach.

Moreover, policymakers should consider the relative advantages and disadvantages of coordination and independence in context, particularly on a function-by-function basis. Coordination of one function may provide advantages that justify the disadvantages, but for a different function the balance may point in another direction. The appropriate tradeoff between (1) avoiding inefficiencies or inconsistencies that might arise from uncoordinated action, and (2) avoiding groupthink/collusion or promoting competition that might arise from independent authority, may differ depending on which function is at issue.

An analysis of agency coordination under NEPA as well as the ESA illustrates some of the tradeoffs of coordinating authority or increasing agency independence, and how these may often differ depending not only on statutory goals but also on the regulatory function at issue. It should be noted, however, that because policymakers, in designing regulatory systems, regularly ignore these differential tradeoffs, empirical evidence with which to assess tradeoffs in any given circumstance is, unfortunately but unsurprisingly, limited. In particular, there is little evidence that would assist evaluation of the tradeoffs of NEPA coordination (or lack thereof) by looking at each function. Accordingly, we also assert more fully in a later chapter[138] that more accurate assessments of the appropriate level of coordination necessarily require employment of a structural adaptive governance framework that promotes systematic monitoring, assessment, and adjustment by policymakers of allocations of authority. Adoption of this adaptive process would provide policymakers and observers alike the opportunity to learn, adjust, and better prognosticate about the tradeoffs of different allocations of authority in the long term. Nonetheless, we make the following preliminary assessments about NEPA coordination based on the limited evidence available to date.

1. Data Generation, Information Analysis, and Planning

NEPA could be understood as requiring interagency coordination of information generation and planning but not implementation, based on the premise that the administrative costs of coordination for information generation and planning are lower than they are for implementation. This tradeoff might make particular sense if the expectation is that individual agencies will, armed with the planning and information generated through coordination, make better implementation decisions independently than collectively.

Although the process is not faultless, the existing evidence suggests that requiring coordination for NEPA planning and information generation and analysis is particularly valuable. Both policymakers and observers alike continue to be unsatisfied with the quality of planning and information-gathering coordination under NEPA, but there also is substantial evidence that NEPA's coordination requirements nonetheless have been effective at helping agencies make better decisions.[139] More-over, a series of studies has found that NEPA's reliance on interagency communication during planning and information gathering often plays a salutary role.[140]

2. Information Distribution and Compliance Monitoring

In our assessment, NEPA's framework also might benefit from requiring and adequately funding responsible agencies to coordinate both infor-mation dissemination and post-decision monitoring. This extension of coordination requirements appears desirable because of the seemingly significant efficiency and effectiveness advantages of coordinating these activities and the relatively low administrative costs of doing so com-pared to uncoordinated monitoring and dissemination, particularly in contexts such as NEPA, in which agencies are already coordinating other pre-decision governmental functions, such as information gath-ering and planning. This additional coordination would also provide participating authorities opportunities to learn and serve as sources of accountability. We suspect, moreover, that the competition and anti-collusion advantages of uncoordinated monitoring would be relatively modest (though not negligible) in the context of information dissemina-tion and monitoring as compared to other functions.

Although the experience under the ESA regarding coordinated moni-toring is imperfect, most critiques emphasize the need for more or bet-ter coordination rather than less. Undoubtedly, reliance on interagency coordination for monitoring under the ESA's Section 7 has been far from flawless in practice. A 2009 GAO report found that the FWS had not developed mechanisms for systematic tracking of required monitoring reports or for tracking the cumulative harm to most species across regu-latory programs.[141] The report also revealed that the extent to which the FWS actually requires ongoing monitoring is highly variable and, even where it is required, the agency lacks complete monitoring information for many formal consultations.[142] A striking example of the harm from this breakdown in monitoring coordination involves an endangered plant species that had recently "numbered more than 1,400," but "was not found at all" once the action agency finally submitted its required annual report fifteen years later.[143] The FWS was trying to improve its monitoring capabilities, though GAO assessed these efforts as promising but insufficient.[144] FWS staff attributed its weak monitoring and monitoring coordination practices to resource constraints, staff turnover, statutory deadlines, internal agency incentives that prioritized planning and implementation over monitoring, and a (mis)understanding of the FWS' role as advisor to other agencies rather than enforcer.[145]

Although additional interagency coordination for monitoring activities may increase the up-front costs of monitoring, such coordination may also help decrease certain administrative costs (e.g., by minimizing duplication or other inefficiencies) when compared to uncoordinated monitoring. Coordinated monitoring may also help make agency decisions more effective by providing multiple agencies opportunities to learn about the efficacy of management strategies and serve as sources of accountability when a partner agency is not achieving appropriate benchmarks. In contrast, potential efficiency through competition and "groupthink" avoidance advantages from independent exercise of authority are not likely to be especially compelling in the context of monitoring. Perhaps unsurprisingly, then, GAO's proposed solution (in concurrence with others[146]) is not to decrease interagency coordination of monitoring under the ESA, but rather to increase and dedicate more resources to it.[147] It recommended empowering the FWS to systematically track monitoring reports and compile relevant data with the assistance and support of other federal and state agencies.[148] This approach is generally consistent with persistent calls to increase resources for monitoring[149] and other statutorily created approaches to interagency coordination of monitoring.[150]

Of course, personnel at regulated agencies may resist post-project monitoring and adaptive management. As compliance monitoring serves to promote accountability, agency officials may resist such efforts and/or deploy them in ways that seek to obfuscate or minimize past errors. As such, beyond requiring the collection and dissemination of information about compliance monitoring and adaptation, introducing mechanisms to increase interagency coordination of compliance monitoring—particularly more formal and firm forms of coordination that require agencies to consult and consider another's comments or even approval—can be vital for helping curb the shirking of duties by agencies.

3. Implementation

In contrast, it appears to be more contestable whether the advantages under NEPA of interagency coordination of project implementation are worth the disadvantages. There certainly could be substantial efficiency and effectiveness benefits of coordinating or even harmonizing implementation decisions. Still, we postulate that the advantages of independent agency action in implementation are stronger than under-monitoring, since the political process is potentially better at accommodating the different policy preferences than requiring a strong form of coordination under the supervision of CEQ or EPA. Furthermore, the administrative costs of coordinating agency implementation appear at first blush to be more significant. The ESA does offer evidence of the value of requiring coordination of implementation activities. The increased up-front costs of coordinating project implementation requirements derived from the ESA's coordination mandates may yield more effective decisions and perhaps even greater administrative savings in the long term.

This accommodation might be particularly valuable in the context of endangered species protection, however. Although the diffuse, longer-term, intangible, and non-monetary characteristics of environmental resources always raise concerns about regulatory inattention to their value, the advantages of species protection are especially easy to discount compared to more concrete interests. Because regulatory initiatives designed for species protection are particularly susceptible to regulatory failure, the case for requiring coordination throughout the regulatory process is especially strong in the ESA context.

E. Context Matters in Assessing Coordination Tradeoffs

Although we offer some preliminary postulates about the relative advantages of coordinating different functions under NEPA, our primary claim is that policymakers should systematically test and evaluate whether the advantages of requiring coordinated monitoring would be worth the disadvantages. For example, policymakers or scholars could assess existing examples of agencies that have attempted coordinated monitoring after the preparation of NEPA documents or in connection with future pilot projects. We postulate that an optimal allocation of governmental authority might often involve coordinating some functions but not others.

Undoubtedly, such an assessment is fundamentally contextual. Although NEPA may demonstrate the need to increase formal coordination among agencies for additional functions, in particular in post-decision monitoring, in many other circumstances an optimal allocation will involve coordinating some functions but maintaining agency independence for others. In fact, the diversity of agency cultures, distributions of power, and resources makes it difficult to prescribe a one-size-fits-all model for coordination even just under NEPA. For example, certain agencies may be less resistant to or simply better at coordinating with other agencies in post-decision monitoring. Some agencies regularly engage in a high volume of NEPA analyses, and others do so relatively infrequently; some agencies have historically been resistant to NEPA review.[151] Thus, it might reasonably be the case that the coordination of certain functions between certain agencies under NEPA might be more effective than for others.

Varying the extent of coordination among functions should heighten the advantages of coordination while minimizing its disadvantages. Coordinated information gathering, for example, might allow co-regulators to more efficiently pool resources than they could acting independently. If so, a shared information base among those regulators may foster experimentation if each acts independently in putting that information to use, such as in standard setting. Similarly, agency accountability might be optimized by pairing coordination of information gathering with competitive agency enforcement. The former might provide greater access to information about co-regulator activities among coordinating agencies, while the latter provides agencies the incentive to call other agencies to account for drift, shirking, capture, or other forms of regulatory failure.

An example of the potential value of situating disparate agency functions at different points along the coordination–independence dimension is reflected in the debate over whether multiple intelligence agencies should be required to report to a single supervisor, the Director of National Intelligence. The 9/11 Commission and the Center for Strategic International Studies expressed concerns that such coordination might suppress innovation and competition among intelligence agencies. The Commission further posited that enhanced coordination would be likely to discourage opposing views when they are most needed.[152] Others have pointed out, however, that the value of competition may be outweighed by the risk that agencies that take inconsistent approaches in acting on accumulated intelligence will operate inefficiently, if not at cross-purposes, undermining efforts to thwart terrorist attacks.[153] Yet these apparently dueling arguments are not necessarily irreconcilable; detractors of coordination were focused primarily on the gathering and analysis of intelligence information, while proponents focused on governmental action in response to the information gathered. In these circumstances, the arguments for allowing agencies to act independently may be stronger for the information-analysis function than for the implementation function, and effective regime design might seek to limit coordination in the former, but promote it in the latter. In direct contrast to the NEPA example explored in this chapter, intelligence reporting may therefore benefit from less coordination in information gathering and from more in implementation, highlighting the importance of making context-specific assessments of the appropriate allocation of authority for each function.

This case study also helps show that interjurisdictional coordination is not a binary toggle, but rather quite diverse in form and extent. In other words, determinations regarding whether interjurisdictional coordination might be justified should consider not merely whether to coordinate, but the type and extent of coordination. Although NEPA has a specific type of coordination mandate—the formal communication and receipt of comments from other agencies and interested parties— interagency coordination can be adjusted in numerous ways. The form and scope of coordination might vary, for example, from merely mandating that an agency provide notice to empowering an agency to oversee and even veto another's action. Yet coordination might be changed not only in the extent of the hierarchy involved, but also in its frequency, duration, formality, and mandatory or discretionary nature.[154] Of course, these choices regarding the type and extent of coordination might vary and thus often would be appropriately assessed on a function-by-function basis.

Finally, it may be beneficial to consider differentiation of coordination efforts according to function as an alternative to movement along other dimensions, such as the centralization–decentralization dimension. For example, rather than increasing centralization to address perceived issues with interjurisdictional competition, policymakers might rather promote greater coordination among authorities, focusing on those functions deemed detrimentally affected by such competition. Indeed, NEPA can be understood as a limited illustration of such a choice; rather than requiring the consolidation of regulatory authority over private or public actions that may cause environmental harm, it requires agencies to simply coordinate planning and information gathering pertaining to such actions.

In short, scholars and policymakers should not ignore these many dimensional and functional differences by confining their analysis solely to the options of dimensional moves that uniformly cover entire government programs. Unfortunately, with few exceptions,[155] scholars and policymakers who analyze interjurisdictional coordination (under NEPA or otherwise) typically promote increasing either independence or coordination without fully appreciating or even acknowledging the significance of functional jurisdiction.[156] This oversight creates the risk that analysts will overlook opportunities to achieve the optimal balance of policy goals by coordinating some functions, while capitalizing on the exercise of independent authority for others.

PART III

Distinguishing Dimensions

Chapter 6

Differentiating Centralization and Overlap in Swap Regulation

If a patient goes to a physician to address a medical problem, the doctor would likely fail to address the problem effectively if she improperly diagnoses the patient's ailment or, even if she diagnoses it accurately, prescribes a treatment that is not capable of remedying the condition. As the next several chapters explore, regulatory allocations can and have failed for similar reasons.[1] Policymakers misdiagnose the causes of regulatory failure when they either (1) incorrectly map or characterize authority along one or more dimensions, or (2) attribute a problem to placement of authority along one regulatory dimension even though the problem is actually more appropriately associated with a different dimension. Moreover, even if they attribute a problem to the appropriate dimension, the chosen fix is unlikely to work (or to work as effectively as it might have) if they devise a solution that involves restructuring along a different dimension.

An exploration of derivatives regulation in the United States provides an example of the type of problems that may arise from these kinds of misdiagnoses. The chapter helps reveal the value of distinguishing between what we identify as the overlap–distinctness and centralization–decentralization dimensions of governmental authority. Both policymakers and scholars have routinely failed to differentiate between the extent to which governmental jurisdiction overlaps and the extent to which such authority is concentrated or dispersed. Perhaps the most straightforward circumstance in which this confusion occurs is when policymakers seek to address problems related to overlap by seeking to adjust the level of centralization. As detailed earlier, the redundancies made possible by overlapping authority may be an effective way to promote regulatory goals through the creation of a safety net that reduces the risk of capture, agency inaction, or regulatory arbitrage.[2] These duplicative regimes, however, are also likely to increase administrative costs and the costs of compliance for regulated entities, and may even increase the risk of regulatory gaps from agencies seeking to rely on (or blame) the efforts of peer agencies.[3]

Yet policymakers and scholars too often misidentify some or all of these overlap concerns as problems of decentralized authority. Accordingly, a commonly proffered solution to these risks of over-regulation or under-regulation has been to consolidate authority in a centralized institution. These proposals often fail to parse the various tradeoffs between overlap and distinctness or between centralized and decentralized authority. They also ignore the possibility that concerns about overlap might also (and perhaps more effectively) be addressed through various possible reductions of overlap that maintain decentralized authority.

A relatively early example of this phenomenon is reflected in the Hoover Commission report.[4] The Hoover Commission identified overlapping government services as a significant source of waste, confusion, and inconsistency in areas such as banking[5] and food safety regulation,[6] but it only considered and recommended greater consolidation of such authority.[7] In so doing, the Commission played down the reorganization dimension that, under our framework, fit the diagnosed problem—the creation of more distinct authority. Although consolidation is certainly capable of reducing inefficiencies, the retention of multiple authorities, each of whom is assigned a distinct function in a particular substantive area, may be preferable. If policymakers seek to reduce duplication and waste, or other problems associated with overlapping authority, such as fragmentation or regulatory gaps, they should not confine themselves to considering consolidation as a solution. Instead, they could decide to retain the same number of agencies and delegate distinct tasks to each. Policymakers could, for example, delineate more distinct lines of substantive authority, or alternatively allocate distinct functions to different agencies. Conflation of the overlap–distinctness and decentralization-centralization dimensions masks this option.

To more fully illustrate this kind of conflation, this chapter focuses on a more recent, limited reallocation of authority. Moreover, it considers not only how observers too often turn to consolidation to address the perceived ills of overlap, but also other ways that the distinction between the overlap and centralization dimensions can be overlooked. Securities and futures regulation in the United States, particularly before and after changes made under Title VII of the Dodd-Frank Wall Street Reform and Consumer Protection Act of 2010,[8] serves as a subtler but nonetheless valuable illustration of the conflation of the centralization and overlap dimensions.

As detailed in section A of this chapter, for decades, two federal regulatory agencies—the Securities and Exchange Commission (SEC) and the Commodity Futures Trading Commission (CFTC)—have been tasked with a broad suite of governmental functions over distinct substantive areas, with the former agency responsible for regulating securities and the latter for regulating futures.[9] Historically, these financial markets were separate, with different products, market actors, and technical knowledge required by the designated regulators. Over the past several decades, however, the two markets have substantially converged. As a result, scholars and policymakers, including key personnel at the Department of the Treasury, have claimed that the current allocation of federal regulatory authority over securities and futures has been ineffective, inefficient, and unfair.

The adjustment of authority to address pervasive concerns regarding market convergence for securities and futures, reflected in Title VII of the Dodd-Frank Act, took a different (albeit comparably flawed) approach to reorganization than the typical tack of consolidation. As explored in section B of this chapter, Congress focused on addressing jurisdiction over derivative swaps by changing authority primarily along the overlap–distinctness dimension. Congress left regulatory authority decentralized between the SEC and CFTC, but minimized overlap for certain products while institutionalizing jurisdictional overlap for others. For the latter, the CFTC and SEC continue to regulate very similar transactions, essentially performing the same functions, but exercise authority that is divided according to substantive jurisdiction—with the SEC having jurisdiction over "security-based swaps" and the CFTC having jurisdiction over "swaps." However, the CFTC and SEC, in consultation with the Federal Reserve, both retain overlapping (and coordinated) rulemaking authority over "mixed swaps" that have both swap and security-based swap characteristics.

Section B of this chapter then explains how these legislative changes to, and the broader commentary on, US derivatives regulation illustrate the consequences of failing to parse the overlap and centralization dimensions in assessing the tradeoffs of regulatory allocations. Interestingly, a close analysis reveals that Congress's approach to swaps regulation in Dodd-Frank may not be as misguided as the understandably robust critiques of the reorganization suggest. In contrast with many other legislative and scholarly responses to regulatory allocation problems (such as that of the Hoover Commission, considered above), Congress's changes at least demonstrated the potential for considering more than a simplistic choice between consolidation and bifurcation—instead authorizing shifts in the level of overlap as well as coordination.

Nevertheless, Title VII of the Dodd-Frank Act still demonstrates the problem of failing to distinguish between these dimensions and neglecting to systematically consider the positive and negative effects of differing allocations of authority. Regrettably, there is little evidence that congressional actors carefully considered the various tradeoffs of overlapping jurisdiction (or of decentralized authority), of adjusting the extent of overlap or centralization by function, or even of dividing regulatory authority functionally rather than substantively. It is thus predictable that many commenters, including in the Treasury Department, have raised—and continue to raise—significant concerns about the costs of bifurcated authority.

Unfortunately, as detailed in this chapter's section C, both proponents and critics of the allocation of US derivatives oversight have often looked selectively at the particular merits or demerits of existing authority. For example, commenters typically fail to consider whether overlapping authority created desirable safety-net benefits, or whether maintaining decentralized authority would have experimentation or other benefits. As a result, they paint an incomplete picture, and inevitably are unable to provide a comprehensive and coherent assessment of regulatory allocations.

More significantly, the broader scholarly commentary on the allocation of derivatives regulation regularly muddles the overlap and centralization dimensions or fails to systematically consider the tradeoffs of movement along one or another of these dimensions. Like the Hoover Commission, many reflexively turn to regulatory consolidation of the SEC and CFTC as the solution to market convergence. Undoubtedly, increased centralization is capable of sensibly addressing some of the critics' concerns. However, modifying the extent of overlap in (or even coordination of) authority would more appropriately deal with other concerns, while potentially retaining some of the advantages of decentralization when they outweigh those of centralization. Conflation thus may lead to a misdiagnosis of problems with the existing allocation, or the proffering of solutions that needlessly sacrifice advantages of other allocation choices.

Finally, we recognize that politics has regularly been the most directly influential driver of allocations in derivatives regulation, with policymakers tending to avoid employing the coherent analysis of the trade-offs of allocational choices that we suggest. As explained years ago by Professor Roberta Romano, a key political impasse has for decades been the closely guarded division of congressional oversight of the SEC and CFTC.[10] The congressional banking and commerce committees oversee the SEC, while the agricultural committees oversee the CFTC.[11] These committees wield considerable power and attract substantial political donations and lobbying; prominent committee members have often resisted consolidation.[12] As in other regulatory arenas, such forces are likely to ignore or resist reallocations that may eliminate their influence. Nonetheless, though in part the book's purpose is to make the arguments for and against consolidation more salient to policymakers, the offered framework may also reveal alternative configurations that may be less susceptible to political resistance. Accordingly, this chapter explores how concerns about duplicative authority might more effectively pursue alternatives that adjust the extent or type of overlap between such authorities or even the form of coordination between the two agencies. Thus, by limiting their analysis, policymakers and observers of derivatives regulation miss potential opportunities from different regulatory configurations that might better accommodate policy tradeoffs or be more politically viable.

A. The Bifurcation and Evolution of US Securities and Futures Regulation

1. Regulation of Securities and Derivatives

The SEC has been the principal regulator of securities markets in the United States since enactment of its organic statute, the Securities Exchange Act of 1934.[13] The SEC regulates securities, securities markets, derivatives clearing organizations (DCOs), self-regulatory organizations

(SROs), underwriters, and various securities market professionals (including broker-dealers, market-makers, and other intermediaries).[14] Further, the SEC's substantive authority covers investment companies under the Investment Company Act of 1940, investment advisors under the Investment Advisors Act of 1940, and trust indentures under the Trust Indenture Act of 1939.[15] In 2000 Congress enacted the Commodity Futures Modernization Act (CFMA), which, among other things, prohibited the SEC (along with the CFTC) from prospective regulation of the over-the-counter (OTC) swaps market.[16] Although the CFMA provided the SEC with antifraud authority over "security-based swap agreements," such as OTC credit default swaps, it specifically prohibited the SEC "from, among other things, imposing reporting, recordkeeping, or disclosure requirements or other prophylactic measures designed to prevent fraud with respect to such agreements."[17]

The SEC is allocated a fairly comprehensive range of regulatory functions focused on the securities markets, including standard setting, registration and licensing, investigation, and enforcement.[18] The Securities Exchange Act of 1934, for example, gives the SEC the authority to not only register, regulate, and supervise securities professionals, including broker-dealers and transfer agents, but also to regulate and oversee national securities exchanges and securities associations, clearing agencies, and industry SROs.[19] In addition, the Securities Exchange Act established a system of securities registration and ongoing public disclosure through reporting requirements.[20] The SEC also has the authority to establish accounting standards for the preparation of reports and audited financial statements, though it generally defers to the generally accepted accounting principles set by the Financial Accounting Standards Board.[21] Of course, the SEC has the authority to adopt standards through the Administrative Procedure Act's rulemaking process, and brings enforcement actions for violations of the federal securities laws and SEC regulations (including for insider trading, accounting fraud, and providing false or misleading information about securities and the companies that issue them).

2. CFTC

The Commodity Futures Trading Commission Act of 1974 (CFTC Act)[22] created the CFTC and conferred upon it exclusive jurisdiction to regulate futures[23] markets in the United States.[24] The CFTC replaced the US Department of Agriculture's Commodity Exchange Authority, which had been authorized to regulate commodities under the Commodity Exchange Act of 1936 (CEA).[25] Today, the CFTC's jurisdiction includes not only futures contracts for the sale of a commodity and options on such contracts, but also futures exchanges, DCOs, SROs, and the activities of various futures market professionals (such as futures commission merchants, brokers, and traders).[26] Initially created for agricultural commodities, the CFTC approved the first futures contracts on financial assets in 1975.[27] Assets covered by futures contracts have continued to expand, today including contracts involving agricultural products, financial instruments and indices, energy products, and metals.[28] However, as mentioned above, in 2000 Congress enacted the CFMA, which among other things expressly prohibited the CFTC (and SEC) from regulating the OTC swaps market.[29]

Like the SEC, the CFTC is afforded a broad range of regulatory functions, including (1) standard setting; (2) implementation through oversight of futures exchanges and market participants, including DCOs and SROs; (3) permitting or approval authority over new futures products and exchange rules; and (4) investigative and enforcement authority for alleged violations of its authorizing statutes or CFTC regulations.[30] The Division of Market Oversight oversees trade execution facilities, performs market and trade practice surveillance, reviews new and existing exchanges to ensure compliance with core principles, evaluates new products to ensure they are not susceptible to manipulation, and reviews compliance of exchange rules and actions with statutory and regulatory requirements.[31] The Division of Clearing and Intermediary Oversight oversees compliance of DCOs, intermediaries, and futures industry SROs (which include the derivatives exchanges and the National Futures Association).[32] The Division of Enforcement investigates and prosecutes alleged violations of the Commodity Exchange Act (CEA)[33] and of CFTC regulations.[34]

3. Policy Rationale for Bifurcated Allocation

The legislative history for the Securities Exchange Act, CEA, and CFTC Act provides only limited information on Congress' rationale for allocating fairly distinct and decentralized (and fairly uncoordinated) authority over securities and futures. Practically speaking, the White House initially offered the SEC chairman regulatory jurisdiction over the commodity futures industry instead of creating the CFTC.[35] The SEC refused the offer, and Congress soon thereafter created the CFTC to manage the US commodities market.

However, in support of establishing a stand-alone agency to regulate futures, the House Report on the CFTC Act emphasizes the diversity and expertise justification for decentralized authority. The report emphasizes the differential expertise used for futures regulation, stating that futures "require highly specialized skills" and that "no SEC Commissioner is appointed because of expertise in futures trading."[36] Moreover, consistent with the diversity justification for decentralized authority, the report points to significant differences between futures and securities as well as participants within these markets.[37] Commenters similarly attribute this allocation to the fact that the two markets were largely isolated from each other.[38] Because of these differences, the House Report concludes that features of futures and securities and their markets "are, and should remain, entirely different within the respective spheres of regulation."[39]

Over the years, proponents of bifurcated authority have pointed to the diversity, expertise, and experimentation justifications for maintaining decentralized authority in the SEC and CFTC. Some assert that there may be particularized regulatory expertise that varies between commodities and securities regulation.[40] Particularly those involved with or subject to CFTC regulation have raised diversity benefits of bifurcated authority, offering concerns about the fit of the SEC's orientation toward facilitating capital formation and thus price stability and futures markets' function of facilitating transfer of the risk of price changes.[41] These observers suggest that the SEC is not "properly attuned to the particular requirements of futures markets."[42] Some argue that a decentralized approach, allowing the SEC and CFTC to co-exist, can foster product innovation,[43] while others have asserted that it promotes regulatory innovation and a range of regulatory alternatives.[44] Most prominently, commenters point to the CFTC's principles-based approach as a valuable regulatory innovation that might not have occurred or be sustained if not for bifurcated authority.[45]

Finally, some suggest that rivalry and interagency competition promotes regulatory and market efficiency.[46] They claim that competition to attract market participants combined with regulatory avoidance by market actors gives each agency the incentive to reduce regulation to efficient levels.[47] Thus, though the United States is the only jurisdiction to vest futures and securities regulation in separate regulators,[48] some claim this competitive dynamic is an important basis for the prosperity of the US financial industry.[49]

4. Substantial Market Convergence Created Regulatory Overlap

Though initially distinct from one another, there has been a steady convergence of US securities and futures markets. With the introduction of futures contracts based on financial instruments—interest rates, currencies, and stock indices—financial products underlie most trading on commodity futures exchanges today.[50] Financial instruments such as swaps, stock-index futures, and other derivatives have introduced significant uncertainty about the difference between futures and securities.[51] Institutions dominate trading in both markets, trading volume in futures is now concentrated among sophisticated market participants in non-agricultural commodities, and stocks, options, and futures exchanges are merging.[52] The two markets have become interrelated and reactive to each other, so that "new financial linkages may cause a crisis in one market to unexpectedly spill over elsewhere."[53] In fact, a principal finding of the Brady Commission, the Presidential task force set up to investigate the stock market crash of October 1987, was that the markets for stocks, stock index futures, and options had become a single market in an economic sense.[54]

As the markets have become linked, so has regulatory oversight. Transactions like single-stock futures trading are handled jointly by broker-dealers on securities exchanges and futures commission merchants on commodity exchanges, so that some entities and their products are now regulated by both the SEC and CFTC.[55] "Under certain conditions, transactions in stock index futures (regulated by the CFTC) and transactions in the underlying stocks (regulated by the SEC) are virtually interchangeable."[56] This market convergence has resulted in the convergence of regulatory authority that was once fairly distinct.

5. Regulatory Decentralization, Overlap, and Conflict

As the markets have converged, the SEC and the CFTC have also "waged almost constant war over the boundaries of their respective jurisdictions."[57] The increasing complexity and hybridization of financial products made such jurisdictional determinations "increasingly problematic"[58] and spawned a history of jurisdictional disputes between the two agencies. For example, in 1975 the CFTC asserted jurisdiction over futures contracts over the objection of the SEC.[59] Subsequently, in 1981, the SEC approved the trading of options on the Chicago Exchange that the CFTC had previously determined to be "commodities."[60] The futures industry challenged the SEC, and Court of Appeals for the Seventh Circuit held that the CFTC had exclusive jurisdiction.[61]

In tension with the claimed benefits of interagency competition noted above,[62] the agencies sought to coordinate their regulatory activities to clarify distinct lines of authority. Most prominently, they agreed in 1981 through the Shad-Johnson Accord to a division of jurisdiction over stock index futures and a prohibition of single-stock futures and narrow-based stock index futures.[63] Congress codified this jurisdictional arrangement through the Futures Trading Act of 1982 but subsequently repealed it through the CFMA.[64] As a prologue to its modification of authority in Dodd-Frank, Congress mandated joint CFTC–SEC oversight of the single-stock futures and narrow-based indices of securities that the Shad-Johnson Accord had prohibited. Nonetheless, conflicts between the two agencies have continued.[65]

6. Arguments for Consolidation

At least in part in response to market convergence and the resulting conflict,[66] calls for the consolidation of the SEC and CFTC have proliferated.[67] Among policymakers, a bill attempting to merge the agencies was first introduced in 1990.[68] The US Government Accountability Office (GAO) dedicated a study to the merger in 1995.[69] The Treasury Department in its prominent 2008 report, "Blueprint for a Modernized Financial Regulatory Structure," called for the consolidation of the SEC and CFTC,[70] and several legislators championed the idea in the lead-up to enactment of the Dodd-Frank Act.[71]

Most of these proposals emphasize market convergence as a rationale for regulatory convergence.[72] However, a wide range of policy justifications have been offered for merger. Some proponents of consolidation identified concerns regarding the inefficiency of bifurcation, pointing out the duplicative compliance costs for market participants[73] and administrative inefficiencies from duplication of regulatory effort,[74] interagency conflict,[75] and even perhaps from lost economies of scale.[76]

Others emphasized the unfairness to market participants from lack of uniform treatment.[77] Some claimed differential treatment by the SEC and CFTC harmed US markets by impairing the risk analysis of market participants,[78] impeding lending,[79] and inducing market volatility.[80] Relatedly, some stated that the existence of two authorities hindered US capacity to negotiate with other countries.[81] In contrast to those who suggest that bifurcation promotes market innovation and competitiveness, some suggest that the existence of two regulators, or perhaps their independence and competition,[82] might hinder product innovation and US market competitiveness vis-a-vis other countries.[83]

Many critics of the allocation emphasized concerns regarding regulatory gaps and under-regulation.[84] A number of critiques seem to focus on the existence of regulatory gaps due not to the organization of authority but rather to the absence of authority delegated to either regulator.[85] Some commenters maintain, however, that the existence of two agencies has led each to fail to observe and/or respond to inter-market problems.[86] They contend that "a single regulator would be better able to monitor overall market conditions and the performance and financial health of market participants."[87] Few, however, distinguish these claims of under-regulation from possible under-regulation that may be caused by the existence of a regulatory commons problem, in which both agencies have the authority to regulate but do not.

On the other hand, some observers raise concerns that the bifurcation of authority has led to excessive regulation. Some of this literature might simply be criticism of the extent of US regulation, that is, that the orientation of the United States toward these markets is not sufficiently laissez faire, as compared, perhaps, to other countries.[88] However, some critics seem at least to suggest the possibility that the existence of two agencies has led to more regulation than one agency would have produced.[89]

B. Dodd-Frank Title VII: A Plausible but Likely Flawed Reorganization

1. Increased Overlap and Coordination

Despite these many critiques, Congress has never merged the two agencies. In 2010, it adopted a very different approach to the reorganization of the SEC and CFTC. Title VII of the Dodd-Frank Act attempts to clarify the regulatory jurisdiction of the SEC and CFTC over the derivatives market[90] and expand regulation of derivatives to include transactions formerly deregulated by the CFMA.[91] Congress largely maintained decentralized authority, allocating essentially distinct or overlapping authority to the SEC and/or CFTC depending on the type of transaction—a "swap,"[92] "security-based swap,"[93] or "mixed swap"[94]—and its associated market participants. Swaps and major swap participants are subjected to regulation by the CFTC[95] while security-based swaps[96] and major security-based swap participants are regulated by the SEC.[97] The Dodd-Frank Act seeks to make this authority distinct with limited overlap, expressly granting the CFTC jurisdiction over puts, calls, and options on securities exempted by the SEC under its organic statute and its jurisdiction over products exempted by the CFTC under its own organic statute.[98] Each agency maintains its fairly thorough complement of regulatory authority within its respective substantive sphere, including standard setting,[99] licensing, compliance monitoring, and enforcement.[100]

Although the CFTC and SEC respectively regulate swaps and security-based swaps in fairly distinct silos, the Dodd-Frank Act allows for some overlap. One area of overlap is that the CFTC and SEC are required to act jointly to define certain key terms.[101] Moreover, each agency retained the authority to bring antifraud enforcement actions for some transactions for which they do not engage in prospective regulation.[102] The Act also provides the SEC with access to certain information in the possession of the CFTC and CFTC-regulated entities, such as DCOs, derivatives contract markets, and swap data repositories.[103] Nonetheless, for swaps and security-based swaps, each agency is granted fairly distinct substantive authority.

In contrast, the Dodd-Frank Act grants the CFTC and the SEC, in consultation with the Federal Reserve, joint rulemaking authority over mixed swaps that contain characteristics of both swaps and security-based swaps.[104] Moreover, Dodd-Frank also mandates substantial inter-agency coordination, again with a particular emphasis on mixed swaps. Beyond required coordination on defining key terms, the CFTC and the SEC must adopt joint regulations "that are comparable to the maximum extent possible"[105] regarding mixed swaps.[106] Further, the SEC and CFTC are required to "consult and coordinate to the extent possible" with each other regarding any non-joint regulations pertaining to swaps or security-based swaps.[107] If either the CFTC or SEC considers a regulation or order by the other to contravene the statute, it may seek judicial review of the decision.[108] In 2018, the agencies signed a memorandum of under-standing to update the scope of coordination and information sharing between the agencies in exercising their joint authority, providing for the possibility of meetings, informal consultations, and written requests.[109]

2. Justifications for Dodd-Frank's Reorganization

Unfortunately, no comprehensive policy justifications were offered in the legislative history for the Dodd-Frank Act supporting Congress' organizational choices for regulation of swaps, especially varying the extent of distinct and overlapping authority for particular instruments. Various industry and labor representatives testified in favor of merger of the SEC and CFTC.[110] Only a few offered justifications for the proposal's level of distinct or overlapping authority.[111]

A few did discuss some benefits of coordination, particularly the harmonization process in which the SEC and CFTC had been engaging before passage of the Dodd-Frank Act. Though cautioning that harmonization could lead to overlapping over-regulation, the chairman of the Chicago Mercantile Exchange testified that it also could and should avoid duplication, increase market efficiency, and eliminate regulatory gaps that merger would not have addressed.[112] The claim regarding regulatory gaps is consistent with the findings of the Financial Crisis Inquiry Commission, which concluded that the key regulatory failure in the derivatives sector contributing to the financial crisis was Congress's ban on regulating OTC derivatives.[113] Others briefly testified that coordination could help avoid regulatory gaps[114] and inconsistencies,[115] simplify compliance, and eliminate waste.[116]

More significantly, the Obama administration did not offer much of a policy defense of its eventually adopted reorganization proposal for the swaps markets. In hearings on the Dodd-Frank Act, Treasury Secretary Timothy Geithner suggested that the reorganization was intended to address "gaps and inconsistencies in the regulation" of futures and securities.[117] He acknowledged the benefits of merger but stated that the reorganization proposal would help "solve most of the substantive problems that exist" and was "a necessary step toward any effort to merge anyway."[118] The administration thus indicated that it understood the reorganization as primarily establishing parallel and distinct jurisdiction between the SEC and CFTC as an incremental step toward consolidation.[119] Other than a few passing references to seeking to avoid duplication,[120] few policy reasons were offered for establishing primarily distinct authority for most products, nor for the creation of overlap over mixed swaps.

Geithner and other officials provided more, but nonetheless limited, justifications for coordination. The Treasury Secretary did contend that coordination would help reduce conflict and promote uniform treatment, and pointed to the more recent attempts by the agencies and Treasury to increase consistency, including joint public hearings and reports.[121] He also asserted that "to ensure that all classes of swaps face similar constraints, we have required the SEC and CFTC to issue joint rules on the regulation of swaps, swap dealers, and major swap participants."[122] A representative of the Federal Reserve System stated that harmonization would help avoid costs for market participants and regulatory gaps.[123] Though not explaining how, the 2018 SEC–CFTC memorandum of understanding states that coordination is intended to promote "market innovation and fair competition," "efficiency in regulatory oversight," "the introduction of novel derivative products," and "the functioning of the underlying markets."[124]

3. Review of and Response to Dodd-Frank Reorganization

Perhaps unsurprisingly, much of the commentary after the passage of Dodd-Frank continues to contend that the problems with derivatives regulation in the United States remain after, or are even exacerbated by, the legislative changes. Some critics regard Dodd-Frank's failure to consolidate the SEC and CFTC into a combined capital markets regulator as one of its greatest weaknesses.[125] Dodd-Frank has been criticized as inefficient for keeping multiple regulators for similar products and activities,[126] as well as for inducing duplicative compliance costs for both market participants[127] and the agencies themselves.[128] Commenters continue to contend that it results in unfair, uneven treatment for similar activities.[129] Some have raised concerns regarding continued regulatory gaps—namely the absence of sufficient regulation of OTC derivatives[130]—which some identify as one of several risks caused by Dodd-Frank's failure to centralize regulatory authority.[131] Meanwhile, some Dodd-Frank critics state that the continued bifurcation prompts over-regulation of OTC derivatives, with the "burdens of the reforms" likely leading to the "isolation of US OTC derivative markets" that are also less competitive.[132]

Despite the requirements of coordination in the regulatory process, a number of observers find coordination to still be lacking, if not worse than before the Dodd-Frank reorganization. The GAO concluded that "the same types of challenges the agencies have faced historically in separately regulating the interconnected markets" persist.[133] GAO studies have found that though the agencies have coordinated on their swaps and security-based swaps rulemakings as required by the Dodd-Frank Act, coordination between the agencies could still be substantially improved.[134] A number of market participants who contributed to GAO-organized discussion groups contended that requiring more rigorous forms of coordination (i.e., joint rulemaking) would have helped address their concerns regarding compliance costs and market efficiency, though others retorted that these benefits would be outweighed by the costs from increased decision-making delays.[135] Some studies conclude that "Dodd-Frank perpetuated and deepened the regulatory divide,"[136] due to "interagency friction, jurisdictional and court battles," and "market surveillance and oversight challenges."[137] The conservative Mercatus Center contends that Dodd-Frank's failure to adopt mechanisms requiring harmonization has compounded the lack of interagency coordination between the SEC and the CFTC.[138] Indeed, some analyses have found inconsistences between the new regulations promulgated by the CFTC and SEC.[139]

4. Failing to Systematically Assess Overlap and Centralization

Though problematic for other reasons, Title VII of the Dodd-Frank Act may not be as misplaced a reallocation of authority as the significant majority of commenters on the reorganization contend. By clarifying each agency's jurisdiction and making at least parts of it distinct, Dodd-Frank may have partially addressed possible compliance and administrative redundancy costs as well as concerns regarding over-regulation from the existence of duplicative authority. Moreover, these changes illustrate that policymakers have many alternatives for shifting authority other than bifurcated authority or consolidation. In particular, it is plausible to address administrative and market efficiency concerns arising from duplication of authority by minimizing overlap for certain regulatory activities (in this case, dedicating the CFTC to managing swaps and the SEC to managing security-based swaps). It may also be reasonable to authorize overlapping authority for certain market activities, if the safety-net benefits of that overlap are worth the additional costs of duplicative regulation. Finally, Congress could plausibly seek to address concerns regarding interagency conflict and inconsistency by requiring, through the Dodd-Frank Act, more formal coordination between the CFTC and SEC in rulemaking processes.

On the other hand, Title VII of the Dodd-Frank Act nonetheless also exemplifies how policymakers can miss the opportunity to weigh the tradeoffs of allocations of authority systematically. On a basic level, there is not even an analysis in the legislative record of the relative advantages of maintaining a largely decentralized regime rather than consolidating the SEC and CFTC. Consolidation of the two agencies might have promoted regulatory economies of scale and addressed the risks of inconsistent regulation due to lack of uniformity; but it might also have reduced the diversity, expertise, or experimentation benefits of decentralized authority. Congress never expressly considered the tradeoffs between retaining decentralized authority (as Dodd-Frank did) and consolidating authority in the hands of a single regulator (as the 2008 Treasury report and others recommended).

Likewise, there is little evidence that Congress based its choices in redistributing authority between the SEC and CFTC on a complete assessment of the merits and demerits of authorizing distinct authority for swaps and security-based swaps and overlapping authority for mixed swaps. It is certainly possible that safety-net benefits might justify the additional administrative costs of creating overlapping and coordinated authority for mixed swaps (but not generally for swaps or security-based swaps). However, there is limited mention in the legislative record even of the advantages or disadvantages of overlap,[140] let alone that Congress relied on such justifications in its reallocation.

Similarly, though it is not the focus of this chapter, Congress's choice to require some form of coordination between the agencies certainly might be reasonable. However, Congress did not articulate the reasons for its particular coordination choices, or why more coordination (or more formal and/or rigid coordination strategies, such as more joint regulation) would not be more successful (as GAO has since suggested).[141] Accordingly, though Congress's approach might conceivably have been an appropriate accommodation of the allocation tradeoffs in derivatives regulation, its failure to coherently assess the advantages and disadvantages of each dimensional choice makes that unlikely.

In fact, Congress might have considered the advantages and disadvantages of these allocation choices on a function-by-function basis. For instance, rather than make the choice of overlap vary depending on the type of market transaction—swap, security-based swap, or mixed swap—it could have considered the tradeoffs of dividing regulatory authority functionally.[142] Moreover, as explored in chapters 3 through 5, the tradeoffs of varying types and degrees of overlap likely differ by government function. For example, the advantages and disadvantages of authorizing the SEC and CFTC to exercise duplicative standard-setting authority will likely differ from those resulting from overlapping compliance monitoring and enforcement functions.

C. Assessing the Commentary on Derivatives Regulation

Similarly, the scholarly and policy literature on regulation of securities and futures at best looks selectively at the advantages or disadvantages of dual-agency regulation of futures and securities. However, many also conflate the overlap and centralization dimensions, failing to contemplate the possibility of addressing concerns about duplication by making dual authority more distinct rather than consolidated.

1. Failure to Assess Allocation Comprehensively

A failure to disaggregate the different components of authority at a minimum causes critics and policymakers too often to focus on one advantage or disadvantage of the allocation but neglect or overlook others. As noted earlier, many critics have undoubtedly detailed particular problems associated with the allocation of authority before and after the Dodd-Frank Act. Yet most of these, as one scholar characterized the detailed report provided by Hank Paulson (George W. Bush's Treasury Secretary), lack "the serious, detailed policy analysis necessary to support many of its specific proposals," and explain "neither why different agencies currently follow different regulatory approaches for different industries nor why virtually all of these approaches should be abandoned in the future."[143]

Moreover, too often those that do evaluate allocations of authority do not assess the tradeoffs of such allotments, even within a particular dimension of authority. For example, critics of bifurcation do not generally weigh the potential diversity, expertise, and experimentation benefits that would be sacrificed if the SEC and CFTC were consolidated, typically only exploring the benefits of consolidation. As a result, they do not coherently assess the tradeoffs of centralized versus decentralized authority, let alone how the tradeoffs of overlapping authority might influence that assessment.

2. Conflating Overlap and Centralization

Even more importantly, scholars and policymakers fail to distinguish between overlapping and decentralized authority in attacking or defending the distribution of authority between the CFTC and SEC, both before and after Dodd-Frank. Unfortunately, past commentary has blurred the lines between decentralization and overlap. While some critiques are appropriately characterized as concerns regarding the extent of decentralization, others are more appropriately associated with overlapping authority. Because these were not disaggregated, commenters did not see or carefully consider other possible reconfigurations of authority that might address the problems with existing authority—possibly better, or at least in ways that are more viable politically, than consolidation.

Many of the critiques of both the pre– and post–Dodd-Frank allocations are best associated with the decentralized nature of derivatives regulation: (1) administrative inefficiencies not from redundant regulatory efforts but from the forfeiting of economies of scale (i.e., spreading the costs of regulating over a larger pool of regulated activities); (2) unfairness due to lack of uniform treatment of similarly situated regulated entities; and (3) market inefficiencies (e.g., volatility) and ineffective market regulation due to differential treatment. Some of the claimed problems, however, are more appropriately linked with the existence of *overlapping* authority, including: (1) market inefficiencies for regulated entities due to duplicative compliance costs; (2) administrative inefficiencies due to the duplication of regulatory effort; (3) the existence of regulatory gaps due to regulatory commons dynamics; and (4) over-regulation due to the existence of multiple regulators. Yet other problems might be equally associated with decentralization and a lack of coordination, such as allegations of under-regulation due to a "race to the bottom" between regulators.[144] However, even commenters who have attempted to make more comprehensive assessments of the tradeoffs of consolidation of the financial markets imply that the only choice is between either a fragmented, decentralized system or a centralized, consolidated framework.[145]

Consider, for example, an assessment not of whether the SEC and CFTC should be combined, but rather of the tradeoffs resulting from having these agencies overlap. Importantly, both critics and proponents of the distribution of regulatory authority, before and after Dodd-Frank, largely ignore whether there are any advantages of overlapping jurisdiction. It is perhaps not surprising that opponents of bifurcated authority would neglect the redundancy benefits of overlapping authority in raising problems with it.

Proponents of bifurcation, however, have largely responded by either rejecting the claimed benefits of centralization[146] or asserting other advantages of the existing allocation. As detailed earlier, some point to the diversity, expertise, and/or experimentation advantages of decentralized authority.[147] Other proponents focus on the advantages of interagency competition.[148] Still others, in contrast, focus on the advantages of coordinating authority to minimize such rivalry.[149] Few proponents even address the features of the allocation related to the extent of overlap,[150] while others claim that there is no overlap and therefore no need for consolidation.[151] In taking such positions, many proponents appear to be conflating decentralization with overlap (and incidentally coordination or independence).[152] This leads them to fail to evaluate whether or not there are any advantages to overlapping SEC and CFTC authority, and whether any such advantages are worth the disadvantages.

Of course, consolidating the agencies would markedly (but not completely) affect any analysis of whether the authority should be coordinated or should overlap. That being said, there would still be value in assessing how coordinated or overlapping the authority should be within the newly created unitary agency, as well as with any other authorities regulating other aspects of the financial markets. While combining the SEC and CFTC into one agency may affect the level of coordination (or overlap) between these two regulators, contrary to the assumptions of some proponents,[153] it is by no means a forgone conclusion that consolidation would advance coordination (or reduce overlap). Two divisions within an agency may work independently and even at cross-purposes, and certainly may regulate activities concurrently.

Accordingly, a consolidated allocation is not the only option. In particular, some of the concerns raised by critics might be addressed by modifying the extent of overlap in (or coordination of) authority. For example, some observers have called into question the robustness and efficacy of the CFTC, arguing that a single regulator might be more effective, judging by the CFTC's past performance.[154] However, although establishing a single, well-resourced agency might serve to limit regulatory gaps, providing redundant regulatory authority to two such agencies could offer additional safety-net benefits to mitigate lapses by, or capture of, one of them. Moreover, retaining decentralized but overlapping authority might also serve to retain some of the diversity, expertise, and experimentation advantages of decentralization when they outweigh the advantages of centralization. These choices come with their own set of tradeoffs that should be considered.

In short, the extent to which multiple agencies should regulate aspects of financial markets, and the extent to which they should coordinate in doing so, are different questions from the extent to which such authority should overlap. By limiting their analysis, policymakers and observers of derivatives regulation not only miss important inputs for assessing allocation choices. They also overlook other possible regulatory configurations that might better accommodate policy tradeoffs.

Even if consolidation of the SEC and CFTC would be an effective accommodation of these tradeoffs for regulating derivatives, critics of the existing distribution of authority have missed alternative, and likely more viable, allocations that would reduce overlap and the problems associated with it. Many commenters, including proponents of consolidation, have suggested that consolidation is infeasible in light of political and practical constraints.[155] Resistance to relinquishing jurisdiction by the congressional banking and agricultural committees and the CFTC has proven to be a significant barrier to merger.[156] By not fully exploring other options to minimize duplication, advocates of consolidation lose the opportunity to address at least some of their concerns in a way that has a better chance of being implemented, even if creating more distinct authority would not achieve all of the purported benefits of consolidation. Notably, at least some recognize the opportunities for coordination rather than consolidation, suggesting the possibilities of cooperation between the SEC and CFTC.[157]

None of these analysts, however, have explored the opportunities for (and tradeoffs of) improving the division of authority between the two agencies. For example, to the extent that overlapping authority is unwarranted for securities and futures, critics might seek to remove the overlap for mixed swaps provided in Dodd-Frank through conferring exclusive authority to regulate these transactions to either the SEC or CFTC.[158] In fact, some commenters have indicated that even consolidation of the CFTC and SEC would not markedly address the regulatory gaps that exist in futures and securities regulation in light of the many regulatory entities charged with regulating financial markets.[159] In light of this reality, and short of a wholesale consolidation of all financial regulation, advocates of reform might be better off considering how reductions in overlap (or which forms of coordination) might address some of the more significant problems they observe in the existing regulatory framework.

Additionally, potential allocation alternatives are not limited to variations for each dimension based on substantive jurisdiction. Besides altering the extent of overlap or of coordination based on differences between types of financial products—as Title VII of the Dodd-Frank

Act did—authority could be apportioned differently according to governmental function. As illustrated in chapters 3, 4, and 5, there may be valuable reasons for varying the extent of centralization and overlap (and coordination) in relation to the governmental function at issue. For example, one commenter noted that "effective and timely crisis management depends above all on the quality of information available to the regulator."[160] If true, this assertion might suggest particular advantages to centralizing ambient market monitoring and distribution, but not information analysis or perhaps routine licensing functions, for which such advantages might be weaker. Alternatively, there may be substantial advantages to having overlapping authority for enforcement, but significantly fewer for standard setting. Or perhaps the tradeoffs in standard setting suggest coordination is appropriate, but for enforcement the tradeoffs point to agency independence. The point is that the range of options are many and not merely a simplistic choice between the current distribution and consolidation.

Finally, the CFTC and SEC story illustrates another valuable insight about government organization—that an allocation of authority may need to evolve with fundamental changes in the circumstances under which the initial allocation was made. The SEC and CFTC were created to regulate a variety of products and market actors. Their respective jurisdictions were decentralized and largely divided substantively, as the instruments regulated by each entity were deemed fundamentally different markets, and the justifications for this authority emphasized the expertise and diversity benefits of decentralization. However, the convergence of these markets has converted distinct authority into significant regulatory overlap. As such, the benefits of maintaining existing authority—now decentralized but overlapping—may be weaker or at least different (i.e., emphasizing any redundancy benefits of overlap) than initially anticipated, and the disadvantages would likely change as well. Of course, this shift would not inevitably mean that the now-overlapping authority is inappropriate, as an argument could be made that the advantages of overlap might outweigh the disadvantages. The broader lesson, however, is that even allocations of authority that were once optimal should be revisited and perhaps adjusted as circumstances change.

Chapter 7

Differentiating Centralization and Coordination in National Intelligence after 9/11

Following the 9/11 terrorist attacks, Congress created the 9/11 Commission to investigate the causes of the intelligence community's failure to thwart the assaults. According to the Commission's report, the consensus of expert opinion was that poor communication, inconsistent data collection and circulation, resultant information gaps, and even adversarialism between the various agencies charged with national security intelligence gathering materially contributed to that failure. Congress responded to this poor coordination in information generation, dissemination, and analysis by adopting the Intelligence Reform and Terrorism Prevention Act (IRTPA), which resulted in the most significant transformation of the structure of the federal government's intelligence community in more than fifty years.[1] IRTPA's principal innovation was the creation of the Office of the Director of National Intelligence (ODNI), to be headed by the Director of National Intelligence (DNI).

Despite the repeated articulation of concerns regarding inadequate coordination, much of the remedial focus by Congress and observers, both before and after IRTPA, has been on centralization. In particular, the authority that IRTPA vested in the DNI represented an effort primarily (though not exclusively) to centralize authority over some aspects of intelligence information management. Contemporaneous analysis of the 9/11 attacks, including analysis by policymakers who accepted many of the 9/11 Commission's recommendations in enacting IRTPA, conflated these two dimensions of authority. Moreover, subsequent evaluation of IRTPA's merits (or demerits) have perpetuated that failure to distinguish between the dimensions, and therefore to assess accurately whether the statute was an appropriate response to the structural defects that contributed to 9/11.

Centralization is not the same as coordination. They are end points of different dimensions and, as chapter 2 describes, present different, context-specific policy tradeoffs.[2] If policymakers and scholars conflate these dimensions, they are prone to misunderstand or ignore the tradeoffs of restructuring authority along either one. They are also likely to propose or adopt reforms that are unresponsive to the problems that spurred dissatisfaction with existing allocations of authority. For example, they may attribute the risks of uncoordinated agency action (such as the failure of different components of the intelligence community to exchange information with one another) to decentralization and therefore reallocate authority to make it more centralized, without ever alleviating the dysfunctions resulting from uncoordinated action. Pre-existing problems may continue, if, absent coordination, subunits of a newly centralized agency replicate the mistakes that plagued the activities of multiple decentralized agencies. Worse yet, greater centralization may needlessly sacrifice the upsides of a decentralized configuration, such as a diversity of approaches capable of prompting policy innovation. These mistakes matter, as they may thwart even well-intentioned institutional reforms.

This chapter explores how the intelligence community's structure affects information generation, dissemination, and analysis.[3] It makes several key points. First, it illustrates how policymakers' conflation of two dimensions (centralization and coordination) and failure to differentiate allocational choices according to function can mask relevant policy tradeoffs and generate reorganizations that fail to address the problems that prompted them. Second, it demonstrates that different structural configurations may be appropriate even for what appear to be related functions, such as information generation, dissemination, and analysis. Third, it describes the unique attributes of the coordination–independence dimension—the availability of multiple forms of coordination and the need to consider inter-functional coordination—and how they may affect distribution of authority along this dimension.

Section A of this chapter provides background on the structure of the nation's intelligence apparatus before 9/11. Section B describes the principal congressional responses to 9/11, which sought to address a perceived lack of coordination by intelligence agencies in the dissemination of information on terrorist threats, culminating in the adoption of IRTPA in 2004. Section C explores the problems that stemmed from conflation of the centralization and coordination dimensions by both policymakers responsible for IRTPA's enactment and scholars assessing both the intelligence failures that contributed to 9/11 and Congress's response to them. It also addresses their failure to consider allocating authority differently along those two dimensions for each of the three information management functions (generation, dissemination, and analysis) and the resulting inability to meaningfully assess the comparative risks and advantages of alternative restructuring options.

Section D concludes by suggesting appropriate structural configurations for each of the three functions based on recognition of the differences between centralization and coordination and the policy tradeoffs entailed in situating each function along those dimensions. We suggest that, based on the concerns articulated by the 9/11 Commission, Congress, and many scholars, an appropriate intelligence information management structure would at least provisionally reflect (1) decentralized authority for information generation and analysis but centralized authority for information dissemination; (2) coordination of information generation and dissemination; and (3) independent, concurrent agency analyses of terrorist risks but hierarchically coordinated high-level analysis for final evaluation of such risk assessments. Finally, section E analyzes how the coordination dimension differs from the other two and why those differences matter.

A. Pre-9/11 Allocation of Authority to Generate, Disseminate, and Analyze Intelligence Information

Before the 9/11 attacks, many components of the federal intelligence community, which was then composed of at least fifteen agencies, had the authority to manage information concerning threats to the nation's security, particularly information relating to threats of terrorism.[4] Under the National Security Act of 1947, the Central Intelligence Agency (CIA) had the responsibility to coordinate "the intelligence activities of the several Government departments and agencies in the interest of national security." That mandate included the duty to make recommendations to the National Security Council on how to coordinate the intelligence activities of the different agencies, to "correlate and evaluate" such intelligence, and to provide for its "appropriate dissemination" within the government.[5] An executive order issued by President Reagan also sought to vest in the CIA, under the supervision of the Director of Central

Intelligence (DCI), the responsibility to coordinate the generation, dissemination, and analysis of intelligence information.[6] Notwithstanding delegation of this authority to the CIA under the 1947 Act, other agencies would "continue to collect, evaluate, correlate, and disseminate departmental intelligence."[7] This legislation did not differentiate structurally among generation, compilation (or aggregation), dissemination, and analysis.[8] In each case, the authority was to be decentralized (in that individual agencies would be authorized to perform all three functions) but purportedly coordinated by the CIA. Because the statute did not define what "departmental intelligence" meant for each agency, it was not clear whether individual agencies' generation, dissemination, and analysis responsibilities were supposed to be distinct or overlapping. The Federal Bureau of Investigation (FBI) and the CIA dealt with domestic and foreign intelligence, respectively, but, as noted below, that dividing line was in some instances blurry.

In fact, in the years preceding 9/11, the actual exercise of information-related functions was somewhat different from this conception, as the CIA's coordinating role for all three intelligence-related functions remained largely unfulfilled. The authority to generate intelligence information was decentralized; each agency was authorized to collect information through sources such as human contacts, intercepted communications, satellite and spy plane images, public sources such as web pages, and covert operations.[9] In some instances, the authorization also overlapped in that multiple agencies collected the same kinds of information. The CIA, for example, was responsible for collecting intelligence concerning threats originating outside the United States.[10] But the Department of Defense's Defense Intelligence Agency also collected foreign-military intelligence for the military services and defense planners,[11] and the National Security Agency (NSA) collected signals intelligence information for members of the policymaking and military communities.[12] The FBI's mandate was different; it was responsible for collecting information on foreign terrorist activity within the United States, in addition to its domestic law enforcement responsibilities.[13] But other agencies also collected internal intelligence. The Immigration and Naturalization Service, for example, had the authority to identify terrorist threats in its tracking of foreign student visa compliance.[14] Finally, the exercise of these agencies' intelligence collection efforts was largely uncoordinated, resulting in intelligence gaps. The FBI and the NSA quarreled, for example, about which of them should collect communications about potential terrorist activity between individuals within the United States, leading to gaps in that information base.[15]

The authority for analysis of intelligence information reflected the same characteristics. The dissemination of intelligence information was generally absent, but to the extent that it occurred, it also appears to have been ad hoc, partially overlapping, decentralized, and poorly coordinated. To a considerable extent, each agency relied on the information it collected itself to identify and respond to terrorist threats and failed to share that information with other agencies. The FBI and the CIA, for example, were authorized to provide a broad range of intelligence information they had collected to the Federal Aviation Administration (FAA) to help it assess threats to aviation safety. But the FAA received little useful information through these channels.[16] The FBI even instructed its agents to withhold information from the FAA concerning the 9/11 terrorists.[17]

The FBI and the CIA also frequently failed to communicate their intelligence findings to each other.[18] After Congress established the CIA in 1947, the agency would focus on foreign intelligence matters, while the FBI was charged with domestic law enforcement.[19] Congress created this jurisdictional divide in part to avoid an "intelligence monopoly" that would evoke images of the Gestapo.[20] Nevertheless, the mandate of the DCI (who also served as the CIA Director) included coordinating the efforts of the intelligence community.[21]

The anticipated coordination failed to materialize due to insufficient delegation of authority to the DCI (such as control over the budgets of the other intelligence agencies)[22] and rivalrous interagency relationships that hindered efforts to coordinate information dissemination.[23] The two agencies were notoriously at loggerheads from the CIA's inception.[24] Their internal cultures differed and, in Brian Tamanaha's portrayal, they "harbor[ed] mutual distrust. Information-sharing across agencies grates against the very ethos and incentives operating within the [intelligence community], which prizes secrecy [. . .] and in which ownership of information translates into influence and career advancement."[25]

The lack of coordination between the FBI and the CIA in exchanging information was exacerbated by the increasing overlap of their authority over time as the distinction between "foreign" and "domestic" threats became increasingly archaic.[26] The FBI's efforts to clarify that jurisdictional dividing line met with resistance from the CIA.[27] Dysfunctional information exchanges between the two agencies affected efforts to combat terrorism as well as to assess whether Iraq under Saddam Hussein possessed weapons of mass destruction. According to the commission that investigated faulty intelligence concerning Iraq's possession of those weapons, the CIA had difficulty obtaining information from the FBI "at the vital fault line between foreign and domestic intelligence," a lack of cooperation that was "reminiscent of the 'void' that the September 11 attack plotters operated in to achieve their objectives."[28]

In short, pre-9/11 intelligence information generation, dissemination, and analysis authority was decentralized, partially overlapping, and largely uncoordinated, and the law did little to distinguish among the different information-related functions in defining the relationships among intelligence agencies. There was some effort to minimize overlap, and both statutes and executive orders tasked the CIA Director with coordinating the activities of the relevant agencies in performing all three functions. Strains persisted among the different agencies, however, especially the CIA and the FBI, hampering efforts to coordinate any of these functions.[29] The 9/11 attacks highlighted these deficiencies.[30]

B. Post-9/11 Reforms to the Structure of the Intelligence Community

1. Creation of the Department of Homeland Security

Less than a month after 9/11, President Bush created the position of Homeland Security Advisor to enhance coordination within the intelligence community.[31] But some members of Congress sought to move in a different direction. They introduced legislation to create a new cabinet-level homeland security agency.[32] President Bush and his advisors initially resisted this approach,[33] insisting that better coordination would preclude the need for major structural reconfiguration.[34] Perhaps fearing the political cost of opposing a dramatic response to 9/11, the White House in 2002 changed tack and proposed the creation of a new Department of Homeland Security (DHS) into which twenty-two existing agencies would be merged.[35] This effort culminated in the passage of the Homeland Security Act of 2002 (HSA).[36]

Though not clearly differentiating between dimensions or functions, DHS's creation appears to have been an effort to centralize intelligence information management, although the HSA secondarily sought to enhance coordination. The Act centralized aspects of information generation, dissemination, and analysis. It vested in a new, high-level Under Secretary for information analysis and infrastructure protection within DHS authority to "establish collection priorities and strategies for information" relating to terrorism threats,[37] and to disseminate information analyzed by DHS to other federal agencies with homeland security responsibilities.[38] Finally, the HSA centralized information analysis. Although it did not preclude the intelligence agencies from analyzing the information they generated, it tasked the Under Secretary with analyzing and integrating intelligence information from other federal agencies and disseminating that analysis throughout the intelligence community.[39]

At the same time, the HSA sought greater coordination in dissemination—and apparently also in analysis—of information. It ordered the undersecretary to coordinate with the federal intelligence agencies and with law enforcement agencies at all levels of government.[40] It sought to create federal, state, and local partnerships "to maximize the benefits of information gathering and analysis to prevent and respond to terrorist attacks."[41] It also pursued "increased efforts to share homeland security information,"[42] ostensibly to "avoid duplicating existing information systems."[43] The statute directed the President to prescribe and implement procedures for the "sharing" of homeland security information among federal agencies, including DHS.[44] These and related provisions seem designed to bolster coordination in both the dissemination and analysis of intelligence information.

2. The 9/11 Commission

Criticisms of the HSA's reorganization efforts soon surfaced. Some charged that the HSA's centralizing thrust did not go far enough for any of the three information-related functions. It neither consolidated intelligence collection and analysis in DHS nor vested it with the authority to compel access to or submission of specific data from other agencies.[45] Congress responded. It created the National Commission on Terrorist Attacks upon the United States (better known as the 9/11 Commission) in the Intelligence Authorization Act for Fiscal Year 2003 to examine the causes of the government's 9/11 failures and recommend corrective measures.[46]

The Commission's final report, issued in 2004, attributed the attacks partly to intelligence failures, all of which reflected inadequate coordination among the intelligence agencies. One failing was that the agencies did not effectively communicate with one another to aggregate (or pool) intelligence information. Before 9/11, intelligence information sharing "was not a priority,"[47] especially for the FBI, which shared very little information with the rest of the community.[48] The CIA also failed to disseminate reports tracking terrorist movements.[49] At least one expert interpreted the report as highlighting a "disastrous" lack of interagency communication, especially between the FBI and the CIA.[50]

Another defect was that breakdowns in information collection led to intelligence gaps. According to the Commission, neither of the agencies responsible for identifying foreign or domestic threats prioritized "identifying foreign threats to domestic targets."[51] Intelligence collection was "still organized around the collection disciplines of the home agencies, not the joint mission,"[52] impairing the government's capacity to identify foreign threats to domestic sources.[53] Relatedly, the Commission bemoaned the failure to "pool" analysis of matters such as the 9/11 attackers' travel plans, resulting in missed opportunities to thwart the plot.[54] One CIA operative complained that "no one looked at the bigger picture; no analytic work foresaw the lightning that could connect the thundercloud to the ground."[55]

A third problem the Commission identified was a multitude of problematic inconsistencies in data collection and dissemination techniques among and within the agencies. It criticized the lack of uniform security clearance standards and questionnaires, for example.[56] A fourth issue the Commission described was a prevailing mindset in which intelligence agencies felt that they "owned" the information they gathered and an incentive structure that impaired sharing because there were risks, but no consequences, for failing to do so.[57] In summary, the Commission likened the different intelligence agencies to specialists in a hospital, each ordering tests, looking for symptoms, and prescribing medication, but lacking an attending physician who makes sure they "work as a team" in patient treatment.[58] Along with its other criticisms, this metaphor suggests that the Commission's primary concern was inadequate coordination.[59]

3. The Intelligence Reform and Terrorism Prevention Act of 2004

Congress enacted IRTPA a swift five months after the Commission issued its report.[60] The statute significantly altered the intelligence community's structure, including aspects that relate to intelligence information management.[61] IRTPA responded to the Commission's criticisms of the intelligence community's uncoordinated information management practices by centralizing, and to a somewhat lesser extent, coordinating intelligence management.[62] A key structural change was eliminating the DCI and replacing it with the DNI, who would serve as the head of the intelligence community[63] and exercise direct oversight authority over the CIA.[64] The legislation's increased centralization extends to all three information-related functions as it vests in the DNI the authority to "determine requirements and priorities for, and manage and direct the tasking of, collection, analysis, production, and dissemination of national intelligence by elements of the intelligence community," including "resolving conflicts in collection requirements and in the tasking of national collection assets of the elements of the intelligence community."[65] With limited exceptions, the Act affords the DNI access to all intelligence related to national security collected by any federal agency.[66] The DNI is responsible for disseminating information such as foreign intelligence data collected under the Foreign Intelligence Surveillance Act of 1978 so that it may be used efficiently and effectively.[67] IRTPA also created a new National Counterterrorism Center (NCTC) within the ODNI to assist "in establishing requirements for the intelligence community for the collection of terrorism information,"[68] "disseminat[ing] terrorism information" throughout the executive branch,[69] and "serv[ing] as the primary organization [...] for analyzing and integrating all terrorism-related intelligence possessed or acquired by the United States Government except intelligence pertaining exclusively to domestic threats.[70] IRTPA also centralized other functions in the DNI, such as funding.[71]

Although it moved the allocation of authority further towards centralization for each of these functions, the individual agencies retain the authority to perform information generation, dissemination, and analysis. IRTPA directs the DNI to "establish objectives, priorities, and guidance for the intelligence community to ensure timely and effective collection, processing, analysis, and dissemination (including access by users to collected data [. . .] and analytic products generated by or within the intelligence community) of national intelligence."[72] IRTPA also directs the DNI to "manage and direct the tasking of, collection, analysis, production, and dissemination of national intelligence by elements of the intelligence community," and for resolving conflicts in collection requirements.[73] Information management authority therefore remains to some extent decentralized in each agency, but is under the direction of the DNI.[74] Intelligence pertaining exclusively to domestic terrorism remained within the FBI's domain.

Although most of its focus was on centralization, IRTPA did modestly alter and clarify the allocation of information-analysis authority along the coordination–independence dimension. IRTPA requires the DNI to increase coordination, but Congress emphasized doing this primarily through consolidation.[75] Nonetheless, it did make the authority to analyze intelligence subject to more hierarchical coordination. To ensure accurate analysis, IRTPA requires the DNI to implement standardized analytic methods and tradecraft policies and procedures and "to ensure that analysis is based upon all sources available."[76] Nonetheless, even with respect to analysis, IRTPA left considerable discretion and thus independence in individual agencies to conduct their own analysis, requiring competitive analysis[77] so that "differences in analytic judgment are fully considered and brought to the attention of policymakers."[78] Thus, notwithstanding several weak nods to more hierarchical coordination, the principal focus of IRTPA's text was on centralizing more intelligence information management activity in the ODNI.[79]

C. Conflation, Confusion, and Faulty Policy Analysis: The Devil Is in the Details

IRTPA's adoption did not quell criticisms of the intelligence community's structure. A persistent complaint was that its components still did not effectively communicate with each other or integrate their efforts to collect, disseminate,[80] and analyze information concerning terrorist threats.[81] The DNI's own inspector general concurred in this evaluation.[82] Turf battles and insistence on restricted access by other agencies continued to plague the effort to coordinate intelligence information dissemination and analysis.[83] The reluctance of the FBI and the CIA to exchange information remained problematic.[84] The intelligence community's erroneous conclusion that Iraq had developed weapons of mass destruction (which the Weapons of Mass Destruction (WMD) Commission attributed to uncoordinated information collection and analysis),[85] failure to halt an airplane-bombing attempt on Christmas Day 2009,[86] and the Boston Marathon bombing of 2013 fed this narrative.[87] Although some evaluations of IRTPA have been more positive,[88] the problems that plagued intelligence information management before 9/11—weak interagency communication, adversarialism, and inconsistency and gaps in information gathering—did not disappear in the wake of its adoption.[89]

Substantial blame for IRTPA's failure to remedy the intelligence failures that prompted its structural reforms likely lies in the absence of systematic assessment of the tradeoffs of allocations along different dimensions and for different functions. Absent that kind of evaluation, the result is likely to be, as in this case, dimensional conflation and missed opportunities to optimize government performance by differentiating functional allocations of authority enumerated throughout this book. The devil really is in the details. In particular, the Commission, Congress, and most observers have routinely missed the important distinction between the centralization and coordination dimensions when assessing and allocating authority within the intelligence community, and largely failed to parse information generation, dissemination, and analysis. As a result, they have offered solutions that are incongruent with identified problems or have missed opportunities to consider allocations that differ with the governmental function at issue.

1. Congress's Inadequate Evaluation of Reorganization Alternatives

On an elementary level, Congress provided limited analysis of the comparative advantages and disadvantages of the existing regime and available restructuring options. The House Report on IRTPA describes the statute's aim as allowing the DNI to "coordinate and manage all aspects of intelligence operations," and to "improve information-sharing of intelligence across the government" by "break[ing] down stovepipes and promot[ing] the fullest information sharing possible."[90] IRTPA would "strengthen[ ] intelligence analysis."[91] But the report lacks any analysis of why the allocations of authority chosen would necessarily accomplish these goals, whether the advantages of those allocations would outweigh their costs, and whether alternative configurations were considered and rejected. One committee member warned that Congress must go beyond "vague guidance to the executive branch" to ensure better information sharing.[92]

The Conference Committee Report's discussion of the rationale for structural reorganization, less than a page long, was even flimsier. It stated that IRTPA's reforms were "designed to achieve horizontal integration or 'matrix management' for the Executive Branch—meaning seamless coordination across departmental lines against interdisciplinary problems epitomized by terrorism."[93] But it did not engage in critical comparative evaluation of the advantages and disadvantages of available restructuring alternatives.

The legislative history indicates that Congress relied heavily on the 9/11 Commission's report.[94] The report did at least identify problems with the existing regime and assessed how its recommendations would address them. As we explain in the next two subsections, however, the Commission's analysis was itself flawed, reflecting dimensional conflation and inadequate differential treatment of the three information-related functions.

2. Dimensional Conflation by the 9/11 Commission and Congress

The 9/11 Commission and Congress identified a number of problems associated with a lack of coordination (which they consequently appropriately addressed by improving): a lack of interagency communication, gaps in intelligence, lack of harmonization in information collection and circulation, and agency rivalry. Nonetheless, they routinely confused coordination and centralization in their analyses and prescriptions, choosing to address the structural coordination problems they identified primarily (though not exclusively) through increased centralization.

Both the 9/11 Commission and Congress conflated coordination and centralization.[95] IRTPA instructed the DNI to "coordinate" the intelligence community's performance of "services the DNI determines can be more efficiently accomplished in a consolidated manner."[96] The statute thus expressly assumes that agency coordination and consolidation are the same. The legislative history also reflects congressional conflation. The House Committee Report suggests that increasing centralization would address concerns regarding lack of coordination by creating a "strong" DNI whose "primary responsibility will be to coordinate the efforts of foreign and domestic intelligence functions."[97] IRTPA would give the DNI "clear authority" over collection activities, all-source analysis, and information sharing (i.e., presumably, dissemination).[98] The Committee bemoaned the absence of "a single, tightly knit organization," implying a need to centralize. It added that the National Security Act of 1947 failed to "specify a unified management structure for coordinating the capabilities of the other intelligence agencies which existed at that time."[99] Because the Committee seemingly equated unification with centralization, its analysis conflates centralization and coordination.[100] Its support for a single organization, followed by a call for coordination, highlights that confusion.[101]

Both the 9/11 Commission and Congress also focused primarily on increasing centralization, even though they mainly identified coordination problems with the preexisting regime. The 9/11 Commission identified intelligence information problems linked to inadequate coordination as factors that contributed to 9/11. A logical response would have been to vary the type and/or extent of interagency communication or harmonization in allocating data generation responsibilities, exchanging the information each agency collected, and analyzing the information each produced. Yet the Commission's recommendations focused to a significant extent on increased centralization. For example, it endorsed vesting greater power in the DNI to "reallocate" information generation efforts.[102] The ODNI would take charge of "pooling all-source intelligence, foreign and domestic," suggesting centralization of the aggregation/dissemination function.[103] Finally, the Commission urged greater centralization of information analysis by urging that an arm of the ODNI, which would "absorb a significant portion of the analytical talent now residing" in agencies such as the CIA, should "lead strategic analysis" through the preparation of "net assessments."[104]

We therefore agree with former federal appellate court judge Richard Posner's assessment that the Commission's recommendations, largely codified in IRTPA, reflect a mismatch between the problems it identified (inadequate coordination) and the solutions it urged (greater centralization). As Posner put it, "the cure may not fit the disease."[105] A more congruent response would have been to concentrate on fostering greater coordination among the intelligence services.[106]

3. Functional Conflation by the 9/11 Commission and Congress

The Commission and ostensibly Congress also failed to clearly define or distinguish information management functions in assessing preexisting regimes or prescribing reallocations to address any limitations. Indeed, although a consensus developed after 9/11 that the government's failure to thwart the attacks resulted from an absence of information sharing among the different elements of the federal intelligence community,[107] the use of the term "information sharing" by analysts has often been ambiguous. The first DNI, for example, concluded that "the failure to 'connect the dots' resulted in part from [...] a failure to share [...] information [...] both within and between agencies."[108] The White House's first response to 9/11 similarly emphasized the need for enhanced coordination, but lacked precision as to which particular features or functions of the intelligence community were the focus of concern.[109]

Nor did the Commission carefully analyze whether structural reforms for one function were justified for other information-related functions. For example, its report claimed that one advantage of centralizing information-related functions is its capacity to address a shortage of experts with sufficient skills.[110] It is not clear why that justification does not apply equally to all three information-related functions, and yet the report seems to urge less centralization of generation than dissemination or analysis. On the other hand, the Commission acknowledged a "serious disadvantage" to its centralization of authority in the ODNI— the concentration of too much power in one place[111]—but overlooked the possibility of managing that problem by adjusting the level of centralization by function. The congressional committee reports on IRTPA also reflect little effort to parse whether allocations of authority should differ by function.[112] The upshot was consistent failure to distinguish among the information generation, dissemination, and analysis functions in assessing the tradeoffs of alternative allocations.

4. Critics' Conflation of Dimensions and Failure to Separate Functions

Observers of the intelligence community, the 9/11 Commission, and Congress have similarly conflated coordination and centralization and have neglected to clearly delineate and explain how to structure the different information-related functions. Dimensional conflation concerning intelligence information management predates the 9/11 Commission's report. For example, some critics of the HSA supported increased centralization of intelligence analysis to address concerns that interagency rivalries were hindering effective performance of that function and to shake up the turf-conscious intelligence community,[113] even though centralized jurisdiction without coordination may not mute such rivalries. Similarly, some feared that decentralized information generation and analysis in DHS would result in redundancy and duplicative effort,[114] but redundancy is the product of overlapping authority, and distinct decentralized authority can avoid it. In addition, in criticizing IRTPA, one scholar appears to have assumed that "diffused," decentralized authority was necessarily independent.[115]

Even those whom we have identified as perceiving conflation by the 9/11 Commission and Congress have overlooked distinctions between certain dimensions or functions. Although we agree with Judge Posner that the Commission and Congress conflated centralization with coordination, we think he may also have conflated these dimensions, as well as the different intelligence-gathering functions. According to Posner, centralization may "reduce diversity and competition in the gathering and analysis of intelligence data, limit the spectrum of threats given serious consideration, and deprive the President of a range of alternative interpretations of ambiguous and incomplete data to consider."[116] This observation creates the very risk that is the essence of Posner's criticism of Congress—conflating centralization and coordination.[117] Although diversity of approach is a byproduct of decentralization,[118] we consider the degree of competition engendered by multiple agencies addressing the same problem to be primarily a function of whether their activities are coordinated or independent. If decentralized authority is coordinated, it may not yield competitive analysis. To the extent Posner favors greater competition, his proposal for more coordination therefore seems counterproductive.

Combining criticism of centralized information "gathering and analysis," as Posner does, also risks masking the different tradeoffs involved in choosing appropriate points on the centralization and coordination dimensions for each function. Although IRTPA centralized information generation, dissemination, and analysis, the centralization of dissemination authority was greater than for the other two functions, notwithstanding the addition of a coordination overlay. Simply characterizing the 9/11 Commission Report and IRTPA as centralizing vehicles thus risks losing the capacity to consider the optimal balance of advantages and disadvantages of different points along that dimension for each of the three functions separately. As we indicate in the last section of this chapter, we believe that the argument for independence is stronger for information analysis than for dissemination (a point with which Posner himself may agree). Finally, although Posner favored better coordination, he did not acknowledge that coordination can take many forms and therefore neglected to consider whether one form of coordination (such as communication) is preferable to another (such as hierarchical control), and whether the answer should differ for the three information management functions.

D. Differentiating Agency Relationships for Information Generation, Dissemination, and Analysis

Restructuring intelligence information management authority, like all restructuring efforts, necessarily entails tradeoffs.[119] It is impossible to assess these tradeoffs meaningfully, however, if dimensions are conflated and functional differences ignored. Both the 9/11 Commission and Congress largely, though not exclusively, focused on addressing the numerous coordination problems they identified through initiatives that primarily increased centralization. This conflation of coordination and centralization led Congress to adopt measures that were not well suited to address the problems identified. Policymakers also missed the opportunity to accommodate the tradeoffs of allocating along the centralization and coordination dimensions by failing to differentiate sufficiently among intelligence information-related functions.

In this section, we offer a potential allocation that primarily focuses on coordination opportunities, predicated as an attempt to address the longstanding concerns articulated by the 9/11 Commission, Congress, and many scholars about the absence of coordination in the intelligence community. Nonetheless, we also identify circumstances under which changes in the level of centralization or continued reliance on independent authority may be appropriate. In short, we suggest that a better approach for addressing policymakers' concerns about intelligence information management would be to create (1) more decentralized, overlapping, and coordinated information generation authority; (2) more centralized, overlapping, and coordinated dissemination authority; and (3) more decentralized, overlapping, and independent authority to analyze information.

Though not the focus of this chapter, we should note that we see value in providing some level of overlapping authority for all three functions. That is because, in light of analyses by others suggesting the advantages of redundancy in this context,[120] we are convinced that the safety-net advantages of overlap with respect to all three functions justify the inefficiencies that may result from duplicative effort. Increasing the chance of avoiding the devastating consequences of a terrorist attack by vesting multiple agencies with the authority to generate and analyze information in particular is worth the additional expenditures incurred as a result of that overlap.[121] This structure protects against the risk that a single agency responsible for generation or analysis will miss important evidence of a threat or misconstrue the meaning of the evidence it has gathered.[122]

The next question is whether authority should be centralized or decentralized. Here, we provide different structures for generation and analysis on the one hand, and dissemination on the other. Centralization fosters economies of scale, has the potential to promote accountability by making one entity responsible for key decisions (although it can also increase the risk of capture),[123] and can increase consistency in approach (e.g., by creating authority to establish one set of standards for classifying information as confidential).[124] Centralization comes at a cost, however.[125] It may sacrifice expertise that decentralized agencies have developed through prior experience (e.g., foreign threats for the CIA and domestic threats for the FBI).[126] It can also reduce the diversity of viewpoints and approaches and squelch the experimentation that spurs innovation.[127]

Differentiating structural allocations on a function-by-function basis may make it easier to strike an appropriate balance. Decentralization of information generation has the potential to take advantage of the diversified expertise of individual agencies that centralization could impair.[128] It increases the chance that one or more agencies will devise innovative approaches to information gathering or uncover important clues that could be missed in a single agency's exclusive pursuit of intelligence information. These advantages may outweigh any loss of economies of scale[129] and the absence of uniformity. The development of different, novel approaches may be particularly important in responding to shifts in the communication strategies of those posing national security threats.[130] A similar balance of advantages and disadvantages arguably cuts even more strongly in favor of decentralized intelligence analysis. Diverse analytical approaches seem particularly critical, as multiple analysts with different preconceptions may interpret the same information in disparate ways.[131] In addition, decentralization may be advisable because of the burdens that would be imposed on any one entity made responsible for analyzing intelligence information collected government-wide.[132] Perhaps for that reason, Judge Posner identifies "size and heterogeneity as limits on the optimum degree of centralization."[133]

The balance of advantages and disadvantages differs for information dissemination. The issue here is how to ensure that each agency has appropriate access to information generated by the others, so that each has the capacity to analyze the most complete set of relevant data and thereby "connect the dots." The goal is to prevent a repetition of 9/11, which might have been avoided if agencies such as the FBI and the CIA each knew what the other had discovered. On the other hand, there is also a concern regarding ensuring the confidentiality of sensitive information related to national security. Centralization allows the government to take advantage of economies of scale in its efforts to aggregate data. It makes little sense for each agency to distribute its work to every other agency when a centralized entity such as the DNI can collect the work of each agency, determine which other entities in the intelligence community should have access, and then distribute it to them. Centralized dissemination also facilitates uniformity in matters such as the establishment of a platform for information submission to a central entity such as the DNI or the formatting of such information. Conversely, the advantages of decentralization seem less salient for dissemination than for generation or analysis. There is likely to be less potential for productive innovation through the participation of multiple entities, and diverse approaches to dissemination seem less important than for generation and, especially, analysis.

For the final dimension, coordination–independence, we treat analysis differently than generation and dissemination. The combination of decentralized information generation and enhanced coordination may preserve many of the advantages of decentralization while mitigating its costs.[134] Coordination can mitigate the risk that multiple agencies with overlapping mandates operate in ways that create gaps in information generation. It can promote accountability by reducing opportunities for an agency to free-ride on the efforts of others and by allowing each agency to be aware of and check the activities of others. If greater hierarchical control over generation is desirable to prevent information gaps or to promote consistency, the DNI might be vested with the authority to develop standards for information generation or to suggest (or even mandate) that an agency investigate a particular problem. The advantages of acting independently appear less compelling for information generation, as groupthink is perhaps not as likely to thwart effective information generation as it is information analysis.

The case for coordinated information dissemination is, if anything, even stronger. Vesting in the DNI the power to compel information submission can combat free riding and promote accountability, both by the agencies required to submit their findings to the DNI and by the DNI itself. Mandatory, hierarchical coordination, such as a requirement that information collected by each agency be pooled in a single entity such as the DNI, may help ensure that one entity sees the big picture and "connects the dots."[135] Such a mandate may be necessary to combat the traditional reluctance of individual agencies to share their information with, and disclose their sources to, others in the intelligence community, which has historically stemmed from traditional interagency rivalries and incentives to hoard information to prevent others from claiming credit for it.[136]

On the other hand, coordination imposes transaction costs lacking in independent structures. The risk of groupthink in this context seems minimal; there is not likely to be much room for innovative policy in developing strategies for the aggregation of information generated by different members of the intelligence community.[137] Some have suggested, however, that hierarchical forms of information submission may create delays and that an incentive-based approach that relies on voluntary submission is a better option.[138] If experience suggests that the costs of particular forms of coordination are considerable (either for generation or dissemination), the question would be whether they are outweighed by the accountability and other advantages, or whether less hierarchical forms of coordination are more likely to provide a better accommodation of these tradeoffs.

In our view, the advantages and disadvantages of coordination and independence align differently for information analysis. Avoiding groupthink may be critical in an area in which the nature of threats is unlikely to remain constant and the past may be an unreliable guide to the future.[139] Independence among intelligence agencies "appear[s] to create a competitive market for intelligence."[140] Acting DNI David Gompert remarked in 2010 that "competitive analysis avoids single points of failure and unchallenged analytic judgments. The lack of competing analytical judgments was a criticism by several post-9/11 commissions."[141] Competition may boost agency morale,[142] especially if credit is afforded to those whose innovations enhance national security. Because the management of intelligence involves uncertainty, change, and potentially catastrophic risk in the event of an intelligence failure, the lost advantages of competition seem more serious than the adverse consequences of free riding, particularly if, as we have suggested it should be, authority to analyze intelligence information is overlapping so that one agency's rigor can compensate for another's laxity.

Of course, applying the lesson from this case study of the need for more fine-tuned, contextual analysis of allocational tradeoffs, we should note that information analysis, like other functions, involves a range of activities, some of which may be more appropriately coordinated even while allocating others independently. For example, even if (as we suggest) it might be appropriate to vest independent risk assessment authority in various intelligence agencies, it would nonetheless be appropriate to recognize the value of hierarchical coordination, if not centralization, in the ultimate analysis of such risk assessments to determine which assessment to rely on in strategic planning or operational implementation.[143]

E. The Unique Attributes of the Coordination–Independence Dimension

We close by noting two ways the coordination dimension differs from the other two. First, both the centralization–decentralization dimension, which is about scale, and the overlap–distinctness dimension, which is about the extent to which authority coexists in multiple entities, present a spectrum of choices that more easily lend themselves to dimensional analysis. Authority may be centralized in one entity, allocated to a few, or decentralized in many. Similarly, organizational structure may reflect greater or lesser amounts of overlap, both substantively and functionally. Coordination is more heterogeneous; it can be assessed in terms of its scope, formality, duration, hierarchy, voluntariness, and/or frequency.[144] It can range from exchange of information to required group consensus before any agency may act. Accordingly, policymakers addressing a problematic absence of coordination would need to identify not only the extent but also the type of coordination that reflects the best set of tradeoffs in the particular context. If hierarchical coordination of information analysis, for example, risks inducing groupthink, increasing mandatory communication instead may be capable of increasing efficiency and taking advantage of pooled expertise without squelching the competition that promotes opportunities for policy innovation.

A second way the coordination dimension differs is that this dimension, unlike the other two, necessarily entails interactions between agencies. Thus, as noted in chapter 2, because it is about intergovernmental relations, unlike the other two dimensions, coordination can occur (or not occur) between functions (e.g., an agency in charge of standard setting can coordinate with another in charge of implementation). The presence or absence of such inter-functional coordination can influence the effectiveness of the exercise of the affected functions. IRTPA is illustrative. It seeks to "ensure that sufficient relationships are established between intelligence collectors and analysts to facilitate greater understanding of the needs of analysts."[145] In other words, the absence of effective communication between those who develop and those who analyze information increases the risk that intelligence failures like those that preceded 9/11 will recur. In passing IRPTA, Congress recognized the value of inter-functional coordination (in this case, between information gathering and analysis).

Structural reforms of the intelligence community alone will not eliminate threats to our national security.[146] But they can mitigate obstacles to more effective intelligence management by placing the components of the intelligence community in the best position to succeed. Alternative structural configurations reflect different ways to balance the values of situating authority at different points along the three dimensions and of differing functional relationships among agencies. By failing to distinguish between dimensions such as coordination and centralization (as well as functions such as information generation, dissemination, and analysis), both analysts and policymakers have prescribed reallocations that are poorly adapted to addressing the concerns they have identified. They have also missed opportunities to consider alternative configurations that might better accommodate the many competing concerns that animate important governmental activities like intelligence gathering.

Chapter 8

Differentiating Coordination and Overlap in Banking Regulation

As noted in chapter 6, dimensional conflation may prompt regulatory reforms that fail to address the deficiencies that spurred them. This chapter addresses the consequences of failing to appreciate the differences between the overlap–distinctness and coordination–independence dimensions of regulatory authority, or to compare the advantages and disadvantages of restructuring authority along each dimension. Conflation of these two dimensions, which is common,[1] may compromise a regulatory program's capacity to achieve its goals and mask the policy options and tradeoffs of structuring authority along one, another, or multiple dimensions.

Several examples highlight the risks of conflating the coordination–independence and overlap–distinctness dimensions. First, greater co-ordination may have some value in addressing wasteful duplication of overlapping effort, but it may not do so as efficiently or effectively as the creation of distinct authority (and in fact may exacerbate inefficiencies or propagate other risks associated with coordination).[2] Second, changing the extent to which authority is distinct or overlapping would likely be a poor choice for inducing greater competition between coordinating agencies, which can be accomplished most directly by increasing the in-dependence of those agencies. Third, if one is concerned about the risks from independent, overlapping authority of subjecting a regulated entity to conflicting regulation[3] and subjecting different regulated entities to non-uniform regulation,[4] carving out distinct realms of authority may reduce the risk of conflict but still may leave the allocation subject to uniformity concerns; increasing coordination would likely be necessary to promote such uniformity.

This chapter identifies two additional types of problems that have re-sulted from congressional efforts to address the perception of excessive overlap in federal regulation of the safety and soundness of depository institutions primarily by increasing agency coordination instead of creating more distinct authority.[5] In the wake of the financial crash of 2008, Congress sought to improve financial regulation,[6] ensure the safety and soundness of depository institutions, and bolster systemic risk oversight[7] by enacting Title I of the Dodd-Frank Wall Street Reform and Consumer Protection Act [8] Legislators and financial regulatory experts linked excessive overlap among the independent authorities of the prudential financial regulators to (1) wasteful duplication of effort; (2) multiple regulators imposing inconsistent and conflicting regulation; and (3) regulatory arbitrage (i.e., the ability of depository institutions to structure transactions or choose charters in ways that subjected them to one regulator rather than another) that enhanced the risk of individual firm and systemic failure.

Despite this diagnosis of excessive overlap, Title I did not seek to decrease overlap. Instead, it created the Financial Stability Oversight Council (FSOC) to coordinate existing prudential regulators' activities. We argue that two different mistakes help explain the apparent failure of these changes to address the perceived shortcomings of US prudential regulation. First, policymakers and scholars identified duplicative, conflicting, and inconsistent regulation arising from overlapping prudential regulatory authority as a crucial issue. As we characterize authority, these problems actually stemmed from the combination of overlapping and independent authority. As a result, significantly increasing coordination was a plausible response. In adopting Dodd-Frank, however, Congress resorted to weak coordination rather than more robust modes of coordination that would likely have been more effective in promoting greater consistency. Second, Congress seems never to have considered reducing overlap to avoid the imposition of conflicting regulation on a single depository institution by multiple regulators. Analysts attributed problematic regulatory arbitrage to overlap, when in fact it resulted from distinct authority. They thereby misidentified and sought to respond to a problem by moving authority in precisely the wrong direction along the overlap–distinctness dimension if indeed they wanted to address regulatory arbitrage.

As to the first problem, it is worth noting that greater coordination among overlapping regulators, if designed properly, may minimize duplicative inefficiency and reduce inconsistent and conflicting regulation.

Coordination could, for example, avoid duplicative inspections by multiple regulators. Likewise, consensus regulatory standards could mitigate conflicting and inconsistent regulation. Dodd-Frank did not effectively address inefficiency, conflict, or inconsistency problems, however, because the form of coordination it chose was inadequate to the task. In addition, even effective coordination comes at a price. Coordination requirements increase transaction costs, potentially negating the efficiency gains of the division of labor, and can generate anti-commons and groupthink risks. This chapter thus reinforces our argument that allocation choices, particularly along the coordination dimension, are not only about whether to coordinate, but also about the extent and type of coordination.

A more direct and politically feasible way to address inefficiency and conflicting regulation resulting from overlap would have been to create more distinct authority by dividing it along substantive or functional lines. Such an approach would also have reduced the risk of groupthink that coordination tends to foster. Had Congress chosen more distinct authority to address inefficiency and conflicting regulation, it still could have resorted to greater coordination to minimize cross-industry inconsistency.

Congressional deliberations do not appear to have included any meaningful weighing of the policy advantages and risks of addressing waste, conflict, and inconsistency through either greater coordination or less overlap. Had legislators done so, those more concerned with improving efficiency and eliminating conflicting regulation may have favored more distinct authority. Those more concerned with preserving the regulatory safety net that overlap produces may have devoted their efforts to choosing a form of coordination likely to effectively reduce conflicting and inconsistent regulation.[9] Congress's apparent failure to consider the likely consequences of restructuring financial regulation along each dimension precluded informed choices among available structural options.

With respect to the second problem, although many attribute regulatory arbitrage to excessive overlap,[10] we believe that a structure that allows a regulated entity's choice of one regulator to disable another regulator's authority is more appropriately regarded as decentralized, independent, and distinct. As such, the creation of even more distinct authority would not be an appropriate solution for minimizing arbitrage, and might even heighten depository institutions' ability to engineer the regulatory process to gain access to the weakest regulation. Attempting to address arbitrage through coordination was not irrational, given the largely independent nature of the prudential regulators' authority. But given the weak form of coordination reflected in Title I, a more promising solution may have been to create more overlap by, for example, subjecting each financial institution to substantive supervision by multiple regulators. As counterintuitive as that solution may sound in light of persistent criticisms of excessive overlap, it might have been attractive to those more concerned about the contributions of arbitrage (and the resulting weak regulation) to the 2008 financial crash than about duplication and inconsistency.

Section A of this chapter describes the allocation of federal prudential regulatory authority before the adoption of Title I. Section B details criticisms of the problems attributed to the excessive overlap that predated Title I, as well as recommended reforms. Section C discusses the financial crash of 2008, and Congress's response in Title I. Section D analyzes the extent to which Title I's failures are linked to the adoption of mismatched regulatory solutions or misidentified problems. Section E argues that reducing overlap was a more direct and perhaps more effective way to minimize duplication and conflict than the weak form of coordination created by Title I, although it risked weakening the regulatory safety net. But an increase in overlap may have addressed arbitrage more effectively than the weak form of coordinated, distinct authority created by Title I. Congress apparently failed to consider whether creating more overlap was a desirable way of eliminating opportunities for regulatory arbitrage and combatting capture, notwithstanding the potential for continued duplication of effort and inconsistent and conflicting regulation.

A. US Regulatory Authority over Depository Institutions before the Financial Crisis

Although financial regulation is designed to accomplish several goals, this chapter focuses on regulation of the safety and soundness of individual financial institutions such as banks, savings and loans, credit unions, and thrifts.[11] "Safety-and-soundness" regulation is directed at ensuring the health of a financial institution and preventing institutions from taking on excessive risk.[12] It includes establishing capital requirements, overseeing risk and liquidity management, monitoring investment portfolios, and fostering adequate internal controls.[13]

The structure of this aspect of financial regulation has long been the subject of dissatisfaction and controversy in the United States.[14] Congress has made various entities responsible for assuring the safety and soundness of depository institutions.[15] The National Bank Act of 1863 created the Office of the Comptroller of the Currency (OCC), which grants charters (a prerequisite to taking deposits and making loans) to national banks[16] and conducts oversight to assure sound operation. The Federal Reserve Act of 1913 created the Federal Reserve Board (FRB) to protect against runs on banks with deteriorating financial conditions that are members of the Federal Reserve System (FRS). The Banking Act of 1933 created the Federal Deposit Insurance Corporation (FDIC) to insure the deposits of participating banks and to regulate state banks that are not members of the FRS.[17] Legislation enacted during the 1930s also created federal regulators for certain depository institutions that had previously been the sole responsibility of state regulators, including thrifts and credit unions.[18] After massive thrift failures in the 1980s, the Financial Institutions Reform, Recovery, and Enforcement Act of 1989[19] created the Office of Thrift Supervision (OTS) to improve oversight of these institutions.[20]

The result was a decentralized system of prudential, or safety-and-soundness, regulators[21] with partially overlapping and, at most, loosely coordinated jurisdiction.[22] Before Dodd-Frank's enactment, each depository institution was regulated by at least two agencies. For example, the primary regulator for national banks is OCC, which charters and supervises them.[23] OCC is authorized to adopt regulations to prevent unsound banking practices, conduct onsite examinations, issue cease and desist orders, impose fines, remove officers and directors, and revoke charters.[24] National banks are also within the jurisdiction of FDIC. It administers the federal deposit insurance system under the Federal Deposit Insurance Act, which vests it with backup regulatory authority over all insured depository institutions,[25] including the right to terminate insurance coverage of institutions engaged in unsafe and unsound practices.[26] FRB also regulates national bank holding companies under the Gramm-Leach-Bliley Act.[27] The primary prudential regulator for state banks that are members of the FRS is FRB, but FDIC exercises backup authority over those with federal deposit insurance, and state regulators issue their charters and also engage in safety-and-soundness regulation.[28] State-chartered banks are regulated by the state chartering agency if they are not members of the FRS, by FDIC if they are federally insured, and by FRB if they take the form of holding companies.[29] Before the passage of Title I, the primary regulator for thrifts was OTS, although FDIC had backup authority for federally insured thrifts.[30]

One observer aptly described the system as "a complex patchwork quilt incorporating multiple federal and state regulators with sometimes overlapping jurisdiction,"[31] with the "specific regulatory configuration depend[ing] on the type of charter the banking institution chooses."[32] For example, a banking group's parent holding company would be regulated by FRB, while its subsidiary national bank would be regulated by both OCC and FDIC (its insurer), and its subsidiary state-chartered bank would be under the jurisdiction of the chartering state and either FDIC or a Federal Reserve Bank (depending on whether the state bank is a member of the FRS). Each agency "has a specific mission and focus, leading examiners for the agencies to pursue different objectives."[33]

B. Criticisms of Prudential Financial Regulation

Congress created the foregoing system for ensuring the safety and soundness of depository institutions in statutes adopted between 1863 and 2002.[34] By the middle of the first decade of the twenty-first century, the consensus of financial regulatory experts was that federal safety-and-soundness regulation was overly decentralized and overlapping,[35] creating three problems: inefficiency, conflicting and/or inconsistent regulation, and regulatory arbitrage. This section summarizes those critiques to lay the groundwork for analysis of Title I's structural reforms in the wake of the crash and of whether those reforms went awry as a result of dimensional conflation.

To address the problems linked to excessive overlap, some analysts urged "better communication and coordination across agencies."[36] Cognizant of these concerns, Congress, in the Financial Services Regulatory Relief Act of 2006 directed the Comptroller General to study the regulatory system, including the impact of charter differences[37] on the regulation of depository institutions, and to "consider the efficacy and efficiency of consolidation of financial regulators."[38] After convening a Comptroller General's Forum, the US Government Accountability Office (GAO) responded in 2007 with a report detecting "a need to modernize the financial regulatory system [. . .] to promote a more coherent and integrated structure."[39]

GAO identified overlap in prudential regulation as a recurring concern,[40] linking it with three problems. First, GAO noted concerns about "duplication of effort [. . .] by [. . .] multiple regulators" in areas such as reporting requirements, which also resulted in unnecessary burdens for regulated institutions. GAO later deemed this inefficiency to be a "principal concern with the regulatory structure for safety and soundness [. . .] oversight."[41] Numerous other observers have agreed.[42]

Second, GAO concluded that overlap was responsible for inconsistent and conflicting regulatory treatment of depository institutions. Part of the problem appears to have been that different firms offering similar financial products[43] were treated differently (although we attribute this problem to decentralized and distinct authority, much as we attribute regulatory arbitrage to decentralized, distinct, and uncoordinated regulation).[44] But GAO and others have also criticized the negative repercussions of subjecting a single financial institution to conflicting requirements by multiple regulators,[45] which produced inconsistencies in examination policies and practices,[46] methods for assessing loan loss reserves, and regulators' practices for referring cases to the Department of Justice.[47]

Third, GAO expressed concern about regulatory arbitrage. This criticism dated back at least to the 1949 Hoover Commission's report attributing the ability of commercial banks "to capitalize by playing the supervisors off against one another" to the "crazy quilt of overlapping jurisdiction and responsibility" among prudential regulators.[48] New depository institutions choose their regulator when they decide which charter to obtain.[49] These institutions may also switch, or convert, their charters upon obtaining regulatory approval.[50] This situation challenged regulators to ensure that regulatory differences were based on legitimate business differences, and were not merely "an attempt to give one type of institution a competitive advantage over others."[51] Not all resisted the temptation. Financial regulators, some of which are funded by chartering fees,[52] encouraged depository institutions to convert their charters "to enlarge their stables of regulatory clients," resulting in "domestic regulatory arbitrage and lax regulation."[53] Former FRB Chairman Arthur Burns referred to the prudential regulatory structure as a "competition in laxity."[54] According to Professors Coffee and Sale, a structure that allows financial institutions to subject themselves to the most accommodating regulator "can be defended as desirable if one believes that regulators inherently overregulate,[55] but not if one believes increased systemic risk is a valid concern."[56]

C. The Financial Crisis of 2008 and Dodd-Frank's Coordination Requirements

The financial crash of 2008 highlighted the need for financial regulatory reform. Whatever its causes,[57] which remain the subject of debate,[58] the crisis impaired the solvency of financial institutions and created a liquidity and credit crunch.[59] Analysts who focused on how regulatory structure may have contributed to the crisis identified problems along all three dimensions, but concerns about inefficient regulatory duplication, inconsistency, and arbitrage, which observers linked to overlap, were a continued theme.[60]

In response to the crash and criticisms attributing regulatory duplication, inconsistency, and arbitrage to excessive overlapping authority, Congress enacted the Dodd-Frank Act in 2010, Title I of which was designed to protect against excessive risk taking by depository institutions.[61] Early drafts of the bill would have replaced all existing bank regulators with a single Financial Institution Regulatory Authority, but Congress chose not to significantly centralize safety-and-soundness regulation.[62] Instead, Title I created a new agency, FSOC, to address gaps in regulatory supervision of large, complex financial institutions and non-bank financial institutions.[63] It authorizes FSOC to designate nonbank financial institutions as "systemically important" financial institutions (SIFIs) according to criteria such as capital requirements and asset tests.[64] FSOC may recommend to FRB the establishment of heightened prudential standards for SIFIs relating to matters such as leverage, concentration, short-term debt limits, risk-based and contingent capital, and public disclosure requirements.[65]

Title I's principal structural innovation was to charge FSOC with coordinating efforts to detect systemic stress and identifying firms whose failure might trigger system-wide problems.[66] FSOC is responsible for collecting information from its member agencies[67] and other regulatory agencies and, if necessary, directing the newly created Office of Financial Research (OFR) within the Treasury Department to collect information from bank holding companies and nonbank financial companies.[68] It is charged with providing direction to and requesting data and analyses from OFR to support FSOC's work and with facilitating information sharing among the member agencies. FSOC's tasks include (1) recommending to member agencies general supervisory priorities and principles reflecting the outcome of their discussions and (2) making non-binding recommendations to primary financial regulators to apply new or heightened safeguards for practices that could create or increase risks to US financial markets.[69] Finally, Title I directs FSOC to provide a forum for discussion and analysis of emerging market developments and financial regulatory issues, and for resolution of jurisdictional disputes among member agencies.[70]

Notwithstanding these coordination functions, FSOC has very limited leverage over the prudential regulators. Apart from the ability to demand information from member agencies, its coordinating authority is non-hierarchical, given the non-binding nature of its substantive recommendations.[71] Perhaps most importantly, a prudential regulator may refuse to adopt FSOC's recommendations as long as it explains why it is doing so.[72]

D. The Dodd-Frank Act's Failure to Address Regulatory Inefficiency, Inconsistency, and Arbitrage Effectively

Assessing financial regulation in the wake of Dodd-Frank, a group led by former FRB Chairman Paul Volcker lamented that the foundational elements of the regulatory structure had still not changed since the 1930s.[73] The group charged that the statute's main focus "was to strengthen and expand the scope of regulation, not to rationalize the regulatory frame-work."[74] Dodd-Frank could have been designed to comprehensively address excessive decentralization and overlap among the prudential regulators deemed by many observers to be responsible for inefficiency, inconsistency, and arbitrage.[75] Congress could have responded to these problems by altering the structure of safety-and-soundness regulation by reallocating authority along multiple dimensions. Instead, it chose only to increase coordination among the prudential regulators.

Many observers have concluded that FSOC's coordinating authority did not appreciably ameliorate the inconsistency, inefficiency, or arbi-trage problems identified as problematic before 2010.[76] According to the Treasury Department, overlap among the authorities of the prudential regulators continued to create duplicative inefficiencies after Dodd-Frank.[77] For example, OFR and FRB continued to conduct "unnecessar-ily duplicative analyses."[78] In addition, FRB, OCC, and the Consumer Financial Protection Bureau (CFPB) have engaged in overlapping data collection efforts, notwithstanding efforts to coordinate, so that differ-ent agencies have requested the same data in different formats, creating problems for depository institutions.[79] FRB and the primary pruden-tial regulators have also exercised overlapping authority in conducting holding company examinations.[80] Overlap also contributed to a lack of accountability among regulators.[81]

Nor did Dodd-Frank solve the problem of inconsistent regulation de-rived from overlapping authority among the prudential regulators. In-consistencies in the examination of depository institutions (e.g., because of divergent methods for assessing the adequacy of loan loss reserves) can produce disparate conclusions about an institution's soundness.[82] Indeed, some might argue that Dodd-Frank exacerbated the risk of in-consistency by subjecting thrifts to oversight by both the primary pru-dential regulator (FDIC or OCC) and FRB instead of just by OTS.[83]

The third problem attributed to overlap was regulatory arbitrage. Title I sought to address it in a couple of ways. First, by abolishing OTS, the statute essentially subjected thrifts and national banks to identical regulation by OCC. An institution could no longer seek more lenient federal regulation by converting its charter from a national bank to a thrift, although it could still convert to a state charter. Second, Title I limited charter conversions by depository institutions subject to formal enforcement actions or to a memorandum of understanding involving a significant supervisory matter.[84] The solution was incomplete, however.[85] Depository institutions in good standing retain the ability to structure their activities and to choose charter types that place them under the jurisdiction of one prudential regulator or another. Many well-rated institutions fell outside the scope of both Title I and related regulatory guidance, and, according to the International Monetary Fund (IMF), a steady stream of conversions continues.[86]

For all of these reasons, the IMF deemed Dodd-Frank to be "an opportunity lost," which left "overlapping mandates" and responsibilities in place.[87] According to the Volcker Alliance, the "antiquated" post-Title I regulatory structure replicated "many of the same weaknesses exposed by the financial crisis," creating opportunities for regulatory capture, jurisdictional conflict, "competition in laxity," and a lack of accountability.[88] President Bush's Treasury Secretary, Hank Paulson, concluded that a framework with less duplication that restricted the ability of financial firms to choose their own regulators "would have worked much better" than primary reliance on coordination to prevent replication of the problems believed to be responsible for the crash.[89]

E. Avoiding Dimensional Confusion and the Opportunity for More Distinct Authority

The financial crisis of 2008 cannot be attributed wholly, or perhaps even principally, to the structural configuration of safety-and-soundness regulation. Regulatory structure can play a role, however, in regulatory failures. As GAO recognized before the crash, "while structure is not the determining factor in the success of efforts to provide efficient and effective regulation, it can facilitate or hinder regulators' efforts."[90] Financial regulatory experts almost uniformly linked overlap among the prudential regulators before Dodd-Frank to undesirable duplication of regulatory effort, regulatory conflict and inconsistency, and regulatory arbitrage opportunities for institutions seeking access to the weakest regulatory regime possible.

Congress could have tried to address these structural concerns through one of several broad approaches to reduce duplication of effort and inconsistent regulation: greater centralization, more coordination, or less overlap. Each of these choices was potentially problematic, however. Efforts to centralize faced formidable political obstacles; coordination has the capacity to add administrative costs and squelch the kind of beneficial competition among the prudential regulators that some observers had praised.[91] And the creation of more distinct authority risked weakening the safety net that is often a desirable byproduct of overlap. Furthermore, a reduction of overlap tends to exacerbate, not alleviate, problems associated with regulatory arbitrage.

Congress chose greater coordination by creating FSOC, but in light of recurrent post–Dodd-Frank criticisms, it is worth exploring whether Congress missed the opportunity to adopt structural reforms along the overlap–distinctness dimension, which might have offered a more promising approach than either centralization or the creation of FSOC as a coordinating entity. This section analyzes whether structural reforms along each dimension were well suited to addressing the problems that spurred calls for reform—inefficiency, conflict, and inconsistency (discussed in subsection 1) and arbitrage (discussed in subsection 2). Although centralization might have been capable of addressing all of these problems, it was not a politically viable solution and might have forfeited some of the advantages of decentralized regulation even if it had been. Greater coordination among the prudential regulators—the approach selected by Congress—likewise has the capacity to reduce inefficiency (by reducing duplication of effort), to minimize conflict and inconsistency, and to eliminate at least some opportunities for arbitrage. However, the authority Title I vested in FSOC was insufficient to effectively accomplish any of these goals. Moreover, it may have increased the transaction costs of regulatory implementation and run the risk of inducing groupthink.

After briefly discussing proposals for greater centralization or coordination of prudential regulatory authority, this section focuses on the third restructuring option, which would have entailed movement along the overlap–distinctness dimension. Even though critics of the pre-2010 regulatory landscape attributed inefficiency, conflict and inconsistency, and arbitrage to excessive overlap, Congress appears to have given short shrift to this option, if it considered it at all. We believe that reduction of overlap would have been a more direct response to reducing duplication of effort among the prudential regulators, as well as inconsistent regulation, than either centralization or coordination, although it would likely have come at the price of weakening the regulatory safety net that often accompanies overlap. At a minimum, more thorough consideration by legislators of a reduction in overlap would have prompted a more informed policy debate about the best way to respond to inefficiency and inconsistency.

Movement along the overlap–distinctness dimension also had the potential to address regulatory arbitrage more effectively than coordination. Thoughtful consideration of that option, moreover, may have revealed a common misdiagnosis of the cause of arbitrage that was likely to generate a solution situated at the wrong pole of this dimension. Although many analysts attribute arbitrage to overlap, we believe it is instead a byproduct of distinct authority. As a result, the creation of more, not less overlap might have minimized arbitrage opportunities. Greater overlap would, of course, have exacerbated concerns about duplication and inconsistency, but those consequences may have been acceptable to those convinced that the most significant flaw in the pre-2010 regulatory system was the absence of a strong regulatory safety net. Policymakers' failure to compare structural solutions along the coordination–independence and overlap–distinctness dimensions masked these policy tradeoffs.

1. Structural Alternatives to Address Inefficiency and Inconsistency

a. Centralization Sacrifices Decentralization Advantages and Lacked Political Viability

In the years preceding the passage of Dodd-Frank, many financial regulatory experts recommended consolidation of federal prudential regulatory authority.[92] Among the options proposed were consolidation of all existing regulators into a single new federal bank agency[93] and a less comprehensive merger of two or more of the prudential regulatory agencies.[94] Supporters of centralization claimed that reducing the number of agencies would (1) enhance efficiency by reducing duplication of effort and promoting economies of scale[95] and (2) promote consistency in regulatory treatment across financial products and institutions.[96] Centralization in a single safety-and-soundness regulator might afford it a greater understanding of systemic risks by eliminating the need for interagency communication.[97] It would also enhance accountability by making one regulator responsible for all aspects of financial regulation.[98]

Opponents of centralization, however, found no evidence that countries with a single prudential regulator have had greater success in preventing or responding to financial crises.[99] In one notable case, the United Kingdom in 2012 dismantled its Financial Services Authority (FSA), which had been created in 1997 as a single integrated regulator for banking, securities, and insurance. The Labour government created the FSA as an experiment in the "radical consolidation of nine previously existing specialist regulators that were responsible for both prudential and business conduct matters."[100] The 2012 decision to carve up the FSA into three agencies responsible for systemic risk and monetary policy issues, prudential regulation, and investor and consumer protection reflected policymakers' conclusion that the integrated regulator had failed to effectively balance effective safety-and-soundness regulation and the protection of consumers against harmful financial products.[101]

In the United States, opponents of centralization argued that it would forfeit the expertise that multiple financial regulators had developed in addressing their corners of the financial markets.[102] It might also fray the rapport that institutions had developed with their traditional regulators, making it more difficult to solicit their cooperation in information gathering and other regulatory functions.[103] Some suggested that the sheer scope of US financial markets would overwhelm the capacities of a single regulator.[104]

Other than to replace OTS as the regulator of thrifts, however, Title I did not reduce the number of prudential regulators or otherwise centralize authority.[105] That choice may have been dictated by political considerations (including, as the Bipartisan Policy Center put it, "the desire of regulatory agencies, Congress, and the financial industry to protect their existing turf and relationships"[106]) that made centralization infeasible.[107] According to President Obama's Treasury Secretary, Tim Geithner, "just about everyone agreed that the current oversight regime was a ridiculously Balkanized mess, but the same tribal warfare that had hobbled the regulatory system would hobble our efforts to rationalize it."[108]

b. FSOC's Coordinating Role Failed to Curtail Inefficiency and Inconsistency

The most significant structural reform reflected in Title I was the creation of FSOC to coordinate federal safety-and-soundness regulation.

Designed properly, improved coordination among multiple regulators might have reduced duplication of effort and minimized inconsistency through the development of congruent regulatory approaches. But the form of coordination adopted may have afforded FSOC too little power to prescribe effective coordinated solutions, and more hierarchical coordination would have entailed other potentially adverse tradeoffs.

The capacity of improved coordination to create more protective prudential regulation was hampered by FSOC's limited authority to compel regulatory actions by its member agencies.[109] Each prudential regulator can reject FSOC recommendations simply by explaining why it wants to do so.[110] By one account, Dodd-Frank vested "heavy reliance on the same financial regulatory agencies that repeatedly failed to impose effective discipline on megabanks in the past."[111] These agencies have prevented, delayed, or weakened the implementation of key protective measures, including addressing (1) incentive structures for executive compensation that encouraged excessive risk taking,[112] (2) reforms to money market rules,[113] and (3) Title I's provisions concerning the Volcker rule (which limits proprietary trading and investments in hedge funds and private equity funds by depository institutions).[114] Implementation of these reforms depended on coordination among "agencies that have found it very difficult to reach consensus in the past," in Arthur Wilmarth's view.[115] The time-consuming nature of coordination itself created delays in addressing emerging risks.[116] Congress's failure to give FSOC greater authority to dictate adoption of these measures by prudential regulators contributed to the continuation of high-risk business strategies.[117] The upshot was that the prudential regulators remained relatively free to pursue their own regulatory approaches, even if the result was duplication of effort and inconsistent treatment by multiple regulators of the same depository institution.

To the extent that FSOC played an effective coordinating role, its efforts may nevertheless have had an unintended adverse byproduct: groupthink. Scholars of financial regulation have argued that, before Dodd-Frank, "a symbiotic relationship between financial leaders and senior regulators produced 'group-think'" that repeatedly led them to bow to the interests of Wall Street.[118] FSOC's creation may have exacerbated that tendency, decreasing the likelihood that prudential regulators would pursue novel and potentially more protective regulatory strategies. According to the Volcker Alliance, the new regulatory framework "was no match for the type of pervasive groupthink among regulators that contributed so significantly to the financial crisis."[119]

Creating a more hierarchical form of coordination would have created risks and advantages. Beyond likely increasing political resistance by existing regulators to more hierarchical coordination, giving FSOC a stronger hand would have reduced the independence of affected regulators still further, which may have squelched competition capable of spurring regulatory innovation[120] and increased groupthink. Competition among regulators can also increase regulatory efficiency and facilitate adaptation by regulated firms to changing conditions.[121] Perhaps the advantages of retaining some competition among prudential regulators outweighed the advantages of forcing them to abide by FSOC's decrees, which may have included eliminating regulatory differences that allowed depository institutions to benefit from weak regulation linked to charter choice. Yet there is little evidence that Congress considered these tradeoffs in choosing coordination as the thrust of its reform efforts.

c. Distinct Authority Might Address Inefficiency and Conflict, but at the Cost of Reducing Safety-Net Advantages

The creation of more distinct authority would have been a third option for addressing duplication and conflicting regulation. Before 2010, each financial institution had a primary regulator and at least one backup regulator.[122] This overlap produced duplication in tasks such as examinations and inconsistencies in data gathering mandates, and sometimes in substantive areas such as capital requirements.

Some financial regulatory experts recommended the creation of more distinct authority divided by substantive jurisdiction. The Bipartisan Policy Center called for assigning a single prudential regulator to each depository institution.[123] Others urged allocation of authority to regulate each sector of the financial services industry to a different agency instead of defining jurisdiction in terms of the nature of the institution and the charter it holds.[124] One version of this option proposed by the FDIC Chairman in 2002 also would have consolidated authority in three federal financial services regulators for banking, securities, and insurance companies choosing a federal charter.[125] Those who opposed the sectoral approach claimed that it would (1) prevent effective monitoring and responses to systemic risk,[126] (2) spur jurisdictional disputes as a result of convergence of financial service providers and products,[127] (3) exacerbate inefficiency by creating duplication of efforts to address common activities or goals across sectors,[128] (4) generate regulatory capture,[129] or (4) suppress regulatory experimentation.[130]

Another option was to allocate authority in accordance with the different regulatory objectives of market stability, safety and soundness, and business conduct regulation.[131] Under this approach, the prudential regulator would oversee safety-and-soundness aspects of financial regulation whether an institution is involved in banking, insurance, or securities-related activity. A variation of this approach, proposed by the Treasury Department in 2008, would have consolidated regulatory authority in a single new Prudential Financial Regulatory Agency, a new Conduct of Business Regulatory Agency, and FRB, which would be responsible for market stability regulation.[132] Although Treasury urged the delineation of "clear regulatory dividing lines," it acknowledged that prudential and market stability regulation can overlap because individual institutional failures can adversely affect the economy as a whole.[133] Treasury recommended increased coordination among the reconfigured financial regulators to avoid duplication of effort and promote consistent regulatory approaches.[134]

Proponents of an objectives-based system claimed it would increase regulatory effectiveness by linking regulatory objectives to regulatory structure. It ostensibly would create economies of scale within each area[135] and address arbitrage concerns by making all institutions subject to the same regulator within each area (safety and soundness, business conduct, and market stability).[136] Skeptics feared, however, that an objectives-based structure would hinder regulators' appreciation and oversight of the linkages among the different regulatory categories,[137] lead to regulatory gaps,[138] and squelch the competition among regulators that can produce experimentation and innovation.[139]

Yet another approach would have been to create distinct authority over different regulatory functions. Different prudential regulators might have been charged with information gathering, monitoring, standard setting, charter issuance, and enforcement. Such an allocation would avoid duplication and conflict, and allow each agency to develop expertise in the exercise of its assigned functions. As far as we know, this functional approach did not receive serious consideration in deliberations over the Dodd-Frank Act, although some past reform proposals touched on differentiation of authority by function.[140] Like other solutions based on distinct authority, the alignment of authority in accordance with regulatory function can best avoid the pitfalls of overlap if each regulator's authorities are clearly delineated, providing predictability by clarifying which regulator has jurisdiction over various aspects of an institution's operations.[141] The Basel Committee's Core Principles for Effective Banking Supervision reflect this point, declaring that "an effective system of banking supervision has clear responsibilities and objectives" for each regulator.[142]

As policymakers responded to the 2008 financial crisis by considering structural reform, they should have explored which configuration promised the best results in light of the tradeoffs implicated by restructuring along all three regulatory dimensions.[143] Assuming that centralization in one mega-prudential regulator was not feasible, Congress should have focused on whether greater coordination or more distinct authority represented a better chance of effectively addressing duplication, conflict, and inconsistency. Coordination might have been an effective mechanism for responding to these ills in light of the independent authority exercised by the prudential regulators before the passage of Dodd-Frank, but the authority granted to FSOC did not take full advantage of this potential, and even if it had, it would have likely come at the expense of greater transaction costs and a heightened risk of groupthink. More distinct authority would have been capable of generating greater regulatory efficiency, reduced risk of conflicting regulation,[144] and enhanced regulator accountability, but reduced overlap would have run the risk of weakening the safety net provided by concurrent regulatory authority.[145] Requiring greater coordination by distinct regulators would more likely address regulatory inconsistency resulting from the imposition of varying burdens on competing categories of financial institutions. Cognizance of the existence of and differences among all three dimensions of regulatory authority would have sharpened policymakers' analysis of these tradeoffs both between and within dimensions.

Of course, the choices of overlapping or distinct and coordinated or independent authority, are not simple binary alternatives. Variations in the nature or degree of required cooperation are likely to produce different tradeoffs. Legislators may not have appreciated that a politically expedient solution based on a form of coordination that did not significantly invade the turf of existing prudential regulators would undercut Title I's effectiveness in addressing threats to financial stability. Had they understood those risks, they might have been willing to allow FSOC to dictate solutions notwithstanding the reduction in regulatory competition this may have induced, or to resort to more distinct authority instead of an ineffective form of enhanced coordination.[146]

Likewise, the choices were not limited to either zero overlap or complete overlap. For example, even if Congress decided that more distinct authority was preferable at the federal level to minimize duplication and conflicting regulation, it might have been able to avoid substantially weakening the safety net provided by concurrent regulatory authority by retaining (or creating) state authority to supplement the oversight provided by each depository institution's exclusive federal safety-and-soundness regulator.[147] The Treasury Department in 2008 urged the creation of authority for state regulators to address business conduct issues associated with federally chartered institutions.[148] Dodd-Frank also granted overlapping powers to CFPB and state officials to adopt and enforce consumer financial protection laws.[149] Similar accommodations might have been provided to accompany the elimination of overlapping federal safety-and-soundness regulation. A regime of overlapping federal and state regulation may combat regulatory capture and operate as a "fail safe" mechanism.[150] Certainly, overlapping federal and state authority is likely to generate some of the same inefficiency and inconsistency risks between levels of government that overlapping authority creates among federal prudential regulators. The issue is whether those consequences are outweighed by the safety net and accountability advantages that overlap provides. Even if policymakers are not willing to create entirely parallel federal and state regulatory systems, they might authorize states to perform some regulatory functions, such as investigation and enforcement of standards.[151] As GAO has pointed out, "some types of concurrent jurisdiction, such as enforcement authority, may be less burdensome to institutions than others, such as ongoing supervision and examination."[152] Similarly, it may be advisable to differ the degree of overlap among federal prudential regulators according to regulatory function.

2. *Increasing, Not Reducing Overlap to Address Arbitrage*

In addition to combatting inefficiency and inconsistency, Title I sought to reduce regulatory arbitrage, which critics of the pre-2010 system also attributed to overlapping prudential regulatory authority.[153] This consensus assessment seems mistaken, however. Overlap exists when two or more regulators have concurrent authority to exercise the same regulatory function over a subject or activity.[154] The problem with regulatory arbitrage is that a regulated entity's choice of, for example, which charter to seek, triggers the authority of one regulator (e.g., one principal prudential regulator) and disables that of another. If that choice did not affect concurrent jurisdiction, regulated entities would gain no advantage by bringing themselves within the jurisdiction of the weakest regulator. Thus, regulatory arbitrage is more properly described as the byproduct of decentralized and distinct authority.

If this assessment is correct, then an effort to reduce overlap is not an appropriate structural response to regulatory arbitrage. The appropriate options would be (1) centralizing authority to reduce the number of regulators from whom regulated entities such as depository institutions can "game the system" by seeking favorable treatment,[155] (2) requiring coordination to minimize differences in regulatory approach, or (3) *increasing* overlap (e.g., by requiring approval of an activity by two or more regulators). Many experts urged centralization, but that solution was apparently a political non-starter, and again would sacrifice decentralization advantages. Congress instead chose to create FSOC as a coordinating entity, but as the discussion above indicates, it did not give that Council sufficient authority to be an effective coordinator. Not only was the loose coordinating authority exercised by FSOC unlikely to significantly reduce inefficient and inconsistent regulation. It was also not up to the task of effectively minimizing opportunities for arbitrage because each prudential regulator remained relatively unconstrained in pursuing its own version of prudential regulation, without being compelled to abide by minimum mandatory standards.

Had Congress analyzed the situation comprehensively, it might have realized that a third solution to arbitrage was available along the overlap–distinctness dimension: the creation of more overlap. That approach may seem counterintuitive, given consistent complaints linking the financial crisis to excessive overlap. Indeed, more overlap might have exacerbated the inconsistency and inefficiency that were two of the three principal drivers of the adoption of Title I. But had analysts properly attributed the third driver of regulatory reform—arbitrage—to distinct rather than overlapping authority, they would have been more likely to recognize increased overlap as a potentially viable solution. Careless descriptions of the dimensions of authority may thus lead to misdiagnosis of regulatory failures (e.g., too much overlap, when the real problem is authority that is too distinct) and failure to identify appropriate regulatory solutions (e.g., increased, not reduced overlap to address arbitrage).

Although increased overlap would have heightened the risk of duplicative regulation and inconsistent treatment of each depository institution, it had the capacity to reduce the adverse consequences of arbitrage, including regulatory capture and weak regulation. Requiring each financial institution to conform to the requirements of two or more regulators would have created a safety net. If one regulator is captured or otherwise fails to address a problem adequately, another with concurrent authority can step into the breach.[156] Overlapping jurisdiction can combat regulatory inertia and make each regulator more reluctant to respond favorably to interest-group pressure because co-regulators may cast adverse light on that behavior.[157] Finally, concentration of authority in a single agency removes checks and balances against abuses of that authority.[158] Moreover, overlap could have been retained for functions (such as enforcement) for which a safety net is deemed most important, even if it were eliminated for other functions such as information gathering or distribution.

The choice facing policymakers—had they considered creating greater overlap as a response to arbitrage—should have been whether, for any particular governmental function, the safety-net advantages of overlap were likely to exceed the efficiency and consistency losses it can spur. If policymakers had concluded that a significant cause of the financial crisis was weak regulation spurred by arbitrage opportunities linked to charter choice, it would have made sense to consider sacrificing the efficiency and consistency gains of decreased overlap in favor of promoting stronger financial regulation through increased overlap.[159] If the increased overlap option were chosen, policymakers might seek to alleviate the increased risk of regulatory inconsistency through tailored forms of coordination, such as differing the form of coordination by function.[160] Moreover, they could have adjusted the form of coordination to further minimize the risk of capture, such as by avoiding vesting one agency with veto power over the imposition of regulatory safeguards by others, so that the capture of that agency would disable the authority of those with concurrent jurisdiction.[161] There is no evidence, however, that Congress engaged in a meaningful evaluation of that tradeoff. Systematic consideration of reform options along all three dimensions would have been more likely to generate that debate.

PART IV

An Integrated and Comparative Capstone

Chapter 9

Varying Climate Change Governance

The in-depth case studies in parts II and III each focused on a specific element of our framework for characterizing and assessing allocations of authority. Chapters 3, 4, and 5 revealed insights from distinguishing among governmental functions in situating authority along one of the three dimensions of authority. Chapters 6 through 8 explained how parsing these dimensions can allow scholars and policymakers to more clearly assess the tradeoffs of allocations implicated by alternative configurations. Nonetheless, these case studies also confirmed that regulatory allocations inevitably raise questions involving dimensions or functions beyond the designated focus of each chapter.

As an inchoate regime seeking to respond to a critical social policy conundrum, climate change governance is a useful concluding case for an integrated, comparative evaluation of the advantages and disadvantages of defining agency jurisdiction along all of the dimensions for different governmental functions. Anthropogenic climate change poses perhaps the most complex, far-reaching, and profound set of environmental challenges the world has ever faced.[1] Considerable evidence substantiates the position that anthropogenic climate change already has caused harm to human and natural systems and will have increasingly severe effects over the coming decades. Climate change will continue to create stresses not only for the physical environment, but also for government institutions and programs dealing with myriad aspects of human existence.[2] The regulatory and management strategies being devised to address climate change are either undeveloped or in their infancy, an opportune policy space for considering how to allocate legal authority both among and within these levels of government. Because of its relative incipiency, climate change governance also serves as a useful initial exploration of and bridge to the adaptive governance infrastructure that we explore in detail in the conclusion.

Climate change governance is likewise useful for demonstrating how the policy tradeoffs of allocations of authority will often vary considerably even for addressing different aspects of the same larger social problem. This chapter addresses three climate-related challenges—adaptation, mitigation, and geoengineering. Adaptation strategies seek to reduce the level of harm resulting from climate change.[3] Mitigation strategies aim to weaken the force of climatic change, primarily through abatement of greenhouse gas (GHG) emissions.[4] For our purposes, geoengineering refers to deliberate and large-scale intervention strategies for manipulating the global climate system.[5]

Each area of climate governance presents different regulatory challenges. Adaptation actions, which tend to be deployed locally, are largely characterized by local environmental and economic benefits and harms. Mitigation strategies provide environmental benefits that may be either global or local in scale, but the economic harms caused by such regulation tend to be localized. Geoengineering activities, which may be deployed unilaterally even by a single individual, pose global environmental risks but are likely to be spurred by the promise of local environmental and economic benefits.

This chapter illustrates how, because of these differences, the tradeoffs of structural governance options will vary, as should responsive governance structures, both dimensionally and functionally. For adaptation, in light of the wide diversity of and uncertainty accompanying most climate effects, a decentralized infrastructure would likely be appropriate for most functions; overlapping authority of key functions with federal primacy may best exploit redundancy benefits; while certain forms of interjurisdictional coordination will be especially valuable for managing cross-jurisdictional effects.

In contrast, mitigation's concern with curtailing global emissions and countering collective-action problems suggests a more robust role for centralized standard setting, supplemented by state authority to take advantage of the experimentation and diversity rationales for decentralized governance. Overlapping state and federal authority for a broad range of functions is appropriate to accrue safety-net advantages and reduce capture risks, especially absent a binding baseline international regime. Finally, relatively independent allocations of authority for functions such as standard setting, permitting, and enforcement have the capacity to foster a "race to the top" among regulators and to combat groupthink, although an array of coordination strategies for functions such as research funding and information dissemination may be useful in promoting economies of scale and eliminating wasteful duplication of effort.

The risk of unilateral deployment of potentially untried, irreversible, and catastrophic geoengineering technologies counsels in favor of (1) centralized control of research and deployment to minimize cross-jurisdictional spillovers, (2) the redundancy benefits of overlapping authority, and (3) international coordination mechanisms to minimize opportunities for deployment by solitary institutions. Development of research and information analysis on geoengineering technologies, however, is more likely to be suited for independent, decentralized governance to promote diverse research that fleshes out geoengineering's opportunities and risks.

We note at the outset that, although we provide sample allocations, the chapter seeks to be neither exhaustive nor conclusive about the appropriate allocations of authority for the different aspects of climate change. We extrapolate from the insights provided by earlier chapters to draw inferences and propose configurations for managing climate change strategies that we believe are plausible and justifiable. Nonetheless, we do not offer definitive prescriptions for structuring intergovernmental relationships in each climate-related area. Rather, the chapter aims to show how the framework offered in this book helps parse the potential tradeoffs for different types of governance problems and to identify some of the issues, tradeoffs, and opportunities that might be missed without our framework. The proposals offered here are merely illustrative of the context-specific and experience-based solutions that policymakers and scholars should be able to generate through the kind of reasoned analysis of policy and values tradeoffs that our analytical framework is intended to induce.

A. Adaptation

Even if no additional GHGs were emitted, preexisting emissions are anticipated to lead to unprecedented and unpredictable changes to ecological, water, and coastal resources as well as public health, public infrastructure, agriculture, and immigration.[6] These effects are expected to place substantial stress on private and public institutions, and may eventually outstrip the capacity of programs and institutions to deal with them.[7] In particular, climate change is upending the assumptions upon which some existing laws, policies, and programs are based. These assumptions go beyond simply the magnitude of a problem society faces or the size of the resource commitment needed to meet the resulting challenges. As one of us has previously pointed out, "agencies regularly adopt strategies that subsequent data may demonstrate are insufficient or for which background conditions shift such that the strategy is no longer as effective as previously expected."[8] The mismatch between regulatory programs built on assumptions that past conditions will remain relatively stable in the future—what some have called "stationarity"[9]— will likely extend beyond natural resource management to a host of other regulatory contexts.

Consistent with the pattern chronicled in parts II and III of the book, most commentary on the distribution of climate adaptation governance largely ignores the potential opportunities from parsing the various governmental functions and dimensions of authority. Much of the growing literature on adaptation governance explores issues other than allocation questions, such as the appropriate decision-making procedures,[10] leadership,[11] the design of policy instruments,[12] adaptation funding,[13] and the diffusion of knowledge or norms across diverse networks of public and private actors.[14] Unsurprisingly, the scholarship that considers allocation questions tends to concentrate on whether to centralize or decentralize authority. Some observers do contemplate the tradeoffs of overlapping authority and others promote coordination, though rarely as a distinctive choice from other dimensions. In fact, some of the literature on climate adaptation governance conflates these different dimensions.[15] Virtually none of it contemplates the possible gains from differentiating by function in allocating authority.

In our view, the existing allocation of authority in the United States may be able to manage a few substantive areas of climate change's effects (and the considerable uncertainty surrounding them), as well as yield appropriate coping strategies. But allocations of authority among governmental institutions will likely need to change considerably for many other areas.[16] Although these adjustments will undoubtedly vary, in general, effective adaptation governance will involve substantial decentralization, allowing for coordination and overlapping authority for certain functions.

1. Emphasis on Decentralization with a Few Centralized Functions

As the effects of climate change and strategies for managing them will often be location-specific, many adaptation programs will often be more appropriately decentralized. Some legal scholars have considered whether authority for adaptation governance should be nationally centralized or vested in regional or local authorities.[17] Similarly, political scientists and sociologists refer to questions of scale, "multilevel governance," "distributed governance" and "polycentricity."[18]

The effects of climate change on specific locations, such as a particular ecosystem or issue area, will be highly variable and contextual.[19] Accordingly, adaptation governance must manage especially high levels of uncertainty.[20] These characteristics provide strong reasons to maintain or increase local and state control over adaptation planning, implementation, and information analysis functions. Moreover, despite decades of scientific evidence and many governmental reports identifying a lack of governmental planning for and activity on climate change adaptation,[21] adaptation planning and management are still fairly undeveloped.[22] As agencies begin to address climate challenges in new contexts or under changed conditions, it makes sense to put a premium on experimentation and innovation and to provide information on the efficacy of different strategies. Decentralization can leverage local knowledge, be tailored to local conditions and preferences, and provide opportunities for regulatory experimentation.

While some commenters have considered creating, or reallocating to, a dedicated public agency for adaptation,[23] most support dispersing much of adaptation governance to local authorities[24] or to agencies in relation to their substantive areas of competence.[25] In light of these tailoring, experimentation, and expertise advantages, some scholars contend, and we agree, that adaptation by default should be addressed through decentralized authority whenever it can be exercised effectively at that level, and that centralization likely should occur only when the national government can perform particular functions better.[26]

On the other hand, centralization for certain functions may leverage economies of scale and provide uniformity advantages. Climate change may provide the impetus for centralized authority because it is projected to accelerate change, prompt ecological migration and interjurisdictional spillovers, and transform ecological processes that transcend jurisdictions. It is also likely to spur adaptation strategies by some local authorities, such as the construction of physical infrastructure that may have collateral effects on other jurisdictions.[27] It is therefore likely to increase conflicts driven by differences in regulatory or management strategies that create externalities.[28] In light of the greater uncertainty, wider scale of effects, and more frequent interjurisdictional conflicts, increasing federal authority to address particular problems or for certain governmental functions may be desirable.[29]

In the United States, a few policymakers have recommended modest increases in centralization for certain adaptation functions and substantive areas. Perhaps the most prominent example is in the only comprehensive climate change bill ever adopted by either house of Congress: Waxman-Markey's American Clean Energy and Security Act of 2009 (ACES).[30] ACES, which was approved by the House of Representatives but died in the Senate, would have increased executive oversight and control over federal and state adaptation for natural resources by granting the President, the Council on Environmental Quality (CEQ), and Department of the Interior authority over funding, planning, and standard setting. It would have established a Natural Resources Climate Change Adaptation Panel tasked with developing a Natural Resources Climate Change Adaptation Strategy.[31] Each federal agency member would have been required to develop a plan consistent with the Strategy.[32] State natural resources adaptation plans consistent with the Strategy would have been eligible for federal implementation funding.[33]

Plan implementation, however, would have remained largely decentralized. Each federal agency or state adaptation plan would have been left to the individual authority to implement and enforce.[34] Likewise, ACES would have maintained several federal information-generation and dissemination programs—a National Climate Service within the National Oceanic and Atmospheric Administration (NOAA), a Global Change Research Program, and a National Climate

Change and Wildlife Science Center in the US Geological Survey—
that relied more on interagency coordination than centralization.[35]

The underlying premise of ACES, to employ strategic use of centralization rather than across-the-board consolidation, is sensible. Although
the particular functions to centralize will undoubtedly vary by substantive regulatory area, we expect that there are strong collective action reasons to centralize certain functions. As each of us has argued elsewhere,
given the wide variety of causes, varied local effects, and substantial
range of jurisdictions affected, managing the effects of climate change
may be a paradigmatic example of such a collective-action problem.[36]
Indeed, despite many governmental reports urging more adaptation
planning and activity, planning has just begun to occur.

We think it will likely often be the case that the advantages of centralized information distribution, including economies of scale, will outweigh the disadvantages of decreased diversity and experimentation.
Such authority might be housed in NOAA, CEQ, or the federal Environmental Protection Agency (EPA). Thus, in contrast with all previous
approaches to information dissemination (including ACES'), we suggest
that centralization of information dissemination, at least at the federal
level, might be more appropriate than reliance on a decentralized, overlapping, and coordinated infrastructure.[37]

Moreover, varying increases in centralization of authority for scientific research, financing, planning, and standard setting, as proposed in
ACES[38] and by some scholars,[39] may be warranted. Nonetheless, such
increases in centralization need not be absolute, except in rare cases.
As explored in section A.2. below, allowing for limited overlap between
state and federal authorities for these functions might be a more effective accommodation of the economies-of-scale and uniformity advantages of centralization and the expertise, diversity, and experimentation
advantages arising from decentralized authority. Scholars who have
urged more centralized adaptation planning have generally not pushed
for preemption of localized institutions.[40] Given substantial uncertainty
about the localized effects of climate change and the effectiveness of
management strategies in addressing them, the impetus for local implementation and permitting to provide opportunities for experimentation
and interjurisdictional learning remains strong—or has perhaps grown
stronger.[41]

2. Mostly Overlapping Authority but with Primacy to Particular Authorities

In limited instances, for functions such as information dissemination or implementation, minimizing inefficiencies by fully allocating distinct adaptation authority to a particular institution or level of government will likely provide more advantages than any redundancy advantages of overlapping authority. Certainly, some adaptation scholars continue to rely on the "matching principle" detailed in chapter 4, which seeks to match regulatory jurisdiction to the single entity with the appropriate scope for addressing an environmental problem.[42] Some recognize that overlap may produce inefficiencies, conflict, and confusion.[43] Indeed, climate change is likely to increase and complicate interactions between existing jurisdictional authorities, and in some instances ecological shifts will lead to new conflicting regulatory overlap and management responses that are incongruous or counterproductive.[44] Accordingly, efficiency and effectiveness considerations may suggest that adaptation information dissemination should be largely undertaken through a fairly distinct federal program, and adaptation implementation through relatively distinct decentralized authority, as proposed in ACES.

However, as evidenced in chapter 4, strategic reliance on modest levels of overlap for many functions might accommodate the advantages of centralized authority without sacrificing all of the diversity and experimentation advantages of decentralization. Multiple scholars have emphasized the advantages of overlap or polycentricity of adaptation authorities, including increased resilience in the face of disturbance, uncertainty, or surprise.[45] Several legal scholars support overlapping federal and state authority, avoiding rigid and exclusive divisions between national and regional jurisdictions, and increasing resilience.[46] The substantial escalation in uncertainty and prospective irreversibility of harm to ecological resources that accompany climate change militate in favor of reliance on a redundant regulatory system. The risk that a solitary program will neglect an important aspect of the problem is significant, and overlapping jurisdiction can provide a crucial safety net by increasing the chance that at least one agency with the jurisdiction to address a climate-related problem has taken steps to do so. Moreover, decentralized, overlapping regimes can enhance the "policy space" needed for effective adaptation efforts.[47]

Concurrent jurisdiction is likely to be particularly valuable where the risks of under-regulation are notably high, such as those addressing high-cost or irreversible effects or the management of nonrenewable resources, especially if those effects are linked to the activities of powerful market actors capable of convincing regulators to ratchet down government intervention in activities such as the development of beachfront property vulnerable to sea-level rise.[48] Such adaptation contexts are likely to be common, especially for natural resource threats.[49]

As chapter 4 explores, policymakers might profitably decrease regulatory overlap of particular governmental functions in order to lessen collective-action problems (such as shirking by multiple regulators with overlapping jurisdiction), while maintaining limited overlap of substantive authority to promote interagency accountability and redundancy advantages.[50] For many functions, assigning overlapping authority but primacy to one institution or level of government may accommodate concerns regarding inefficiency and regulatory inaction while leveraging the diversity and experimentation advantages of decentralization as well as the redundancy advantages of overlap.[51] Allocating overlapping authority with federal primacy for standard setting and funding and state primacy for implementation and enforcement, as provided in ACES, may reasonably navigate the advantages and disadvantages of the centralization and overlap dimensions. Such an approach might also most successfully balance the efficiency advantages of unitary governance with the redundancy advantages of overlapping authority.[52]

3. Coordinating Information, Funding, Planning, and Standard Setting

Interjurisdictional coordination of adaptation functions, through limited federal oversight or required state harmonization, might provide substantial advantages in managing cross-jurisdictional effects. In the adaptation context, government reports and scholars have roundly criticized lack of coordination as a barrier to better governance[53] or called for increased coordination to promote information sharing and avoid fragmentation.[54] In addition, policymakers have established programs that promote interjurisdictional collaboration on information generation, dissemination, and planning. These include the US Global Change

Research Program, a federally funded climate research effort sponsored by thirteen federal agencies,[55] and the now-disbanded Interagency Climate Change Adaptation Task Force.[56] Although federal agency participants in the Task Force lacked direct oversight or authority over others' adaptation activities, the Task Force served as a venue for federal agencies to communicate, brainstorm, and develop recommendations for the President on potential federal adaptation strategies. The Task Force called for additional collaboration and coordination among federal agencies and endorsed allocating to the federal government a key role in coordinating with other stakeholders to address climate change.[57] Other regulators have made similar appeals for agency collaboration to prepare and plan for climate change effects.[58]

Despite these calls for additional coordination, few have explored the possible forms of coordination (and tradeoffs of these alternatives) that could be employed in adaptation governance. At a minimum, it probably should include communication between authorities, but might also involve oversight by more central federal authorities or required harmonization between regulators addressing cross-jurisdictional effects. For example, ACES would have made adaptation planning and standard setting more hierarchical by requiring federal-agency natural-resource adaptation plans to be approved by the President and state natural resource adaptation plans to be approved by the Interior Secretary.[59]

Moreover, policymakers will have to consider which functions to coordinate. Especially in substantive regulatory areas in which the information-gathering and distribution functions are not consolidated in a unitary regulatory authority, there is likely to be a strong case for mandating or promoting coordination and sharing of information in areas of intersecting jurisdiction. Even so, retaining decentralized and overlapping information generation and dissemination systems and attempting to overcome their weaknesses through coordination may be less advantageous than a more consolidated strategy. ACES proposed reliance on federal coordination of disparate information-generation and dissemination efforts by an array of new councils, panels, and agencies.[60] In our view, such a system, overlaid on an already decentralized regulatory system, risks creating an inefficient, confusing, and unnecessarily repetitive array of information generation and dissemination. A requirement that agencies integrate adaptation into already-mandated plans would perhaps be more useful than establishing a new planning process, perhaps with cross-jurisdictional impacts addressed through interagency coordination.

An assessment of the advantages and disadvantages of coordinated authority might point to its use for other functions, however. Coordinating adaptation financing among regulatory authorities to prepare for and respond to the effects of climate change will likely provide significant advantages in limiting duplicative spending, as resources inevitably remain limited. At least in some regulatory contexts, mandating or otherwise promoting communication and cooperation over adaptation planning and standard setting may limit conflicting and counterproductive strategies. Coordination could take the shape of requiring all applicable regulators to sign off on standards adopted. For implementation and enforcement, it could also include each agency agreeing to bind itself to implementing and/or enforcing the mutually agreed-upon plans or standards.

Nonetheless, there are reasons to be cautious about wholesale endorsement of rigorous coordination for adaptation. In some circumstances, close coordination among agencies with intersecting jurisdiction might create unnecessary regulatory costs, vulnerabilities to groupthink, or lax interjurisdictional accountability as agencies adopt a more cooperative relationship with other regulators.[61] Moreover, close coordination may hinder regulators' ability to tailor management strategies to their particular situations and sacrifice some experimentation advantages of decentralized governance. As a result, the advantages of close cooperation—as compared to information generation and dissemination, financing, planning, and standard setting—are likely to be less evident for information analysis, implementation, or permitting. Perhaps for those reasons, ACES would have kept adaptation implementation largely independent and decentralized.[62]

B. Mitigation

In contrast with adaptation strategies, efforts to mitigate climate change through reducing individual source GHG emissions will impose local costs, but the resulting advantages may or may not be localized.[63] Climate mitigation efforts will have universally undifferentiated effects on atmospheric GHG concentrations.[64] Nevertheless, mitigation may be more beneficial in places that are facing climate threats (such as coastal areas vulnerable to sea-level rise) than in others; some places may even be harmed by mitigation if they would benefit from changes such as falling temperatures that extend crop growing seasons.[65] Even if localized costs provide localized benefits, however, those benefits cannot be confined to the locus of emissions-reduction activity.

Mitigation governance structures need to address several problems. First, one jurisdiction's failure to abate GHG emissions will exacerbate climate risks to other jurisdictions by increasing GHG concentrations responsible for adverse effects on physical, social, and economic systems.[66] Second, because a jurisdiction requiring GHG emission reductions cannot capture all of the benefits of doing so, and because a jurisdiction making no effort to reduce its own emissions will benefit from others' reductions, mitigation efforts face free-rider and public-goods problems.[67] Individual actors may have incentives to avoid incurring the economic costs of reducing their own emissions while reaping the environmental benefits of reductions by others.[68] The risk of under-regulation is exacerbated by the susceptibility of individual regulators to capture by powerful economic interests such as fossil fuel producers.[69] These dynamics suggest the desirability of regulatory structures that create a safety net to counter that risk. Third, the imminent need to reduce atmospheric GHG concentrations and the unprecedented challenges posed by climate change suggest that governance structures might appropriately seek to foster, for some functions, the experimentation and policy innovation associated with decentralized governance.[70] These distinctive features of climate mitigation seem to militate in favor of a governance framework that is more heavily tilted than in the adaptation context toward centralization, overlap, and coordination for certain functions, but with strategically allocated decentralized, distinct, or independent authority for other functions.

1. Existing International and National Governance Mechanisms

GHG emissions are subject to control at multiple governance levels. Parties to the United Nations Framework Convention on Climate Change (UNFCCC), including the United States, agreed to limit GHG emissions, but did not commit to specific reduction measures.[71] The 1997 Kyoto Protocol, which the United States never ratified, required aggregate GHG emission reductions by developed nations and imposed quantitative emission targets for these parties,[72] but those commitments mostly expired in 2012. In the 2015 Paris Agreement, the parties to the UNFCCC agreed to submit "nationally determined contributions" to reduce GHG emissions, which would be implemented through domestic mitigation measures.[73] These pledges, however, are voluntary and unenforceable,[74] and fundamental questions remain about the regime's impact in light of the United States' stated intent in 2017 to withdraw from the accord in 2020.[75] Nonetheless, it is a universally established governance framework characterized by decentralized, overlapping, and weakly coordinated authority. In light of space constraints, this section primarily focuses on US domestic climate governance, relying on the existing international regime as a baseline for considering domestic allocation alternatives. We do, however, explore international geoengineering governance in the next section, as this aspect of climate governance is particularly inchoate, both domestically and internationally, and the combination of global catastrophic risk and potential localized benefits makes the interjurisdictional implications of geoengineering particularly salient.

US mitigation governance is also somewhat decentralized and overlapping, but it is independent in important respects. Following the Supreme Court's ruling in *Massachusetts v. EPA*[76] that EPA is empowered under the Clean Air Act (CAA) to regulate GHGs, EPA issued a finding that GHG emissions endanger public health and welfare.[77] That finding triggered EPA's authority to regulate new motor vehicle emissions, which EPA, in conjunction with the National Highway Traffic Safety Administration, has done by issuing various centralized standards.[78] That authority is largely distinct, as the CAA preempts most state regulation of tailpipe emissions, with limited exceptions for more stringent EPA-approved standards issued by California and adopted by other states.[79]

Regulatory authority over stationary sources is generally more decentralized, overlapping, and independent. The Supreme Court's endorsement of EPA's authority to regulate some aspects of stationary source GHG emissions[80] paved the way for EPA's adoption of uniform federal standards for major new or modified stationary sources,[81] as well as issuance of the Clean Power Plan (CPP), in which EPA sought to restrict GHG emissions from existing electric generating plants.[82] The Supreme Court stayed the CPP before it went into effect, however,[83] and after President Trump's election, EPA proposed to repeal and replace, with significantly weaker controls, both its new source standards for power plants[84] and the CPP.[85] If an administration successfully repealed the Endangerment Finding, EPA's authority to regulate GHG emissions under the CAA would be completely disabled. If, as it has proposed doing, the Trump administration successfully revokes California's waiver from the CAA's preemption of state vehicle emission standards,[86] regulatory authority over mobile-source GHG emissions would be centralized in EPA.

EPA's near-complete withdrawal from the mitigation arena has shifted the locus of action to the states. The CAA preserves state overlapping authority to adopt independent standards for regulating stationary sources that are more stringent than EPA's.[87] Some states, led by California, have exercised that authority,[88] and those efforts have accelerated as states have sought to fill the vacuum created by EPA's withdrawal from climate mitigation.[89]

Given the piecemeal (and rapidly waning) federal effort to restrict GHG emissions, state supplementation efforts, and the uncertain future of state regulation of motor vehicle emissions, the rest of this section sketches some credible applications of our framework for designing mitigation governance. This analysis is informed primarily by the characteristics of climate mitigation described at the beginning of this section: local costs with effects that extend beyond the enacting jurisdiction. That dynamic creates a significant risk of cross-jurisdictional externalities and free-riding behavior that militates in favor of the adoption of minimum federal emission control standards. The current disinterest in federal mitigation regulation, however, reinforces the value of creating a safety net by authorizing decentralized, overlapping, and independent state authority to engage in more rigorous abatement efforts.

2. Centralization of Many Functions but Key Roles for Decentralized Authorities

As previous chapters have suggested, there are often good reasons to centralize information generation and dissemination to take advantage of economies of scale[90] and ensure effective distribution of information on climate science and GHG abatement technologies.[91] At least until the Trump administration reduced access to scientific information by removing links to and references to that information from agency websites,[92] the federal government performed these functions in the mitigation context.[93] Effective mitigation governance would almost certainly start by reversing the Trump administration's abdication of the federal government's information generation and dissemination capacities.

Centralized collection and dissemination of information about the success or failure of federal and state emissions control policies also makes sense as a means of publicizing innovative solutions.[94] There is perhaps less reason to centralize information analysis, as exercise of that function by scientific experts and policymakers at multiple levels of government may engender innovative takes on how to develop effective and efficient GHG emission reduction strategies.[95]

The cross-jurisdictional impacts of GHG emissions also strongly militate for adopting federal mandatory minimum-emission control standards.[96] One state's failure to limit its sources' emissions increases the risk of adverse climate effects elsewhere. Conversely, the benefits of one state's efforts to control emissions would largely be enjoyed outside of the adopting jurisdiction. The anticipated result is an undersupply of mitigation efforts.[97] Federal standards would minimize the risk of under-regulation. Further, absent federal standards, GHG abatement efforts would likely be affected by a race to the bottom, with states relying (if states are concerned about climate risks at all) on other states' controls.[98]

For reasons discussed in section B.3 of this chapter, there are good reasons not to make most federal GHG emission standard-setting authority exclusive. Given the extensive range of sources responsible for GHG emissions, the value of experimentation militates in favor of allowing the states to adopt standards that supplement EPA's.[99] Some EPA standards themselves incorporate mechanisms empowering decentralized authorities. Federal emission standards need not specify particular sources' obligations but can delegate such subsidiary standard setting to states. The CPP, for example, established statewide emission caps for electricity-generating facilities, but afforded the states considerable discretion to allocate reduction responsibilities among individual sources.[100] In addition, the CPP would have allowed states to craft cap-and-trade programs that would have further decentralized determinations concerning specific source controls.[101] The diversity of approaches enabled by multiple-state standard setting may weigh in favor of the adoption of standards that carve out a significant role for discretionary state choices, which, if successful, could then be exported to other states.

Centralized enforcement of federally adopted standards is supported by expertise and economies-of-scale advantages, as well as by the federal government's superior resource capacity to engage in protracted proceedings against well-financed alleged violators.[102] As the next section argues, however, overlapping federal and state enforcement authority for state-adopted standards may have useful safety-net and capture-resistance advantages.

3. Mostly Federal Baselines, with State Primacy for Certain Functions

For mitigation governance, most functions will likely benefit from concurrent federal and state roles, though opportunities exist for allocating either federal or state agencies primacy and even distinct authority for particular functions. We have sketched out a rationale for relatively distinct authority in one area: the enforcement of federally promulgated GHG emission control standards. We also anticipate that the federal government will take the lead in disseminating scientific and technical information about climate change effects and technological means of reducing them, primarily for efficiency reasons. There is no reason, however, to prevent lower levels of government from supplementing those efforts with additional intergovernmental exchanges. Some US states and localities have provided access to climate information that the Trump administration removed from the websites of federal agencies, reflecting the value of safety nets even for the management of information on the causes and effects of climate change, as well as on techniques for abating it.[103] State dissemination of information on regulatory successes, especially those involving innovative policy approaches, would be particularly useful. Likewise, EPA's analysis of scientific and technical studies, or of the fate of international, federal, or state mitigation policies and strategies, should not preclude additional analyses by state officials, who may glean different lessons than those EPA provides.

Substantial reasons support overlapping authority for most other mitigation-related functions. Perhaps the most important characteristics of climate mitigation in determining the appropriate allocation of standard-setting authority are the risks of free-riding behavior by the states and of regulatory capture at both the federal[104] and state levels. The risk that under-regulation stemming from either dynamic could prompt significant adverse effects suggests that in most contexts, the safety-net advantages of overlapping standard-setting authority would likely outweigh distinct authority's capacity to avoid duplication of effort and conflicting standards. The potential for such conflict is low because a stationary source would at most be subject to two standards—EPA's and that of the state in which it is located. And if the performance standards cap emissions, compliance with the more stringent standard will also satisfy the weaker one.

One possible exception to this inclination toward overlapping standard-setting authority concerns emissions from nationally marketed products such as new motor vehicles. Avoiding inconsistent standards for manufacturers of those products may justify more extensive preemption than the floor preemption that we have argued should apply (and does currently apply under the CAA)[105] to stationary sources of GHGs.[106] These concerns explain the CAA's preemption of state tailpipe emission standards for all states except California.[107] Yet Congress carved out a role for California to adopt more stringent standards (and for other states to adopt them if approved by EPA) to honor the state's past role as a policy innovator and allow it to continue to experiment in the future.[108] Numerous analyses have found significant value in that compromise solution. It ensures that no auto manufacturer will have to grapple with more than two standards in its production and marketing strategies (and complying with California's more stringent controls ordinarily would also satisfy federal controls).[109] At the same time, it preserves California's role as a "laboratory" of experimentation in auto emission regulation.[110]

More generally, EPA's efforts to weaken GHG emission limits for some vehicles on the ground that they are too onerous[111] highlights the importance of preserving supplemental state regulatory power. The accountability advantages of federal–state overlap might favor a similar configuration to control emissions over other nationally marketed products or to mandate energy-efficient products such as electric appliances, although no state may have the extensive history of policy entrepreneurship in those areas that California has pioneered in regulating auto emissions.

A comparison with the laws governing stratospheric ozone depletion is instructive. By joining the Montreal Protocol,[112] the United States committed to phasing out production and consumption of ozone-depleting substances that increase exposure to ultraviolet radiation associated with health and ecosystem risks.[113] The United States sought to fulfill those commitments in Title VI of the 1990 CAA amendments,[114] which phased out manufacture, marketing, and use of those substances.[115] Notwithstanding the treaty-based origins of US commitments, Congress did not preempt more stringent state standards for ozone-depleting chemicals, other than for the program's initial two-year period.[116] The rationale for preserving state authority to restrict GHG emissions is even stronger absent the kind of robust, binding international standards reflected in the Montreal Protocol.[117] The importance of the safety net provided by overlapping federal and state standard-setting authority for GHG emissions is strengthened by both the non-specific nature of the commitments made under the Paris Agreement and the Trump administration's stated intention to withdraw from it as of November 2020. Such a withdrawal would weaken the federal government's incentives to adopt standards that may be necessary to avoid the worst climate change impacts.

Planning and implementation authority are also good candidates for overlap. An approach analogous to the CPP's emission reduction mechanism would afford the states primacy in planning that is essentially the same as when they adopt state implementation plans (SIPs) for criteria pollutants under the CAA.[118] That endeavor involves distributing allowable statewide emissions among regulated sources.[119] Although requiring EPA approval of state plans and implementing actions to ensure conformity to statutory goals is advisable, policymakers could make it clear that EPA's review is intended to be deferential and not to interfere with legitimate state policy choices. Such a structure provides two levels of review that minimize capture risks. Implementation of supplemental standards would reasonably be the distinct responsibility of the enacting state. The need for a safety net would be less salient because, under the structure we envision, states would only be authorized to adopt, plan for, and implement standards more stringent than baseline federal standards.

Finally, enforcement authority might appropriately be either overlapping or distinct, depending on the nature and purpose of the standards. Efficiency advantages arguably justify distinct authority to enforce federally adopted standards.[120] Both levels of government should be able to enforce standards that a state adopts as part of the regulatory authority delegated to it by EPA, as the CAA currently allows for obligations derived from SIPs.[121] Dual enforcement authority in that context provides safeguards against inactivity by either level of government due to inadequate resources or capture that arguably outweigh the increase in administrative costs resulting from the maintenance of dual enforcement mechanisms, at least if policymakers are convinced of the value, as we are for climate mitigation, of precautionary regulation.[122] Policymakers more concerned about administrative inefficiencies or excessive government intervention in markets may, of course, reach different conclusions about the advisability of overlapping enforcement structures.

4. Mostly Coordinated Authority, with Independence When the Risk of Inaction Is Unacceptable

Some forms of coordination would almost certainly be advisable for effective mitigation governance, although relatively independent authority would likely be valuable for functions whose exercise is critical to effective efforts to reduce the risks of widespread climate-related harm and for which the benefits of policy innovation are potentially significant. If EPA were to adopt state obligations similar to the CPP's statewide GHG emission caps, but vest states with planning and implementation discretion, it would be apt for EPA to review state performance and, in some instances, act in lieu of a state failing to satisfy its obligations. EPA already performs similar functions under the CAA.[123] Similar hierarchically coordinated permitting authority would be appropriate for stationary sources regulated by a state to meet emission caps and similar obligations imposed on the state, rather than directly on emissions sources. Such authority may enhance state accountability, prevent shirking, and leverage EPA's expertise in assessing the adequacy of state actions.

As we noted in chapter 4, providing EPA a robust but narrowly tailored oversight role while reducing its duty to duplicate underlying functions primarily performed by states may simultaneously best accommodate the redundancy advantages of overlap while reducing inefficiencies. At the same time, there are persuasive reasons to allow states to use their planning and permitting processes to independently impose more stringent source-specific duties. Independent implementation of those strategies would be a counterpart to the independent state standard-setting authority discussed later in this section.

It may be inefficient for regulators at both levels of government to pursue simultaneous enforcement actions against the same regulated entity, as well as unfair to subject a source to contemporaneous (and potentially conflicting) enforcement actions. Identifying the appropriate nature of that coordination is perhaps less clear. The CAA requires communication between federal and state enforcement officials, allowing both EPA and the states to enforce SIPs but requiring EPA to notify the state and wait at least thirty days before pursuing enforcement.[124] The Clean Water Act (CWA) goes further, affording primacy to state enforcement of state-issued discharge permits.[125] Some federal pollution control statutes, including the CAA,[126] allow the federal government in some cases to "over-file" if it deems state-imposed sanctions to be inadequate, notwithstanding the inefficiencies and unfairness that may result from sequential enforcement actions.[127] Deciding whether to allow such sequential enforcement for GHG mitigation requires balancing efficiency and fairness considerations against concerns about inadequate enforcement by one governmental level. Because we favor granting states considerable discretion to devise tailored policy solutions consistent with (and extending beyond) federal mitigation goals, and because we are concerned that resource shortages and anti-regulatory ideology have hampered federal enforcement capacity, we tilt toward the CWA's robust state primacy model. Further, states should retain independent authority to enforce their own obligations that extend beyond federal floors.

A loose form of coordination may also be desirable for information generation. Federal–state coordination in setting a research agenda can help avoid wasteful expenditures on studies that EPA is already performing or of which it is otherwise aware. Similar coordination within the federal government may also be desirable. Communication among federal agencies may facilitate efficient allocation of federal research dollars and production of studies that operate synergistically to fill research gaps. Coordination between EPA and state agencies, or among federal agencies, can facilitate efficient pooling of research resources (which also provides a rationale for coordinated funding). There may also be value in EPA prodding states to assist it in plugging information gaps in areas such as ambient monitoring. Nevertheless, states should be free to extend their own research agendas into areas in which they perceive critical information needs to exist.

Providing opportunities for communication via information dissemination also has value. There is likely little glory in claiming credit for being the best at independently distributing information on the results of scientific studies conducted by others, for example, so the cost-saving advantages of the coordinated federal distribution of such information are probably of overriding importance. However, concerns that an agency or governmental level may suppress rather than disseminate information (as some suggest the Trump administration has done[128]) militate for allowing other authorities to do so independently. Similarly, as we have argued at length in chapter 7, the tradeoffs in allocating authority to analyze information appear to favor overlapping, independent authority even more strongly, as the differing skill sets, experiences, and points of view fostered by independent analysis are likely to reduce groupthink and spark innovative insights and policy solutions.

Finally, relatively independent standard-setting authority seems desirable. Most of the advantages associated with coordination appear to be relatively modest in this standard-setting context. Other than for regulation of nationally marketed products, as discussed below, there seems little need for either federal–state or interstate harmonization of mitigation standard setting. The floor preemption discussed in section B.3 in this chapter would eliminate the risk of a race to the bottom. Interjurisdictional communication, whether it is voluntary or mandatory, or participation in the adopting jurisdiction's standard-setting processes by another unit of government, would likely do little to reduce free-riding risks. Communication may be more useful in pooling resources and expertise so that each jurisdiction that is engaged in standard setting need not reinvent the wheel.

These marginal efficiency advantages of coordination, however, need to be weighed against its costs. The principal problem with coordinated standard setting, particularly if it takes the form of interjurisdictional consensus requirements or a federal veto over state standards, is that it creates obstacles to the adoption of standards that are urgently needed to abate the environmental harms posed by GHG emissions. Even rigorous procedural requirements can create disincentives to action by making it costlier to pursue. Independent standard setting thus acts as a palliative to the risk of government inaction, which, under the Trump administration, is all too apparent.

An additional, if perhaps less cogent, advantage of independent standard setting might be providing opportunities for policy innovation on matters such as the design of a carbon tax.[129] Independent standard setting (above the minimum federal floor) can also combat groupthink, opening the door to important policy breakthroughs. In light of the substantiated urgent need for robust climate mitigation strategies and our general predisposition toward promoting cost internalization (even if it is at the expense of over-regulation), these benefits of independent standard-setting authority between federal and state governments may well outweigh the harmonization and/or efficiency advantages of coordination.[130]

The balance may differ for standards (such as mobile-source emission standards) for which it seems advisable to avoid imposing multiple state standards that could create burdensome marketing challenges for auto manufacturers or similar product suppliers. As noted above, an attractive compromise may be to allow a policy leader such as California to adopt its own, more stringent standards under a hierarchically coordinated regime requiring EPA approval employing a deferential review standard.[131] Such a solution might achieve a tolerable degree of uniformity while fostering competition and innovative policy measures by states that are at great risk of climate-related damage, that want to respond to public support for vigorous regulation, or that take pride in their reputations as progressive environmental policy leaders.

C. Geoengineering

The United Kingdom's Royal Society defines geoengineering (or climate engineering) as "the deliberate large-scale manipulation of the planetary environment to counteract anthropogenic climate change."[132] Solar radiation management (SRM) involves reducing the amount of solar radiative energy that reaches the Earth's surface to offset the trapping of infrared radiation caused by rising GHG concentrations, such as by dispersing sulfate aerosol particles in the stratosphere to enhance surface reflectivity of the sun's radiation[133] or modifying cloud structures to reduce their retention of solar radiation.[134] The other major category of geoengineering is CO_2 removal (CDR), which would remove and sequester CO_2 from the atmosphere through techniques such as seeding the oceans with iron to spur the growth of phytoplankton capable of absorbing CO_2.[135]

Because no geoengineering technique has been tested at larger than a laboratory scale, the effects of deploying these technologies is uncertain.[136] The nature and scope of those effects are likely to be significantly different for the two categories of geoengineering, however. SRM technologies have the capacity to create adverse effects at a planetary scale,[137] including altered weather patterns, damage to the stratospheric ozone layer, irreversible effects on biodiversity, and dimming of light.[138] Moreover, once deployment of SRM technologies begins, it may be impossible to stop using them without triggering massive, sudden temperature increases.[139] In contrast, the characteristics of most forms of CDR appear to be analogous to those addressed by climate mitigation strategies, with largely localized costs and primarily global benefits.[140] As a result, the governance issues posed by CDR and mitigation are likely to be similar. As a key purpose of this chapter is to demonstrate how our analytical framework suggests different organizational choices for different aspects of climate governance, we focus here on the considerations that should illuminate the creation of governance structures for SRM forms of geoengineering.

The overarching considerations for structuring SRM governance appear to be (1) uncertainty about the nature and likelihood of potentially catastrophic and irreversible effects from deployment; (2) the global scope of those effects; and (3) the ability of one actor, which stands to enjoy concentrated beneficial effects from SRM deployment, to pursue it without the participation or consent of others who may be adversely affected.[141] These characteristics distinguish SRM governance challenges from those involving both mitigation and adaptation. For mitigation, the main problem is combatting the inclination to let others bear the economic burdens of cutting GHG emissions.[142] Both adaptation and geoengineering seek to reduce local climate-related problems (such as sea-level rise), but while the effects of adaptation actions will be primarily local, SRM deployment may have devastating global impacts.

The distinctive aspects of geoengineering governance suggest that, for most functions, international control of SRM technologies probably should generally be characterized by (1) overlapping authority that provides redundancy; (2) centralization, which fosters the capacity to control collective-action problems such as cross-jurisdictional externalities; and (3) coordinated structures to provide obstacles to unilateral deployment. Research and information analysis authority, however, should likely be decentralized and independent to take advantage of the diversity and innovation benefits available through those allocations.

1. The Lack of Existing SRM Governance Mechanisms

Geoengineering governance mechanisms are sorely lacking,[143] both internationally and in the United States.[144] Policymakers have largely neglected geoengineering due to uncertainty about effectiveness,[145] fears about potentially dramatic effects, and concerns that discussion of geoengineering raises moral hazard problems by providing an excuse to avoid developing mitigation and adaptation strategies.[146] Attention to geoengineering options is accelerating, however, as mitigation and adaptation efforts flounder, making the need to craft effective governance structures for geoengineering particularly urgent.[147] As one climate scientist remarked, "no credible prognosis has emerged to explain how such governance might emerge."[148]

Scholars, think tanks, and government-sponsored researchers have begun to weigh in on appropriate reforms to address aspects of geoengineering activity such as research,[149] but few of the resulting policy recommendations have been incorporated into governance mechanisms.[150] Even when the allocation of authority has been analyzed, consideration of the various dimensions[151] and functions has been rare.[152] The following sections explore governance options for geoengineering for each dimension and for multiple regulatory or management functions.

2. Addressing Cross-Border Impacts through Centralized SRM Governance

A key characteristic of research into and use of SRM technologies is the breadth of their potential adverse effects. SRM deployment, and even research experiments into its use, by one jurisdiction risks triggering adverse effects around the globe. Centralized governance is the classic mechanism for forcing internalization of adverse cross-jurisdictional impacts.[153] It also fosters uniform regulatory approaches that may prevent inequities arising from differing constraints by jurisdiction.

The arguments for centralized SRM governance are probably strongest for standard setting.[154] Because of the significant global risks posed by SRM technologies, all governments ideally should be subject to uniform constraints on their use that minimize the risk of cross-jurisdictional externalities.[155] As noted in chapter 4, Congress long ago recognized the need for centralized federal standard setting for interstate air and water pollution to address collective-action problems. Likewise, a strong argument exists for subjecting SRM research and deployment to federal regulation, perhaps even preempting state or local governments from authorizing such activities.[156] Centralized standard-setting authority can avoid regulatory gaps arising from uncoordinated, decentralized efforts to address the problem.[157] The risks associated with SRM technologies are likely to outweigh the diversity and experimentation advantages of decentralized state standard setting. Fostering large-scale regulatory experimentation for radical SRM technologies seems ill-advised. Internationally, the capacity for more centralized standard setting differs in that there is no international institution capable of unilateral imposition of binding SRM research or deployment standards. Rather, any such constraints must derive from treaty mechanisms, which we characterize in chapter 2 as a coordinating device.

Similar considerations appear to apply to implementation of centrally adopted standards.[158] In the domestic context, the fact that the benefits of SRM deployment will tend to be local while the environmental risks remain broader suggest that SRM implementation governance also might be centralized. If so, planning for project development and enforcement of standards and permit conditions would logically be centralized in the federal government, too.

Centralization also seems appropriate for other functions, at both the international and national levels. For the foreseeable future, the financing of SRM technologies is likely to be confined to research rather than deployment. Centralized international research funding could result in an equitable sharing of research costs and also take advantage of economies of scale. Absent an agreement like the Kyoto Protocol's Clean Development Mechanism for funding mitigation efforts, however, the burden of geoengineering-research funding is likely to fall on individual nations. In the United States, a centralized federal research effort may be justifiable on capacity, coherence, accountability, and credibility grounds.[159] Further, the federal government can issue grants with conditions that appropriately balance research benefits and risks.[160]

On the other hand, though a case can be made for centralized governance of research on the use and effects of SRM techniques, that allocation appears more contestable.[161] Decentralizing research may engender diverse approaches and leverage the differing expertise of agencies such as EPA and NOAA. Such a structure—perhaps combined with a coordination mechanism requiring authorization by a federal agency other than the one conducting research[162]—may provide the greatest opportunities for exploring promising technologies while minimizing environmental risks.[163] At the international level, SRM research inevitably will be somewhat decentralized but might be constrained by treaty-based coordination, much as we suggest it would be for standard setting and implementation, as the dividing line between research and deployment is anything but clear.[164]

For reasons explored in chapter 7, contrasting structures are likely appropriate for dissemination and analysis of information about the risks and benefits of SRM technologies. Both internationally (among nations) and domestically (primarily among federal agencies), decentralized information analysis enhances the prospects for diverse approaches that lead to analytical breakthroughs and leverage the expertise of different analysts.[165] In contrast, a more centralized infrastructure for information dissemination would foster economies of scale and avoid unnecessary duplication of effort. The entity or entities charged with aggregating and disseminating research on the viability and effects of SRM might also collect the analyses of others and engage in a meta-level analysis to provide an overview that may provide the basis for centralized standard setting and implementation decisions.[166]

3. Addressing the Risk of Catastrophic Impacts through Overlapping Authority

The potential magnitude of and the level of uncertainty about the environmental impacts of SRM geoengineering activities suggest a particularly precautionary orientation that is congruent with the safety-net advantages of overlapping authority. Relatedly, appropriately designed overlapping authority can also counter the risks of regulatory inaction and capture. At both the international and domestic levels, overlapping authority to conduct research into the viability and risks of SRM technologies would likely enhance opportunities to produce, replicate, and verify research breakthroughs concerning SRM techniques and effects that might justify any duplication of effort and diffusion of responsibility that overlap may create. Although the discovery of effective SRM technologies has the potential to reduce long-term climate risks, policymakers considering the degree of overlap should keep in mind that SRM research projects that involve activities such as atmospheric dispersal of sulfate particles themselves may create adverse physical impacts. As suggested below, that risk may cut in favor of imposing a regime of hierarchical coordination on the deployment of even SRM research, such as vesting an international or national body with veto power over individual projects, or at least requiring governments considering SRM research to solicit the input of and allow participation in authorization proceedings by other governments.

Overlapping authority to engage in information analysis seems even less contestable. Multiple analyses of the same research can counter the risk that one analyst with a vested interest in resorting to SRM technologies will play down its risks. The environmental risks that conducting research creates will not accompany analysis of its results. On the other hand, broad dissemination of information concerning the mechanisms and effects of SRM technologies heightens the risk that the information will fall into the hands of someone willing to deploy SRM prematurely. A precautionary approach therefore may suggest that even analysis should be confined to a relatively small number of entities.

As chapter 4 illustrates, floor preemption for standard setting is the norm in the United States for conventional environmental pollution control management. Similarly, no state should be able to undercut federal standards for the approval or implementation of SRM initiatives.[167] It is less clear that SRM governance should follow the lead of more traditional US environmental governance regimes by allowing states to block SRM projects through the adoption of more stringent standards. In other contexts, such as nuclear power plant construction, Congress has created distinct federal regulatory authority to balance environmental risks with considerations such as energy production and national security needs.[168]

We nevertheless tentatively favor allowing states to apply more stringent standards to projects within their borders. First, SRM projects are characterized by local benefits and wider-scale costs, a combination that should mitigate concerns that individual states will impose more stringent SRM controls for self-interested reasons that diverge from the national interest. Second, authorizing states to block projects within their borders creates a safety net and protects against capture in a context involving environmental risks of unprecedented magnitude.[169] As chapter 2 notes, concurrent regulatory jurisdiction is most compelling in contexts in which the costs of under-regulation are high, as with those posing high-cost or irreversible effects.

To the extent that the safety net rationale for overlap is compelling, it would also militate in favor of overlapping inspection and compliance-monitoring authority. If the federal government is vested with hierarchically coordinated project approval authority, as suggested in the next section, both the federal entity that approved a research project and regulators in the state in which a project is located should be afforded site access to assess compliance with federal (and any more-stringent, supplemental state) standards. Enforcement authority also might be shared. The federal government's authority to enforce its own standards and permit conditions obviously makes sense. Federal enforcement protects against the risk that a state with strong incentives to promote SRM in light of its local benefits will fail to uncover, disclose, or take action to halt noncompliance despite its potential to create cross-jurisdictional harms. If the safety net benefits of overlap justify concurrent federal and (more stringent) state standard-setting authority, however, they would also appear to argue for allowing a state to enforce its own, more stringent standards in the absence of federal enforcement.

4. Addressing the Risk of Unilateral Action through Coordinated Governance

The third critical factor that should guide allocation of SRM governance authority is the ease with which someone may deploy SRM technologies absent regulatory restriction, and the potential divergence between that actor's interests and those of the larger global community.[170] Individual nations, states, or even private actors may favor pursuit of SRM solutions that benefit them even if they pose catastrophic global risks.[171] One might predict such behavior if an implementing nation or state is experiencing, or expects to experience, severe adverse climate effects and the cost of pursuing a geoengineering solution, such as dispersing sulfate aerosol particles, is relatively low.[172]

As we describe below, coordination of several functions may be a promising way to address this concern of unilateral action. Although mandatory harmonization requirements in particular may reduce even fruitful SRM activity and undoubtedly increase administrative costs, it may be a necessary tradeoff for certain functions such as implementation to minimize the risk of devastating deployment. Moreover, less hierarchical forms of coordination, such as comment and consultation requirements, may be employed to pool resources and expertise, and to harmonize governance efforts as a means of minimizing inconsistency. For various functions these advantages may outweigh the additional administrative costs, groupthink risk, and barriers to intergovernmental competition and policy innovation associated with coordination. For functions such as information analysis, however, the tradeoffs may plausibly point to more independent authority.

In both the international and domestic contexts, the advantages of coordinated dissemination of research results appear to be robust.[173] Just as in chapter 7 we recommended coordination within the US intelligence community to identify and address terrorist threats, coordinated dissemination of information internationally and domestically about SRM research or deployment is essential to informed consideration of whether to allow its use. Dissemination of information about the risks that accompany SRM may deter governments from engaging in high-risk unilateral action.[174] These benefits may justify administrative coordination costs, and the risk of groupthink appears to be relatively low for dissemination of research results.[175]

Whether to support information generation through coordinated research by multiple entities on SRM viability and risks may be a closer call. On the one hand, independent research combats groupthink and may spur competition resulting in innovative research techniques. On the other hand, research coordination can facilitate pooling of resources and expertise,[176] prioritization of research inquiries, and avoidance of duplicative effort.[177] Moreover, coordinated research efforts may minimize research-related risks. We therefore favor research coordination akin to what we recommend later in this section for SRM deployment.

The case for independent analysis of geoengineering research results appears to be stronger. Independent analysis can combat groupthink and any rush to endorse risky (or suppress useful) SRM technologies. Nations not facing imminent climate disasters are more likely than those with more immediate problems to highlight the global risks of geoengineering projects and to argue that their potential benefits do not justify those risks, while those facing emergencies will likely tack in the opposite direction. Independent analysis can serve as a check against both forms of bias.[178]

Hierarchical coordination through treaty-based norms is the most likely form of international standard setting for SRM technologies, although such an undertaking currently faces considerable political obstacles.[179] There is, nonetheless, some precedent for such a venture. A resolution adopted in 2008 pursuant to a 1996 protocol to a convention to prevent marine dumping[180] prohibited ocean fertilization, except for research activities.[181] Another model is the 1987 Montreal Protocol,[182] which commits parties to phasing out ozone-depleting substances, but leaves implementation to individual parties.[183] International establishment but national implementation of standards restricting SRM technologies should mitigate concerns about international micromanagement.[184] International coordination, such as adoption of non-binding principles for good research and deployment practices, may balance the need for information and precautionary approaches to SRM research and deployment. Domestically, coordination is only an issue if states are allowed to adopt standards that exceed minimum federal standards or if multiple federal agencies issue standards governing SRM research. Such coordination may take the form of consultation to avoid conflicting federal and state standards or disparate standards by federal agencies with distinct authority that otherwise could trigger regulatory arbitrage.

To mitigate the risk that a nation may unjustifiably skew application of standards in favor of project approval, international implementation might be coordinated by inviting input from the international community on proposed project approvals by individual nations. It may also be appropriate to vest in an international entity the authority to mediate disputes among proponents and opponents before their approval (or rejection), or to provide a forum for all governments to provide input before a neutral convener.[185] Such procedures will enhance accountability by governments considering project approval and allow them to benefit from the expertise of those who may not have had access to licensing or permitting processes at a lower governmental level.

As alluded to in section C.2 of this chapter, it may be advisable to vest coordinating authority to approve or disapprove individual research projects in the United States in a single federal agency such as the US Global Change Research Program or the Office of Science and Technology Policy, even if multiple agencies are authorized to conduct SRM research experiments. Such an arrangement would create a strong form of hierarchical coordination capable of promoting efficiency in the allocation of research dollars and limiting research discordance.[186] As chapter 4 illustrates, vesting primacy in one level of government through hierarchical coordination with limited oversight by another can minimize the costs of overlap. Requiring authorization by a single federal agency would perhaps make it easier to pursue a precautionary approach, which is arguably appropriate in light of the uncertainty over and potential irreversibility of the effects of SRM deployment.[187]

On the other hand, as we learned in chapter 8, independently exercised overlapping authority can strengthen regulatory safety nets by requiring regulated entities (in this case, SRM project proponents) to pass through multiple regulatory gates. To maintain coordination's advantages while avoiding a structure that vests only one entity with the power to block risky projects, project review and approval authority might be vested in an agency that is not itself engaged in or authorized to conduct research, to minimize potential conflicts between research promotion and regulatory control. This structure is reflected in the laws governing nuclear proliferation, in which different agencies have research and regulatory roles.[188]

Enforcement may benefit from coordination. Internationally, governments should be able to initiate proceedings through national forums to enforce treaty obligations or domestic standards. Nations may be able to pool resources and expertise to initiate or intervene in domestic enforcement proceedings.[189] International adjudicatory forums might even be available to pursue alleged violations of principles of customary international law.[190] In the United States, however, control over individual enforcement cases should be allocated exclusively to a federal permit-issuing entity but concurrently to federal and state officials if states are vested with any permitting authority, as under the federal pollution control laws.

D. Lessons

The crafting of climate governance mechanisms should be driven by assessments of the differing tradeoffs of alternative dimensional and functional structures presented by the disparate challenges posed by climate change adaptation, mitigation, and geoengineering. In all three areas, governance should deal with the uncertainty and potentially unprecedented scope of climate change impacts (and, in the case of SRM, efforts to address them). However, climate adaptation requires governance structures oriented toward addressing relatively localized costs and benefits; mitigation efforts arise in the context of projected local costs and largely global benefits; while SRM technologies require regimes that manage activities expected to create local benefits and potentially massive global costs.

Governance structures in each area should include processes for adjusting initial allocations of authority as new information emerges about the capacity of existing structures to meet governance goals or about the successes or failures of different governance mechanisms. Adaptive governance is particularly important when regulation addresses uncertain risks whose salience may change over time.[191] Thus, "build[ing] international cooperation and norms from the bottom up, as knowledge and experience develop," may best suit geoengineering governance.[192] Yet, as we explain in the conclusion, the success of governance mechanisms in addressing virtually any social problem may hinge on the capacity of the broader governance structure to integrate systematic learning about the efficacy of allocations of authority over time.

Conclusion

As the diverse examples in this book demonstrate, decisions concerning how best to allocate or reallocate authority among different government entities are critical to the functioning of government programs. The frequency with which policymakers resort to reorganization as a response to government failure attests to the salience of institutional allocations as a policy response. Notwithstanding their importance, analysis of the implications of these choices is often flawed or incomplete. We wrote this book in an effort to illuminate the choices facing policymakers as they consider allocation options in light of our belief that well-structured programs are likely to better foster regulatory or management goals in ways that promote important values such as effectiveness, efficiency, fairness, and legitimacy. As stated in the introduction, this book has five main objectives.

A. Speaking the Same Language

First, the book provides a common terminology and taxonomy for the use of those who establish or analyze interjurisdictional relations. This common language should facilitate coherent dialogue about the advantages and disadvantages of particular allocations, without interlocutors talking past each other. In this sense, the book provides a basic but important intervention in the large and growing literature on interjurisdictional institutional design—most prominently the literature on federalism. It explains how scholars and policymakers largely conflate the related but differing dimensions of authority, as well as ignore the many linked but varying sets of governmental functions. The book also illustrates how these misteps occur when scholars and policymakers characterize authority as well as when they analyze the tradeoffs of situating authority along different dimensions (and points within a dimension).

B. Understanding the Dimensions and Functions of Authority

Relatedly, in exploring this framework in a variety of contexts, the book discerns a number of descriptive insights that substantiate the value of the framework we offer. In exploring the centralization–decentralization dimension, we have learned that assessing the appropriate degree of centralization of agency authority should depend on more than just how to allocate authority between governmental levels—between federal or state authority, for example. This dimension, which frequently involves the scale at which governance will occur, also presents choices within a level of government. That is, decentralization can be vertical, but it can also be horizontal. Authority within the federal government, for instance, can be more or less centralized. Even within a specific agency, an assessment weighing the advantages and disadvantages of centralizing authority may yield dividends.

In investigating the overlapping–distinct dimension, consideration of how functional jurisdiction interacts with overlapping authority particularly reveals insights and opportunities. The overlap–distinctness dimension raises inherent scope questions, such as, what is the extent to which two or more regulators share substantive and functional jurisdiction? Overlapping authority can only exist if both substantive and functional jurisdiction coincide. Proponents and detractors of overlapping authority evidently often misunderstand the extent to which authority actually overlaps by neglecting to consider its substantive and functional components. Moreover, by understanding the interaction between functional jurisdiction and overlap, policymakers can explore alternative approaches for adjusting the extent of overlap in ways that might minimize some of its disadvantages while retaining more of the advantages. As explored in chapters 4 and 6, policymakers might lodge the same substantive jurisdiction in two institutions but keep such authority distinct by allocating certain functions to one and other functions to the other. Yet another option might be to reduce overlap for certain functions but maintain or increase it for those functions for which redundancy is especially beneficial, such as standard setting or enforcement, in many cases.

In addition, we describe each of the dimensions as continua, not binary choices between centralized or decentralized, overlapping or distinct, and coordinated or independent authority. Although we maintain the general utility of this construct, we also acknowledge that the coordination–independence dimension, in particular, which turns largely on the nature of interactions among agencies, may not involve a single-factor assessment of more or less coordination. Rather, it is more heterogeneous than the other two dimensions. As explored in chapters 2 and 5, coordination and independence involve multiple indicia, with the level of coordination being potentially greater if such activities are more formal, mandatory, frequent, lengthy, or hierarchical. Further exploration of the possible advantages and disadvantages of these various components of coordination, and how they may interact, would undoubtedly be fruitful. Moreover, as we examined in chapter 7, because the coordination–independence dimension is about intergovernmental relations, unlike the other two dimensions, coordination can occur (or not occur) between functions. The presence or absence of interfunctional coordination can influence the effectiveness of the exercise of the affected functions, as chapter 7's analysis of the reform of the nation's intelligence apparatus in the wake of 9/11 reveals.

C. Evaluating Policy Tradeoffs of Differing Dimensional and Functional Allocations

A third general aim of this project was discerning a number of normative postulates about how particular allocations of authority may be warranted in certain circumstances. The case studies explored in parts II and III generate both general precepts and more specific, contextualized prescriptions. In chapters 3 through 5, we assert and illustrate how functional jurisdiction matters in assessing the tradeoffs of allocating authority along a particular dimension. In chapters 6 through 8, we explain and explore various ways that failing to parse the different dimensions of authority can lead to misdiagnoses of problems, confused or myopic debate about the tradeoffs of alternative allocations, and/or missed opportunities that might more effectively or pragmatically address identified allocations concerns.

In addition to these assessments about how best to allocate authority along each dimension for particular functions, the case studies yielded some ideas that cut across the dimensions of authority. First, in some settings, policymakers will find opportunities to adjust one dimension of authority to address or reduce certain shortcomings of another. In chapter 4, for example, we explain how narrowly tailored coordination might be used to reduce the potential disadvantages from reducing overlap between federal and state authority over enforcement under the Clean Air Act (CAA) and Clean Water Act (CWA). Instead of the significant duplication of enforcement that is currently possible under these laws, policymakers could authorize states to assume virtually all direct permit enforcement when certified by the Environmental Protection Agency (EPA) as being capable of robust enforcement. This would significantly reduce the extent of overlap, which might have efficiency advantages but raises potential risks to efficacy from not having a sufficient safety net. However, pairing this change with restrained coordination through limited but mandatory permit enforcement review by EPA could help maintain some of the efficacy advantages of redundant authority while minimizing its efficiency costs. The judicious use of overlap and coordination would give the federal and state agencies relatively distinct authority over enforcement as compared to the existing allocation, which might provide much of the current safety-net advantages of overlap while helping minimize administrative disadvantages.

Of course, in other contexts, different shifts in a dimension might be warranted to reduce the same or different risks and adverse consequences of allocations of authority along a different dimension. In chapter 3, we observed that policymakers may be able to secure the advantages of decentralized enforcement, including policy experimentation—while avoiding duplication, inefficiency, and inequities stemming from differences in enforcement strategy—by creating minimal overlap but requiring at least some coordination of effort. Similarly, in chapter 8, we suggest the possibility of pairing an increase in overlap between federal regulators of depository institutions to reduce the risk of regulatory arbitrage with limited coordination of certain functions, such as joint inspection, to alleviate the risk of conflict and inconsistency from the overlap.

Our case studies also reveal that there might be opportunities to adjust along a dimension on a function-by-function basis to maximize the advantages of each end of the dimension. For example, as chapter 7 illustrates, independent intelligence information analysis may be a desirable way of preventing groupthink, but coordination may be essential to both information dissemination and implementation (effective responses based on the results of that analysis). Alternatively, combining a relatively centralized allocation for one function (such as standard setting) with a decentralized allocation for another (such as implementation) might most ably accommodate the economies of scale and uniformity advantages of centralization with the experimentation and expertise advantages of decentralization.

Finally, the case studies make clear that, even for allocations of authority that were once sound, policymakers may need to restructure allocations as the underlying circumstances for the regulatory regime change. Chapter 6 may be the clearest illustration of this phenomenon. Federal law originally decentralized and divided substantive jurisdiction for financial securities and futures between the Securities Exchange Commision and the Commodity Futures Trading Commission. According to the legislative history, Congress created this allocation primarily to take advantage of the expertise and diversity advantages of decentralization and the efficiency advantages of distinct authority. Because the securities and futures markets largely converged in subsequent decades, what had been fairly distinct authority shifted to overlapping jurisdiction. Accordingly, the policy tradeoffs of the allocation likely fundamentally shifted, warranting a new assessment of the underlying tradeoffs, and perhaps a realignment commensurate with the change in circumstances.

Although we believe that the insights from the application of the framework developed in this book are valuable and pioneering, we also recognize that inevitably we are only able to glean moderate normative guidance for future allocations or reallocations of regulatory authority. The framework enables observers and policymakers to work through a number of suppositions about the tradeoffs of different allocations. And in chapter 9 we offer our own postulates about how allocations of authority should play out differently in addressing different types of regulatory problems, even in the same substantive realm—in that case, the various forms of climate change governance. Yet we think our framework makes evident that there is a scarcity of empirical analyses exploring the tradeoffs of allocations in particular settings on which to ground most postulates. Although there undoubtedly is a general scarcity of "empirical investigation into the creation and design of public institutions," as Donald Moynihan has put it,[1] this shortage is perhaps exacerbated by the confusion and conflation of dimensions and functions that we suggest is prevalent.

D. Fostering Empirical Inquiry and Evaluation

As such, a fourth aim of the book is that it can offer a template for the proliferation of future empirical inquiry by scholars and policy analysts incrementally investigating the advantages and disadvantages of certain allocative configurations in particular settings. In this sense, it is of a piece with the long line of prior calls to rely on empirical methods to assess public administration, dating back to Woodrow Wilson's declaration that public administration is a science.[2] Although we regard the Trump administration's 2018 reorganization plan as deeply flawed, as the introduction explains, we agree with its call for the accumulation of "more evidence about what works and what needs to improve in order to inform mission-critical decisions and policies."[3]

One possible research design might explore the effectiveness of overlapping enforcement in serving as a safety net using the pollution control context studied in chapter 4. The investigation would first need to identify state enforcement decisions and place them in categories ranging from diligent to lax enforcement. Analysts could then examine how often the federal government over-filed on a state decision (i.e., sought more stringent remedies or liabilities). The study would need to assess whether there were any differences between the varying statutory approaches. Under the CAA and CWA, EPA is not legally required to give any deference to state determinations, while under the Resource Conservation and Recovery Act (RCRA) it must provide more deference to states (and substantial deference in some jurisdictions). The study could also examine whether any federal over-filing led to different penalties under the different statutory designs. Finally, the study might consider assessing the disadvantages of the duplicative federal program, perhaps as compared to advantages in over-filing and/or any differences between the CAA/CWA and RCRA schemes.

Another example might involve investigative assessments of the tradeoffs of interjurisdictional coordination for the information distribution function. The study might map the scope of governmental infrastructure in a particular regulatory area, gauge the extent and type of coordination between any governmental portals, and assess the efficacy of such coordination in information dissemination. The assessment might be comparative, considering the relative efficacy of the coordination in dissemination as contrasted with a less (or differently) coordinated but otherwise similar regulatory program.

Of course, a fundamental impediment to these empirical analyses for scholars and analysts is acquisition of the basic information on the performance of government institutions needed to make such assessments. To some degree, pointing out this obstacle might reflect a critique of the limited transparency of government institutions. Yet it is more elemental. Most regulatory agencies do not, nor have the incentive to, collect even basic information about the performance of their programs.[4] Even when they do, they are often starved for resources and may thus be inclined to subordinate the kind of investigation needed to assess ongoing programs to tasks such as meeting statutory deadlines and other responsibilities.[5]

E. Fostering Experimentalism and Learning about the Structure of Public Governance

The fifth and perhaps most fundamental ambition of this project is to suggest a framework for assessments of allocations of authority that regulators and policymakers can and should embed into the governance process itself. The case studies and examples explored in the book demonstrate a broad need for an adaptive approach to governance. Governance should integrate feedback loops that require and/or otherwise incentivize some or all regulatory institutions to systematically monitor and assess the efficacy of allocations in accommodating the tradeoffs or otherwise realizing the ends for which they were proposed. The success of such a process requires concrete legislative commitment in the form of adequate funding, some of which may be dedicated to the assessment and adjustment process we envision.

The preceding chapters make the affirmative case to policymakers that tradeoffs exist along the dimensions of authority and often differ by function. A structural adaptive governance framework augments this potential for maximizing the public benefits of government programs.

"Adaptive governance" reflects the need to monitor government operations, evaluate the resulting feedback, and make appropriate adjustments.[6] Much of the literature on adaptive governance and resilience theory, particularly in the context of adaptive management, tends to focus on process, that is, those features of the legal system that govern the procedures of decision making.[7] So, too, have many prior attempts to improve or legitimize administrative regulation, starting with the Administrative Procedure Act (APA).[8] Recently, we supplemented this prevailing emphasis on process and "procedural legal adaptive capacity" by exploring the tradeoffs of "substantive legal adaptive capacity," that is, the "degree to which statutory goals are capable of accommodating change."[9]

Our focus here, however, is on aspects of the legal system that are "structural" or organizational.[10] A structural adaptive governance framework would oblige policymakers to prioritize regulatory objectives and declare why a proposed allocation of authority is tentatively expected to best achieve the prioritized goals. As detailed in Figure 2.5, these identified objectives include not just general or even more concrete notions of regulatory efficiency, effectiveness, fairness, or accountability. Ultimately, policymakers should articulate sufficient guidance to support the allocation of authority developed, including which advantages or disadvantages of a particular dimension are of primary value or concern. For example, in deciding in a given program the extent to which authority between regulators should overlap for a particular function, legislators may declare they are (or are not) significantly more concerned about the risks of under-regulation, regulatory arbitrage, and agency capture as compared to the additional regulatory costs and risk of a regulatory commons that overlap may induce. In such a circumstance, that determination would reasonably support an allocation of authority providing for more (or less) overlapping jurisdiction to multiple authorities.

The key component of this experimentalist governance framework is the systematic monitoring and assessment of allocations to evaluate their efficacy. Experience with the administration of a particular program may either confirm or refute the degree to which an allocation of authority has promoted programmatic goals in light of actual experience. This kind of regulatory information infrastructure could be incrementally integrated into the statute or regulation authorizing the allocation or reorganization.[11]

However, in our view, a requirement for monitoring and assessment of government allocations would be better established as part of a general-operation statute applicable to all agencies. Our ambition is for such legislation to develop the status of a "super-statute" that situates structural adaptive governance as a cornerstone of the administrative state.[12] As an overarching framework presiding over the activity of most agencies, it would be somewhat akin to the APA.[13] Crucially, however, its focus on enhancing structural adaptive capacity via the monitoring and assessment of organizational allocations of authority would be entirely different from the APA's procedural focus on the regulation of agency decision-making processes.

Such a program would also be a more firmly and systematically embedded version of the sporadic succession of Presidential initiatives seeking to review and potentially restructure administrative organization, from the Hoover Commission[14] to the most recent Trump administration's executive order directing a comprehensive reorganization of the federal administrative state and its 2018 reorganization plan.[15] Yet this mandate would be substantially different from its predecessors. Previous initiatives have often been ad hoc, and most have not sought to comprehensively apply to all federal agencies and programs. A more comprehensive program is vital for promoting systematic learning that may shed light on the success or failure of existing institutional configurations, suggest future directions within an agency or program, and provide experiential information that can be shared more broadly within and across jurisdictions. Cross and pan-governmental distribution of systematic learning can help policymakers responsible for structuring government programs avoid repeating past mistakes and foster experimentation, which, if successful, may be transferable to a wide range of regulatory or management contexts.

Moreover, none of the prior mechanisms referred to above has relied on a systematic framework for comprehending and assessing allocations of authority. Many of these previous initiatives, such as the Trump administration's proposed reorganization,[16] implicitly or explicitly disfavor the existence of multiple, overlapping, and intersecting jurisdiction, with little or any supporting explanation other than conclusory, unrevealing, and disparaging references to inefficiencies and redundancies. As exhibited in our case studies, however, any efficiency advantages of eliminating duplicative authority ought to be balanced against potential gains from overlapping authority. Similarly, many past reorganization initiatives failed to examine the range of coordination alternatives available between such authorities or to recognize the downsides of coordination. Any advantages from increased coordination among government institutions should be weighed against its disadvantages (including increased administrative costs and risk of groupthink) and the opportunity costs of not creating agency independence.

Virtually none of the previous efforts to engage in large-scale reorganization of the federal bureaucracy has investigated whether interagency relationships should vary by function. As detailed in the introduction, the Trump plan purports to strive for a comprehensive review of alternative options for restructuring the federal administrative state and to eschew a "one size-fits all" approach,[17] but its recommendations are dominated by what appear to be rote calls for greater centralization, and reflect little or no attention to the possibility of varying structural configurations based on function.

Finally, adopted requirements for the review of allocations of regulatory authority have at times been imposed to advance a deregulatory agenda untethered to any empirical assessment of the tradeoffs of existing or proposed allocations. The narrow focus of these statutes and Presidential orders, of which the Trump executive order and reorganization plan are archetypal examples, is to reduce government controls on market behavior or devolve federal authority, without any evaluation of the tradeoffs of such changes.[18] Although it is impossible and even detrimental to completely divorce policy from politics, we believe it is feasible to create an evaluative regime that relies on a relatively objective evaluation of empirical information on past organizational successes and failures as the basis for recommendations that may then be openly debated in the crucible of the policy deliberations of the affected agencies, and, if appropriate, in Congress.

Using the vocabulary of our allocational framework, the structural adaptive governance infrastructure that we recommend would center on three information functions: (1) information generation on the nature of, reasons for, and effects of an existing allocation of authority; (2) collection and distribution of such information; and, finally, (3) analysis and assessment of the existing allocation in light of the policymakers' identified rationale for the allocation. In our view, primary information generation and distribution would best be allocated primarily to a relatively independent and politically insulated agency that is fairly centralized and distinct. In this context, the diversity, experimentation, and expertise advantages of decentralized authority are likely to be modest and outweighed by the uniformity and economies-of-scale advantages of centralized information generation and distribution. Moreover, the authority to conduct these functions should be fairly distinct because the advantage of creating a safety net through redundancy would not seem to be sufficiently robust to justify the inefficiencies that would result from overlapping authority among multiple insulated agencies. Any safety-net advantages, moreover, as discussed below, may already be substantially created through overlap of the information analysis function. Nonetheless, because much of the raw information concerning program implementation would be held by the agencies whose performance is being reviewed, information generation authority by the agency dedicated to allocation assessment would necessarily overlap and need to be coordinated with the activities of these agencies. In contrast, information distribution might be more appropriately centralized, independent, and distinct.

Finally, authority over information analysis should at least initially be decentralized, overlapping, and coordinated. Although the agency primarily tasked with information generation and distribution should also be accorded information analysis authority, we suggest that this function also would be appropriately dispersed among a variety of institutional actors, including the reviewed agencies themselves, for their appraisal and critique. This allocation could be accomplished through an initial assessment by the lead agency, which would be subject to limited coordination via a comment process that subsequently incorporated other perspectives in the assessment document. Ultimately, of course, Congress and the President would have the power to decide if or when any particular allocation of substantive decision-making authority might need to be reallocated in light of such information.

1. Reinvigorating Professionalism about Governmental Structure

Our framework thus suggests a language and structure for the analysis of interjurisdictional relations that will be valuable to outside actors assessing public institutions, but also to those within government who are responsible for implementing and overseeing regulatory activity. The commitment to empiricism that we envision of course would be expected to develop within the agency that is granted primary authority for advancing this adaptive governance infrastructure. However, we also anticipate that the effects of these reforms would help elevate reliance on the provision of evidence and reasoning for allocations of authority throughout the regulatory state and, in our more audaciously optimistic moments, even in deliberations by elected officials.[19]

Employment of this information and learning infrastructure would foreseeably increase the salience of professionals tasked in the administrative state with assessing the tradeoffs and efficacy of allocations of authority. The creation or expansion of authority focused on monitoring, assessing, and distributing information about interjurisdictional relations would necessarily seek to develop and invigorate expertise in assessing allocations of authority and incorporate such methods as relevant within the regulatory state. In this sense, our framework may be viewed as similar to prior proposals seeking to promote increased reliance on empirical methods to assess and advance the practice of public administration, most prominently the rise of policy analysis in public policy programs in the late 1960s.[20] Nonetheless, our focus is less on disciplinary development and more on the operation of government.

The Office of Management and Budget's (OMB) Office of Information and Regulatory Affairs (OIRA)—which, according to a 1993 executive order, "is the repository of expertise concerning regulatory issues, including methodologies and procedures that affect more than one agency"[21]—might seem to be a plausible institution to take the lead in implementing the systematic monitoring and distribution of information about government allocations that we envision. Yet in our view, OIRA would be a poor choice. We believe it is critical to vest the primary responsibility for collating, analyzing, and distributing the results of the learning process described above in an entity that is more nonpartisan, less vulnerable to shifts in the prevailing political winds, and less associated with any particular partisan positions on substantive regulatory issues. Doing so would be consistent with the creation of a civil service insulated from political influence, which some regard as "a seminal development in public management."[22]

OIRA's role in overseeing the adoption of agency regulations has been controversial, to say the least. Proponents of OIRA review have endorsed the capacity of the centralized regulatory review process that OIRA oversees to improve interagency coordination, increase accountability, and improve the substance of rules, as well as the substance of regulation.[23] Others insist, however, that OIRA from its inception has reflected an anti-regulatory bias and elevated efficiency considerations over other values, even when the organic statutes of the agencies whose regulations it reviews create a different values hierarchy.[24] Further, the OMB has frequently been criticized for its lack of transparency and its skewing of access toward the regulated community.[25] We regard transparency as an essential component of the structural adaptive governance framework we endorse.[26] Whether it is the defenses or the criticisms of the OMB's role in regulatory review one finds more persuasive, the splintered assessments of its performance is uncontestable, increasing the risk that its regulatory judgments will not be regarded, at least by some, as objective.

The Congressional Research Service (CRS) and the Government Accountability Office (GAO) currently provide the closest analogues in the federal government to the institution we propose. However, their functions currently are much more limited and ad hoc than the more comprehensive framework we recommend. CRS, whose mission is largely information collection and policy-based analysis and which is regarded as apolitical,[27] is an attractive choice for heading up the enterprise we envision. Indeed, the statute from which CRS derives its authority explicitly requires it to act in nonpartisan fashion,[28] and CRS takes that mandate seriously.[29] CRS is authorized to provide information in response to requests by legislators or congressional committees on recommendations by executive agencies or the President, or on its own initiative in anticipation of requests by legislators or committees.[30] Although that authorization may not allow CRS to respond directly to information requests by agencies or the President, CRS's authorizing statute could easily be amended to allow it to do so. Another option for performing the systematic evaluative tasks that our framework calls for is GAO. Although it typically issues reports at the request of legislators, it also performs work that "is mandated by public laws."[31] Indeed, one of GAO's principal responsibilities is "reporting on how well government programs and policies are meeting their objectives."[32]

Under current statutory authorizations, however, neither of these agencies engages in systematic, continued assessment of allocations of authority throughout the federal administrative state. Accordingly, if either were vested with the information generation, distribution, and analysis functions we propose through this adaptive governance infrastructure, it would need substantial increases in resources to do so to supplement the meager resources currently available for these kinds of assessments within the regulatory agencies. If adopted and adequately funded, our proposed framework would provide a systematic and more comprehensive way to assess the tradeoffs of alternative allocations of authority. Once assessed, policymakers would be armed with better information with which to potentially affirm or adjust those allocations.

Because of its focus on independence, empiricism, and adaptive assessment, to some extent our proposal might evoke Justice Stephen Breyer's call for the formation of a politically insulated and expert-driven federal risk regulation agency, to be tasked with crafting adaptable regulatory strategies that reflect comparative evaluation of available options based on insights gleaned from experience.[33] However, our proposal would limit the substantive jurisdiction of an evaluative entity such as CRS or GAO to the review of allocations of authority, and its functional jurisdiction to information generation, dissemination, and analysis. In other words, it would have no capacity to adopt or implement changes in allocations. More importantly, we are not suggesting, as Justice Breyer appeared to do, that allocation of the responsibility to administer a program for assessing structural adaptive governance will or should be conclusive about the merits of alternative ways of organizing interjurisdictional relations.

2. Accountability in, and Deliberation about, Government (Re)Organization

Of course, agency assessments of the effectiveness of allocations in achieving policymakers' objectives would be far from incontrovertible, even if generated by an entity with a reputation for high-quality and objective work. Nonetheless, we see value in vesting the initial assessment responsibility to an entity insulated but not divorced from politics, and then allowing others to review and challenge the resulting analysis in more political domains. The analyses provided by an agency such as CRS would provide a starting point for considering whether changes in existing allocations are appropriate, and, if so, what they should be. But other agencies or observers both through and after review-and-comment processes undoubtedly would and should review and interrogate such assessments and develop their own appraisals of allocations. The ambition of embedding this framework within the administrative state architecture, however, is to provide a common language for policymakers, scholars, interest groups, and the public. Doing so will facilitate review, critique, and debate about the appropriate program objectives and the optimal balance of the tradeoffs implicated by different configurations.

Such a dialogue can set the stage for more accurate delineations of, and appropriate adjustments to, allocations of authority. Those determinations ultimately should be made in the political process, steeped as they are in evaluation of values tradeoffs. Our hope, however, is that more independent, empirical analyses, informed by the input of relevant stakeholders, will inform the debate in ways that tend not to occur under the current system. One of the reasons why past reorganization efforts have not been rooted in the kind of systematic and empirically supported evaluation we envision may be that Congress, the White House, and the agencies themselves often lack expertise in the policy implications of government organization. Further, even when institutions such as OIRA possess such expertise, they tend to be heavily influenced by political considerations. The learning infrastructure we propose has the potential to make policy analysis a more salient component of legislative and administrative decision-making processes, at least incrementally. At a minimum, the kind of analysis generated by our proposed learning infrastructure should help reveal whether an existing or proposed allocation of authority is reasonably designed to address the identified goals of the allocation or instead reflects a mismatch between the values a particular allocation of authority strives to achieve (such as efficient use of government resources, governmental accountability, or fostering innovative policy approaches) and the structural means chosen to promote those values.

Relatedly, though more contextual evidence of what works and does not work to advance particular goals is needed, we recognize that different policymakers will have disparate goals and assess the relative tradeoffs of allocations differently. As acknowledged in the introduction and evinced in the case studies explored in this book, our substantive pre-commitments include maximizing market cost internalization and erring in favor of over-regulation, rather than under-regulation. These values will often prompt us to favor overlapping authority and the checks available from more hierarchical forms of coordination, particularly in connection with the standard setting and enforcement functions.[34] Indeed, chapter 9, in relying on the prodigious and growing scientific data available, maintains that a range of overlapping and coordinating strategies are necessitated by global anthropogenic climate change (though we also assert that these strategies should vary as contexts differ).

Nonetheless, as several of these examples also illustrate, we appreciate that the advantages of overlapping and coordinated authority are not incontrovertible; that in some circumstances such advantages may be outweighed by other policy considerations; and that such advantages will often have diminishing returns if adopted for every governmental function and every substantive program.[35] As a result, in some circumstances, centralized, distinct, or independent allocations may be more appropriate for particular functions or substantive features (bearing in mind that these dimensional choices are on a continuum rather than binary). We do not contend that our framework provides fixed, objective answers about appropriate tradeoffs or optimal regulatory allocations. Inevitably, such assessments will be contextual, and we certainly do not endeavor to essentialize the appropriateness of allocations of authority in light of the many diverse and evolving contexts that make up intergovernmental relations in administrative regulation.[36]

Others will differ in their assessment of the primacy of fundamental values, as well as in their assessments of the various tradeoffs needed to accommodate these values in allocation decisions. And though we consider the opportunity to inform such debates to be one of the more exciting implications of our proposed allocation framework, we also recognize that increased data about potential configurations and their tradeoffs may answer some but not all of the questions raised (not, at least, at this time). Yet we maintain that reliance on this allocation framework would inform—and when combined with our proposed adaptive governance infrastructure, could fundamentally transform—these deliberations. Elected officials would need to identify which values, policies, and tradeoffs are most appropriate, and such decisions would ultimately be subject to public scrutiny through the democratic process.[37]

In this sense, integrating periodic monitoring and assessment into the regulatory design process through this adaptive governance infrastructure would not only make government regulators more accountable to elected officials. This framework also provides an avenue for legislative policymakers to make administrative agencies more accountable to the public, especially if it is coupled with a statutory mandate for the responsible government entity to perform its task in a transparent manner and make the recommendations it provides to legislators and agencies publicly available. Among the questions that should be the focus of consideration and debate are whether an existing allocation of authority or proposed restructuring integrates metrics for evaluating its performance over time, and whether it accommodates sufficient concrete opportunities to adjust agency inter-relationships in response to changed circumstances or unintended consequences. These evaluative metrics and adjustment opportunities have the potential to help catalyze the democratic process by inducing policymakers to consider and explain structural options in terms of their policy implications instead of on more purely political considerations. Thus, we aspire to contribute to a more robust form of deliberative democracy and policymaking.

Although we appreciate that it would likely not eliminate the influence of politics in allocations of regulatory authority, the hope of the structural adaptive governance infrastructure we propose is to make reason-giving more salient. Scholars and think tanks have described the requirement that administrative agencies articulate reasons for their actions to be a critical component of government accountability.[38] They have suggested that reliance on evidence and reason-giving are the keys to informed and accountable policymaking.[39] Although a similar judicially enforceable requirement that Congress provide reasons for its actions may not be appropriate for separation-of-powers or institutional competence reasons,[40] congressional deliberation and reason giving (at least in statutory text) can both foster informed policy choice and provide a safeguard against arbitrariness.[41] If our framework can facilitate debate about the advantages and disadvantages of available allocations of authority, and clearer explanations of the reasons for the solutions chosen, it can contribute to the achievement of these aspirations in the important context of the institutional design of government authority. Professionals in public administration should find that mission invigorating, given the emphasis in their training on (1) participating and contributing to the policy process; (2) analyzing, synthesizing, and thinking critically in problem solving; (3) articulating and applying a public-service perspective; and (4) communicating and interacting productively with the public.[42] At a minimum, we hope that our analytical framework and the explanation of its value provided in this book will convince scholars and think tanks to craft and recommend to policymakers organizational reform proposals that avoid the flaws of past reorganizations like those surveyed in chapters 3 through 8.

We recognize that systematic collection and assessment of information on the structure of existing governance programs will generate administrative costs. Yet we contend that a desire to avoid these additional costs alone cannot prop up the unremittingly ad hoc improvisation and lack of empirical substantiation that the various case studies and vignettes in this book reveal to be the standard approach to allocations of authority by policymakers throughout the American administrative state. We suggest that the evidence and opportunities for coherent deliberation provided by our recommended infrastructure to elected officials, agencies, and ultimately the public of what allocations of authority work and do not work, both generally and in particular contexts, are worth these costs. This information will allow policymakers to adjust allocations in ways that increase programmatic effectiveness, efficiency, fairness, or accountability. Accordingly, providing adequate resources to those responsible for evaluating organizational reforms, past and future, is critical.

This call to foster adaptive governance and establish a learning infrastructure framework may seem unrealistic to many, particularly in light of the crescendo of partisanship and even intolerance of the past decade in American and global politics. The Trump administration, working with congressional allies, has undoubtedly hastened efforts to "hollow out" government.[43] We confess to concern about the capacity of empiricism and experimentalism to penetrate and shape the cynical politics of institutional design.

But continued technological advances in information generation, dissemination, and analysis[44] increasingly bestow the capacity for understanding and assessing governance. In our view—or at least hope—we may be reaching a transformative moment in American democracy. When the increasingly confounding Trump vortex founders or otherwise expires, many in the American public may be ready to reconnect with reason and evidence to help shape better institutions and advance good governance. Our admittedly ambitious aim is that this adaptive governance infrastructure, relying on our taxonomy for deciphering allocations of authority, will do more than help better (re)organize government. In the wake of receding general confidence in governmental institutions, the lack of substantive policy deliberation among elected officials about allocations of authority, and hostility to science and expertise,[45] our project endeavors to improve governance by injecting evidence, experimentalism, and deliberation into the sometimes dysfunctional but critically important American regulatory system. Reason giving—founded in provisional allocation, empirical assessment, and systematic review and adjustment—can elevate deliberations about allocations of authority, and improve our understanding about, and policymakers' decisions in, reorganizing government.

ACKNOWLEDGMENTS

We thank Clara Platter, our editor at NYU Press, who saw value in our proposal and shepherded it through the approval process. We also thank Amy Klopfenstein, who guided us through the manuscript preparation process, and Martin Coleman, who assisted in editing the book. Although they remain anonymous, we are grateful for the feedback and suggestions provided by the reviewers of the proposal and draft manuscript recruited by NYU Press.

We benefited enormously from the insights provided to us by our academic and professional colleagues. We received critically helpful feedback from participants in workshops at the Georgetown University Law Center; George Washington University Law School; Northwestern University Law School; University of California, Irvine School of Law; University of Colorado Law School; and Yale Law School. Students in Professor Camacho's fall 2017 seminar on Regulatory Design at the Yale Law School also gave us thoughtful input. At the risk of omitting some whose observations aided us, we acknowledge Bruce Ackerman, Vicki Arroyo, Donna Attanasio, Ian Ayres, Lori Brainard, William Buzbee, Christopher Carrigan, Jennifer Chacon, Jamison Colburn, Lawrence Cunningham, Seth Davis, David Driesen, Joel Eisen, Dan Esty, Joshua Galperin, Heather Gerken, Abbe Gluck, Emily Hammond, Oona Hathaway, Christine Jolls, Scott Kieff, Summer Kim, Doug Kysar, Annie Lai, Amanda Leiter, Stephen Lee, Peter Linquiti, Yair Listokin, Timothy Lytton, Jonathan Macey, Jeffrey Manns, David Markell, Dan Markovits, Jennifer Mascott, Jerry Mashaw, Thomas McGarity, Tracey Meares, David Min, Alan Morrison, Anne Joseph O'Connell, Lee Paddock, Nick Parrillo, Richard Pierce, Margot Pollans, Judith Resnik, Michael Robinson-Dorn, Cristina Rodríguez, Susan Rose-Ackerman, Erin Ryan, Scott Schang, David Schleicher, Greg Shaffer, Sidney Shapiro, Charles Taylor, Michael Weiland, Art Wilmarth, and Taisu Zhang for their wise and perceptive critiques of our ideas.

Special thanks are due to research librarians Amy Atchison, Germaine Leahy, and Christina Tsou, as well as Angie Middleton, Veronica Przybyl, Adelina Tomova, and Armon Goharbin for their editorial assistance. We relied heavily on our research assistants, including Aaron Adams, Erin Dykstra, Franklin Krbechek, Nate Krevor, Tyler Liu, Cassie Mastrostefano, Andrea Ringer, Tyler Sniff, Stacy Steep, Arshawn Teymoorian, Jecoliah Williams, and William Yon (who also helped on graphic design).

We also thank both the George Washington University Law School and the University of California, Irvine School of Law for providing financial research support for the project.

Finally, we would be remiss if we did not mention our families, without whose patience we could not possibly have completed this book. Our spouses, Kathleen and Emily, not only allowed us to escape tasks we should have taken on, but also graciously listened to countless conversations about the book's progress (both with them and between ourselves) and then provided advice without which we might have lost our way.

Alejandro Camacho   Robert Glicksman
Laguna Beach, CA   Bethesda, MD

NOTES

INTRODUCTION

1 Exec. Office of the President, "Delivering Government Solutions in the 21st Century: Reform Plan and Reorganization Recommendations" (2018).

2 "Fact Sheet: President Donald J. Trump Is Reforming the Federal Government, Making It More Efficient, Effective, and Accountable" (June 21, 2018), www.white house.gov.

3 "Behind Trump's Plan to Overhaul the Government: Scaling Back the Safety Net," *New York Times*, June 21, 2018, www.nytimes.com.

4 "Fact Sheet." *See, e.g.,* Exec. Order No. 13771, 82 Fed. Reg. 9339 (January 30, 2017).

5 Exec. Office of the President, 5.

6 Gillian E. Metzger and Kevin M. Stack, "Internal Administrative Law," 115 *Michigan Law Review* 1239, 1271–72 (2017).

7 Exec. Order No. 12,291, 3 C.F.R. 127, 128 (1982), reprinted in 5 U.S.C. § 601 (1988). *See generally* Michael A. Livermore and Richard L. Revesz, "Regulatory Review, Capture, and Agency Inaction," 101 *Georgetown Law Journal* 1337 (2013).

8 *See* Thomas W. Merrill, "Presidential Administration and the Traditions of Administrative Law," 115 *Columbia Law Review* 1953, 1971 (2015).

9 Thomas J. Laubacher, "Simplifying Inherently Governmental Functions: Creating a Principled Approach from Its Ad Hoc Beginnings," 46 *Public Contract Law Journal* 791, 798 (2017); Jody C. Baumgartner, "The Vice Presidency in the Twenty-First Century," 44 *Pepperdine Law Review* 561, 574 (2017).

10 US Gov't Accountability Off., GAO-18-427, "Government Reorganization: Key Questions to Assess Agency Reform Efforts," 1, 8 (2018).

11 For examples of such books, see Beryl Radin and Joshua M. Chanin, *Federal Government Reorganization: A Policy and Management Perspective* (2009); Brian J. Cook, *Bureaucracy and Self-Government: Reconsidering the Role of Public Administration in American Politics* (2014); *The Sage Handbook of Organization Studies* (2d ed. Stewart Clegg, Cynthia Hardy and Walter E. Nord eds., 2006); James Q. Wilson, *Bureaucracy: What Government Agencies Do and Why They Do It* (1989); David Osborne and Ted Gaebler, *Reinventing Government: How the Entrepreneurial Spirit is Transforming the Public Sector* (1992).

12 For recent books on federalism, *see, e.g.,* Erin Ryan, *Federalism and the Tug of War Within* (2012); *Preemption Choice: The Theory, Law, and Reality of Federalism's Core Question* (William W. Buzbee ed., 2009); James E. Fleming and Jacob T. Levy, *Federalism and Subsidiarity* (2014).

13 Wilson, 23.

14 Christopher Carrigan, *Structured to Fail? Regulatory Performance under Competing Mandates* 7 (2017).

15 The legal process school of the 1950s, whose canonical sources are teaching materials by Henry Hart and Albert Sacks (Henry M. Hart, Jr. and Albert M. Sacks, *The Legal Process: Basic Problems in the Making and Application of Law* (tent. ed. 1958)), urged allocation of decision-making authority "to the institutions best suited to decide particular questions." Ernest Young, "Institutional Settlement in a Globalizing Judicial System," 54 *Duke Law Journal* 1143, 1149–50 (2005). This movement, however, paid limited attention to the values tradeoffs implicit in comparative institutional analysis and largely focused on the activities of and interactions between courts and legislatures. Guido Calabresi, "An Introduction to Legal Thought: Four Approaches to Law and to the Allocation of Body Parts," 55 *Stanford Law Review* 2113, 2124–25 (2003).

16 Proponents of the "structure and process thesis" considered ways to enhance political control of bureaucratic decisions through legislative monitoring of agencies and the use of administrative procedures to enfranchise important constituencies. *See* Mathew McCubbins, Roger G. Noll, and Barry R. Weingast, "Administrative Procedures as Instruments of Political Control," 3 *Journal of Law, Economics, and Organization*, 243 (1987); *cf*. Richard B. Stewart, "The Reformation of Administrative Law," 88 *Harvard Law Review* 1669 (1975) (an iconic study of the use of procedure to foster stakeholder involvement in the administrative process). These studies, however, did not focus on how alternative ways of structuring interagency relationships can best promote regulatory goals.

17 Some public administration scholars and practitioners have explored the impact of administrative organization, emphasizing analytical policy evaluation using economics, statistics, and decision theory. *See* Metzger and Stack, 1268; Richard Elmore, "Graduate Education in Public Management: Working the Seams of Government," 6 *Journal of Policy Analysis and Management* 69, 69–72 (1986). Many of these efforts, however, have been confined to particular structural components, such as when the safety-net advantages of overlapping authority justify duplication of effort and interagency conflicts or how merging regulatory and non-regulatory missions in a single agency may impair agency performance. *See* Jacob E. Gersen, "Designing Agencies," *in Research Handbook on Public Choice and Public Law* 351 (Daniel A. Farber and Anne Joseph O'Connell eds., 2010) (citing Wilson; Jonathan Bendor, *Parallel Systems: Redundancy in Government* (1985)); Carrigan, 7–9, 11, 23 (surveying the public administration literature on the influence of goal ambiguity).

18 Lester M. Salamon, "The New Governance and the Tools of Public Action: An Introduction," in *Tools of Government: A Guide to the New Governance* 23 (Lester M. Salomon ed., 2002).

19 *See id.;* Neil Gunningham, "Environmental Management Systems and Community Participation: Rethinking Chemical Industry Regulation," 16 *UCLA Journal of Environmental Law and Policy* 319, 333 (1998).

20 *See, e.g.,* Salamon, 23–24; Daniel A. Farber, "What (If Anything) Can Economics Say about Equity?," 101 *Michigan Law Review* 1791, 1794 (2003).

21 *See, e.g.,* Jody Freeman and Laura I. Langbein, "Regulatory Negotiation and the Legitimacy Benefit," 9 *NYU Environmental Law Journal* 60, 63 (2000).

22 Exec. Order No. 13781, § 1, 82 Fed. Reg. 13959 (March 16, 2017).

23 Exec. Office of the President, 11.

24 *Id.,* 4.

25 The plan provides only a bibliography comprising principally general works on government organization and relies on analogies to private-sector organizational change, notwithstanding obvious differences in the missions and capacities of public and private institutions. *See, e.g., id,* 10.

26 Eric Katz, "Tempers Flare as White House Defends Reorg Proposal against Accusations of Stonewalling," *Government Executive,* July 18, 2018, https://www .govexec.com; see also Juana Summers, "Democrats Push Trump Administration to Provide More Details on Government Reorganization Plan," *CNN Politics,* July 18, 2018, https://www.cnn.com (describing comment by Senator Heitkamp that, assuming there were data and analysis behind the plan, "we should have access to that analysis").

27 For example, the plan mentions agency independence and interagency competition each only once, obliquely, depicting the latter in entirely negative terms. Exec. Office of the President, 108, 119.

28 *See, e.g., id,* 13, 23–24 (conflating all three dimensions), 91 (intermingling centralization and overlap).

29 Of the plan's thirty-two specific reorganization proposals, at least twenty (including merging the Departments of Education and Labor) rely wholly or primarily on consolidation of existing agencies or programs. Proposals 1–7, 9–10, 13–14, 17, 15c, 20, 22–25, and 31. Only one proposal (to reorganize the policy function of the Office or Personnel Management) reflects decentralization within the federal government. Only two feature coordination of interagency activities (coordination of federal economic assistance resources, which also would involve consolidation, and establishment of a unified cybersecurity workforce).

30 Katelyn Burns, "Trump's Proposed Government Reorganization Faces Long Road in Congress," *Rewire.News,* July 10, 2018, https://rewire.news (quoting Senator Tom Cole).

31 Katz.

32 See, e.g., Katz (describing joint statement that accompanied the first "minibus" for fiscal year 2019 providing that "no funds provided in this act or any previous act to any agency shall be used to implement" proposal to reallocate authority of the US Army Corps of Engineers); Pub. L. No. 115-141, § 111, 132 Stat. 348, 415 (2018) (prohibiting use of funds provided in the Consolidated Appropriations Act, 2018, to transfer authority of the Bureau of Alcohol, Tobacco, Firearms, and Explosives).

33 Exec. Order No. 11495, 34 Fed. Reg. 18447 (November 20, 1969); Congressional Research Serv., "Federal Emergency Management and Homeland Security Orga-

nization: Historical Developments and Legislative Options" 7 (Henry B. Hogue and Keith Bea eds., 2006).

34   Exec. Order No. 11724, 38 Fed. Reg. 17175 (June 29, 1973); Congressional Research Serv., 12.

35   *See* National Governors' Association, "National Governors' Association Policy Position A.—17: Emergency Preparedness and Response," *1978 Emergency Preparedness Project: Final Report* (1979).

36   Exec. Order No. 12127, 44 Fed. Reg. 19367 (April 3, 1979); Exec. Order No. 12148, 44 Fed. Reg. 43239 (July 24, 1979).

37   *See, e.g.,* US General Accounting Office, RCED-91-43, "Disaster Assistance: Federal, State, and Local Responses to Natural Disasters Need Improvement" 66 (1991); US General Accounting Office, RCED-93-186, "Disaster Management: Improving the Nation's Response to Catastrophic Disasters" (1993); Elizabeth F. Kent, Note, "'Where's the Cavalry?' Federal Response to 21st Century Disasters," 40 *Suffolk University Law Review* 181, 195 (2006).

38   Congressional Research Serv., 65.

39   Donald F. Kettl, "Is the Worst Yet to Come?," 604 *Annals of the American Academy of Political and Social Science* 273, 277 (2006).

40   Pub. L. No. 107-296, § 503(1), 116 Stat. 2135, 2213 (codified at 6 U.S.C. § 313).

41   Kent, 197; Lisa Grow Sun, "Disaster Mythology and the Law," 96 *Cornell Law Review* 1131, 1204–5 (2011); Congressional Research Serv., 20–21.

42   US Congress, House Select Bipartisan Comm. to Investigate the Preparation for and Response to Hurricane Katrina, A Failure of Initiative, 109th Cong., 2nd Sess. 158 (2006).

43   *See* Dara Kay Cohen, Mariano-Florentino Cuéllar and Barry R. Weingast, "Crisis Bureaucracy: Homeland Security and the Political Design of Legal Mandates," 59 *Stanford Law Review* 673, 756 (2006); Richard T. Sylves, "President Bush and Hurricane Katrina: A Presidential Leadership Study," 604 *Annals of the American Academy of Political and Social Sciences* 26, 30–31, 33 (2006).

44   The Post-Katrina Emergency Management Reform Act of 2006, Pub. L. No. 109-295, § 611, 120 Stat. 1355, elevated FEMA's status within DHS, exempted it from the DHS Secretary's reorganizational authority, and afforded its head direct access to the President during emergencies and disasters. Grow Sun, 1204.

45   *See* Kettl, 283–84.

46   *See* Arnold M. Howitt and Herman B. "Dutch" Leonard, "Katrina and the Core Challenges of Disaster Response," 30:1 *Fletcher Forum of World Affairs* 215, 220 (2006).

47   Cohen, Cuéllar, and Weingast, 756; Gregg P. Macey, "Environmental Crisis and the Paradox of Organizing," 2011 *B.Y.U. Law Review* 2063, 2113.

48   *See* Cohen, Cuéllar, and Weingast, 742; Robert J. Rhee, "Catastrophic Risk and Governance After Hurricane Katrina: A Postscript to Terrorism Risk in A Post-9/11 Economy," 38 *Arizona State Law Journal* 581, 613 (2006).

49   Victoria Nourse and Gregory Shaffer, "Varieties of New Legal Realism: Can A New World Order Prompt A New Legal Theory?," 95 *Cornell Law Review* 61, 124 (2009).

50 *See* Judith Resnik, "Accommodations, Discounts, and Displacement: The Variability of Rights as a Norm of Federalism(s)," 17 *Jus Politicum, Revue de droit politique* 209 (2017).

51 *Cf.* Ian Ayres and John Braithwaite, *Responsive Regulation: Transcending the Deregulation Debate* (1992) (suggesting the need for evaluation of opportunities for surgical interventions to address policy tradeoffs that may otherwise be overlooked).

52 *See* Clayton P. Gillette and James E. Krier, "Risk, Courts, and Agencies," 138 *University of Pennsylvania Law Review* 1027, 1040–41, 1069 (1990); Wendy Wagner, Katherine Barnes and Lisa Peters, "Rulemaking in the Shade: An Empirical Study of EPA's Air Toxic Standards," 63 *Administrative Law Review* 99, 108, 151 (2011).

53 Most notably, this inclination takes the shape of more tolerance for overlapping authority and the checks available from certain forms of coordination, and for centralized governance when it is needed to address interjurisdictional externalities.

54 *See* Jonathan L. Marshfield, "Improving Amendment," 69 *Arkansas Law Review* 477, 515 (2016).

55 *See* Richard Briffault, "'What about the "Ism"'? Normative and Formal Concerns in Contemporary Federalism," 47 *Vanderbilt Law Review* 1303, 1314 (1994); Jenna Bednar, "The Political Science of Federalism," 7 *Annual Review of Law and Social Science* 269, 272 (2011).

56 Calabresi, 2121 n. 33. Although Arthur Corbin acknowledged that these empirical tools could not provide definitive answers, he insisted that they can guide those who fashion the law. *Id.*, 2121. *See also* Scott L. Cummings, "The Puzzle of Social Movements in American Legal Theory," 64 *UCLA Law Review* 1554, 1568 (2017).

57 Joshua B. Fischman, "Reuniting 'Is' and 'Ought' in Empirical Legal Scholarship," 162 *University of Pennsylvania Law Review* 117, 119–20 (2013). Scholars in other fields, such as public administration, have also traditionally tended to subordinate empirical analysis to theoretical claims. *See* Brian D. Feinstein, "Designing Executive Agencies for Congressional Influence," 69 *Administrative Law Review* 259, 269 n.39 (2017). More recently, a group of "new legal realist" scholars have promoted interdisciplinary research that "combines empirical research, legal theory, and policy" to support policy development. Howard Erlanger et al., "Is It Time for a New Legal Realism?," 2005 *Wisconsin Law Review* 345 (2005). When they have addressed institutional design, they have often focused on topics such as evaluating the design of private entities such as corporations, *e.g.*, Nourse and Shaffer, "Varieties of New Legal Realism," 86–87, or enhancing stakeholder participation under the new governance model, rather than on the manner in which authority should be allocated among public institutions. *See, e.g.*, Joel Handler et al., "A Roundtable on New Legal Realism, Microanalysis of Institutions, and the New Governance: Exploring Converges and Differences," 2005 *Wisconsin Law Review* 479 (2005).

58 For discussion of adaptive governance literature, see David L. Markell, "Emerging Legal and Institutional Responses to Sea-Level Rise in Florida and Beyond," 42 *Columbia Journal of Environmental Law* 1, 50–51 (2016).

59 *See* Alejandro E. Camacho, "Adapting Governance to Climate Change: Managing Uncertainty through a Learning Infrastructure," 59 *Emory Law Journal* 1 (2009).
60 Sidney A. Shapiro and Robert L. Glicksman, *Risk Regulation at Risk: Restoring a Pragmatic Approach* 16 (2003).
61 *Id.,* 24, 26. As one observer noted, the pragmatists sought "to help contrive new governmental agencies to be used experimentally as means for achieving better results." Jerome N. Frank, "Experimental Jurisprudence and the New Deal," Address Before the Senate of the United States, 78 Cong. Rec. 12412, 12413 (1934).
62 Shapiro and Glicksman, 24–25.
63 Erlanger et al., 357.
64 New governance scholars have endorsed using experimental methodologies to design alternatives to traditional regulation. Victoria Nourse and Gregory Shaffer, "Empiricism, Experimentalism, and Conditional Theory," 67 *SMU Law Review* 141, 146 (2014). In the environmental arena, adaptive management—an iterative, feedback-based technique borrowed from business management, experimental science, systems engineering, and industrial ecology—has emerged as a policy-making tool. Robin Kundis Craig and J.B. Ruhl, "Designing Administrative Law for Adaptive Management," 67 *Vanderbilt Law Review* 1, 17 (2014).
65 Nourse and Shaffer, "Empiricism, Experimentalism, and Conditional Theory," 179–80.
66 Richard J. Pierce, Jr., "Outsourcing Is Not Our Only Problem," 76 *George Washington Law Review* 1216, 1224 (2008).
67 *See* Anne Joseph O'Connell, "Intelligent Oversight," in *The Impact of 9/11 and the New Legal Landscape: The Day that Changed Everything?* (Matthew J. Morgan, ed. 2009) (arguing that the stability of congressional oversight committees provides an obstacle to adoption of organizational reforms of agency structures).
68 *See* Daniel C. Esty, "Red Lights to Green Lights: From 20th Century Environmental Regulation to 21st Century Sustainability," 47 *Environmental Law Review* 1, 3 (2017).
69 *See, e.g.,* Stewart, "The Reformation of Administrative Law," 1670–71, 1673.
70 *See* Emily Hammond and David L. Markell, "Administrative Proxies for Judicial Review: Building Legitimacy from the Inside-Out," 37 *Harvard Environmental Law Review* 313, 323–24 (2013); Sidney A. Shapiro and Richard E. Levy, "Heightened Scrutiny of the Fourth Branch: Separation of Powers and the Requirement of Adequate Reasons for Agency Decisions," 1987 *Duke Law Journal* 387 (1987).
71 *See, e.g.,* William W. Buzbee, "Recognizing the Regulatory Commons: A Theory of Regulatory Gaps," 89 *Iowa Law Review* 1 (2003); Jason Marisam, "Duplicative Delegations," 63 *Administrative Law Review* 181, 223–24 (2011); Anne Joseph O'Connell, "The Architecture of Smart Intelligence: Structuring and Overseeing Agencies in the Post-9/11 World," 94 *California Law Review* 1655, 1691–93 (2006).
72 *See, e.g.,* William A. Birdthistle and M. Todd Henderson, "Becoming A Fifth Branch," 99 *Cornell Law Review* 1 (2013); Michael P. Vandenbergh, "Private Environmental Governance," 99 *Cornell Law Review* 129 (2013).

73 *See, e.g.,* Michael Abramowicz, "Market-Based Administrative Enforcement," 15 *Yale Journal on Regulation* 197 (1998); Richard B. Stewart, "Models for Environmental Regulation: Central Planning Versus Market-Based Approaches," 19 *Boston College Environmental Affairs Law Review* 547 (1992).

74 Alejandro E. Camacho and Robert L. Glicksman, "Legal Adaptive Capacity: How Program Goals and Processes Shape Federal Land Adaptation to Climate Change," 87 *University of Colorado Law Review* 711 (2016).

75 *See, e.g.,* Bruce Ackerman, "The New Separation of Powers," 113 *Harvard Law Review* 633 (2000); Gillian E. Metzger, "The Interdependent Relationship Between Internal and External Separation of Powers," 59 *Emory Law Journal* 423 (2009).

CHAPTER 1: SUBSTANTIVE AND FUNCTIONAL JURISDICTION

1 *See* 1 George Cameron Coggins and Robert L. Glicksman, *Public Natural Resources Law* §§ 6:14–6:17 (2d ed. 2007).

2 *See* Drugs, US Food and Drug Admin., www.fda.gov (accessed December 17, 2018); Cosmetics, US Food and Drug Admin., www.fda.gov (accessed December 17, 2018); Foods, US Food and Drug Admin., www.fda.gov (accessed December 17, 2018) (identifying FDA authorities); "About FSIS," US Food Safety and Inspection Serv., www.fsis.usda.gov (accessed December 17, 2018).

3 Dodd-Frank Wall Street Reform and Consumer Protection Act, Pub. L. No. 111-203, 124 Stat. 1376 (2010).

4 Elizabeth R. Schiltz, "The Paradox of the Global and the Local in the Financial Crisis of 2008: Applying the Lessons of *Caritas in Veritate* to the Regulation of Consumer Credit in the United States and the European Union," 26 *Journal of Law and Religion* 173, 183–84 (2010).

5 Kenneth A. Bamberger and Deirdre K. Mulligan, "Privacy on the Books and on the Ground," 63 *Stanford Law Review* 247, 257 (2011).

6 For a discussion of how different scientific disciplines affect the design and management of natural resource regulatory systems, *see* Eric Biber, "Which Science? Whose Science? How Scientific Disciplines Can Shape Environmental Law," 79 *University of Chicago Law Review* 471 (2012).

7 *See* Timothy P. Duane, "Greening the Grid: Implementing Climate Change Policy through Energy Efficiency, Renewable Portfolio Standards, and Strategic Transmission System Investments," 34 *Vermont Law Review* 711, 743–44 (2010).

8 *See, e.g.,* Joseph P. Liu, "Regulatory Copyright," 83 *North Carolina Law Review* 87, 148 (2004).

9 *See, e.g.,* 42 U.S.C. § 7405 (authorizing EPA grants to state or local agencies to finance programs for the prevention and control of air pollution).

10 The National Institutes of Health awarded $20 billion in 2016 for research grants. National Institutes of Health Data Book, "NIH Budget Mechanism Detail FY 2001–2014," http://report.nih.gov (accessed December 18, 2018). Congress allocated over $7 billion in 2016 to the National Science Foundation (National Science

Foundation, "FY 2017 Budget Request to Congress," 1 (February 9, 2016), https://www.nsf.gov).

11 "In FY 2011, the federal government provided $607 billion in grants to state and local governments." Congressional Budget Office, "Federal Grants to State and Local Governments," 1 (March 2013), www.cbo.gov.

12 US Geological Survey, "About Us," www.usgs.gov (accessed December 18, 2018).

13 National Oceanic and Atmospheric Administration Research, "*About Us*," http://research.noaa.gov (accessed December 18, 2018).

14 Baseline monitoring typically seeks to measure conditions before regulation begins so that the impact of regulation may later be tracked and adjustments made. *See* Daniel Schramm and Akiva Fishman, "Legal Frameworks for Adaptive Natural Resource Management in a Changing Climate," 22 *Georgetown International Environmental Law Review* 491, 495 (2010). *See also generally* J.B. Ruhl and James Salzman, "Gaming the Past: The Theory and Practice of Historic Baselines in the Administrative State," 64 *Vanderbilt Law Review* 1 (2011).

15 *See, e.g.,* National Water Quality Monitoring Council, "Glossary of Water-Quality Monitoring Terms" (November 3, 2016), https://acwi.gov (defining "ambient monitoring" as "all forms of monitoring conducted beyond the immediate influence of a discharge pipe or injection well and may include sampling of sediments and living resources"); Eric Biber, "The Problem of Environmental Monitoring," 83 *University of Colorado Law Review* 1, 9 (2011) (detailing problems with ambient monitoring).

16 *See, e.g.,* National Aeronautics and Space Administration and Smithsonian Astrophysical Observatory, "Tropospheric Emissions: Monitoring of Pollution Mission Overview" (2015), http://tempo.si.edu; National Aeronautics and Space Administration, "Major Air Pollution Studies to Converge Over Denver" (July 3, 2014), www.nasa.gov (describing NASA field studies for ozone levels).

17 *See, e.g.,* "NOAA's National Environmental Satellite, Data, and Information Service (NESDIS): The Nation's Operational Weather Satellite and Information Service," 5 www.legislative.noaa.gov (accessed December 18, 2018).

18 49 U.S.C. § 31306a (2012).

19 US Department of Transportation, Center for Climate Change and Environmental Forecasting, "About the Center," https://climate.dot.gov (accessed December 18, 2018).

20 *See, e.g.,* US Department of Labor, "Agencies and Programs" (accessed December 18, 2018) (discussing Office of Congressional and Intergovernmental Affairs and Office of Public Affairs).

21 *See, e.g.,* Exec. Order No. 12866, § 6, 58 Fed. Reg. 51735 (September 30, 1993).

22 *See* Robert L. Glicksman and Richard E. Levy, *Administrative Law: Agency Action in Legal Context* 385 (2d ed. 2015).

23 42 U.S.C. § 7609 (2012).

24 *See, e.g.,* USDA, "Offices," www.usda.gov (accessed December 18, 2018) (describing the Office of the General Counsel in the Department of Agriculture).

25 *Cf.* US EPA Office of the Administrator/Office of Policy/Office of Strategic En-
    vironmental Management, "Program Evaluation Glossary" (November 1, 2007),
    https://iaspub.epa.gov (defining "planning" as "the process of anticipating future
    occurrences and problems, exploring their probable impact, and detailing poli-
    cies, goals, objectives, and strategies to solve the problems").
26 *E.g.,* Resource Management Planning, 81 Fed. Reg. 89580 (December 12, 2016)
    (codified at 43 C.F.R. pt. 1600) (planning by the Bureau of Land Management);
    "National Forest System Land Management Planning," 77 Fed. Reg. 21162 (Apr. 9,
    2012) (codified at 36 C.F.R. pt. 219) (planning by the US Forest Service).
27 As chap. 5 and the conclusion explore more fully, few agencies are required to
    engage in any form of program assessment or modification, although some execu-
    tive orders require retrospective review for certain rules. *See, e.g.,* Exec. Order No.
    13563, § 6, 76 Fed. Reg. 3821 (January 18, 2011). Certain autonomous agencies like
    GAO, however, do review program performance, though usually at the request of
    Congress and rarely through systematic monitoring, evaluation, and adjustment.
    See US Gov't Accountability Office, "About GAO," www.gao.gov.
28 *E.g.,* 33 U.S.C. §§ 1311(b), 1314(b) (2012) (authorizing EPA to establish standards for
    controlling pollutant discharges to surface water bodies); 42 U.S.C. § 7412(d), (f)
    (2012) (authorizing EPA to set standards for hazardous air pollutant emissions).
29 *See* 5 U.S.C. § 551(4), (5) (2012) (defining rule and rulemaking).
30 *E.g.,* 33 U.S.C. §§ 1342, 1344 (2012) (establishing permit programs for discharges
    of pollutants and dredged or fill material, respectively). *Cf.* US EPA, "Terminol-
    ogy Services" https://iaspub.epa.gov (accessed December 18, 2018) (defining a
    permitting program as "a program [. . .] that issues an authorization, license, or
    equivalent control document to implement the requirements of an environmental
    regulation").
31 *See* 5 U.S.C. § 551(6), (7) (2012) (defining order and adjudication).
32 *See, e.g.,* US EPA, "Terminology Services, https://iaspub.epa.gov (accessed De-
    cember 18, 2018) (defining "monitoring" as "periodic or continuous surveillance
    or testing to determine the level of compliance with statutory requirements").
33 *See, e.g.,* National Water Quality Monitoring Council, "Glossary" (defining
    "compliance monitoring" as monitoring "to ensure the meeting of immedi-
    ate statutory requirements, the control of long-term water quality, the quality
    of receiving waters as determined by testing effluents, or the maintenance of
    standards during and after construction of a project"); "Availability of a Final
    Addendum to the Handbook for Habitat Conservation Planning and Incidental
    Take Permitting Process," 65 Fed. Reg. 35241, 35, 252–53 (June 1, 2000) (defining
    compliance monitoring).
34 *See, e.g.,* 65 Fed. Reg. at 35, 252–23 (defining effect and effectiveness monitoring to
    include whether the action or plan is achieving its stated goals and objectives).
35 *E.g.,* 33 U.S.C. § 1319 (2012) (providing authorities for EPA and states to enforce
    the Clean Water Act); 42 U.S.C. § 7413 (providing similar authority to enforce the
    Clean Air Act).

36 US Securities and Exchange Commission, "About the Division of Enforcement," www.sec.gov (accessed December 18, 2018).

37 Whether an administrative proceeding is best characterized as rulemaking or adjudication may depend on whether the resulting decision turns on legislative or adjudicative facts. *See* 2 Richard J. Pierce, Jr., *Administrative Law Treatise* § 10.5, 937–38 (5th ed. 2010) (explaining the difference between the two).

38 *See, e.g.,* David A. Hyman and William E. Kovacic, "Why Who Does What Matters: Governmental Design and Agency Performance," 82 *George Washington Law Review* 1446, 1471, 1495 (2014) (describing fostering commercial aviation and promoting airline safety as separate "functions" of the FAA but referring to the "enforcement functions" of CFPB).

39 For example, EPA includes Offices for Air and Radiation, Chemical Safety and Pollution Prevention, Land and Emergency Management, and Water, corresponding with its various substantive authorities to regulate air quality, pesticides and toxic substances, solid and hazardous waste, and water quality, respectively. EPA Organization Chart, www.epa.gov (accessed December 18, 2018).

40 In 1993, EPA reorganized the Office of Compliance and Enforcement by centralizing in it enforcement authority that had previously been dispersed among five offices. "US EPA Office of Environmental Justice in the Matter of the Fifth Meeting of the Environmental Justice Advisory Council," 9 *Administrative Law Review American University* 623, 663 (1995).

41 At EPA, these include the Office of Enforcement and Compliance Assurance, the Office of Inspector General, and the Office of Research and Development. These offices are charged with enforcement, investigation, and research, respectively, across the entire range of EPA's substantive authority. *See* Alfred A. Marcus, "EPA's Organizational Structure," 54 *Law and Contemporary Problems* 5, 23 (1991).

42 *See* "Today's IRS Organization," www.irs.gov (accessed December 18, 2018).

43 *See, e.g.,* USDA, "Offices," www.usda.gov (accessed December 18, 2018) (describing the Office of Communications, the Office of Congressional Relations, and the Office of the General Counsel within the Department of Agriculture).

44 "About GAO," www.gao.gov (accessed December 18, 2018).

45 "About USGS," www.usgs.gov (accessed December 18, 2018).

46 *See* "About DOJ," www.justice.gov (accessed December 18, 2018).

47 *See, e.g.,* William W. Buzbee, "The Regulatory Fragmentation Continuum, Westway and the Challenges of Regional Growth," 21 *Journal of Law and Politics* 323, 348 (2005) (discussing "institutional fragmentation," which results from allocation of authority to "diverse institutions such as legislatures, agencies, courts and legally empowered citizens").

CHAPTER 2: THE DIMENSIONS OF ALLOCATIONS OF AUTHORITY

1 Though regulators can coordinate authority *between* governmental functions, the depicted three-dimensional framework only illustrates such relationships for a particular substantive and functional allocation. *See* chap. 2, § C.

2   *But cf.* Arizona v. United States, 132 S. Ct. 2492, 2507 (2012) (recognizing limited state role in policing immigration status).

3   *See, e.g.,* 42 U.S.C. § 7475(d) (2012) (establishing a role for federal land management agencies in an EPA review of state permits approving emissions that might affect federal lands).

4   *E.g.,* 42 U.S.C. §§ 7507, 7543 (2012) (allowing EPA to approve California's tailpipe emission regulation under the Clean Air Act, which other states can follow in lieu of federal restrictions).

5   Examples include stationary source regulation under the Clean Air Act, 42 U.S.C. §§ 7410(a), 7411, 7475(a)(1), 7502(c)(5) (2012), and public land management. *See* 1 George Cameron Coggins and Robert L. Glicksman, *Public Natural Resources Law* § 1:1 (2d ed. 2007).

6   For example, the authority to regulate federally owned lands is typically centralized in the federal government. *See* Robert L. Fischman, "Cooperative Federalism and Natural Resources Law," 14 *New York University Environmental Law Journal* 179, 205 (2005). However, jurisdiction to manage different kinds of federal lands systems (e.g., national parks, national forests, wildlife refuges, and other public lands) has been delegated to (and decentralized among) several federal land management agencies.

7   Jody Freeman and Jim Rossi, "Agency Coordination in Shared Regulatory Space," 125 *Harvard Law Review* 1131, 1146 (2012).

8   Similarly, authority may be more or less decentralized within a single agency, depending on its internal distribution of authority. Likewise, subdivisions within an agency may be aligned at different points along the overlap and coordination dimensions, just as multiple agencies may be so aligned.

9   Subsidiarity is the organizing principle "that a central authority should have a subsidiary function, performing only those tasks which cannot be performed effectively at a more immediate or local level." *Subsidiarity*, Oxford English Dictionary, www.oed.com (accessed December 18, 2018). It is a general principle of European Union law. *See* Consolidated Version of the Treaty on European Union art. 5(3), Feb. 7 1992, 2010 O.J. (C 83) 13.

10 *See, e.g.,* Jeffrey S. Dornbos, "All (Water) Politics Is Local: A Proposal for Resolving Transboundary Water Disputes," 22 *Fordham Environmental Law Review* 1, 17 (2010) (arguing that the Constitution's reservation of non-enumerated powers to the states reflects the subsidiarity principle).

   Although this book focuses on policy considerations, policymakers' ability to centralize authority in the federal government may also be constrained by constitutional limitations, such as those constraining the scope of Congress' regulatory authority under the Commerce Clause (*see, e.g.,* Nat'l Fed'n of Indep. Bus. v. Sebelius, 567 U.S. 519, 547–58 (2012) (finding that Affordable Care Act's individual mandate exceeded federal power to regulate interstate commerce)) or preserving state power under the Tenth Amendment. *See, e.g.,* Printz v. United States, 521 U.S. 898 (1997) (invalidating statutory provision requiring state authorities to perform background checks).

11 *See, e.g.,* Adrian Vermeule, "Local and Global Knowledge in the Administrative State," in *Law, Liberty and State: Oakeshott, Hayek and Schmitt on the Rule of Law* 295, 296, 315 (David Dyzenhaus and Thomas Poole eds., 2015) (explaining that proponents of decentralized authority prefer allocations that take advantage of context-specific knowledge).

12 *See, e.g.,* Jonathan H. Adler, "Jurisdictional Mismatch in Environmental Federalism," 14 *New York University Environmental Law Journal* 130, 136–37 (2005). Some commenters have suggested that these "diversity" advantages of decentralization can also promote equity. *See, e.g.,* Robin Kundis Craig, "Adapting Water Federalism to Climate Change Impacts: Energy Policy, Food Security, and the Allocation of Water Resources," 5 *Environmental and Energy Law and Policy Journal* 183, 196 (2010).

13 *See* New State Ice Co. v. Liebmann, 285 U.S. 262, 311 (1932) (Brandeis, J., dissenting); David L. Markell, "States as Innovators: It's Time for a New Look to Our 'Laboratories of Democracy' in the Effort to Improve Our Approach to Environmental Regulation," 58 *Albany Law Review* 347, 355 (1994); Adler, "Jurisdictional Mismatch," 137.

14 *See generally* Charles M. Tiebout, "A Pure Theory of Local Expenditures," 64 *Journal of Political Economy* 416 (1956); Robert Nozick, *Anarchy, State, and Utopia* (1977); Bruce Johnsen, "The Evolution of Sherman Act Jurisdiction: A Roadmap for Competitive Federalism," 7 *University of Pennsylvania Journal of Constitutional Law* 403, 405 (2004).

15 *See, e.g.,* Gerald E. Frug, *City Making: Building Communities without Building Walls* (1999).

16 *See, e.g.,* Jonathan H. Adler, "The Fable of Federal Environmental Regulation: Reconsidering the Federal Role in Environmental Protection," 55 *Case Western Reserve Law Review* 93, 107 (2004). Others have posited, however, that devolution of regulatory authority can detract from accountability. *See, e.g.,* David Markell, "'Slack' in the Administrative State and Its Implications for Governance: The Issue of Accountability," 84 *Oregon Law Review* 1, 23–47 (2005).

17 *See* Robert L. Glicksman, "From Cooperative to Inoperative Federalism: The Perverse Mutation of Environmental Law and Policy," 41 *Wake Forest Law Review* 719, 729 (2006).

18 Local governments also enacted smoke control ordinances. *Id.,* 729–30.

19 *See, e.g.,* Water Pollution Control Legislation—1971: Hearings on H.R. 11,896, H.R. 11,895: Before the Comm. on Public Works, 92d Cong. 520 (1971); David Schoenbrod, "246 Glorious Cheeses or the Impact of Environmental Regulation on Small and Emerging Business," 5 *Journal of Small and Emerging Business Law* 91, 99 (2001); Ann E. Carlson and Andrew Mayer, "Reverse Preemption," 40 *Ecology Law Quarterly* 583, 609 (2013); Hope M. Babcock, "Dual Regulation, Collaborative Management, or Layered Federalism: Can Cooperative Federalism Models from Other Laws Save Our Public Lands?," 3 *Hastings West-Northwest Journal of Environmental Law and Policy* 193, 199–200 (1996).

20 *See, e.g.*, Riegel v. Medtronic, Inc., 552 U.S. 312, 334 (2008); Rush Prudential HMO, Inc. v. Moran, 536 U.S. 355, 387 (2002); Pegram v. Herdrich, 530 U.S. 211, 237 (2000).

21 *See, e.g.*, Bruesewitz v. Wyeth LLC, 562 U.S. 223, 228 n.15 (2011).

22 *See, e.g.*, Altria Group, Inc. v. Good, 555 U.S. 70, 77 (2008); Lorillard Tobacco Co. v. Reilly, 533 U.S. 525, 541 (2001).

23 *See, e.g.*, Egelhoff v. Egelhoff ex rel. Breiner, 532 U.S. 141, 151 (2001).

24 *See, e.g.*, California Div. of Labor Standards Enforcement v. Dillingham Const., N.A., Inc., 519 U.S. 316, 330 (1997); New York State Conf. of Blue Cross and Blue Shield Plans v. Travelers Ins. Co., 514 U.S. 645, 655–56 (1995).

25 *See, e.g.*, BFP v. Resolution Trust Corp., 511 U.S. 531, 544 (1994).

26 *See, e.g.*, Metrop. Life Ins. Co. v. Massachusetts, 471 U.S. 724, 740 (1985).

27 *See, e.g.*, Nat'l Fed'n of Indep. Bus. v. Sebelius, 567 U.S. 519, 681 (2012) (Scalia, J., dissenting).

28 *See, e.g.*, United States v. Lopez, 514 U.S. 549 (1995). For discussion of a trend toward greater devolution of regulatory authority, *see* Peter H. Schuck, "Introduction: Some Reflections on the Federalism Debate," 14 *Yale Journal on Regulation* 1 (1996). For criticism of that trend, *see* Edward Rubin, "The Myth of Accountability and the Anti-Administrative Impulse," 103 *Michigan Law Review* 2073, 2074 (2005).

29 *See, e.g.*, Freeman and Rossi, 1142.

30 *See* Alejandro E. Camacho, "Transforming the Means and Ends of Natural Resources Management," 89 *North Carolina Law Review* 1405, 1423 (2011).

31 *Cf.* Hannah Jacobs Wiseman and Dave Owen, "Federal Laboratories of Democracy," 52 *U.C. Davis Law Review* 1119, 1135 (2018) (arguing that the experimentation benefits of decentralization are not limited to state and local agencies because "the federal government is itself decentralized in many ways, some of which can enable differentiation and experimentation").

32 *See, e.g.*, Liesbet Hooghe and Gary Marks, "Unraveling the Central State, But How?," Political Science Series, Institute for Advanced Studies, Vienna 6 (2003), http://aei.pitt.edu/530/2/pw_87.pdf; Dornbos, 17; *Environmental Federalism* 259, 263 (Terry L. Anderson and Peter J. Hill eds., 1997).

33 Anne Joseph O'Connell, "The Architecture of Smart Intelligence: Structuring and Overseeing Agencies in the Post-9/11 World," 94 *California Law Review* 1655, 1680 (2006).

34 *See, e.g.*, Daniel C. Esty, "Revitalizing Environmental Federalism," 95 *Michigan Law Review* 570, 614 (1996); Esty, "Toward Optimal Environmental Governance," 74 *New York University Law Review* 1495, 1562 (1999); Adler, "Jurisdictional Mismatch," 148.

35 *See* Robert L. Glicksman and Richard E. Levy, "A Collective Action Perspective on Ceiling Preemption by Federal Environmental Regulation: The Case of Global Climate Change," 102 *Northwestern University Law Review* 579 (2008).

36 Whether a set of issues should be regarded as primarily of national or local concern may be contested. *See, e.g.*, Ngai Pindell, "Nevada's Residential Real Estate Crisis: Local Governments and the Use of Eminent Domain to Condemn Mortgage Notes," 13 *Nevada Law Journal* 888, 900 (2013).

37 *See* J.B. Ruhl, "Climate Change Adaptation and the Structural Transformation of Environmental Law," 40 *Environmental Law* 363, 423 (2009).

38 *See* Boggs v. Boggs, 520 U.S. 833, 838–39 (1997).

39 *See* Bonito Boats, Inc. v. Thunder Craft Boats, Inc., 489 U.S. 141, 162 (1989).

40 *See* Chamber of Commerce of U.S. v. Brown, 554 U.S. 60, 76 (2008).

41 *See* Offshore Logistics, Inc. v. Tallentire, 477 U.S. 207, 233 (1986).

42 *See* United States v. Locke, 529 U.S. 89, 103 (2000).

43 Adler, "Jurisdictional Mismatch," 139; Richard Stewart, *Introduction to Environmental Law, the Economy, and Sustainable Development* 11 (Richard L. Revesz et al. eds., 2000); Daniel A. Farber, "Climate Adaptation and Federalism: Mapping the Issues," 1 *San Diego Journal of Climate and Energy Law* 259, 266 (2009).

44 *See* Richard J. Pierce, Jr., "Regulation, Deregulation, Federalism, and Administrative Law: Agency Power to Preempt State Regulation," 46 *University of Pittsburgh Law Review* 607, 666 (1985).

45 *See* Glicksman and Levy, "A Collective Action Perspective," 599–600.

46 *See id.*, 600–602.

47 *See* Richard B. Stewart, "Pyramids of Sacrifice? Problems of Federalism in Mandating State Implementation of National Environmental Policy," 86 *Yale Law Journal* 1196, 1215 (1977).

48 *See, e.g.,* Kirsten Engel, "State Environmental Standard-Setting: Is there a 'Race' and is It 'to the Bottom'?" 48 *Hastings Law Journal* 271 (1997); Peter P. Swire, "The Race to Laxity and the Race to Undesirability: Explaining Failures in Competition among Jurisdictions in Environmental Law," 14 *Yale Law and Policy Review* 67 (1996).

49 If other states do not lower standards, an individual state is in a better position to attract industry, while if other states lower standards, then the state must act similarly to compete effectively. This dynamic has also surfaced internationally. *See* John H. Knox, "A New Approach to Compliance with International Environmental Law: The Submissions Procedure of the NAFTA Environmental Commission," 28 *Ecology Law Quarterly* 1, 54 (2001).

50 Clean Air Act Amendments of 1977, Pub. L. No. 95-95, 91 Stat. 685 (1977).

51 H.R. Rep. No. 95-294, at 152 (1977). *See also* Hodel v. Virginia Surface Mining and Reclamation Ass'n, 452 U.S. 264, 281–82 (1981).

52 *See, e.g.,* William L. Cary, "Federalism and Corporate Law: Reflections Upon Delaware," 83 *Yale Law Journal* 663, 666 (1974) (shareholder rights against corporations); Lynn LoPucki and Sara Kalin, "The Failure of Public Company Bankruptcies in Delaware and New York: Empirical Evidence of a 'Race to the Bottom,'" 54 *Vanderbilt Law Review* 231, 266 (2001) (bankruptcy law); Laurence H. Tribe, "The Constitutionality of the Patient Protection and Affordable Care Act: Swimming in the Stream of Commerce," 35 *Harvard Journal of Law and Public Policy* 873, 880 (2012) (health care insurance).

53 *See* chap. 2, § C.2.

54 *See* Amy J. Wildermuth, "Is Environmental Law a Barrier to Emerging Alternative Energy Sources?," 46 *Idaho Law Review* 509, 529 (2010).

55 *See, e.g.*, An Act to Improve, Strengthen, and Accelerate Programs for the Prevention and Abatement of Air Pollution, Pub. L. No. 88-206, 77 Stat. 392 (1963).

56 *See, e.g.*, H.R. Rep. No. 89-2170, 4 (1966); H.R. Rep. No. 87-306, 5 (1961).

57 *See* William L. Andreen, "Fables and Federalism: A Re-examination of the Historical Rationale for Federal Environmental Regulation," 42 *Environmental Law* 627, 653 (2012).

58 Glicksman, "From Cooperative to Inoperative Federalism," 730.

59 *See, e.g.*, H.R. Rep. No. 90-728, 12 (1967).

60 *See* Richard J. Lazarus, *The Making of Environmental Law* 67, 70–73 (2004).

61 *See, e.g.*, *The Federalist No. 10*, 54 (James Madison) (E.H. Scott ed., 1894) (defining faction as citizens "united and actuated by some common impulse of passion, or of interest, adverse to the rights of other citizens, or to the permanent and aggregate interests of the community"); Dornbos, 17.

62 Geographically separate jurisdiction provides a straightforward illustration of distinct authority. For example, each state has sovereign police powers (including the authority to regulate land use) within its geographic boundaries. *See, e.g.*, Carolina Trucks and Equipment, Inc. v. Volvo Trucks of N. Am., Inc., 492 F.3d 484, 491–92 (4th Cir. 2007). Accordingly, the authority of an Alaskan municipality to regulate land use is effectively distinct from the authority of a Maine municipality to do the same, even though both regulate land use.

63 *See* Robert L. Glicksman and Richard E. Levy, *Administrative Law: Agency Action in Legal Context* 762 (2d ed. 2015). The APA demands a similar separation of prosecutorial and adjudicatory authority within agencies conducting formal adjudications. 5 U.S.C. § 554(d) (2012).

64 Collins v. Nat'l Transp. Safety Bd., 351 F.3d 1246, 1252 (D.C. Cir. 2003).

65 Cheryl D. Block, "A Continuum Approach to Systemic Risk and Too-Big-to-Fail," 6 *Brooklyn Journal of Corporate, Financial and Commercial Law* 289, 299 (2012).

66 *See generally* 2 and 3 Coggins and Glicksman, ch. 17, 29, 32.

67 33 U.S.C. § 1319 (2012).

68 *See, e.g.*, Robert B. Ahdieh, "Dialectical Regulation," 38 *Connecticut Law Review* 863, 864 (2006).

69 *See, e.g.*, 33 U.S.C. §§ 1311(b), 1342(b) (2012) (delegating standard-setting function primarily to EPA and permitting function primarily to states meeting certain minimum requirements).

70 *See generally* Henry N. Butler and Jonathan R. Macey, *Using Federalism to Improve Environmental Policy* (1996).

71 *Id.*, 48. *See also* Adler, "Jurisdictional Mismatch," 133.

72 Freeman and Rossi, 1150; Jacob E. Gersen, "Overlapping and Underlapping Jurisdiction in Administrative Law," 2006 *Supreme Court Review* 201, 214.

73 *See* chap. 2, § B.2.

74 Todd S. Aagaard, "Regulatory Overlap, Overlapping Legal Fields, and Statutory Discontinuities," 29 *Virginia Environmental Law Journal* 237, 288 (2011); Vermeule, 322.

75 *See* Jason Marisam, "Duplicative Delegations," 63 *Administrative Law Review* 181, 184 (2011); Gersen, 214.

76 Jason Marisam, "Interagency Administration," 45 *Arizona State Law Journal* 183, 223 (2013); Freeman and Rossi, 1150. Overlapping regulatory authority is not the only potential source of multiple regulatory obligations. For example, a facility may be subject to numerous regulatory duties under different statutes even if all statutes are administered by the same agency.

77 *See* Ahdieh, 897.

78 *See* William W. Buzbee, "The Regulatory Fragmentation Continuum, Westway and the Challenges of Regional Growth," 21 *Journal of Law and Politics* 323, 349 (2005). *See also* James M. Buchanan and Yong J. Yoon, "Symmetric Tragedies: Commons and Anticommons," 43 *Journal of Law and Economics* 1, 11–12 (2000).

79 Kirsten H. Engel, "Harnessing the Benefits of Dynamic Federalism in Environmental Law," 56 *Emory Law Journal* 159, 165–66 (2006).

80 William W. Buzbee, "Recognizing the Regulatory Commons: A Theory of Regulatory Gaps," 89 *Iowa Law Review* 1, 5–6 (2003).

81 *See* Buzbee, "The Regulatory Fragmentation Continuum," 348–49.

82 *See* William W. Buzbee, "State Greenhouse Gas Regulation, Federal Climate Change Legislation, and the Preemption Sword," 1 *San Diego Journal of Climate and Energy Law* 23, 30–36 (2009).

83 Ahdieh, 897–98.

84 *See* Buzbee, "Recognizing the Regulatory Commons," 51.

85 *See, e.g.*, Robert A. Schapiro, "From Dualist Federalism to Interactive Federalism," 56 *Emory Law Journal* 1, 17 (2006); Robert A. Schapiro, "Monophonic Preemption," 102 *Northwestern University Law Review* 811, 812–13 (2008); Engel, "Harnessing the Benefits," 162.

86 *See* Freeman and Rossi, 1187; Aagaard, 288.

87 Engel, "Harnessing the Benefits," 162.

88 *See id.*

89 *See, e.g.*, J.B. Ruhl and James Salzman, "Climate Change, Dead Zones, and Massive Problems in the Administrative State: A Guide for Whittling Away," 98 *California Law Review* 59 (2010); Buzbee, "Recognizing the Regulatory Commons," 1; David E. Adelman and Kirsten H. Engel, "Adaptive Federalism: The Case against Reallocating Environmental Regulatory Authority," 92 *Minnesota Law Review* 1796, 1800–1801 (2008).

90 Jared Snyder and Jonathan Binder, "The Changing Climate of Cooperative Federalism: The Dynamic Role of the States in a National Strategy to Combat Climate Change," 27 *UCLA Journal of Environmental Law and Policy* 231, 252 (2009).

91 *See, e.g.*, Blake Hudson, "Reconstituting Land-Use Federalism to Address Transitory and Perpetual Disasters: The Bimodal Federalism Framework," 2011 *Brigham Young University Law Review* 1991, 2037.

92 *See* chap. 2, § B.1.

93 Buzbee, "State Greenhouse Gas Regulation," 53.

94 *See* Freeman and Rossi, 1138; Benjamin Ewing and Douglas A. Kysar, "Prods and Pleas: Limited Government in an Era of Unlimited Harm," 121 *Yale Law Journal* 350, 354 (2011); Michael Doran, "Legislative Organization and Administrative Redundancy," 91 *Boston University Law Review* 1815, 1819 (2011).

95 The desirable amount of overlap is likely to be highly contextual, depending on the cultures and professional backgrounds of agencies and their personnel, and the political context. *See* Eric Biber, "The More the Merrier: Multiple Agencies and the Future of Administrative Law Scholarship," 125 *Harvard Law Review Forum* 78, 80 (2012). The location of the relevant agencies along the other dimensions identified in this book is also likely to be important, such as whether the agencies have cooperative or competitive relationships.

96 *See* Engel, "Harnessing the Benefits," 179; see also Ewing and Kysar, "Prods and Pleas," 410.

97 Alejandro E. Camacho, "Adapting Governance to Climate Change: Managing Uncertainty Through a Learning Infrastructure," 59 *Emory Law Journal* 1, 67–68 (2009).

98 *See* Engel, "Harnessing the Benefits," 178–79.

99 O'Connell, 1677. *See also* Rachel E. Barkow, "Insulating Agencies: Avoiding Capture through Institutional Design," 89 *Texas Law Review* 15, 50 (2010).

100 *See* Aagaard, 294.

101 *See generally* Victor Fleischer, "Regulatory Arbitrage," 89 *Texas Law Review* 227, 252 (2010).

102 *See* Eugene A. Ludwig, "Assessment of Dodd-Frank Financial Regulatory Reform: Strengths, Challenges, and Opportunities for a Stronger Regulatory System," 29 *Yale Journal on Regulation* 181, 189 (2012).

103 *See, e.g.*, Elizabeth K. Brill, "Privacy and Financial Institutions: Current Developments Concerning the Gramm-Leach-Bliley Act of 1999," 21 *Annual Review of Banking Law* 167, 210 (2002).

104 *See* Freeman and Rossi, 1187.

105 *Id.*, 1157.

106 *See* Ann Carlson, "Iterative Federalism and Climate Change," 103 *Northwestern University Law Review* 1097, 1100–1101 (2009).

107 *See* Adelman and Engel, 1820–21; Ahdieh, 892; Engel, "Harnessing the Benefits," 177 (noting that "regulatory activity at one level [. . .] may be a stepping stone to regulation at the governing level that dual federalism proponents label 'optimal'").

108 As compared to the other dimensions, the coordination–independence dimension is less conducive to characterization as a simple spectrum ranging from greater to lesser degrees of coordination because coordination can be measured in different ways, including its frequency, duration, scope, and voluntariness. *See* chap. 2, § C.1.

109 *See* Mark Osler, "Asset Forfeiture in a New Market-Reality Narcotics Policy," 52 *Harvard Journal on Legislation* 221, 239–40 (2015).

110 *See, e.g.*, California Bay-Delta Authority (CBDA), "California Bay-Delta Program Archived Website," www.calwater.ca.gov (accessed December 18, 2018); *see also*

Bradley C. Karkkainen, "Collaborative Ecosystem Governance: Scale, Complexity, and Dynamism," 21 *Virginia Environmental Law Journal* 189, 217–18 (2002).

111 *See, e.g.*, FDA Food Safety Modernization Act, Pub. L. No. 111-353, § 201(a), 124 Stat. 3885, 3923 (2011) (codified at 21 U.S.C. § 421(d)) (requiring the Departments of Homeland Security, Health and Human Services, Agriculture, Commerce, and EPA to coordinate).

112 *See, e.g.*, Drinking Water Security and Safety Amendments, adopted as part of the Public Health Security and Bioterrorism Preparedness and Response Act of 2002, Pub. L. No. 107–188, §§ 401–403, 116 Stat. 594, 682–87 (2002) (requiring coordination, led by EPA, to abate and respond to threats to drinking water infrastructure security).

113 *See, e.g.*, Eugene Bardach, *Getting Agencies to Work Together: The Practice and Theory of Managerial Craftsmanship* (1998); Ruhl and Salzman, 66.

114 *See* Freeman and Rossi, 1184.

115 *See id.*, 1183.

116 *See id.*, 1187 (explaining the risk that agency exercise of discretionary delegated authority will drift away from legislative preferences).

117 *See id.*, 1187–88 (defining shirking as a form of drift that involves inaction). Shirking is often driven by the hope that another regulator will address a problem, relieving the shirker of the need to do so. *See, e.g.*, William W. Buzbee, "Urban Sprawl, Federalism, and the Problem of Institutional Complexity," 68 *Fordham Law Review* 57, 131 (1999).

118 *See* Freeman and Rossi, 1189; Daniel A. Farber and Anne Joseph O'Connell, "Agencies as Adversaries," 105 *California Law Review* 1375, 1420–21 (2017) (recognizing "information generating capacity" of interagency monitoring relationships in overseeing policy decisions, but categorizing such relationships as adversarial).

119 *See* Freeman and Rossi, 1186. *Cf.* Farber and O'Connell, 1419 (noting potential for hierarchical agency relationships with conflict resolution mechanisms to foster democratic legitimacy and accountability).

120 *See* Camacho, "Adapting Governance," 74–75.

121 *Cf.* Thomas McInerney, "Putting Regulation Before Responsibility: Towards Binding Norms of Corporate Social Responsibility," 40 *Cornell International Law Journal* 171, 195 (2007); Maribeth Wilt-Seibert, "Unemployment Compensation for Employees of Educational Institutions: How State Courts Have Created Variations on Federally Mandated Statutory Language," 29 *University of Michigan Journal of Law Reform* 585, 611 (1995).

122 *See generally* Freeman and Rossi; Keith Bradley, "The Design of Agency Interactions," 111 *Columbia Law Review* 745 (2011); J.R. DeShazo and Jody Freeman, "Public Agencies as Lobbyists," 105 *Columbia Law Review* 2217 (2005).

123 Gregg Macey, "Environmental Crisis and the Paradox of Organizing," 2011 *Brigham Young University Law Review* 2063, 2113 (2011) (discussing different definitions in game theory, resource exchange, contingency theory, and transaction cost economics).

124 *See* Freeman and Rossi, 1156. *See also* Vermeule, 319 (referring to "myriad" coordination mechanisms, ranging from conversations to formal interagency memoranda of agreement); David A. Hyman and William E. Kovacic, "Why Who Does What Matters: Governmental Design and Agency Performance," 82 *George Washington Law Review* 1446, 1480 n.143 (2014).

125 *See, e.g.*, Alejandro E. Camacho, "Community Benefits Agreements: A Symptom, Not the Antidote, of Bilateral Land Use Regulation," 78 *Brooklyn Law Review* 355, 364 (2013); Jesse Hahnel and Caroline Van Zile, "The Other Achievement Gap: Court-Defendant Youth and Educational Advocacy," 41 *Journal of Law and Education* 435, 473 (2012).

126 Charlene D. Luke, "The Relevance Games: Congress's Choices for Economic Substance Gamemakers," 66 *Tax Lawyer* 551, 553 n.7 (2013) (discussing frequent collaboration among agencies responsible for enforcing the Internal Revenue Code).

127 *See* Craig W. Thomas, *Bureaucratic Landscapes: Interagency Cooperation and the Preservation of Biodiversity* 24 (2003) (describing non-mandatory interagency cooperation).

128 *See* Freeman and Rossi, 1157.

129 *See* Farber and O'Connell, 1388 (noting the distinction between coordination and conflict: "Conflict may overlap with coordination; potentially adversarial actors may choose—or be forced—to work together. But conflictual agencies may choose not to coordinate in some situations, and coordination need not involve adversarial agencies.").

130 *Id.*, 1385–86. Farber and O'Connell's typology includes as examples of adversarial coordination "monitoring or advisory relationships," in which one agency is authorized to monitor, demand information from, or offer formal advice to another, and relationships that are hierarchical or governed by a conflict resolution mechanism. *See id.*, 1389, 1409, 1418. For example, they characterize the relationship that governs review by the Office of Information and Regulatory Affairs of rulemaking by other agencies as a form of "hard hierarchy." *Id.*, 1407.

131 42 U.S.C. §§ 4321–4370h (2012).

132 *See* Bradley, 757–58.

133 Publication of public notices by agencies in the Federal Register is an obvious example.

134 *E.g.*, "Establishment of the Task Force on Market Integrity and Consumer Fraud," 83 Fed. Reg. 33115 (July 18, 2018); National Endowment for the Arts, Arts and Human Development Task Force, www.arts.gov (accessed December 18, 2018).

135 *See* Freeman and Rossi, 1157; 16 U.S.C. § 6577 (2012) (providing that the Secretary of Agriculture "may consult with" other federal and state agencies in carrying out the Healthy Forests Reserve Program).

136 *See* Freeman and Rossi, 1157; Bradley, 750–56.

137 *See* Bradley, 755 (describing how the Federal Power Act requires the Federal Energy Regulatory Commission to consider input from fish and wildlife agencies before approving plans to construct new hydroelectric dams); Freeman and Rossi,

1158 (citing EPA's duty to solicit other agencies' opinions before promulgating pesticide regulations).

138 The Coordinated Framework for the Regulation of Biotechnology Products is a formal interagency agreement governing commercial biotechnology processes and products. "Coordinated Framework for Regulation of Biotechnology," 51 Fed. Reg. 23302 (June 26, 1986). Some international treaties or interstate compacts exemplify relatively robust forms of harmonization over standard setting. *See, e.g.,* "Colorado River Compact of 1922," 70 Cong. Rec. 324 (1928); "Upper Colorado River Basin Compact," ch. 48, 63 Stat. 31 (1949).

139 *See* Bradley, 755–56.

140 Thomas, 25 ("Scope refers to the range of issues covered [. . .]. Strength refers to the binding nature of the agreements, ranging from verbal or tacit agreements to legally binding documents. Duration refers to the endurance of an agreement.").

141 Others have recognized as much. *See, e.g.,* Farber and O'Connell, 1384 ("We are reluctant to join the celebration of agency coordination, at least not without substantial qualifications.").

142 *See* Camacho, "Adapting Governance," 30–36; Freeman and Rossi, 1182.

143 Richard L. Revesz, "Rehabilitating Interstate Competition: Rethinking the 'Race to the Bottom' Rationale for Federal Environmental Regulation," 67 *New York University Law Review* 1210, 1211–12 (1992). *See also* Nestor M. Davidson, "Cooperative Localism: Federal-Local Collaboration in an Era of State Sovereignty," 93 *Virginia Law Review* 959, 961 (2007).

144 Adler, "Jurisdictional Mismatch," 134.

145 *See, e.g.,* Dara Kay Cohen, Mariano-Florentino Cuéllar, and Barry R. Weingast, "Crisis Bureaucracy: Homeland Security and the Political Design of Legal Mandate," 59 *Stanford Law Review* 673, 710–11 (2006).

146 *See* chap. 2, § A.2.

147 *See generally* Michael A. Heller, "The Tragedy of the Anticommons: Property in the Transition from Marx to Markets," 111 *Harvard Law Review* 621, 622–26 (1998). An anti-commons regime is one "that requires everybody's consent to achieve socially beneficial outcomes." Eyal Benvenisti, "Sovereign and Trustees for Humanity: On the Accountability of States to Foreign Stakeholders," 107 *American Journal of International Law* 295, 312 (2013).

148 *See* chap. 2, § C.1.

149 *See, e.g.,* Hanoch Dagan and Michael A. Heller, "The Liberal Commons," 110 *Yale Law Journal* 549, 590 (2001); Heller, 622–26.

150 *Cf.* Engel, "Harnessing the Benefits," 178–79.

151 *See* Irving Janis, *Victims of Groupthink* 8–9 (1972) (coining the term "groupthink" as a product of cohesive in-groups "when the members' strivings for unanimity override their motivation to realistically appraise alternative courses of action"); Susan Cain, "The Rise of the New Groupthink," *New York Times,* January 15, 2012, www.nytimes.com (citing research showing that brainstorming sessions do not stimulate creativity).

152 O'Connell, 1676. Though Professor O'Connell focuses on this dynamic as a benefit of regulatory redundancy, we believe that it is more properly understood as a feature of independence among regulators.

153 Coordinated information generation, for example, may allow co-regulators to stretch their resources farther than they could acting independently. If so, a shared information base may foster experimentation if each regulator acts independently in performing other functions, such as planning or standard setting.

154 *See, e.g.*, Carlson, 1102.

155 O'Connell, 1676–78.

156 Ahdieh, 890.

157 *Cf.* Marisam, "Interagency Administration," 224.

158 *See* William W. Buzbee, "Asymmetrical Regulation: Risk, Preemption, and the Floor/Ceiling Distinction," 82 *New York University Law Review* 1547, 1555 (2007).

159 *See* 42 U.S.C. § 7543 (2012).

160 *See* 7 U.S.C. § 136v(b) (2012).

161 *See* 49 U.S.C. § 5125 (2012).

162 *See, e.g.*, 33 U.S.C. § 1370 (2012); 42 U.S.C. § 7416 (2012).

163 Even if regulatory power is concentrated in one entity, however, the degree of intra-agency coordination among employees or offices within a single agency remains a relevant consideration.

164 15 U.S.C.A. § 2608(a)(2) (2018).

165 "Light-Duty Vehicle Greenhouse Gas Emission Standards and Corporate Average Fuel Economy Standards," 75 Fed. Reg. 25324 (May 7, 2010). *See* Freeman and Rossi, 1169–73.

166 42 U.S.C. § 7521(a) (2012).

167 49 U.S.C. § 32902(a), (f) (2012).

CHAPTER 3: DECENTRALIZATION AND THE FUNCTIONS OF FOOD REGULATION

1 Exec. Office of the President, "Delivering Government Solutions in the 21st Century: Reform Plan and Reorganization Recommendations," 32 (2018).

2 We use food safety to refer to the degree of health risk resulting from the ingestion of food. For a broader definition of the term, see Emily M. Broad Leib and Margot J. Pollans, "The New Food Safety," 107 *California Law Review* (forthcoming 2019).

3 As chap. 2 indicates, authority may be centralized or decentralized between governmental levels (as in the commonly debated federalism context), within a level of government, or even within a single agency. Accordingly, though the policy tradeoffs discussed in this chapter largely occur in connection with allocations among federal agencies, they are analogous to those involved in federalism and intra-agency contexts.

4 As chap. 2 explains, the asserted advantages of decentralized regulatory authority include what we refer to there as the expertise, diversity, experimentation, and

(between governmental levels) accountability advantages. Centralization may be justified as promoting economies of scale, avoiding collective-action problems, bolstering uniformity and minimizing conflicting regulation, and fostering accountability by diminishing factional influence.

5 US Gov't Accountability Off., GAO-17-74, "Food Safety: A National Strategy Is Needed to Address Fragmentation in Federal Oversight," 5–6 (2017).

6 This chapter's focus is almost entirely on allocation of food safety regulatory authority among federal agencies.

7 For a dated but still largely accurate description of the structure of federal food safety regulation, see Richard A. Merrill and Jeffrey K. Francer, "Organizing Federal Food Safety Regulation," 31 Seton Hall Law Review 61, 91–114 (2000).

8 For charts depicting the agencies and their responsibilities, see US Gov't Accountability Off., GAO-05-212, "Experiences of Seven Countries in Consolidating Their Food Safety Systems," 7–8 (2005); US Gov't Accountability Off., GAO-05-549T, "Steps Should Be Taken to Reduce Overlapping Inspections and Related Activities," 6 (2005).

9 See US Gov't Accountability Off., GAO-04-588T, "Fundamental Restructuring Is Needed to Address Fragmentation and Overlap," 4 (2004) (noting the absence of strategic design).

10 US Gov't Accountability Off., GAO-05-549T, at 1; see also US Gov't Accountability Off., GAO-04-588T, 5.

11 US Gov't Accountability Off., GAO-02-47T, "Fundamental Changes Needed to Ensure Safe Food," 3–4 (2011).

12 Additional state or local regulation at the retail level is also possible.

13 These proposals surfaced as early as 1949. See Merrill and Francer, 118–19. For a chart of subsequent proposals through 1998, see id. 115–18; see also Nat'l Acad. of Sciences (NAS), Ensuring Safe Food: From Production to Consumption Appx. B (1998); Nat'l Acad. of Sciences (NAS), Enhancing Food Safety: The Role of the Food and Drug Administration 325–69 (2010).

14 US Gov't Accountability Off., GAO-T-RCED-94-223, "A Unified, Risk-Based Food Safety System Needed," 1 (1994), GAO-02-47T, 2–3. See also Laurie J. Beyranev and Emily M. Broad Leib, "Making the Case for a National Food Strategy in the United States," 72 Food and Drug Law Journal, 225, 233–34 (2017).

15 NAS, Ensuring Safe Food.

16 Id., 6, 8, 61, 87.

17 Id., 12.

18 Id., 13 Box ES-4, 99 Box 6-3.

19 NAS, Enhancing Food Safety, 315–16.

20 Exec. Order No. 13,100, 3 C.F.R. § 209 (Aug. 25, 1998).

21 President's Council on Food Safety, "Assessment of the NAS Report, Ensuring Safe Food from Production to Consumption" (1999), http://clinton3.nara.gov (emphasis added).

22 Decentralized regulatory authority may create inequities in the treatment of regulated entities under the jurisdiction of different agencies. *See, e.g.*, Merrill and Francer, 127–35.

23 US Govt. Accountability Off., GAO/T-RCED-99-256, "US Needs a Single Agency to Administer a Unified, Risk-Based Inspection System" (1999); *see also* US Gov't Accountability Off., GAO-02-47T.

24 US Gov't Accountability Off., GAO-04-588T, 5-8; US Gov't Accountability Off., GAO-05-549T, 16.

25 *See* US Govt. Accountability Off., GAO-15-180, "Federal Food Safety Oversight: Additional Actions Needed to Improve Planning and Collaboration" 18, 30 (2014).

26 *See* US Govt. Accountability Off., GAO-04-832R, "Posthearing Questions Related to Fragmentation and Overlap in the Federal Food Safety System" 3 (2004).

27 *Id.*, 2.

28 *See* US Gov't Accountability Off., GAO-05-212. The countries were Canada, Denmark, Germany, Ireland, the Netherlands, New Zealand, and the United Kingdom (UK). For further discussion of food safety regulation in other countries, see NAS, *Enhancing Food Safety*, 371–96.

29 US Gov't Accountability Off., GAO-05-212, 3.

30 *Id.*, 3.

31 *Id.*, 21.

32 *See, e.g.*, Timothy M. Hammonds, "It Is Time to Designate a Single Food Safety Agency," 59 *Food and Drug Law Journal* 427, 432 (2004) (urging centralization of "all federal food safety oversight activities").

33 For discussion of several of these, see US Gov't Accountability Off., GAO-05-549T, 5.

34 *See* Merrill and Francer, 66, 119–21.

35 Pub. L. No. 111-353, 124 Stat. 3885 (2011) (codified at scattered sections of 21 U.S.C.).

36 *See, e.g.*, Margot J. Pollans, "Regulating Farming: Balancing Food Safety and Environmental Protection in a Cooperative Governance Regime," 50 *Wake Forest Law Review* 399, 399 (2015).

37 *See, e.g.*, 21 U.S.C. §§ 350g(n)(2), 350i(b) (2012) (rulemaking); *id.* § 2201(a), (c) (information evaluation); *id.* § 350h(a)(1) (standard setting); *id.* § 350h(b)(2)(A), (d) (education and enforcement); *id.* § 2202(a)(1), (3) (research); *id.* 21 U.S.C. § 2224(b)(1) (CDC coordination of foodborne illness surveillance systems and information-sharing).

38 *See, e.g.*, Pollans, 412.

39 US Gov't Accountability Off., GAO-11-289, "Food Safety Working Group Is a Positive First Step but Governmentwide Planning Is Needed to Address Fragmentation," 2–3 (2011). *See also* Thomas O. McGarity and Rena I. Steinzor, "The End Game of Deregulation: Myopic Risk Management and the Next Catastrophe," 23 *Duke Environmental Law and Policy Forum* 93, 98 (2012).

40 US Gov't Accountability Off., GAO-11-289, 12–13.

41 Senator Dick Durbin and Rep. Rosa L. Delauro, "Food Safety is a Matter of National Security," *The Hill*, January 20, 2015, http://thehill.com.

42 Safe Food Act of 2015, S. 287, 114ᵗʰ Cong. (2015).

43 *Id.*, § 2(a)(6), (7).

44 Centralization's supporters frequently claim that it promotes accountability and uniformity and minimizes regulatory gaps. *See, e.g.*, Caroline Smith deWaal, "Food Safety Inspections: A Call for Rational Reorganization," 54 *Food and Drug Law Journal* 453, 454 (1999). But regulatory gaps may also result from legislative failure to delegate adequate authority to agencies sharing jurisdiction, or from the regulatory commons that may accompany overlapping authority.

45 Grace Knofczynski, "Lawmakers Propose a Single Food Safety Administration," *The Regulatory Review*, February 17, 2015, www.theregreview.org.

46 The bill did not define the term function.

47 Safe Food Act of 2015, §§ 101(a), 102(a).

48 *Id.* § 103(c). *Cf.* Jody Freeman and Jim Rossi, "Agency Coordination in Shared Regulatory Space," 125 *Harvard Law Review* 1131, 1153 (2012) (questioning whether the creation of DHS after 9/11 improved the effectiveness or efficiency of national security and whether consolidation of federal financial regulation would be wise).

49 Statement of Al Almanza, Deputy Under Secretary for Food Safety, Before the Subcomm. on Agric., Rural Development, Food and Drug Admin., and Related Agencies, Comm. on Appropriations, US House of Representatives, February 26, 2015, www.fsis.usda.gov; Knofczynski.

50 Office of Management and Budget, "Fiscal Year 2016, Budget of the US Government," 82, www.whitehouse.gov.

51 Ron Nixon, "Obama Proposes Single Overseer for Food Safety," *New York Times*, February 20, 2015.

52 Exec. Office of the President, 33.

53 Nixon.

54 *See* Scott Bass and Alan Raul, "The Single Food Agency: A Modest Dialectic Dialogue," 59 *Food and Drug Law Journal* 453, 453 (2004).

55 Knofczynski. *See also* Nixon (quoting consumer lobbyist concerned about combining "different agencies with different missions under one roof").

56 Hammonds, 430; Nixon (quoting one USDA inspector as fearing that consolidation would "drag us down to [FDA's] minuscule standards."). *See also* Richard Raymond, "Dual Jurisdiction: Also in Need of 'Modernization,'" *Food Safety News*, Jan. 3, 2011, www.foodsafetynews.com; Danny Vinik, "Who's Watching the Chickens?," *Politico*, March 17, 2016. One cabinet secretary predicted that merging FSIS and FDA would "wreak havoc." Merrill and Francer, 168 (remarks of USDA Secretary Dan Glickman).

57 *See, e.g.*, Dara Kay Cohen, Mariano-Florentino Cuéllar and Barry R. Weingast, "Crisis Bureaucracy: Homeland Security and the Political Design of Legal Mandates," 59 *Stanford Law Review* 673, 710–11 (2006); Anne Joseph O'Connell, "The Architecture of Smart Intelligence: Structuring and Overseeing Agencies in the

Post-9/11 World, 94 *California Law Review* 1655, 1724 (2006). *See also* Raymond ("Creating a huge, monolithic, federal agency has been done in recent years. Most don't think it is working out that well.").

58 *See also* Merrill and Francer, 150. We take no position here on whether authority should be consolidated in an executive or stand-alone agency.

59 Centers for Disease Control, "About FoodNet," www.cdc.gov; *cf.* Mariano-Florentino Cuéllar, "Modeling Partial Agency Autonomy in Public-Health Policy-making," 15 *Theoretical Inquiries in Law* 471, 499 (2014).

60 US Gov't Accountability Off., GAO-04-832R, 3.

61 *Cf.* Garrick B. Pursley, "Skeletal Norms," 18 *University of Pennsylvania Journal of Constitutional Law* 353, 384 (2015).

62 *See* Freeman and Rossi, 1152; Merrill and Francer, 165–66; Jason Marisam, "Inter-agency Administration," 45 *Arizona State Law Journal* 183, 224–25 (2013). In 1998, 28 different congressional committees had a hand in food safety oversight. NAS, *Ensuring Safe Food*, 26.

63 Merrill and Francer, 129.

64 *See, e.g.,* Hannah J. Wiseman and Dave Owen, "Federal Laboratories of Democracy," 52 *U.C. Davis Law Review* 1119 (2018) (recognizing that functional differentiation can accommodate the benefits of centralization (such as the economies of scale from centralized funding) and decentralization (such as the experimentation benefits from decentralized planning or implementation).

65 *See* Merrill and Francer, 150–52.

66 Vinik.

67 Hammonds, 431.

68 The same comparative risk assessment benefits may result from centralization of other functions, such as enforcement. Centralized enforcement may reduce the risk that regulators will address relatively less serious violations before they address relatively more serious violations. These benefits need to be weighed against the benefits of decentralized enforcement, discussed below.

69 NAS, *Ensuring Safe Food*, 148, 154, 165, 171, 195, 313.

70 *See* Vinik.

71 NAS, *Enhancing Food Safety*, 153–71.

72 *See* Hannah J. Wiseman, "Regulatory Islands," 89 *New York University Law Review* 1661 (2014).

73 *See* Robert L. Glicksman and Richard E. Levy, "A Collective Action Perspective on Ceiling Preemption by Federal Environmental Regulation: The Case of Global Climate Change," 102 *Northwestern University Law Review* 579, 595–97 (2008); Daphna Renan, "Pooling Powers, 115 *Columbia Law Review* 211, 213 (2015).

74 *See* US Gov't Accountability Off., GAO-15-180, 29–31.

75 *See* 2 George Cameron Coggins and Robert L. Glicksman, *Public Natural Resources Law* § 16:34 (2d ed. 2007).

76 *See* Marisam, 215.

77 US Gov't Accountability Off., GAO-05-549T, 16.

78 US Gov't Accountability Off., GAO-05-212, 21.

79 *See, e.g.,* George A. Hay, "Innovations in Antitrust Enforcement," 64 *Antitrust Law Journal* 7 (1995); Richard Delgado, "Law Enforcement in Subordinated Communities: Innovation and Response," 106 *Michigan Law Review* 1193 (2008).

80 *See* Cynthia Giles, "Next Generation Compliance," *Environmental Forum* 22 (September/October 2013); Robert L. Glicksman and David L. Markell, "Unraveling the Administrative State: Mechanism Choice, Key Actors, and Regulatory Tools," 36 *Virginia Environmental Law Journal* 317, 371–80 (2018).

81 *See, e.g.,* Daniel C. Esty, "Toward Optimal Environmental Governance," 74 *New York University Law Review* 1495, 1562 (1999).

82 US Gov't Accountability Off., GAO-04-832R, 3.

83 NAS, *Ensuring Safe Food,* 80–81.

84 Centralized research results may be distributed to multiple agencies with standard-setting or other risk management responsibilities. *See* Vinik.

85 *See* Jennifer Nou, "Intra-Agency Coordination," 129 *Harvard Law Review* 421, 452, 460 (2015) (discussing policy-specific horizontal specialization).

86 *See* Marisam, 199.

87 *See, e.g.,* Matthew C. Waxman, "National Security Federalism in the Age of Terror," 64 *Stanford Law Review* 289, 344 (2012); Daniel A. Farber and Anne Joseph O'Connell, "Agencies as Adversaries," 105 *California Law Review* 1375, 1422, 1425 (2017).

88 US Gov't Accountability Off., GAO-15-180, 17–18.

89 *Cf.* NAS, *Enhancing Food Safety,* 253 (suggesting that state and local inspections be conducted under uniform federal standards with FDA oversight).

90 *See* US Gov't Accountability Off., GAO-05-212; NAS, *Enhancing Food Safety,* 371–96.

91 US Gov't Accountability Off., GAO-05-212, 4, 15 (Figure 2).

92 *Id.*

93 US Gov't Accountability Off., GAO-05-212, 4, 12, 14, 25.

94 *See* US Gov't Accountability Off., GAO-05-212, 25, 26.

95 *See, e.g.,* US Gov't Accountability Off., GAO-05-212, 17, 19, 20, 21, 23, 24.

CHAPTER 4: THE FUNCTIONS OF OVERLAPPING POLLUTION CONTROL FEDERALISM

1 One study found that the vast majority of home break-ins through locked doors occurred when those doors lacked an additional deadbolt lock. *See* Center for Problem-Oriented Policing, "The Chula Vista Residential Burglary Reduction Project, Chula Vista Police Department" (2001), www.popcenter.org.

2 *See* chap. 2, § B.

3 President Barack Obama, Remarks by the President in State of Union Address, https://obamawhitehouse.archives.gov (January 25, 2011).

4 *See* chap. 4, § B.2.

5 *See* chap. 4, § B.3.

6 42 U.S.C. §§ 7401-7671q (2012).

7 33 U.S.C. §§ 1251-1387 (2012).

8   42 U.S.C. §§ 6901-6992k (2012).
9   *See, e.g.*, Hodel v. Virginia Surface Min. & Reclamation Ass'n, Inc., 452 U.S. 264, 289 (1981); David E. Adelman and Kirsten H. Engel, "Adaptive Federalism: The Case against Reallocating Environmental Regulatory Authority," 92 *Minnesota Law Review* 1796, 1830 (2008); Ann E. Carlson, "Federalism, Preemption, and Greenhouse Gas Emissions," 37 *U.C. Davis Law Review* 281, 284–85 (2003); Patricia Ross McCubbin, "Michigan v. EPA: Interstate Ozone Pollution and EPA's 'NOx SIP Call,'" 20 *St. Louis University Public Law Review* 47, 61–62 (2001). *But cf.* Roderick M. Hills, Jr., "The Political Economy of Cooperative Federalism: Why State Autonomy Makes Sense and 'Dual Sovereignty' Doesn't," 96 *Michigan Law Review* 813, 852 (1998) ("It had never been the case that the federal and state governments operated in 'separate and distinct spheres' pursuing independent and distinct objects with distinct resources.").
10 *See* chap. 2, § A.
11 *See, e.g.*, The River and Harbors Act of 1899, 33 U.S.C. § 407 (2012) (prohibiting the discharge of "refuse matter" without a federal permit, though the program's principal objective was to preserve navigability of waterways, not pollution control); Robert L. Glicksman, "From Cooperative to Inoperative Federalism: The Perverse Mutation of Environmental Law and Policy," 41 *Wake Forest Law Review 719* (2006).
12 These included state common law nuisance, trespass, negligence, and strict liability, and local zoning, smoke control, and pollution-control regulations. *See* Glicksman, 729–30.
13 *See, e.g.*, An Act to Improve, Strengthen, and Accelerate Programs for the Prevention and Abatement of Air Pollution, Pub. L. No. 88-206, 77 Stat. 392 (1963); An Act to Provide Research and Technical Assistance Relating to Air Pollution Control, Pub. L. No. 84-159, 69 Stat. 322 (1955).
14 *See* Glicksman, 730.
15 *See* Robert L. Glicksman and Richard E. Levy, "A Collective Action Perspective on Ceiling Preemption by Federal Environmental Regulation: The Case of Global Climate Change," 102 *Northwestern University Law Review* 579, 600–601 (2008).
16 *See, e.g.*, 33 U.S.C. § 1370 (2012); 42 U.S.C. § 6929 (2012); 42 U.S.C. § 7416 (2012).
17 42 U.S.C. § 7409(b)(1)-(2). Arguably, only EPA can adopt ambient standards for criteria pollutants, although that reading of the statute is not inevitable. Section 116 preserves state authority to adopt "any standard or limitation respecting emissions of air pollutants." *Id.* § 7416(1).
18 *See* Nancy B. Collins and Andrea Hall, "Nuclear Waste in Indian Country: A Paradoxical Trade," 12 *Law and Inequality* 267, 342 (1994).
19 *See* 49 U.S.C. § 5125 (2012).
20 7 U.S.C. § 136v(b) (2012). The CAA also establishes programs that grant exclusive federal jurisdiction over particular substantive areas of air pollution regulation. *See, e.g.*, 42 U.S.C. §§ 7651 to 7651 (2012) (creating federal "cap-and-trade" program for cutting acid-forming emissions from power plants).
21 42 U.S.C. §§ 7521, 7524 (2012).

22 *See id.* § 7543.

23 *See id.* § 7507.

24 Glicksman and Levy, 595–96.

25 *See, e.g.*, 42 U.S.C. § 6981(a) (2012) (RCRA).

26 42 U.S.C. § 7661a(b)(2).

27 *Id.* § 7403(a).

28 *Id.* § 7403(c). The program also requires EPA to ensure the comparability of data collected in different states and obtained from different nations. *Id.* § 7403(c)(2).

29 *Id.* § 7411(b)(1)(A).

30 *Id.* §§ 7501(3), 7502(c)(1).

31 *Id.* § 7475(a)(4).

32 *Id.* § 7416. States rarely adopt pollution standards that are more stringent than federal standards; indeed, some state statutes prohibit it. *See* Jerome M. Organ, "Limitations on State Agency Authority to Adopt Environmental Standards More Stringent than Federal Standards: Policy Considerations and Interpretive Problems," 54 *Maryland Law Review* 1373 (1995). Some states have adopted more stringent standards for emissions of hazardous air pollutants, however. *See* US Gov't Accountability Off., "Clean Air Act EPA Should Improve the Management of Its Air Toxics Program," 33–41 (June 2006), www.gao.gov; Congressional Research Service, "Mercury Emissions from Electric Power Plants: States are Setting Stricter Limits," 1–4 (February 22, 2007), http://congressional.proquest.com.

33 42 U.S.C. §§ 7479(3), 7501(3) (2012).

34 33 U.S.C. §§ 1311(b), 1314(b) (2012).

35 *Id.* § 1370.

36 *Id.* § 1251(a)(2).

37 *Id.* § 1313(c).

38 *Id.* § 1314(a).

39 *Id.* § 1313(c)(3)-(4) (2012).

40 *Id.* § 1313(d)(1)(C).

41 *Id.* § 1313(d)(2).

42 Pronsolino v. Nastri, 291 F.3d 1123 (9th Cir. 2002).

43 42 U.S.C. § 7410 (2012).

44 *Id.* § 7407(a).

45 *See* Ann E. Carlson, "Iterative Federalism and Climate Change," 103 *Northwestern University Law Review* 1097, 1108 (2009).

46 42 U.S.C. § 7410(k).

47 *Id.* § 7410(c).

48 33 U.S.C. § 1329(b) (2012).

49 *Id.* § 1329(b)(2)(A).

50 Pronsolino v. Nastri, 291 F.3d 1123 (9th Cir. 2002).

51 33 U.S.C. § 1313(e).

52 42 U.S.C. § 7661a(b) (2012).

53 33 U.S.C. § 1342(b).

54 *Id.* § 1342(b), (d).
55 EPA, "About NPDES," www.epa.gov.
56 42 U.S.C. § 7661a(d) (2012).
57 *Id.* § 7661d(a)-(b).
58 33 U.S.C. § 1342(c) (2012); 42 U.S.C. § 7661a(e).
59 In addition, the CAA (42 U.S.C. § 7604), CWA (33 U.S.C. § 1365), and RCRA (42 U.S.C. § 6972) authorize private parties with standing to file suit against permittees for permit violations. Though many of the considerations raised in this book may parallel those for assessing the allocation of authority between private and public parties, including the tradeoffs of overlapping private and public enforcement, such analyses are beyond the scope of this book.
60 42 U.S.C. § 6973(a) (2012).
61 *Id.* § 6928(a)(1).
62 *Id.* § 6928(a)(2).
63 *Id.* § 6972; Blue Legs v. EPA, 668 F. Supp. 1329 (D.S.D. 1987), *aff'd on other grounds*, 867 F.2d 1094 (8th Cir. 1989).
64 Harmon Indus., Inc. v. Browner, 191 F.3d 894 (8th Cir. 1999).
65 United States v. Power Eng'g Co., 303 F.3d 1232, 1240 (10th Cir. 2002).
66 *See, e.g.*, 42 U.S.C. § 7413(b) (2012).
67 David M. Bearden et al., "Environmental Laws: Summaries of Major Statutes Administered by the Environmental Protection Agency," Congressional Research Service Report 7-5700, 17 (2013).
68 42 U.S.C. § 7413(a)(3).
69 EPA may file civil enforcement actions even with respect to SIP requirements after notifying the alleged violator and the state. *Id.* § 7413(a)(1). It may pursue criminal enforcement of both federally issued and state issued requirements. *Id.* § 7413(c). *Cf.* 33 U.S.C. § 1319(a)(1) (2012) (giving EPA exclusive authority under the CWA to enforce federal requirements and concurrent authority with states over permit requirements); *id.* § 1319(c) (providing for federal CWA criminal enforcement).
70 Mike Soraghan, "Enforcement would end under Trump plan—former EPA chief," *Energywire* (March 20, 2017), www.eenews.net.
71 33 U.S.C. § 1281(g) (2012).
72 For example, responsibility for financing wastewater treatment construction transitioned to state and local governments in 1989. *Id.* § 1383(a); Bearden et al., 29.
73 *See* 33 U.S.C. § 1329(i)(1); US Gov't Accountability Off., GAO-16-697R, "Environmental Protection Agency: Status of Efforts to Address Nonpoint Source Water Pollution through the Section 319 Program" (2016), www.gao.gov.
74 42 U.S.C. § 7410(a)(5)(A)(i) (2012).
75 *Id.* § 7410(a)(5)(A)(ii).
76 *See, e.g.*, Robert L. Glicksman and Matthew R. Batzel, "Science, Politics, Law, and the Arc of the Clean Water Act: The Role of Assumptions in the Adoption of a Pollution Control Landmark," 32 *Washington University Journal of Law and Policy* 99, 114–16 (2010).

77 42 U.S.C. § 7431.

78 *See, e.g.,* H.R. Rep. No. 95-294, 151 (1977).

79 *Cf.* Solid Waste Agency of N. Cook County v. US Army Corps of Eng'rs, 531 U.S. 159, 195 (2001) (Stevens, J., dissenting) ("The destruction of aquatic migratory bird habitat, like so many other environmental problems, is an action in which the benefits (*e.g.*, a new landfill) are disproportionately local, while many of the costs (*e.g.*, fewer migratory birds) are widely dispersed and often borne by citizens living in other States. In such situations, described by economists as involving 'externalities,' federal regulation is both appropriate and necessary.").

80 The dormant Commerce Clause precludes state legislation that purports to restrict the amount of pollution emitted in another state. *See, e.g.,* Pacific Merchant Shipping Ass'n v. Goldstene, 639 F.3d 1154, 1178 (9th Cir. 2011).

81 *See, e.g.,* H.R. Rep. No. 95-294, 152 (1977); 116 Cong. Rec. 32,901 (1970) (remarks of Sen. Muskie); Hodel v. Virginia Surface Mining and Reclamation Ass'n, 452 U.S. 264, 281–82 (1981); Rancho Viejo, LLC v. Norton, 323 F.3d 1062, 1069 n.7 (D.C. Cir. 2003); Gibbs v. Babbitt, 214 F.3d 483, 501 (4th Cir. 2000).

82 *See* Glicksman and Levy, 600–601.

83 EPA's latest proposal to revise the definition of CWA "waters" conspicuously disregards the overlap dimension by posing a false choice between federal and state authority. "Revised Definition of 'Waters of the United States,'" 84 Fed. Reg. 4154 (Feb. 19, 2019). *But see* S. Rep. No. 89-192, 6 (1965) (supporting minimization of overlap in motor vehicle pollution regulation in response to industry concerns about the potential for a patchwork of conflicting state and federal standards). *See also* H.R. Rep. No. 90-728, 8, 22 (1967).

84 Jonathan H. Adler, "The Fable of Federal Environmental Regulation: Reconsidering the Federal Role in Environmental Protection," 55 *Case Western Reserve Law Review* 93, 107–11 (2004). Professor Adler also raises concerns that federal "ceiling" preemption could inhibit more stringent, and possibly more efficient or effective, state measures. Jonathan H. Adler, "Jurisdictional Mismatch in Environmental Federalism," 14 *New York University Environmental Law Journal* 130, 169–75 (2005).

85 *See, e.g.,* Adler, "Jurisdictional Mismatch," 139–51. Professor Sovacool likewise details the assumptions of advocates of exclusive state authority who emphasize experimentation, diversity, accountability, equity, and competition arguments on behalf of decentralization. Benjamin K. Sovacool, "The Best of Both Worlds: Environmental Federalism and the Need for Federal Action on Renewable Energy and Climate Change," 27 *Stanford Environmental Law Journal* 397, 429–38 (2008).

86 *See, e.g.,* Sovacool, 418–29 (emphasizing cost internalization, preventing races to the bottom, economies of scale, and uniformity advantages); John P. Dwyer, "The Practice of Federalism Under the Clean Air Act," 54 *Maryland Law Review* 1183, 1219 (1995) (highlighting economies of scale, cost internalization, and uniformity). *Cf.* Edward Rubin and Malcolm Feeley, "Federalism: Some Notes on a National Neurosis," 41 *UCLA Law Review* 903, 914 (1994) (arguing that "standard argu-

ments for federalism" are actually "arguments that specific national policies are best implemented by decentralized decision-making"); Sandra B. Zellmer, "The Devil, the Details, and the Dawn of the 21st Century Administrative State: Beyond the New Deal," 32 *Arizona State Law Journal* 941, 1048 (2000).

87 *See, e.g.,* Daniel C. Esty, "Revitalizing Environmental Federalism," 95 *Michigan Law Review* 570, 620 (1996).

88 *See, e.g.,* Robert A. Schapiro, "Toward a Theory of Interactive Federalism," 91 *Iowa Law Review* 243, 251 (2006).

89 *See, e.g.,* Jody Freeman and Jim Rossi, "Agency Coordination in Shared Regulatory Space," 125 *Harvard Law Review* 1131, 1138 (2012); Benjamin Ewing and Douglas A. Kysar, "Prods and Pleas: Limited Government in an Era of Unlimited Harm," 121 *Yale Law Journal* 350, 354 (2011); Michael Doran, "Legislative Organization and Administrative Redundancy," 91 *Boston University Law Review* 1815, 1819 (2011); William W. Buzbee, "State Greenhouse Gas Regulation, Federal Climate Change Legislation, and the Preemption Sword," 1 *San Diego Journal of Climate and Energy Law* 23, 53 (2009).

90 Adelman and Engel, 1844–49; Sovacool, 450; Katherine A. Trisolini, "All Hands on Deck: Local Governments and the Potential for Bidirectional Climate Change Regulation," 62 *Stanford Law Review* 669, 745–46 (2010).

91 Kirsten H. Engel, "Harnessing the Benefits of Dynamic Federalism in Environmental Law," 56 *Emory Law Journal* 159, 179 (2006).

92 Engel, 178–79, 181; Sovacool, 450; Todd S. Aagaard, "Regulatory Overlap, Overlapping Legal Fields, and Statutory Discontinuities," 29 *Virginia Environmental Law Journal* 237, 294 (2011); Anne Joseph O'Connell, "The Architecture of Smart Intelligence: Structuring and Overseeing Agencies in the Post-9/11 World," 94 *California Law Review* 1655, 1677 (2006).

93 *See, e.g.,* Engel, 184.

94 Adelman and Engel, 1823. Even some of these assertions do not seem to distinguish the advantages of overlap from those of other dimensions of authority. For example, some suggest diversity, experimentation, and autonomy, which we suggest are actually advantages of decentralization, to be advantages of overlap. *See, e.g.,* Sovacool, 448–49; Engel, 182–83. Scholars have also claimed that overlap can provide economies of scale (a benefit more appropriately associated with centralization) and improved dialogue (a benefit more appropriately associated with coordination). *See* Sovacool, 449–51; Engel, 170–73.

95 William W. Buzbee, "Contextual Environmental Federalism," 14 *NYU Environmental Law Journal* 108, 126 (2005).

96 Freeman and Rossi, 1150; Jacob E. Gersen, "Overlapping and Underlapping Jurisdiction in Administrative Law," 2006 *Supreme Court Review* 201, 214; Jason Marisam, "Duplicative Delegations," 63 *Administrative Law Review* 181, 184 (2011).

97 Marisam, 223; Freeman and Rossi, 1150.

98 James M. Buchanan and Yong J. Yoon, "Symmetric Tragedies: Commons and Anticommons," 43 *Journal of Law, Economics & Policy* 1, 11–12 (2000); Robert B.

Ahdieh, "Dialectical Regulation," 38 *Connecticut Law Review* 863, 897–98 (2006); Matt Bogoshian and Ken Alexa, "The Essential Role of State Enforcement in the Brave New World of Greenhouse Gas Emission Limits," 27 *UCLA Journal of Environmental Law and Policy* 337, 341 (2009); William W. Buzbee, "Recognizing the Regulatory Commons: A Theory of Regulatory Gaps," 89 *Iowa Law Review* 1, 5–6, 51 (2003).

99 *See e.g.*, Robert A. Schapiro, "From Dualist Federalism to Interactive Federalism," 56 *Emory Law Journal* 1, 17 (2006); Robert A. Schapiro, "Monophonic Preemption," 102 *Northwestern University Law Review* 811, 812–13 (2008); Aagaard, 288.

100 See chap. 2, § B.1.

101 Engel, 165–66.

102 Henry N. Butler and Jonathan R. Macey, "Externalities and the Matching Principle: The Case for Reallocating Environmental Regulatory Authority," 14 *Yale Law & Policy Review* 23, 66 (1996).

103 *See, e.g.*, Aagaard, 286–300.

104 Dual federalism's "most fundamental tenet [. . .] is that the state and federal governments have distinct, mutually exclusive realms of regulatory jurisdiction." Christopher K. Bader, "A Dynamic Defense of Cooperative Federalism," 35 *Whittier Law Review* 161, 165 (2014).

105 *See* Adelman and Engel, 1830–31; William W. Buzbee, "Brownfields, Environmental Federalism, and Institutional Determinism," 21 *William & Mary Environmental Law and Policy Review* 1, 60 (1997).

106 Bogoshian and Alexa, 347–48; Buzbee, "Contextual Environmental Federalism," 125, 128; Engel, 178–181.

107 *Cf.* Freeman and Rossi, 1146–47 (discussing the potential for inefficiency and conflict from overlapping authority in antitrust law, but alternatively noting the value of relying on the diverse expertise of two agencies in setting food safety standards).

108 *See* chap. 4, § B.3.

109 540 U.S. 461, 469 (2004).

110 *Id.*, 506–7 (Kennedy, J. dissenting).

111 *Id.*, 506–7.

112 *Id.*, 507.

113 *Id.*, 518.

114 The state has the discretion to select a different BACT on remand that may be acceptable to EPA.

115 Of course, the tradeoffs of the extent of overlap are likely to be relevant in assessing not only the relationship between federal and state agencies but also between administrative agencies within a particular government (e.g., federal) or between governments at a similar scale (e.g., states).

116 *See, e.g.*, Jerome M. Organ, "Subsidiarity and Solidarity: Lenses for Assessing the Appropriate Locus for Environmental Regulation and Enforcement," 5 *University of St. Thomas Law Journal* 262, 277 (2008).

117 *See* Robert R. Kuehn, "The Limits of Devolving Enforcement of Federal Environmental Laws," 70 *Tulane Law Review* 2373, 2379–80 (1996). *Cf.* Enforcement of Environmental Laws: Hearing before the S. Comm. on Environment and Public Works, 105 Cong. Rec. 64–65 (1997) (Prepared Statement of Lois J. Schiffer, Assistant Attorney General, Environment and Natural Resources Division) (detailing successful examples of synergistic federal and state enforcement).

118 Jared Snyder and Jonathan Binder, "The Changing Climate of Cooperative Federalism: The Dynamic Role of the States in a National Strategy to Combat Climate Change," 27 *UCLA Journal of Environmental Law and Policy* 231, 236, 246 (2009); Vivian E. Thomson and Vicki Arroyo, "Upside-Down Cooperative Federalism: Climate Change Policymaking and the States," 29 *Virginia Environmental Law Journal* 1 (2011).

119 The centralization advantages of a unitary federal allocation are relevant here because movement along one dimension (here, toward centralization) can influence evaluation of the net advantages and disadvantages of movement along another dimension (here, the overlap–distinctness dimension). Policymakers should consider the tradeoffs involved in situating authority along each of the dimensions in tandem with one another.

120 *See, e.g.*, Environmental Law Institute, State Constraints: State-Imposed Limitations on the Authority of Agencies to Regulate Waters Beyond the Scope of the Federal Clean Water Act (May 2003), www.eli.org. *Cf.* Congressional Research Service, Managing Electronic Waste: Issues with Exporting E-Waste, 1, 2, 6 (February 6, 2008), http://congressional.proquest.com (describing state efforts to regulate e-waste not subject to RCRA regulation).

121 *See* chap. 4, § A.4.

122 At least for the CAA and CWA, such information gathering and ambient monitoring might sensibly be allocated toward the more centralized end of that spectrum, in light of the associated core advantages of uniformity and economies of scale, as well as the more muted experimentation and diversity advantages. However, for specific monitoring or research functions for which states have particular expertise, it might be more sensible to devolve such distinct authority.

123 Office of the Administrator, EPA, "EPA Kicks Off Website Updates," News Release (April 28, 2017), www.epa.gov; Valerie Volcovici, "Trump Administration Tells EPA to Cut Climate Page from Website," *Reuters* (January 24, 2017), www.reuters.com.

124 *See* chap. 4, § B.2.

125 *See* Carlson, "Iterative Federalism and Climate Change," 1134; National Research Council of the National Academies, "State and Federal Standards for Mobile-Source Emissions," 264–65 (2006).

126 Further, movement along another dimension of authority may address concerns implicated by overlap, or vice versa. For example, reductions in functional overlap may often be beneficially accompanied by establishing coordination mechanisms among agencies sharing substantive authority.

127 *See* S. Rep. No. 91-1196, 18, 21 (1970) (noting roles for both federal and state enforcement).

128 *See* 42 U.S.C. § 7413(b) (2012) (CAA); 33 U.S.C. § 1319(a)(1) (2012) (CWA).

129 30 U.S.C. §§ 1201–1328 (2012).

130 For example, the Office of Surface Mining has been reluctant to exercise its take-
back authority under SMCRA, even in circumstances of repeated state deficiency.
See, e.g., W. Virginia Highlands Conservancy v. Norton, 161 F. Supp. 2d 676, 681
(S.D.W. Va. 2001); 190 F. Supp. 2d 859, 870 (S.D.W. Va. 2002); 238 F. Supp. 2d 761,
764 (S.D.W. Va. 2003).

131 Harmon Indus., Inc. v. Browner, 191 F.3d 894 (8th Cir. 1999).

CHAPTER 5: NEPA, THE ESA, AND THE TRADEOFFS OF
INTERAGENCY COORDINATION

1 42 U.S.C. §§ 4321-4370 (2012).

2 NEPA.gov, "Environmental Impact Statements Filed through 2012," ceq.doe.gov;
National Association of Environmental Professionals, "Summary of NAEP Annual
National Environmental Policy Act (NEPA) Report for 2016" (2017), www.naep.org.

3 *See* chap. 5, § A.

4 *See* chap. 5, § B.2.

5 This case study will focus on how the assessment of the advantages and disadvantages of coordination will differ depending on the government function under
consideration, even though NEPA and the ESA may inevitably raise additional
questions involving other dimensions of regulatory authority.

6 16 U.S.C. §§ 1531-1544 (2012).

7 Jody Freeman and Jim Rossi, "Agency Coordination in Shared Regulatory Space,"
125 *Harvard Law Review* 1131, 1189 (2012).

8 *Id.,* 1183.

9 Maribeth Wilt-Seibert, "Unemployment Compensation for Employees of Educational Institutions: How State Courts Have Created Variations on Federally
Mandated Statutory Language," 29 *University of Michigan Journal of Law Reform*
585, 611 (1995); Thomas McInerney, "Putting Regulation Before Responsibility:
Towards Binding Norms of Corporate Social Responsibility," 40 *Cornell International Law Journal* 171, 195 (2007).

10 See Freeman and Rossi, 1186–89; Alejandro E. Camacho, "Adapting Governance
to Climate Change: Managing Uncertainty Through a Learning Infrastructure," 59
Emory Law Journal 1, 74–75 (2009).

11 42 U.S.C. § 4332(2)(C) (2012).

12 *Id.* An environmental impact statement must meaningfully assess the environmental effects of the proposed action, any unavoidable adverse environmental effects should the proposal be implemented, and a reasonable range of alternatives
to the proposed action. *Id.* § 4332(2)(C)(i)–(v).

13 *See, e.g.,* Bradley C. Karkkainen, "Toward a Smarter NEPA: Monitoring and
Managing Government's Environmental Performance," 102 *Columbia Law Review*

903, 904–5 (2002); Joseph Sax, "The (Unhappy) Truth about NEPA," 26 *Oklahoma Law Review* 239 (1973); Philip Michael Ferester, "Revitalizing the National Environmental Policy Act: Substantive Law Adaptations From NEPA's Progeny," *16 Harvard Environmental Law Review* 207 (1992); Philip Weinberg, "It's Time to Put NEPA Back on Course," *New York University Environmental Law Journal* 99, 110–12 (1994).

14 42 U.S.C. §§ 4342–4347 (2012); 40 C.F.R. § 1500.3. CEQ has promulgated implementing regulations for NEPA and provided guidance to federal agencies on compliance with NEPA's requirements. *See* 40 C.F.R. §§ 1500-1517.7.

15 42 U.S.C. § 4332(2)(C). *See also* 40 C.F.R. § 1503.1(a)(1).

16 NEPA's regulations provide for the appointment of a lead agency where more than one federal agency proposes or is involved in the same action or is involved in a group of actions directly related to each other. 40 C.F.R. § 1501.5(a)(1)–(2).

17 Cooperating agencies must assist lead agencies in the preparation of an EIS. 40 C.F.R. § 1501.6.

18 *Id.* § 1501.6(a)(1)–(2).

19 *Id.* § 1503.2.

20 *Id.* § 1501.6(b)(1)–(2).

21 *Id.* § 1501.6(b)(3).

22 42 U.S.C. § 4332(2)(C) (2012). CEQ regulations also mandate that agencies "cooperate with State and local agencies to the fullest extent possible to reduce duplication between NEPA and State and local requirements," including by engaging in joint planning processes, joint environmental research and studies, joint public hearings, and joint environmental assessments. 40 C.F.R. § 1500.4(n); *id.* § 1500.4(h); *id.* § 1506.2(b)(1)–(4).

23 CEQ, "The National Environmental Policy Act: A Study of Its Effectiveness After Twenty-five Years," 21 (1997), http://digital.library.unt.edu.

24 40 C.F.R. § 1507.3(a).

25 *Id.* § 1507.3(a).

26 *See, e.g.,* Environmental Law Institute, "NEPA Success Stories: Celebrating 40 Years of Transparency and Open Government," 14 (August 2010), https://www.eli .org; Hal Delaplane, "Partnering Facilitates SPR Pipeline EA," 18 *US Department of Energy NEPA Lessons Learned Quarterly Report* 4–5 (1999), https://energy.gov; Roger Twitchel, "NEPA Helps to Protect Sagebrush Steppe Ecosystem," 36 *U.S. Department of Energy NEPA Lessons Learned Quarterly Report* 18 (2003), https:// energy.gov.

27 P. Lynn Scarlett, "National Environmental Policy Act: Enhancing Collaboration and Partnerships" 1, presented at Rocky Mountain Mineral Law Foundation Special Institute on the National Environmental Policy Act (October 2010), http:// lynnscarlett.com.

28 CEQ, "National Environmental Policy Act," ix.

29 *Id.*

30 *Id.*, 22.

31 *Id.*, ix.
32 Helen L. Serassio, "Legislative and Executive Efforts to Modernize NEPA and Create Efficiencies in Environmental Review," 45 *Texas Environmental Law Journal* 317, 321 (2015).
33 *Id.*
34 *Id.*
35 *Id.*
36 *Id.*, 327.
37 CEQ, "Memorandum for the Heads of Federal Agencies, Cooperating Agencies in Implementing the Procedural Requirements of the National Environmental Policy Act," 1 (January 30, 2002), http://www.fws.gov.
38 *Id.*, 2.
39 *Id.*
40 The NEPA Task Force, "Modernizing NEPA Implementation" (September 2003), https://ceq.doe.gov.
41 *Id.*, 26.
42 Scarlett, 3.
43 Nancy H. Sutley, Chair, CEQ, to Heads of Federal Departments and Agencies, "Improving the Process for Preparing Efficient and Timely Reviews under the National Environmental Policy Act," 34 (March 6, 2012), www.whitehouse.gov.
44 Serassio, 328.
45 *Id.*, 330.
46 *See* David J. Hayes, "Leaning on NEPA to Improve the Federal Permitting Process," 45 *Environmental Law Reporter News and Analysis* 10018, 10019 (2015).
47 Exec. Order No. 12604, 77 Fed. Reg. 18885 (March 22, 2012).
48 Hayes, 10020–21.
49 *See* Fixing America's Surface Transportation Act, Pub. L. No. 114-94, 129 Stat. 1312 (2015) (seeking to streamline environmental review and permitting for transportation infrastructure).
50 Exec. Order No. 13807, 82 Fed. Reg. 40463 (August 15, 2017); OMB, "Memorandum of Understanding Implementing One Federal Decision under Executive Order 13807" (April 10, 2018).
51 *See* "Update to the Regulations for Implementing the Procedural Provisions of the National Environmental Policy Act," 83 Fed. Reg. 28591 (June 20, 2018) (publishing CEQ's Advance Notice of Proposed Rulemaking).
52 Karkkainen, 954, 946–47.
53 *Id.*, 957.
54 *Id.*, 950.
55 EPA, Environmental Impact Statement (EIS) Database, NEPA, https://cdxnodengn.epa.gov (accessed December 18, 2018).
56 *See* Karkkainen, 938; CEQ, "National Environmental Policy Act," 31.
57 40 C.F.R. § 1505.2(c).
58 *Id.* § 1505.3.

59 *See, e.g.,* CEQ, "National Environmental Policy Act," 31; Sarah E. Light, "NEPA's Footprint: Information Disclosure as a Quasi-Carbon Tax on Agencies," 87 *Tulane Law Review* 511, 571 (2013). *See generally* Eric Biber, "The Problem of Environmental Monitoring," 83 *University of Colorado Law Review* 1 (2011).

60 40 C.F.R. § 1505.3.

61 Ronald Bjorkland, "Monitoring: The Missing Piece: A Critique of NEPA Monitoring," 43 *Environmental Impact Assessment Report* 129 (2013).

62 National Forest Foundation, "A Roadmap for Collaboration Before, During and After the NEPA Process" 24 (October 2013), www.nationalforests.org.

63 Karkkainen, 954; Bjorkland, 129; CEQ, "Collaboration in NEPA: A Handbook for NEPA Practitioners" 23 (October 2007), http://energy.gov.

64 Bjorkland, 129; National Forest Foundation, 24.

65 *See* Karkkainen, 907–8; Robert L. Glicksman, "Bridging Data Gaps Through Modeling and Evaluation of Surrogates: Use of the Best Available Science to Protect Biological Diversity Under the National Forest Management Act," 83 *Indiana Law Journal* 465, 524 (2008).

66 40 C.F.R. § 1502.9(c).

67 *Id.*

68 *See, e.g.,* K. Jack Haugrud, "Perspectives on NEPA: Let's Bring a Bit of Substance to NEPA—Making Mitigation Mandatory," 39 *Environmental Law Reporter News and Analysis* 10638 (2009); Forester, 258–59; Eric Pearson, "Section 102(1) of the National Environmental Policy Act," 41 *Creighton Law Review* 369, 383–84 (2008).

69 *See, e.g.,* Matthew J. Lindstrom, "Procedures Without Purpose: The Withering Away of the National Environmental Policy Act's Substantive Law," 20 *Journal of Land, Resources, and Environmental Law* 245 (2000). *But see* California Environmental Quality Act, Cal. Pub. Res. Code §§ 21000–21177 (2016) (incorporating implementation requirements that state/local agencies mitigate environmental harm); New York's State Environmental Quality Review Act, N.Y. Envtl. Conserv. L. §§ 8-0101 to 8-0117 (2016) (same).

70 Winter v. Natural Res. Def. Council, Inc., 555 U.S. 7 (2008); Robertson v. Methow Valley Citizens Council, 490 U.S. 332 (1989); Vermont Yankee Nuclear Power Corp. v. Natural Res. Def. Council, Inc., 435 U.S. 519, 558 (1978).

71 James T.B. Tripp and Nathan G. Alley, "Streamlining NEPA's Environmental Review Process: Suggestions for Agency Reform," 12 *New York University Environmental Law Journal* 74, 76–77 (2003).

72 Nicholas C. Yost, *NEPA Deskbook* 7 (3d. ed. 2005).

73 Presidents have progressively limited the power of CEQ, and Congress has routinely appropriated limited funds and staff. *Id.*

74 42 U.S.C. §7609 (2012). In creating this authority, Congress stated: "It is essential that mission-oriented Federal agencies have access to environmental expertise in order to give adequate consideration to environmental factors." S. Rep. No. 91-1196, 43 (1970).

75 Yost, 8; EPA, "Environmental Impact Statement Rating System Criteria" (April 7, 2017), www.epa.gov.

76 Moreover, if EPA determines that the lead agency has not sufficiently revised the proposal so that the project remains environmentally unsatisfactory, EPA must refer the matter to CEQ for mediation. 42 U.S.C. §7609(b) (2012).

77 16 U.S.C. § 1536(a)(2) (2012).

78 *Id.*

79 FWS, "Section 7 Consultation: A Brief Explanation" (last updated April 14, 2015), www.fws.gov. Informal consultation is, however, optional. 50 C.F.R. § 402.13(a).

80 FWS, "Section 7 Consultation."

81 *Id.*

82 *Id.*; 50 C.F.R. § 402.13(a).

83 FWS, "Section 7 Consultation"; 16 U.S.C. § 1536(c)(1).

84 50 C.F.R. § 402.14(a), (b)(1)-(2); FWS, "Section 7 Consultation."

85 50 C.F.R. § 402.14, (c), (g)(5).

86 FWS, "Section 7 Consultation," 79; 16 U.S.C. § 1536(b)(3)(A).

87 50 C.F.R. § 402.14(i).

88 *Id.*

89 Bennett v. Spear, 520 U.S. 154, 169–70 (1997).

90 16 U.S.C. § 1536(o).

91 50 C.F.R. § 402.14(h)(3).

92 *Id.*; 16 U.S.C. § 1536(b)(3)(A).

93 16 U.S.C. § 1536(b)(3)–(4); 50 C.F.R. § 402.14.

94 FWS, "Section 7 Consultation."

95 Bennett v. Spear, 520 U.S. 154, 169 (1997).

96 *See id.*

97 *Id.*, 170. The taking prohibition is codified at 16 U.S.C. § 1538(a)(1)(B) (2012).

98 *See* 16 U.S.C. § 1536(e)–(h); 50 C.F.R. pt. 450.

99 16 U.S.C. § 1536(o)(2).

100 Freeman and Rossi, 1158. *See also* Eric Biber, "Too Many Things to Do: How to Deal with the Dysfunctions of Multiple-Goal Agencies," 33 *Harvard Environmental Law Review* 1, 52–57 (2009) (contrasting interagency coordination under ESA as "agency as regulator" and under NEPA as "agency as lobbyist.").

101 *See, e.g.,* Jeremy Brian Root, "Limiting the Scope of Reinitiation: Reforming Section 7 of the Endangered Species Act," 10 *George Mason Law Review* 1035, 1036 (2002).

102 Jacob W. Malcom and Ya-Wei Li, "Data Contradict Common Perceptions about a Controversial Provision of the Endangered Species Act," 112 *Proceedings of the National Academy of Sciences* 15844, 15846 (2015).

103 US Gov't Accountability Office, GAO-05-732T, "Endangered Species Act: Successes and Challenges in Agency Collaboration and the Use of Scientific Information in the Decision Making Process," 10 (2005); US Gov't Accountability Office, GAO-09-225R, "Endangered Species Act: Many GAO Recommendations Have Been Implemented, but Some Issues Remain Unresolved," 2 (2009).

104 Malcom and Li, 15844.

105 *Id.*

106 *Id.*, 15846–47.

107 *Id.*, 15847.

108 *Id.*, 15848.

109 *Id.*

110 US Gov't Accountability Off., GAO-05-732T, 10.

111 *Id.*

112 *Id.* at 8; US Gov't Accountability Off., GAO-09-225R, 2.

113 "Notice of Availability of a Final Addendum to the Handbook for Habitat Conservation Planning and Incidental Take Permitting Process," 65 Fed. Reg. 35242, 35243, 35253 (June 1, 2000).

114 *Id.*, 35,254.

115 *See* Eric Biber, "The Problem of Environmental Monitoring"; Alejandro E. Camacho, "Can Regulation Evolve? Lessons from a Study in Maladaptive Management," 55 *UCLA Law Review* 293, 324–25 (2007).

116 50 C.F.R. § 402.16(a)–(d).

117 *Id.* § 402.16(b).

118 *Id.* § 402.16(a), (d).

119 *Id.* § 402.16(c).

120 Karkkainen, 903.

121 A mitigated finding of no significant impact relies on contemplated mitigation measures to reduce the threshold level of significance that triggers the obligation to prepare an EIS. *See* Karkkainen, 934.

122 *Id.*, 927. The little empirical work that has been done suggests that "most EIS forecasts were presented in narrative language too vague or imprecise to be empirically verifiable or falsifiable" or were "fairly accurate" only thirty percent of the time. *Id.*, 928 (citing Paul J. Culhane et al., *Forecasts and Environmental Decisionmaking: The Content and Predictive Accuracy of Environmental Impact Statements* 96, 111–16, 228–31 (1987)).

123 *See, e.g.,* 4 Cal. Code Reg. § 15097(d).

124 *See, e.g.,* Sarah Langberg, "A 'Full and Fair' Discussion of Environmental Impacts in NEPA EISs: The Case for Addressing the Impact of Substantive Regulatory Regimes," 124 *Yale Law Journal* 716, 753–54 (2014); National Forest Foundation, 7–9.

125 In fact, CEQ regulations expressly require agencies to "reduce excessive paperwork" and delay." 40 C.F.R. §§ 1500.4–1500.5. *See also* CEQ, "Collaboration in NEPA," 5.

126 CEQ, "National Environmental Policy Act," x; CEQ, "Collaboration in NEPA," 5.

127 CEQ, "Collaboration in NEPA," 5.

128 CEQ, "National Environmental Policy Act," x; CEQ, "Collaboration in NEPA," 5.

129 *See* CEQ, 4; CEQ, "Collaboration in NEPA," 4; National Forest Foundation, 7–9.

130 Ron Deverman et al., "Environmental Assessments: Guidance on Best Practice Principles," 45 *Environmental Law Reporter News and Analysis* 10142, 10153 (2015).

131 Freeman and Rossi, 1182.

132 Merrell v. Thomas, 807 F.2d 776, 779 (9th Cir. 1986).

133 Douglas Cty. v. Babbitt, 48 F.3d 1495, 1506 (9th Cir. 1995).

134 Camacho, "Adapting Governance," 30–36.

135 David A. Weisbach and Jacob Nussim, "The Integration of Tax and Spending Programs," 113 *Yale Law Journal* 955, 994–95 (2004).

136 Anne Joseph O'Connell, "The Architecture of Smart Intelligence: Structuring and Overseeing Agencies in the Post-9/11 World," 94 *California Law Review* 1655, 1676–78 (2006).

137 *See* Richard L. Revesz, "Rehabilitating Interstate Competition: Rethinking the 'Race to the Bottom' Rationale for Federal Environmental Regulation," 67 *New York University Law Review* 1210, 1211–12 (1992); Jonathan H. Adler, "Jurisdictional Mismatch in Environmental Federalism," 14 *New York University Environmental Law Journal* 130, 134 (2005).

138 *See* Conclusion.

139 *See, e.g.,* Serge Taylor, *Making Bureaucracies Think: The Environmental Impact Statement Strategy of Administrative Reform* (1984); Council on Environmental Quality, *The National Environmental Policy Act: A Study of Its Effectiveness After Twenty-Five Years* ix (1997); Council on Environmental Quality, *Environmental Quality, Environmental Impact Statements: An Analysis of Six Years' Experience by Seventy Federal Agencies* (1976); Council on Environmental Quality, *Fourth Annual Report* (1973).

140 *See* Michael C. Blumm and Stephen R. Brown, "Pluralism and the Environment: The Role of Comment Agencies in NEPA Litigation," 14 *Harvard Environmental Law Review* 277 (1990); Michael C. Blumm and Marla S. Nelson, "Pluralism and the Environment Revisited: The Role of Comment Agencies in NEPA Litigation," 37 *Vermont Law Review* (2013).

141 US Gov't Accountability Office, GAO-09-550, "Endangered Species Act: The U.S. Fish and Wildlife Service Has Incomplete Information about Effects on Listed Species from Section 7 Consultations," 11–24 (2009).

142 *Id.,* 11.

143 *Id.,* 15.

144 *Id.,* 24–25.

145 *Id.,* 13–14.

146 *See* Jason Totoiu, "Quantifying, Monitoring, and Tracking 'Take' Under the Endangered Species Act: The Promise of a More Informed Approach to Consultation," 41 *Environmental Law* 165, 192–93 (2011).

147 US Gov't Accountability Off., GAO-09-550, 27.

148 *Id.*

149 *See* Camacho, "Adapting Governance," 38, 40–42.

150 Examples of interagency coordination of monitoring abound. *See, e.g.,* 16 U.S.C. §§ 1642(c)(3), (d)(3), (e)(3)-(4), 1643(c), 1645(b)-(c), (d)(3) (2012) (national forest management); 16 U.S.C. §§ 1431(b)(5), 1440(b)(1)(A) (2012) (national marine

sanctuaries); 22 U.S.C. § 9010 (2012) (child abduction); 42 U.S.C. § 247d-5(a)(3) (B)(i) (2012) (antimicrobial resistance); 42 U.S.C. § 290aa(e)(1) (2012) (substance abuse); 42 U.S.C. § 300aa-2 (a)(7) (2012) (vaccination and immunization); 42 U.S.C. § 247b-21(a)(3)(C) (2012) (mosquito control); 42 U.S.C. § 13001b(d)(1) (2012) (regional children's advocacy centers); 42 U.S.C. § 7707(a) (2012) (seismic research).

151 The Federal Energy Regulatory Commission, for instance, has generally been resistant to NEPA review, failing to adopt a policy about complying with NEPA until 1987 and aggressively asserting in court its independence from CEQ regulations. *See* Paul W. Parfomak, "Interstate Natural Gas Pipelines: Process and Timing of FERC Permit Application Review," *Congressional Research Service* 3 (January 16, 2005).

152 O'Connell, 1685.

153 *See* Freeman and Rossi, 1135; Aaron J. Saiger, "Obama's 'Czars' for Domestic Policy and the Law of the White House Staff," 79 *Fordham Law Review* 2577, 2588 (2011).

154 *See* chap. 4, § C.3.

155 *See, e.g.,* Arnold M. Howitt and Herman B. "Dutch" Leonard, "Katrina and the Core Challenges of Disaster Response," 30 *Fletcher Forum of World Affairs* 215, 220 (2006).

156 *See, e.g.,* J.R. DeShazo and Jody Freeman, "Public Agencies as Lobbyists," 105 *Columbia Law Review* 2217, 2221, 2232, 2253 (2005).

CHAPTER 6: DIFFERENTIATING CENTRALIZATION AND OVERLAP IN SWAP REGULATION

1 Regulatory failure may be attributable to non-structural factors such as procedural infirmities, lack of resources, and the use of inadequate tools or control methodologies, but this chapter and the next two concentrate on structural problems with derivatives regulation, management of information relating to threats to national security, and regulation of the safety and soundness of depository institutions.

2 *See* chap. 2, § B.2.

3 *See* chap. 2, § B.1.

4 In 1949, a commission headed by former President Herbert Hoover engaged in detailed study of agency organization. US Comm'n on the Organization of the Executive Branch of the Government, "The Hoover Commission on Organization of the Executive Branch of the Government" (1949).

5 *Id.,* Appendix N 116.

6 *Id.,* 250–51. *See also* Richard A. Merrill and Jeffrey K. Francer, "Organizing Federal Food Safety Regulation," 31 *Seton Hall Law Review* 61, 118 (2000).

7 *See* US Comm'n on the Organization of the Executive Branch of the Government, Appendix N 116. *See also* Steven A. Ramirez, "Depoliticizing Financial Regulation," 41 *William and Mary Law Review* 503, 564 n. 371 (2000); Elizabeth F. Brown, "The Tyranny of the Multitude Is a Multiplied Tyranny: Is the United States

Financial Regulatory Structure Undermining U.S. Competitiveness?," 2 *Brooklyn Journal of Corporate, Financial, and Commercial Law* 369, 378 (2008).

8 Dodd-Frank Wall Street Reform and Consumer Protection Act, Pub. L. No. 111–203, 124 Stat. 1376 (2010). Title VII of the Dodd-Frank Wall Street Reform and Consumer Protection Act of 2010 is also called the Wall Street Transparency and Accountability Act; the larger act is commonly known as the Dodd-Frank Act.

9 The Federal Energy Regulatory Commission (FERC)'s jurisdiction over energy-related derivatives also overlaps with that of the CFTC, with the dividing line between the two agencies' jurisdictions arguably being even more unclear than that between the CFTC and SEC. *See* Alexia Brunet and Meredith Shafe, "Beyond Enron: Regulation in Energy Derivatives Trading," 27 *Northwestern Journal of International Law and Business* 665 (2007). Regulation of energy derivatives raises parallel issues as (and reinforces the central claim of) this chapter. *Cf.* Meric Sar, "A Regulatory Retreat: Energy Market Exemption from Private Anti-Manipulation Actions Under the Commodity Exchange Act," 22 *Fordham Journal of Corporate and Financial Law* 605, 633 (2017); "Key Legal Issues Facing the Administration in 2013: Environment, Energy and Natural Resources," 43 *Environmental Law Reporter News and Analysis* 10395, 10396–97 (2013).

The Department of Labor's regulatory authority over investment of retirement assets under the Employee Retirement Income Security Act of 1974 also overlaps with CFTC and SEC derivatives regulation. *See* Anita Krug, "The Other Securities Regulator: A Case Study in Regulatory Damage," 92 *Tulane Law Review* 229 (2017).

10 *See* Roberta Romano, "The Political Dynamics of Derivative Securities Regulation," 14 *Yale Journal on Regulation* 279 (1997).

11 *Id.*, 284.

12 *Id.*, 284–85; Jerry W. Markham, "Merging the SEC and CFTC—A Clash of Cultures," 78 *University of Cincinnati Law Review* 537, 552, 558–93 (2009).

13 15 U.S.C. §§ 78a-78qq (2012).

14 US Dep't of the Treasury, "Blueprint for a Modernized Financial Regulatory Structure," 58–60 (March 2008).

15 *Id.*, 57.

16 *Id.*, 46–47; Mark Jickling, "The Merger of the SEC and the CFTC: A Pro/Con Analysis?," 90–222, 3 (April 23, 1990).

17 SEC, "Derivatives" (accessed December 18, 2018), www.sec.gov.

18 US Gov't Accountability Off., GAO-16-175, "Financial Regulation: Complex and Fragmented Structure Could Be Streamlined to Improve Effectiveness" (2016).

19 US Dep't of the Treasury, 56.

20 *Id.*

21 *Id.*

22 Commodity Futures Trading Commission Act of 1974, Pub. L. No. 93-463, 88 Stat. 1389 (1974).

23 Though statutorily undefined, a "future" or "futures contract" generally refers to a highly standardized agreement between two parties to buy and sell a specific asset at a specified price before or upon some set future date. US Dep't of the Treasury, 44.

24 *Id.*

25 Commodity Exchange Act, Pub. L. No. 74-675, 49 Stat. 1491 (1936).

26 US Dep't of the Treasury, 44–45, 49–52.

27 *Id.*, 44.

28 *Id.*

29 *See id.*, 46–47. As OTC swaps including "credit default swaps" were traded directly between two parties, "there was no central repository of information and no way for regulators or counterparties to determine if an individual counterparty would be able to honor its swap obligations." Joshua Macey, Note, "Playing Nicely: How Judges Can Improve Dodd-Frank and Foster Interagency Collaboration," 126 *Yale Law Journal* 806, 815 (2017). The CFTC eventually described "this lack of transparency [as] a major contributor to the 2008 financial crisis." *Id.*, 816.

30 US Dep't of the Treasury, 45.

31 US Commodity Futures Trading Comm'n, "CFTC Organization" (accessed December 18, 2018), www.cftc.gov.

32 *Id.*

33 Commodity Exchange Act, Pub. L. No. 74-675, 49 Stat. 1491 (1936).

34 US Commodity Futures Trading Comm'n, "CFTC Organization, Programs and Functions."

35 John D. Benson, Comment, "Ending the Turf Wars: Support for a CFTC/SEC Consolidation," 36 *Villanova Law Review* 1175, 1175 (1991); Roberta S. Karmel, "The Future of the Securities and Exchange Commission as a Market Regulator," 78 *University of Cincinnati Law Review* 501, 502 (2009–10).

36 H.R. Rep. No. 93-975, 71 (1974). The Department of Agriculture was similarly seen as lacking expertise, in addition to being subject to a potential conflict of interest. *See* Romano, 336–37.

37 H.R. Rep. No. 93-975, 71.

38 Mark Jickling, Congressional Research Serv., 95-698E, "Merging the CFTC and the SEC?," 2 (June 9, 1995).

39 H.R. Rep. No. 93-975, 71. *See also* Henry Eschwege, Director, Resources and Economic Development Division, GAO, Commodity Futures Trading Commission, Statement before the Senate Comm. on Agriculture and Forestry, 571–72 (May 20, 1974).

40 Lawrence A. Cunningham and David Zaring, "The Three or Four Approaches to Financial Regulation: A Cautionary Analysis against Exuberance in Crisis Response," 78 *George Washington Law Review* 39, 50 (2009); Terrence Duffy, "The Effective Regulation of the Over-The-Counter Derivatives Market," Prepared statement before the House Subcomm. on Capital Markets, Insurance, and Government Sponsored Enterprises, Comm. on Financial Services 138 (June 9, 2009).

41 *See* Jickling, "Merging the CFTC and the SEC?," 1, 4–5.

42 Jickling, "The Merger of the SEC and the CFTC," 12.

43 Romano, 282, 383.

44 Cunningham and Zaring, 49–50.

45 *See* US Dep't of the Treasury, 109; Bart Chilton, Comm'r, CFTC, "Let's Not 'Dial M for Merger': CFTC's Principles-Based Regulation—A Success Story," before the Futures Indus. Ass'n, Law and Compliance Luncheon (November 13, 2007), www.cftc.gov.

46 Jickling, "The Merger of the SEC and the CFTC," 13–14; Cunningham and Zaring, 49–50; Jickling, "Merging the CFTC and the SEC?," 4.

47 *See* Romano, 282; Edward J. Kane, "Regulatory Structure in Futures Markets," 4 *Journal of Future Markets* 367, 383 (1984).

48 John C. Coffee, Jr. and Hillary A. Sale, "Redesigning the SEC: Does the Treasury Have a Better Idea?," 95 *Virginia Law Review* 707, 720 (2009).

49 Jickling, "The Merger of the SEC and the CFTC," 13.

50 *See* Markham, 587; Jickling, "Merging the CFTC and the SEC?," 2.

51 US Dep't of the Treasury, 107; Jickling, "Merging the CFTC and the SEC?," 2–3; Jickling, "The Merger of the SEC and the CFTC," 3.

52 US Dep't of the Treasury, 108–9.

53 Jickling, "Merging the CFTC and the SEC?," 2–3.

54 Jickling, "The Merger of the SEC and the CFTC," 3.

55 Markham, 587–88.

56 Jickling, "Merging the CFTC and the SEC?," 2–3.

57 Benson, 1175; Daniel A. Farber and Anne Joseph O'Connell, "Agencies as Adversaries," 105 *California Law Review* 1375, 1379 (2017) (noting that the two agencies "have long tussled over jurisdiction, including early disputes over which agency should regulate futures contracts based on securities").

58 US Dep't of the Treasury, 107.

59 *Id.*

60 *Id.*

61 Board of Trade of Chicago v. SEC, 677 F.2d 1137 (7th Cir. 1982), *vacated as moot,* 459 U.S. 1026 (1982).

62 *See* chap. 6, § A.3.

63 US Dep't of the Treasury, 107.

64 *Id.*, 108.

65 *Id.*

66 Thomas A. Russo and Marlisa Vinciguerra, "Financial Innovation and Uncertain Regulation," 69 *Texas Law Review* 1431, 1495 (1991).

67 *See, e.g.,* Chi. Mercantile Exch. v. SEC, 883 F.2d 537, 544 (7th Cir. 1989); Benson, 36; US Dep't of the Treasury, 115; Roberta Karmel, Professor, Brooklyn Law School, "Harry Cross Visiting Professor Lecture," 9 (January 29, 2009), www .law.washington.edu; Bipartisan Policy Center, "Dodd-Frank's Missed Opportunity: A Road Map for More Effective Regulatory Architecture," 44 (2014), http://

bipartisanpolicy.org; Eric Hammesfahr, "Former regulators favor SEC, CFTC merger," *CQ Roll Call*, (October 6, 2014).

68 H.R. 4477, Markets and Trading Reorganization and Reform Act, 101st Cong. (1989–90). Bills of the same name were reintroduced in subsequent Congresses.

69 *See* US Gov't Accountability Off., GAO-10-410, "Clearer Goals and Reporting Requirements Could Enhance Efforts by CFTC and SEC to Harmonize Their Regulatory Approaches" (2010).

70 US Dep't of the Treasury, 106.

71 Senator Michael D. Crapo, Modernizing the U.S. Financial Regulatory System: Statement before Senate Comm. on Banking, Housing and Urban Affairs, 32 (February 4, 2009); Press Release, "Frank and Capuano introduce legislation to merge the SEC and CFTC," (November 29, 2012), http://democrats.financialservices. house.gov (statement of Rep. Barney Frank).

72 *See* US Dep't of the Treasury, 106. Whereas the markets were truly distinct in the 1930s at the time of enactment of the federal securities laws and the CEA, Treasury noted, the bifurcation stopped operating effectively after futures trading began to expand beyond agricultural commodities in the 1970s. *Id. See also* Jickling, "Merging the CFTC and the SEC?," 1.

73 *See* Romano, 283; Jickling, "Merging the CFTC and the SEC?," 3; Cunningham and Zaring, 50.

74 *See* Jickling, "Merging the CFTC and the SEC?," 3; US Dep't of the Treasury, 106. Some, however, were skeptical that merger would significantly reduce costs. *See* Markham, 605.

75 *See, e.g.,* Jickling, "Merging the CFTC and the SEC?," 3; US Gov't Accountability Off., GAO-16-175, 42; William J. Brodsky, "A Real Regulatory Redundancy," *Wall Street Journal*, October 19, 2007.

76 *See, e.g.,* Kai Kramer, "Aren't We Still in the 'Garden of the Forking Paths'? A Comment on Consolidation of the SEC and CFTC," 4 *Houston Business and Tax Law Journal* 410, 442–44 (2004).

77 *See* Volcker Alliance, Reshaping the Financial Regulatory System: Long Delayed, Now Crucial 22 (2015), https://volckeralliance.org; Brodsky, A19; US Gov't Accountability Off., GAO-16-175, 42–43.

78 *See* US Dep't of the Treasury, 109.

79 *Id.*

80 *Id.*

81 *See id.*; Cunningham and Zaring, 39–40.

82 *See* US Dep't of the Treasury, 108; US Gov't Accountability Off., GAO-16-175, 42.

83 Jickling, "The Merger of the SEC and the CFTC," 6.

84 US Dep't of the Treasury, 109.

85 The Financial Crisis Inquiry Report: Final Report of the National Commission on the Causes of the Financial and Economic Crisis in the United States xxiv, 48 (2011); US Dep't of the Treasury, 46–47; Duffy, "The Effective Regulation," 138.

86 US Dep't of the Treasury, 109; Steven Davidoff Solomon, "Paradigm Shift: Federal Securities Regulation in the New Millennium," 2 *Brooklyn Journal of Corporate Finance and Commercial Law* 339, 356 (2008); Cunningham and Zaring, 50; Kenneth W. Dam, "The Subprime Crisis and Financial Regulation: International and Comparative Perspectives," 10 *Chicago Journal of International Law* 581, 599 (2010); Jickling, "The Merger of the SEC and the CFTC," 4.

87 Jickling, "The Merger of the SEC and the CFTC," 4; *see also* Jickling, "Merging the CFTC and the SEC?," 1, 2–3.

88 *See, e.g.,* Brown, 377–80; Romano, 342.

89 *See, e.g.,* US Dep't of the Treasury, 109–13.

90 Davis, Polk and Wardwell LLP, "Summary of the Dodd-Frank Wall Street Reform and Consumer Protection Act, Enacted into Law on July 21, 2010," 52 (2010), www.davispolk.com.

91 SEC, Derivatives.

92 15 U.S.C. §8321(b) (2012).

93 *Id.* § 8341(3).

94 15 U.S.C. §§ 78c(a)(68)(D), 8302(a)(8) (2012). *See also* US Dep't of the Treasury, 52–53.

95 7 U.S.C. §6s(d) (2012); *see also* US Dep't of the Treasury, 53. Swaps includes credit default swaps, interest rate swaps, and total return swaps on a broad range of asset categories.

96 15 U.S.C. §78o-10(d). A security-based swap is a swap based on (1) a narrow-based security index, (2) a single security or loan, or (3) the occurrence, nonoccurrence, or extent of the occurrence of certain events relating to a single issuer of a security or the issuers of securities in a narrow-based security index. *Id.* § 78c(a)(68).

97 *Id.* § 78o-10(d). *See also* US Dep't of the Treasury, 53. Certain products that contain elements of both commodities contracts and securities, however, remain regulated by the SEC as securities. Davis, Polk and Wardwell LLP, "Summary of the Dodd-Frank," 54.

98 15 U.S.C. § 8302(b)(1), (b)(2) (2012). *See also* Davis, Polk and Wardwell LLP, "Summary of the Dodd-Frank," 54.

99 15 U.S.C. § 8302(f).

100 7 U.S.C. § 6b-1(a) (2012); 15 U.S.C. § 8302(a)(4). *See also* Davis, Polk and Wardwell LLP, "Summary of the Dodd-Frank," 61, 62.

101 15 U.S.C. § 8302(d)(1). *See also* SEC, Derivatives.

102 7 U.S.C. § 6b-1(d) (CFTC); 15 U.S.C. § 78o-10(*l*)(1)(D) (SEC). *See also* Davis, Polk and Wardwell LLP, "Summary of the Dodd-Frank," 54; SEC, Derivatives.

103 7 U.S.C. §§ 7(d)(23), 7(k)(3), 24(c)(7)(C) (2012). *See also* SEC, Derivatives.

104 15 U.S.C. § 8302(a)(8); *see also* US Gov't Accountability Off., GAO-16-175, 23. The SEC characterizes mixed swaps as "security-based swaps that also have a commodity component." 15 U.S.C. § 78c(a)(68)(D).

105 15 U.S.C. § 8302(d)(2)(D).

106 *Id.* § 8302(a)(8). The SEC and CFTC must also prescribe joint regulations on trade repository recordkeeping requirements (*id.* § 8302(d)(2)(B)) and books and records requirements for swap entities related to security-based swap agreements. *Id.* § 8302(d)(2)(C). The Financial Stability Oversight Council has authority to resolve conflict over any of these joint regulations. *Id.* § 8302(d)(3).

107 *Id.* § 8302(a)(1), (2). Though Dodd-Frank requires the agencies to treat "functionally or economically similar products or entities [. . .] in a similar manner," it also specifically declines to require them to be treated "in an identical manner." *Id.* § 8302(a)(7)(A), (B).

108 *Id.* § 8302(c)(1)(A). The two agencies must also consult the Federal Reserve Board on many of their joint and non-joint actions (*see, e.g.,* 12 U.S.C. § 5471(b) (2012)), and with other regulators on capital and margin rules (7 U.S.C. § 6s(e) (2012)) and promulgating their joint rules. 15 U.S.C. § 8302(a)(6) (2012).

109 "Memorandum of Understanding between the U.S. Securities and Exchange Commission and the U.S. Commodity Futures Trading Commission regarding Coordination in Areas of Common Regulatory Interest and Information Sharing" (June 28, 2018).

110 *See, e.g.,* Enhancing Investor Protection and the Regulation of Securities Markets: Testimony before Senate Comm. on Banking, Housing, and Urban Affairs, 10, 82, 96, 320, 322 (March 10, 2009).

111 *See* Randolph C. Snook, Executive Vice President of the Securities Industry and Financial Markets Association, Industry Perspectives on the Obama Administration's Financial Regulatory Reform Proposals, Hearing Before the House Comm. on Financial Services 104 (July 17, 2009); Damon A. Silvers, American Federation of Labor and Congress of Industrial Organizations, Enhancing Investor Protection and the Regulation of Securities Markets: Testimony before the Senate Comm. on Banking, Housing, and Urban Affairs, 326 (March 10, 2009).

112 Terrence A. Duffy, "Prepared Statement before the House Comm. on Agriculture, Hearing to Review Proposed Legislation by the U.S. Department of Treasury Regarding the Regulation of Over-the-Counter Derivatives Markets" 63, 138 (September 17, 22, 2009).

113 The Financial Crisis Inquiry Report, xxiv. This Commission was created by Congress and the President to examine the causes of the financial crisis.

114 Kenneth C. Griffin, Over-the-Counter Derivative: Modernizing Oversight to Increase Transparency and Reduce Risks: Hearing before Senate Subcomm. on Securities, Insurance, and Investment, Comm. on Banking, Housing, and Urban Affairs, 137 (Responses to Written Questions of Chairman Reed).

115 T. Timothy Ryan, Enhancing Investor Protection and the Regulation of Securities Markets: Statement before Senate Comm. on Banking, Housing, and Urban Affairs, 10 (March 10, 2009).

116 Richard Baker, Industry Perspectives on the Obama Administration's Financial Regulatory Reform Proposals, Hearing Before the House Comm. on Financial Services 159 (July 17, 2009).

117 Secretary Timothy F. Geithner, Department of the Treasury, The Administration's Proposal to Modernize the Financial Regulatory System: Hearing before Senate Comm. on Banking, Housing and Urban Affairs 57 (June 18, 2009).

118 *Id.*

119 Though creating similar parallel authority might make future consolidation easier, the move to exclusivity would not do so.

120 *See, e.g.,* Gary Gensler, Chairman, CFTC, Regulatory Perspectives on the Obama Administration's Financial Regulatory Reform Proposals, Part I, Hearing before House Comm. on Financial Services 54 (July 22, 2009).

121 Geithner, 78. *See also* Duffy, "Prepared Statement," 63.

122 Geithner, 78.

123 Patricia White, Associate Director, Division of Research and Statistics, Federal Reserve, Responses to Written Questions of Chairman Jack Reed, Over-the-Counter Derivatives: Modernizing Oversight to Increase Transparency and Reduce Risks: Hearing Before Subcomm. on Securities, Insurance, and Investment, Senate Comm. on Banking, Housing, and Urban Affairs 10 (June 22, 2009).

124 Memorandum of Understanding, 1.

125 Bipartisan Policy Center, "Dodd-Frank's Missed Opportunity," 12.

126 *See, e.g.,* Bipartisan Policy Center, "Dodd-Frank's Missed Opportunity," 5.

127 US Gov't Accountability Off., GAO-16-175, 46; Louise Bennetts, "Regulatory Fragmentation, the Balkanization of Financial Markets and the Competitiveness of the American Financial Services Sector," Statement before the House Subcomm. on Oversight and Investigations of the House Comm. on Financial Services, (March 4, 2014), www.cato.org.

128 US Gov't Accountability Off., GAO-16-175, 46.

129 Volcker Alliance, 22.

130 Alan Blinder, "Financial Entropy and the Optimality of Over-Regulation," in D. Evanoff, A. Haldane, and G. Kaufman (eds.), *The New International Financial System: Analyzing the Cumulative Impact of Regulatory Reform* 3, 16 (2016).

131 Volcker Alliance, 2; *see also* Bipartisan Policy Center, "Dodd-Frank's Missed Opportunity," 5.

132 Christian Johnson, "Regulatory Arbitrage, Extraterritorial Jurisdiction, and Dodd-Frank: The Implications of US Global OTC Derivative Regulation," 14 *Nevada Law Journal* 542 (2014).

133 US Gov't Accountability Off., GAO-16-175, 47.

134 *Id.,* 44–45.

135 *Id.,* 47.

136 *See* Bipartisan Policy Center, "Dodd-Frank's Missed Opportunity," 82.

137 Volcker Alliance, 22.

138 Mercatus Center, Dodd-Frank: What It Does and Why It's Flawed, 77 (Hester Peirce and James Broughel eds., 2013), http://mercatus.org.

139 US Gov't Accountability Off., GAO-16-175, 44–45; Macey, "Playing Nicely," 821, 833; Bennetts.

140 *See* chap. 6, § B.2.

141 *See* US Gov't Accountability Off., GAO-16-175, 47.

142 *See* chap. 6, § C.2.

143 Joel Seligman, "The SEC in a Time of Discontinuity," 95 *Virginia Law Review* 667, 673 (2009).

144 *See* chap. 6, §§ A.5, B.3.

145 *See, e.g.,* John C. Coffee, Jr., "Competition Versus Consolidation: The Significance of Organizational Structure in Financial and Securities Regulation," 50 *Business Lawyer* 450 (1995); Cunningham and Zaring, 51. Cunningham and Zaring do identify three or four approaches to financial regulation, but differentiate them as either fragmented, centralized, or consolidated. *See id.*, 42–44. *See also* Jickling, "The Merger of the SEC and the CFTC," 13–14.

146 *See, e.g.,* Jill E. Fisch, "Top Cop or Regulatory Flop? The SEC at 75," 95 *Virginia Law Review* 785, 788–89 (2009); Chilton.

147 *See* US Gov't Accountability Off., GAO-16-175, 120; Markham, 587.

148 *See chap. 6,* § A.3.

149 Arguably, in requiring the SEC and CFTC to coordinate over mixed swaps, Congress through Dodd-Frank implicitly considered the benefits of retaining the independence necessary for interagency competition to be outweighed by the advantages of such coordination between the two agencies.

150 *But see* Chilton (advocating in passing for a focus on increasing harmonization and improving coordination rather than consolidation, though even then not considering the potential tradeoffs of overlap or coordination).

151 *See, e.g.,* Duffy, 138.

152 *See, e.g.,* Yuliya Guseva, "Destructive Collectivism: Dodd-Frank Coordination and Clearinghouses," 37 *Cardozo Law Review* 1693, 1706–11 (2016).

153 *See, e.g.,* Romano, 283.

154 Jickling, "The Merger of the SEC and the CFTC," 9.

155 *See, e.g.,* John C. Coffee, Jr., "Enhancing Investor Protection and the Regulation of Securities Markets," Prepared statement before the Senate Comm. on Banking, Housing, and Urban Affairs, (March 10, 2009); Kenneth Rosen, "Cooperation Before Consolidation in Investor Protection," 90 *Tulane Law Review* 1211 (2016); Seligman, 673.

156 Markham, 552, 558–93.

157 *See* chap. 6, § B.2.; Rosen, 1227–34; Mary L. Schapiro, Chairman, SEC, SEC Oversight: Current State and Agenda: Hearings before the House Subcomm. on Capital Markets, Insurance, and Government Sponsored Enterprises, Comm. on Financial Services 43 (July 14, 2009).

158 Lynn E. Turner, Former Chief Accountant, SEC, Enhancing Investor Protection and the Regulation of Securities Markets: Prepared statement before Senate Comm. on Banking, Housing, and Urban Affairs 225, 236. Similarly, critics might (or might not) find that some form of coordination between the SEC and CFTC required by the Dodd-Frank Act is still worth it despite the lack of overlap.

159 *See, e.g.,* Jickling, "Merging the CFTC and the SEC?," 3.
160 *Id.,* 5.

CHAPTER 7: DIFFERENTIATING CENTRALIZATION AND
COORDINATION IN NATIONAL INTELLIGENCE AFTER 9/11

1 The term "intelligence community" is defined in 50 U.S.C. § 3003(4) (2012) to include the ODNI; the CIA; the NSA; the DIA; the Office of Intelligence and Analysis of the DHS; DoD offices conducting reconnaissance programs; and the intelligence elements of the armed forces, the FBI, the DEA, and the DOE.

2 This chapter focuses on conflation of concerns regarding inadequate coordination and excessive decentralization. However, conflation of other aspects of these dimensions is also possible, though less likely. For example, certain problems associated more appropriately with excessive decentralization, such as lost economies of scale, would be poorly addressed through greater coordination.

3 The chapter's emphasis is not on the intelligence community's planning for, formulation of, or implementation of responses to the information it generates, distributes, and analyzes.

4 These included many of the agencies included in the current statutory definition of the intelligence community. *See* Anne Joseph O'Connell, "The Architecture of Smart Intelligence: Structuring and Overseeing Agencies in the Post-9/11 World," 94 *California Law Review* 1655, 1660 (2006).

5 National Security Act of 1947, Pub. L. No. 80-253, § 102(d), 61 Stat. 495, 498.

6 Exec. Order No. 12333, United States Intelligence Activities, §§ 1.3(a)(1), 1.5(g), 1.8(a), 46 Fed. Reg. 59941, 59946 (Dec. 4, 1981). The order directed all agencies to give the CIA Director "access to all [intelligence] information." *Id.* § 1.6(a). It also required the Director to coordinate information analysis, ensuring "competitive analysis [. . .] so that diverse points of view are considered fully and differences of judgment within the Intelligence Community are brought to the attention of national policymakers." *Id.* § 1.5(k).

7 Pub. L. No. 80-253, § 102(d)-(e).

8 Throughout this book, we treat information compilation and dissemination as a single function meant to encapsulate those agency activities centered on assembling and distributing existing information, as those two activities typically operate in tandem. Nonetheless, as the book does for information generation, dissemination, and analysis, one might consider, if the tradeoffs might vary in a particular circumstance, further distinguishing information compilation (collection of information generated by diverse sources) and dissemination (distribution of that aggregated information) as separate functions.

9 O'Connell, 1661; Richard A. Posner, *Preventing Surprise Attacks: Intelligence Reform in the Wake of 9/11*, 99 (2005). For depictions of the authority of components of the intelligence community during the Cold War and as of 2005, see National Commission on Terrorist Attacks upon the United States, *The 9/11 Commission Report* 73–102, 407–8 (2004), https://9-11commission.gov, and Report of the

Comm'n on the Intelligence Capabilities of the United States Regarding Weapons of Mass Destruction 579–82 (March 31, 2005), https://fas.org, respectively.

10 *See* § 102 of the National Security Act of 1947 (codified at 50 U.S.C. § 3036(d) (2012)).

11 The DIA's role is "to provide coordination and reduce duplication among the military services' intelligence units." O'Connell, 1661 n.22.

12 Report of the Comm'n on the Intelligence Capabilities, 579–80; Dara Kay Cohen, Mariano-Florentino Cuéllar and Barry R. Weingast, "Crisis Bureaucracy: Homeland Security and the Political Design of Legal Mandates," 59 *Stanford Law Review* 673, 682 (2006).

13 That authority was derived from the Foreign Intelligence Surveillance Act of 1978, Pub. L. No. 95-511, 92 Stat. 1783.

14 National Commission on Terrorist Attacks, 80–81.

15 *See* Robert F. Blomquist, "Congressional Oversight of Counterterrorism and Its Reform," 11 *Roger Williams University Law Review* 1, 30 (2005); National Commission on Terrorist Attacks, 87–88, 142.

16 National Commission on Terrorist Attacks, 83.

17 *Id.*, 274–75.

18 This problem may have been due in part to legal barriers to interagency communication, such as the absence of any mechanism by which the FBI could share with the CIA evidence about foreign intelligence operations uncovered during a grand jury investigation. Craig S. Lerner, "Calling a Truce in the Culture Wars: From Enron to the CIA," 17 *Stanford Law and Policy Review* 277, 285 (2006). Some agencies performed poorly even aside from deficient interagency coordination. The 9/11 Commission Report, for example, criticized the FBI's intelligence collection, dissemination, and analysis mechanisms as "woefully inadequate." National Commission on Terrorist Attacks, 77.

19 Grant T. Harris, Note, "The CIA Mandate and the War on Terror," 23 *Yale Law and Policy Review* 529, 531 (2005).

20 Harris, 531 (quoting Rhodri Jeffreys-Jones, *The CIA and American Democracy* 32 (2d ed. 1998)).

21 *Id.*, 531–32.

22 *Id.*, 532.

23 *See generally* Thomas Fingar, "Office of the Director of National Intelligence: From Pariah to Piñata to Managing Partner," in *The National Security Enterprise: Navigating the Labyrinth* 186 (Roger Z. George and Harvey Rishikoff eds., 2d ed. 2017).

24 Lerner, 284. The State Department and the Pentagon also opposed the CIA's creation. Aziz Z. Huq, "Structural Constitutionalism as Counterterrorism," 100 *California Law Review* 887, 907 (2012).

25 Brian Z. Tamanaha, "'Are We Safer from Terrorism?' No, but We Can Be," 28 *Yale Law and Policy Review* 419, 428 (2010); *see also* National Commission on Terrorist Attacks, 267 (describing additional inadvertent lack of communication).

26 Harris 555; *see also* Patricia M. Wald, "Analysts and Policymakers: A Confusion of Roles?," 17 *Stanford Law and Policy Review* 241, 251 (2006) (discussing conflict over responsibility for gathering foreign intelligence on US soil). For a discussion of another example of how convergence of the jurisdictions of multiple agencies can affect their performance, see chap. 6, § C.2.

27 Harris, 555.

28 Report of the Comm'n on the Intelligence Capabilities, 297.

29 Lerner, 284.

30 *See* Helen Fessenden, "The Limits of Intelligence Reform," 84 *Foreign Affairs* 106, 107 (2005).

31 Cohen, Cuéllar, and Weingast, 684–85.

32 *Id.*, 687. Calls for centralization of authority also followed Pearl Harbor, leading to the CIA's creation. O'Connell, 1659 n.15.

33 Cohen, Cuéllar, and Weingast, 687–88.

34 *Id.*, 688–89.

35 *Id.*, 690–91, 723.

36 Pub. L. No. 107-296, 116 Stat. 2135. *See generally* Jonathan Thessin, "Department of Homeland Security," 40 *Harvard Journal on Legislation* 513 (2003).

37 Pub. L. No. 107-296, § 201(d)(10).

38 *Id.* § 201(d)(9).

39 *Id.* § 201(d)(1), (9). *See also* S. Rep. No. 107-175, at 12 (2002).

40 Pub. L. No. 107-296, § 201(d)(17).

41 *Id.* § 891(b)(10) (codified at 6 U.S.C.A. § 481(b)(10) (2012)).

42 "Homeland security information" includes information relating to existence, prevention, disruption, or responses to terrorist threats. 6 U.S.C. § 482(f)(1).

43 Pub. L. No. 107-296, § 891(b)(12).

44 6 U.S.C. § 482(a)(1)(A), (b)(1).

45 Thessin, 528.

46 Pub. L. No. 107-306, §§ 601–2, 604, 116 Stat. 2383, 2408 (2002).

47 National Commission on Terrorist Attacks, 328.

48 *Id.*, 80, 358.

49 *Id.*, 268.

50 *See* Fessenden, 117.

51 National Commission on Terrorist Attacks, 263, 267.

52 *Id.*, 408 ("The importance of all-source analysis cannot be overstated. Without it, it is not possible to 'connect the dots.'").

53 The Commission also criticized information generation by individual agencies. *See, e.g., id.*, 77 (charging that the FBI's information systems were "woefully inadequate").

54 *Id.*, 353.

55 *Id.*, 277.

56 *Id.*, 422; *see also id.*, 388 (concerning exit data for visas). Constraints on the release of information may also exist for legitimate reasons, such as source protection.

57 *Id.*, 417.

58 *Id.*, 353.

59 Others used different metaphors to suggest inadequate hierarchical coordination. *See, e.g.,* Project on National Security Reform, "Toward Integrating Complex National Mission: Lessons from the National Counterterrorism Center's Directorate of Strategic Operational Planning," 31 (February 2010), https://cdn1.nyt.com (describing counterterrorism as "an orchestra without a conductor"); Richard A. Posner, *Uncertain Shield: The U.S. Intelligence System in the Throes of Reform* 12–14 (2006) (stating that "the 9/11 Commission wanted the [DNI] to be like a corporate CEO").

60 Pub. L. No. 108-458, 118 Stat. 3638 (2004).

61 *See* O'Connell, 1730–32; Report of the Comm'n on the Intelligence Capabilities, 35; Fingar, 189; Posner, *Uncertain Shield*, 13–14.

62 Congress adopted many of the 9/11 Commission's recommendations. *See* Martin E. Halstuk and Eric B. Easton, "Of Secrets and Spies: Strengthening the Public's Right to Know About the CIA," 17 *Stanford Law and Policy Review* 353, 388 (2006).

63 50 U.S.C. § 3023(a)(1), (b) (2012).

64 For diagrams comparing the structure of the US intelligence system before and after IRTPA's adoption, see Posner, *Uncertain Shield*, 12–15.

65 50 U.S.C. § 3024(f)(1)(A)(ii) (2012).

66 *Id.* § 3024(b).

67 *Id.* § 3024(f)(6).

68 *Id.* § 3056(f)(1)(H).

69 *Id.* § 3056(f)(1)(D).

70 *Id.* § 3056(d)(1), (g)(1)(G).

71 *Id.* § 3024(c)(1)(B), (5)(A). "The DNI can direct money to those programs he thinks need the money the soonest." Fessenden, 114. IRTPA also authorizes the DNI to make unilateral transfers of money and personnel among agencies. *Id.* For a discussion of IRTPA's transfer of authority over budgetary and personnel matters to the DNI, see O'Connell, 1667–68.

72 50 U.S.C. § 3024(f)(1)(A)(i) (2012).

73 *Id.* § 3024(f)(1)(A)(ii). IRTPA precludes the DNI from "abrogat[ing] the statutory responsibilities" of departmental heads. Pub. L. No. 108-458, § 1018, 118 Stat. 3670–71. According to one source, Congress created a position with "a fancy title" but replicated "the structural weakness within the intelligence community pre-9/11." Jay Kramer, "The Director of National Intelligence and Congressional Oversight of the Intelligence Community: Much Needed Statutory Clarifications and Necessary Institutional Reforms," 20 *Kansas Journal of Law and Public Policy* 452, 466 (2011).

74 *See, e.g.,* 50 U.S.C. § 3024(g)(1).

75 *Id.* § 3024(r).

76 *Id.* § 3024(h)(1)(A)-(B).

77 *Id.* § 3024(h)(1)(C). *See also id.* § 3024 note (endorsing "alternative analysis (commonly referred to as 'red-team analysis'")).

78 *Id.* § 3024(h)(3).
79 The provision of IRTPA that defines the ODNI's duties does not even refer to coordination. *Id.* § 3025.
80 *See* Markle Found, Task Force, "Mobilizing Information to Prevent Terrorism: Accelerating Development of a Trusted Information Sharing Environment," 1 (2006), www.markle.org (concluding that "systematic [. . .] information sharing remains more of an aspiration than a reality").
81 *See* Tamanaha, 425.
82 *Id.*, 426.
83 *Id.* (noting "analysts' and collectors' desire to closely protect their most secret sources").
84 *See id.*, 428.
85 John D. Negroponte and Edward M. Wittenstein, "Urgency, Opportunity, and Frustration: Implementing the Intelligence Reform and Terrorism Prevention Act of 2004," 28 *Yale Law and Policy Review* 379, 392 (2010).
86 Tamanaha, 430; Negroponte and Wittenstein, 413.
87 Senator Susan Collins blamed inadequately coordinated information dissemination for the Boston event. Greg Miller, "Watch was urged for bomb suspect," *Washington Post*, April 25, 2013.
88 *See, e.g.*, Negroponte and Wittenstein, 415; Marshall Curtis Erwin, Congressional Research Serv., Intelligence Issues for Congress, CRS Report No. RL33539, 5 (2013), www.fas.org; Fingar, 192. In 2017, GAO removed the establishment of effective mechanisms for sharing terrorism-related information from its high-risk list because of "significant progress" in sharing such information among federal, state, local, tribal, international, and private-sector actors. US Gov't Accountability Off., GAO-17-317, High-Risk Series: Progress on Many High-Risk Areas, While Substantial Efforts Needed on Others 4 (2017).
89 *See, e.g.*, Negroponte and Wittenstein, 403; Fingar, 186 (noting persistence of problematic institutional attitudes and rivalries).
90 H.R. Rep. No. 108-724, pt. 1, 150 (2004).
91 *Id.*, 150.
92 *Id.*, 190 (additional views of Rep. Holt). Another member questioned the efficacy of "creat[ing] another bureaucracy at the top of the Intelligence Community, another stovepipe." *Id.*, 198 (dissenting views of Rep. LaHood).
93 H.R. Rep. No. 108-796, 242 (2004).
94 *See, e.g., id.*, 147, 149.
95 *See* Leonard J. Long, "Posner's Economic Reflections on U.S. Intelligence Reform," 24 *Queensland Law Reporter* 407, 421 (2006).
96 50 U.S.C. § 3024(r) (2012).
97 H.R. Rep. No. 108-724, pt. 1, at 143, 149.
98 *Id.*, 143.
99 *Id.*
100 *See, e.g., id.*, 147.

101 The 9/11 Commission also conflated the two dimensions, depicting redundancies within the intelligence community as a liability, in part because they decrease information sharing. O'Connell, 1658. But redundancy results from overlap, and inadequate information exchanges may result from poor coordination. Reducing overlap would not necessarily generate more coordinated information exchanges. Others have criticized interagency competition as inefficient, see, e.g., Negroponte and Wittenstein, 401, even though allocating distinct authority to the competing agencies can minimize duplicative effort while retaining competition in a function such as information analysis. The advantages of competition flow from independently structured decentralized agencies, not redundancy (i.e., overlap).

102 9/11 Commission Report, 409.

103 *Id.*, 404, 409.

104 *Id.*, 404.

105 Posner, *Preventing Surprise Attacks*, 153. Posner charged that the Commission ignored the "unalloyed disaster" of centralizing authority in the DHS and centralized control of illegal drugs in a drug "czar." *Id.*, 10, 50. *See also* Long, 421. For a discussion of the problems stemming from "the gargantuan new conglomeration" of agencies housed within the DHS, see Susan B. Glasser and Michael Grunwald, "Department's Mission Was Undermined from the Start," Washington Post, December 22, 2005.

106 Posner, *Preventing Surprise Attacks*, 199–201.

107 *See, e.g.* Fingar, 187.

108 Negroponte and Wittenstein, 384; *see also* Tamanaha, 423; William C. Banks, "The Death of FISA," 91 *Minnesota Law Review* 1209, 1243 n.228 (2007).

109 *See, e.g.*, National Commission on Terrorist Attacks, 327. The committee reports accompanying the HSA's adoption also reflect no indication that Congress considered different structures for generation, dissemination, and analysis of intelligence information. H.R. Rep. No. 107-609, 89–90 (2002); S. Rep. No. 107-175, 23–25 (2002). *See also* H.R. Rep. No. 107-796, 242 ("The conference report gives the DNI strong authority, [. . .] such as unambiguous authority to task collection and analysis.").

110 National Commission on Terrorist Attacks, 401.

111 *Id.*, 406.

112 *See, e.g.*, H.R. Rep. No. 108-274, pt. 1, 143 (2004) (explaining that to achieve effective coordination of foreign and domestic intelligence functions, "the [DNI] will have clear authority over Intelligence Community [. . .] collection activities, all-source analysis, information classification, information sharing, and information management technologies and standards"). The Committee identified "information sharing" and analysis as separate functions, *id.*, 150, but did not assess whether their performance should be structured in the same way or differently. It also noted the value of "analytic competition and allowing room for diversity," *id.*, 153, but did not explain how IRTPA's allocations would promote that goal or whether alternative structures might have done so more effectively.

113 Thessin, 528–29.

114 *Id.*, 529.

115 *See* Huq, 909 (arguing that IRTPA "failed to address excessive interservice diffusion of intelligence functions" and that the Pentagon "actively resisted" the DNI's coordinating efforts).

116 Posner, *Preventing Surprise Attacks*, 43.

117 Others analyzing IRTPA appear to have conflated the centralization and coordination dimensions in other ways, such as by attributing an increase in the risk of groupthink to greater centralization. *E.g.*, O'Connell, 1676. But decentralization by itself does not protect against groupthink; a decentralized but heavily coordinated allocation may also be susceptible. Groupthink tends to result from insufficient independence among decentralized decisionmakers.

118 As Posner put it, diversity contributes to "a broader range" of analytical perspectives. Posner, *Preventing Surprise Attacks*, 155.

119 Tamanaha, 429; *see also* Posner, *Uncertain Shield*, 208.

120 Lerner, 289; O'Connell, 1731.

121 *See* Lerner, 289 (arguing that "duplicative agencies [. . .] may end up doing the same thing, but this is precisely the way other fail-safe institutions, like nuclear power plants and air traffic control systems, work").

122 *See* O'Connell, 1677–78, 1731.

123 Cohen, Cuéllar, and Weingast, 753; *but cf.* Posner, *Uncertain Shield*, 79 (arguing that layering a new bureaucracy over intelligence agencies may diffuse responsibility).

124 Posner, *Uncertain Shield*, 63–64.

125 O'Connell, 1688–89.

126 *Cf.* Lerner, 289 (noting comparative advantages of different agencies engaged in paramilitary activities).

127 *See* O'Connell, 1676.

128 *See* Posner, *Uncertain Shield*, 60 (discussing "specialized intelligence capabilities").

129 Indeed, combining inconsistent missions in a single organization may create diseconomies of scale. Posner, *Preventing Surprise Attacks*, 150.

130 *See, e.g.*, Elimma C. Ezeani, "Responding to Homegrown Terrorism: The Case of Boko Haram," 22 *Annual Survey of International and Comparative Law* 1, 17 (2017).

131 *See* Posner, *Preventing Surprise Attacks*, 47 (arguing that the 9/11 Commission "was unaware of the benefits of diversity"); Cohen, Cuéllar, and Weingast, 752–53.

132 *See* Tamanaha, 429; *cf.* Cohen, Cuéllar, and Weingast, 711 (noting that centralization can make an agency "harder to manage" and that "sheer size" can frustrate coordination efforts). The latter point suggests that choices along one dimension can affect the viability of choices along another.

133 Posner, *Preventing Surprise Attacks*, 144, 150.

134 Posner, *Uncertain Shield*, 71.

135 *See* Posner, *Preventing Surprise Attacks*, 142 (discussing the need to pool fragmentary data to assess threats accurately).

136 *Id.*, 145–46.

137 Budgeting and planning may also benefit from coordination. *Id.*, 48.

138 *See id.*, 153–54; Project on National Security Reform Guiding Coalition, "Legal Affairs Roundtable Series on National Security Transformation," 135 (2011), www .americanbar.org.

139 O'Connell, 1731 ("Analysis of collected information seems the most competitive of the community's tasks and prone to group-think.").

140 *Id.*, 1658; *see also* Posner, *Uncertain Shield*, 60.

141 Erwin, 4. CRS suggests that balancing unnecessary redundancy (which results from overlap) and retention of competitive analysis (which is a goal of independent allocations of authority) poses continuing challenges. But policymakers can avoid redundancy through more distinct authority, while allowing multiple agencies to compete in information analysis. The bigger challenge may be balancing eliminating redundancy and preserving a safety net.

142 Lerner, 290.

143 This kind of high-level aggregation and review of the analytical products of individual agencies may counter the possibility that an agency may discount a "rival" agency's analysis due to distrust or reluctance to assist a perceived competitor's efforts.

144 *See* chap. 2, § C.1.

145 50 U.S.C. § 3024(h)(4) (2012).

146 *See* Posner, *Preventing Surprise Attacks*, 157–58.

CHAPTER 8: DIFFERENTIATING COORDINATION AND OVERLAP IN BANKING REGULATION

1 *See, e.g.*, Veronica Root, "Coordinating Compliance Incentives," 102 *Cornell Law Review* 1003, 1029 (2017) (noting that "the traditional concern regarding inter-agency coordination is with 'overlapping delegations of power'"). Others have noted the risk of conflating different features of authority and sought to avoid doing so. *See, e.g.*, Daniel A. Farber and Anne Joseph O'Connell, "Agencies as Adversaries," 105 *California Law Review* 1375, 1384 n.54 (2017) (professing a desire to "resist the impulse to conflate conflict and fragmentation," attributing conflict to various forms of "adversarial" coordination, and arguing that use of the term fragmentation to describe division of authority is often unclear).

2 Increasing coordination instead of creating more distinct authority, on the other hand, may not be as effective as distinct authority at minimizing administrative costs or addressing risks of a regulatory commons or conflicting regulation. Choosing to restructure along one dimension rather than another inevitably involves making such tradeoffs.

3 Conflicting regulation occurs when a regulated entity is subject to multiple regulatory mandates that are either impossible to comply with simultaneously or whose objectives are incompatible.

4 Non-uniformity (or inconsistency) may occur in two contexts. First, it may occur when regulatory mandates apply differently to multiple regulated entities (such as

depository institutions) that provide similar services or engage in similar activities, but each of which is subject to a different regulator. Second, it may also occur if a single regulated entity is subject to multiple mandates that do not conflict with one another. If a regulated entity is subject to two sets of performance standards, one of which is more stringent than the other, the mandates lack uniformity (or consistency) but do not necessarily conflict (though may be viewed as conflicting if each mandate reflects an effort to strike a balance among competing values).

5   Other examples of mismatched regulatory solutions that may be a byproduct of conflating these dimensions might be identifying (1) excessive coordination as a problem but requiring more (or less) overlap, (2) insufficient coordination as a problem but requiring more overlap, or (3) too much overlap as a problem but requiring less coordination.

6   Financial regulation involves "oversight over financial institutions' financial condition and risk management practices" to ensure "the safe and sound operations of [. . .] financial institutions." US Dep't of the Treasury, "Blueprint for a Modernized Financial Regulatory Structure," 157 (2008), www.treasury.gov.

7   "Systemic risk is risk to an entire financial system or market, as opposed to the collapse of one firm within that market." Roberta S. Karmel, "The Controversy over Systemic Risk Regulation," 35 *Brooklyn Journal of International Law* 823, 825 (2010).

8   Pub. L. No. 111-203, §§ 101–76, 124 Stat. 1376, 1391–1442 (2010). Title I of the Dodd-Frank Wall Street Reform and Consumer Protection Act is individually known as the Financial Stability Act of 2010.

9   As § E.1.c below explains, whether coordination promotes or frustrates the safety net and capture resistance benefits of overlapping authority depends on both the risks that a safety net is designed to address as well as the form of coordination chosen.

10 *See, e.g.*, Jody Freeman and Jim Rossi, "Agency Coordination in Shared Regulatory Space," 125 *Harvard Law Review* 1131, 1185 (2012) ("Arbitrage refers to the possibility that regulated entities will seek to take advantage of situations of shared or overlapping authority to get the best deal possible, or play agencies against one another in an effort to drive regulatory standards downward.").

11 US Gov't Accountability Off., GAO-09-216, Financial Regulation: A Framework for Crafting and Assessing Proposals to Modernize the Outdated US Financial Regulatory System 4 (2009).

12 *See* Robert F. Weber, "Structural Regulation as Antidote to Complexity Capture," 49 *American Business Law Journal* 643, 663 (2012). This kind of regulation, which dates back to the 1860s, "is believed to contribute to a more stable broader economy." Mark Jickling and Edward V. Murphy, Congressional Research Serv., R40249, Who Regulates Whom? An Overview of US Financial Supervision, Summary, 6 (December 8, 2010).

13 US Gov't Accountability Off., GAO-16-175, Complex and Fragmented Structure Could Be Streamlined to Improve Effectiveness 10 (Table 1).

14 Bipartisan Policy Center, Economic Policy Program, Financial Regulatory Reform Initiative, "Dodd-Frank's Missed Opportunity: A Road Map for a More Effective Regulatory Architecture" 30 (2014), https://bipartisanpolicy.org (noting dozens of restructuring proposals dating to the 1930s).

15 The US has an unusually large number of prudential regulators. Robert C. Hockett, Oversight of the Financial Stability Oversight Council: Due Process and Transparency in Non-Bank SIFI Designations, Testimony before the House Subcomm. on Oversight and Investigations, Comm. on Financial Services 7 (November 19, 2015), https://papers.ssrn.com. For depictions of their overlapping jurisdictions, see US Gov't Accountability Off., GAO-16-375SP, "2016 Annual Report: Additional Opportunities to Reduce Fragmentation, Overlap, and Duplication and Achieve Other Financial Benefits," 8, 64 (2016). For a history of federal regulation of depository institutions, see US Dep't of the Treasury, "Blueprint," 32–37.

16 Michael S. Barr, Howell E. Jackson, and Margaret E. Tahyar, *Financial Regulation: Law and Policy* 159 (2016).

17 US Gov't Accountability Off., GAO-16-175, 105. FDIC also oversees insured state-chartered banks that are not members of the Federal Reserve. *Id.*

18 US Gov't Accountability Off., GAO-16-175, 105–6.

19 Pub. L. No. 101-78, 103 Stat. 183.

20 US Gov't Accountability Off., GAO-16-175, 106.

21 Prudential supervision is meant to assure that depository institutions are adequately capitalized and liquid, do not take excessive risks, and "are otherwise safe and sound." Bipartisan Policy Center, "Dodd-Frank's Missed Opportunity," 20.

22 *See, e.g.,* US Gov't Accountability Off., GAO-09-216, 22; US Gov't Accountability Off., GAO-05-61, Financial Regulation: Industry Changes Prompt Need to Reconsider US Regulatory Structure 8 (2005).

23 Jickling and Murphy, Summary, 6.

24 US Dep't of the Treasury, "Blueprint," 40; Jickling and Murphy, 15.

25 US Dep't of the Treasury, "Blueprint," 41; US Gov't Accountability Off., GAO-16-175, 17 n.23. The Federal Deposit Insurance Fund is designed primarily for resolving (i.e., seizing and liquidating or selling the assets of) failed or failing institutions. Jickling and Murphy, 15; Cheryl D. Block, "A Continuum Approach to Systemic Risk and Too-Big-to-Fail," 6 *Brooklyn Journal of Corporate, Financial and Commercial Law* 289, 329 (2012).

26 US Dep't of the Treasury, "Blueprint," 41.

27 Jickling and Murphy, 16.

28 State as well as federal regulators may charter and supervise depository institutions. Jickling and Murphy, 40; Hockett, 7.

29 Jickling and Murphy, 16. FRB acts as the "umbrella regulator for financial holding companies." *Id.* FDIC is also the primary prudential regulator for state savings banks. US Dep't of the Treasury, "Blueprint," 41.

30 US Gov't Accountability Off., GAO-09-216, 9, 11.

31 Block, 298; *see also id.*, 328.

32 US Gov't Accountability Off., GAO-05-61, 31–32 (2005); *see also* Block, 316.

33 Bipartisan Policy Center, "Dodd-Frank's Missed Opportunity," 20.

34 US Gov't Accountability Off., GAO-09-216, 6–7 (Figure 1) lists and describes the relevant statutes.

35 *See, e.g.*, John C. Coffee, Jr. and Hillary A. Sale, "Redesigning the SEC: Does the Treasury Have a Better Idea?," 95 *Virginia Law Review* 707, 716 (2009).

36 US Gov't Accountability Off., GAO-05-61, 10, 15–16.

37 Bank charter types include commercial banks, thrifts, credit unions, and industrial loan companies. US Gov't Accountability Off., GAO-08-32, 6–7 (2007), "Industry Trends Continue to Challenge the Federal Regulatory Structure"; *see also* Barr, Jackson and Tahyar, 165 (describing the differences).

38 Pub L. No. 109-351, § 1002, 120 Stat. 1996, 2009.

39 US Gov't Accountability Off., GAO-08-32, 2.

40 *Id.*, 1.

41 US Gov't Accountability Off., GAO-16-175, 34–35.

42 *See, e.g.*, Bipartisan Policy Center, "Dodd-Frank's Missed Opportunity," 21; US Dep't of the Treasury, "Blueprint," 1, 28, 89; Harvey L. Pitt, "Bringing Financial Services Regulation into the Twenty-First Century," 25 *Yale Journal on Regulation* 315, 321 (2008); John L. Douglas, "The Role of a Banking System in Nation-Building," 60 *Maine Law Review* 511, 527 (2008).

43 *See* US Gov't Accountability Off., GAO-08-32, 21; *see also id.*, 18 (discussing how product convergence helped create blurred jurisdictional boundaries, conflicting requirements, and competitive imbalances).

44 *See, e.g.*, Rose Marie Kushmeider, "The US Federal Financial Regulatory System: Restructuring Federal Bank Regulation," 17(4) *FDIC Banking Rev.* 1, 7 (2005), www.fdic.gov.

45 *See* US Gov't Accountability Off., GAO-16-175, 31. For example, lenders were subject to different approaches by prudential regulators screening data to determine whether they violated fair lending laws. *Id.*, 33. *See also* Lawrence A. Cunningham and David Zaring, "The Three or Four Approaches to Financial Regulation: A Cautionary Analysis against Exuberance in Crisis Response," 78 *George Washington University Law Review* 39, 82–83 (2009).

46 US Gov't Accountability Off., GAO-16-175, 31–32.

47 *Id.*, 32–33. *See also* US Dep't of the Treasury, "Blueprint," 172; Eric A. Posner and E. Glen Weyl, "Benefit-Cost Paradigms in Financial Regulation," 43 *Journal of Legal Studies* S1, S11–12 (2014).

48 2 Comm'n on Organization of the Executive Branch of the Government, Regulatory Commissions, Appendix N, Task Force Report on Regulatory Commissions, 116 (1949) (recommending possible combination in one agency of all federal bank supervisory activities). Congress created the Hoover Commission to help

eliminate duplication and overlap of government functions. Pub. L. No. 80-162, §§ 9(2)-(3), 10, 61 Stat. 246 (1947).

49 Jickling and Murphy, 1; US Dep't of the Treasury, "Blueprint," 37.

50 Jickling and Murphy, 34–35.

51 US Gov't Accountability Off., GAO-08-32, 30.

52 Jickling and Murphy, 7.

53 Arthur E. Wilmarth, Jr., "The Financial Services Industry's Misguided Quest to Undermine the Consumer Financial Protection Bureau," 31 *Review of Banking and Financial Law* 881, 933 (2012); Barr, Jackson and Tahyar, 176.

54 Barr, Jackson and Tahyar, 176; *see also* Kushmeider, 8; US Gov't Accountability Off., GAO-16-175, 61; *see also* US Dep't of the Treasury, "Financial Regulatory Reform: A New Foundation: Rebuilding Financial Supervision and Regulation," 5 (2009), www.treasury.gov (arguing that regulatory fragmentation allowed depository institutions "to shop for the regulator of their choice").

55 Some observers apparently do. *See, e.g.,* Edward J. Kane, "Regulatory Structure in Futures Markets: Jurisdictional Competition Among the SEC, the CFTC, and other Agencies," National Bureau of Economic Research, Working Paper No. 1331, 5, 30 (1984). Thus, the pre-Dodd-Frank regime has some defenders.

56 Coffee and Sale, 725–26.

57 The Treasury Department's 2009 report discusses contributing factors. *See* US Dep't of the Treasury, "Financial Regulatory Reform"; *see also* Barr, Jackson and Tahyar, 58–70; Coffee and Sale, 731–49 (surveying "what went wrong").

58 Barr, Jackson and Tahyar, 63.

59 US Gov't Accountability Off., GAO-16-175, 114.

60 Bipartisan Policy Center, "Dodd-Frank's Missed Opportunity," 15, 61; "Secretary Geithner Introduces Financial Stability Plan," US Dep't of Treasury Press Release, TG-18 (February 10, 2009), www.treasury.gov.

61 The relevant portions of Dodd-Frank are at Pub. L. No. 111-203, §§ 101–56, 124 Stat. 1376 (2010).

62 Jickling and Murphy, 3. Dodd-Frank abolished OTS, but split authority to oversee thrifts among OCC, FDIC, and FRB. US Gov't Accountability Off., GAO-16-175, 15, 37.

63 Non-banks "offer loans or other sources of capital, but do not have a bank charter and do not rely on deposits for their own funding." Edward V. Murphy, Cong. Research Serv., R42083, Financial Stability Oversight Council: A Framework to Mitigate Systemic Risk 2 (2013), https://fas.org. For a description of FSOC's purposes and duties, see Pub. L. No. 111-203, § 112(a)(1); S. Rep. No. 111-176, 47 (2010). *See generally* Donald N. Lamson and Hilary Allen, "The Financial Stability Oversight Council: Completely New or Déjà Vu?," *Banking Rep. (BNA)* (May 24, 2011).

64 Pub. L No. 111-203, § 213(a). *See also* S. Rep. No. 111-176, 48 (2010); Murphy, 9.

65 S. Rep. No. 111-176, 47 (2010).

66 Jickling and Murphy, 3; *see also* S. Rep. No. 111-176, 2–3, 47 (2010); H.R. Rep. No. 111-517, 865 (2010). Before Dodd-Frank, no federal agency was responsible for analyzing risks to the financial system as a whole. *See* Block, 316 n.131.

67 These include all of the pre-Dodd-Frank prudential regulators (except OTS), as well as the Treasury Department, the SEC, the CFTC, CFPB, and, as non-voting members, various state officials. Pub. L. No. 111-203, § 111(b).

68 Pub. L. No. 111-203, §§ 152–153; Bipartisan Policy Center, "Dodd-Frank's Missed Opportunity," 15.

69 Pub. L. No. 111-203, § 120(a).

70 *Id.*, § 112(a)(2).

71 Jickling and Murphy, 24. FSOC's designation of a SIFI is binding in that it is a prerequisite to FRB's application of heightened prudential regulatory standards.

72 Pub. L. No. 111-203, § 120(c)(2).

73 The Volcker Alliance, "Reshaping the Financial Regulatory System: Long Delayed, Now Crucial," 1 (2015), www.volckeralliance.org; *see also id.*, 10, 12; Block, 328 n.191.

74 Volcker Alliance, 3.

75 *See* US Gov't Accountability Off., GAO-16-175, 30.

76 *See* Volcker Alliance, 1; US Gov't Accountability Off., GAO-16-175, ii; Hockett, 8.

77 *See* US Dep't of Treasury, "A Financial System that Creates Economic Opportunities: Banks and Credit Unions" 30 (2017), www.treasury.gov; *see also* US Gov't Accountability Off., GAO-16-175, 63. Similar criticisms have been made about the creation of DHS. *See, e.g.*, Dara Kay Cohen, Mariano-Florentino Cuéllar and Barry R. Weingast, "Crisis Bureaucracy: Homeland Security and the Political Design of Legal Mandate," 59 *Stanford Law Review* 673, 742 (2006); Freeman and Rossi, 1153–54.

78 GA0-16-175, iii.

79 *Id.*, 36–37.

80 *Id.*, 34–35, 75, 78–79; Kushmeider, 7.

81 US Gov't Accountability Off., GAO-16-175, 86.

82 *Id.*, ii, 31.

83 *Id.*, 37.

84 *Id.*, 62–63.

85 Hockett, 10.

86 US Gov't Accountability Off., GAO-16-175, 62; Saule T. Omarova, "The Dodd-Frank Act: A New Deal for a New Age?," 15 *North Carolina Banking Institute* 83, 88 (2011).

87 IMF, *Financial Sector Assessment Program: Detailed Assessment of Observance of the Basel Core Principles for Effective Banking Supervision*, IMF Country Report No. 15/89, 5 (2015), www.imf.org; *see also* Bipartisan Policy Center, "Dodd-Frank's Missed Opportunity," 47 (diagram showing remaining "overlapping mandates and requirements").

88 Volcker Alliance, 20–21.

89 *Id.*, 2 (quoting Henry M. Paulson, Jr., *On the Brink: Inside the Race to Stop the Collapse of the Global Financial System* (2013)).

90 US Gov't Accountability Off., GAO-05-61, 113; *see also* Andrew Godwin, Timothy Hose and Ian Ramsay, "A Jurisdictional Comparison of the Twin Peaks Model of Financial Regulation," 18 *Journal of Banking Regulation* 103, 123 (2017).

91 *See, e.g.*, US Gov't Accountability Off., GAO-08-32, 28 (recognizing argument that competition among prudential regulators allowed financial institutions "to offer a diverse range of products and services").

92 *See* Karmel, 838.

93 *See, e.g.*, H.R. 1227, Bank Regulatory Consolidation and Reform Act of 1993, 103rd Cong. (1993–94); *see also* US Dep't of the Treasury, "Financial Regulatory Reform," 22.

94 US Gov't Accountability Off., GAO-05-61, 76–78, 129–30.

95 *Id.*, 113; US Dep't of the Treasury, "Blueprint," 141.

96 *See* US Gov't Accountability Off., GAO-09-216, 55. Equating centralization with reduction of overlap risks conflating the two dimensions and masking the trade-offs involved in minimizing overlap by movement along two different dimensions. *See also* chap. 6.

97 US Dep't of the Treasury, "Blueprint"; US Gov't Accountability Off., GAO-09-216, 55. One critique of the pre-Dodd-Frank regime was that it was difficult for any agency to track risks across charter types or financial market sectors. *See* US Gov't Accountability Off., GAO-05-61, 124.

98 *See* US Gov't Accountability Off., GAO-05-61, 131.

99 Jickling and Murphy, 3.

100 See Michael W. Taylor, "Regulatory Reform in the U.K.," 18 *North Carolina Banking Institute* 227, 228 (2013).

101 *Id.*, 235; *see also* Hilary J. Allen, "Financial Stability Regulation as Indirect Investor/Consumer Protection Regulation: Implications for Regulatory Mandates and Structure," 90 *Tulane Law Review* 1113, 1128 (2016); Arthur E. Wilmarth, Jr., "Turning a Blind Eye: Why Washington Keeps Giving in to Wall Street," 81 *University of Cincinnati Law Review* 1283, 1397 (2013).

102 *See* US Gov't Accountability Off., GAO-09-216, 56; Hockett, 8; US Gov't Accountability Off., GAO-05-61, 123.

103 Hockett, 8.

104 US Dep't of the Treasury, "Blueprint," 141.

105 *See* Freeman and Rossi, 1148.

106 Bipartisan Policy Center, "Dodd-Frank's Missed Opportunity," 11; *see also id.*, 30 (referring to inertia and turf battles).

107 *See* Cunningham and Zaring, 99–100.

108 Volcker Alliance, 12.

109 US Gov't Accountability Off., GAO-16-175, iii, 66, 81–85; Volcker Alliance, 18.

110 Pub. L. No. 111-203, § 120(c)(2); Bipartisan Policy Center, "Dodd-Frank's Missed Opportunity," 37.

111 Arthur E. Wilmarth, Jr., "A Two-Tiered System of Regulation Is Needed to Preserve the Viability of Community Banks and Reduce the Risks of Megabanks," 2015 *Michigan State Law Review* 249, 323.

112 Seletha R. Butler, "Business Ethics: Conceptualize Governing with the Ethic of Care and Justice," 12 *New York University Journal of Law and Business* 99, 105 (2015).

113 *See* Volcker Alliance, 18–19.

114 Pub. L. No. 111-203, § 619 (§ 13(b)(1)(A)-(B)). *See* "Prohibitions and Restrictions on Proprietary Trading and Certain Interests in, and Relationships With, Hedge Funds and Private Equity Funds," 79 Fed. Reg. 5536 (January 13, 2014). Regulators subsequently further weakened the Rule (Wilmarth, "A Two-Tiered System," 327), and have proposed to weaken it still further. "Proposed Revisions to Prohibitions and Restrictions on Proprietary Trading and Certain Interests in, and Relationships With, Hedge Funds and Private Equity Funds," 83 Fed. Reg. 33432 (July 17, 2018).

115 Wilmarth, "A Two-Tiered System," 328.

116 US Gov't Accountability Off., GAO-16-175, 31.

117 Wilmarth, "A Two-Tiered System," 333; *see also id.*, 339.

118 Arthur E. Wilmarth, "The Dodd-Frank Act's Expansion of State Authority to Protect Consumers of Financial Services," 36 *Journal of Corporate Law* 893, 908 (2011).

119 Volcker Alliance, 27.

120 *See, e.g.*, US Gov't Accountability Off., GAO-16-175, 13; US Gov't Accountability Off., GAO-08-32, 18.

121 Kane, 30; Mark Jickling, "The Merger of the SEC and the CFTC: A Pro/Con Analysis?," Cong. Research Serv. 90-222, 10 (1990).

122 For depictions of the overlapping jurisdictions of prudential regulators after Dodd-Frank, see US Gov't Accountability Off., GAO-16-175, 14 (Table 2), 19 (Figure 3); Jickling and Murphy, 4.

123 Bipartisan Policy Center, "Dodd-Frank's Missed Opportunity," 28–29.

124 *See* US Gov't Accountability Off., GAO-05-61, 129–30; US Gov't Accountability Off., GAO-08-32, 9–10; Barr, Jackson and Tahyar, 75.

125 US Gov't Accountability Off., GAO-08-32, 40.

126 US Dep't of the Treasury, "Blueprint," 27; Volcker Alliance, 14.

127 US Dep't of the Treasury, "Blueprint," 27.

128 *Id.*, 27–28.

129 US Dep't of the Treasury, "Financial Regulatory Reform," 22.

130 US Gov't Accountability Off., GAO-05-61, 130.

131 An "objectives-based approach" focuses on regulatory goals by "addressing particular market failures." US Dep't of the Treasury, "Blueprint," 13; Coffee and Sale, 723–24.

132 US Dep't of the Treasury, "Blueprint," 137–38. For an evaluation of this proposal, see Cunningham and Zaring, 74–83.

133 US Dep't of the Treasury, "Blueprint," 157; *see also* US Dep't of the Treasury, "Financial Regulatory Reform," 21.

134 *See* US Dep't of the Treasury, "Blueprint," 139, 142, 146; *see also* US Gov't Account-ability Off., GAO-08-32, 43–44.

135 US Gov't Accountability Off., GAO-05-61, 130; Barr, Jackson and Tahyar, 76.

136 Barr, Jackson and Tahyar, 76; US Gov't Accountability Off., GAO-05-61, 130.

137 US Gov't Accountability Off., GAO-08-32, 38.

138 Barr, Jackson and Tahyar, 76–77.

139 US Gov't Accountability Off., GAO-05-61, 130. The creation of distinct authority need not impair beneficial competition among regulators if they are allowed to exercise that authority independently of one another. A regulatory innovation applicable to one product or sector might prove attractive to a regulator exercising distinct authority over another product or sector, even if the innovation would need to be massaged to fit a different regulatory context.

140 *See, e.g.,* US Gov't Accountability Off., GAO-05-61, 75–76 (1994 Treasury De-partment proposal). The European Union has attempted functional allocation of prudential regulation. *See* European Banking Authority, "About Us," http://www.eba.europa.eu/ (accessed December 18, 2018); Jens Dammann, "The Bank-ing Union: Flawed by Design," 45 *Georgetown Journal of International Law* 1057, 1074 (2014).

141 *Cf.* US Dep't of Treasury, "A Financial System," 30 (recommending "more clearly defined regulatory mandates"). Changes over time in the services regulated firms provide or the environment in which they operate pose a risk that the lines of distinct authority as initially drawn may become problematic.

142 Basel Committee on Banking Supervision, "Core Principles for Effective Banking Supervision," 21 (2012), www.bis.org.

143 *Cf.* Cunningham and Zaring, 51.

144 Creating distinct authority would not have been tailored to address inconsistent treatment by multiple regulators of similarly situated depository institutions be-cause each regulator could still have exercised its distinct, independent authority to adopt regulatory requirements that varied from co-regulators' efforts. Certain forms of coordination would have been more appropriate responses to reducing such risks of inconsistency.

145 Allocation of authority along the coordination–independence dimension can affect the regulatory safety nets that overlapping authority is capable of provid-ing in different ways. Coordinated authority may protect against the risk that no regulator will address a problem if the coordination results in a division of responsibility among co-regulators that assures that no risk remains outside the purview of all regulators. Independent authority, however, is likely better situated to assure that one regulator will address a risk that a co-regulator with overlap-ping authority neglects. In addition, the type of coordination matters, as the analysis in this chapter of the limited nature of FSOC's authority demonstrates. Coordination via an interagency council may increase certain risks of regulatory capture but hierarchical forms of coordination (e.g., requiring another agency's concurrence) may decrease it.

146 *See also* Jill Fisch and Eric Roiter, "A Floating NAV for Money Market Funds: Fix or Fantasy?," 2012 *University of Illinois Law Review* 1003, 1027–28 (2012); Wilmarth, "A Two-Tiered System," 336.

147 "Historically, states serving as a laboratory for experiment justified the preservation of a state banking system." US Dep't of the Treasury, "Blueprint," 160.

148 *Id.*, 180.

149 Wilmarth, "The Dodd-Frank Act's Expansion," 948.

150 *Id.*, 949–50.

151 *See* US Dep't of the Treasury, "Blueprint," 180. *See, e.g.,* 12 U.S.C.A. § 25b(i) (2012) (authorizing only the OCC to exercise direct administrative oversight over national banks, but allowing state attorneys general to *enforce* non-preempted state laws against banks).

152 US Gov't Accountability Off., GAO-09-216, 57.

153 *See* chap. 8, § B.

154 *See* chap. 2, § B.2.

155 Bipartisan Policy Center, "Dodd-Frank's Missed Opportunity," 30.

156 *See* Catherine M. Sharkey, "Agency Coordination in Consumer Protection," 2013 *University of Chicago Legal Forum* 329, 334; US Gov't Accountability Off., GAO-16-175, 13.

157 Todd S. Aagaard, "Regulatory Overlap, Overlapping Fields, and Statutory Discontinuities," 29 *Virginia Environmental Law Journal* 237, 294 (2011); US Gov't Accountability Off., GAO-09-216, 73.

158 Volcker Alliance, 4; Cunningham and Zaring, 112.

159 *See, e.g.,* Brett H. McDonnell, "The Promise and Perils of Top-Down Capital Regulation," 55 *Washburn Law Journal* 385, 389 (2016); John H. Cochrane, "Challenges for Cost-Benefit Analysis of Financial Regulation," 43 *Journal of Legal Studies* S63, S73 (2014); Erik F. Gerding, "The Dialectics of Bank Capital: Regulation and Regulatory Capital Arbitrage," 55 *Washburn Law Journal* 357, 358 (2016); Zachary J. Gubler, "Public Choice Theory and the Private Securities Market," 91 *North Carolina Law Review* 745, 807 (2013); Wulf A. Kaal, "Hedge Fund Regulation Via Basel III," 44 *Vanderbilt Journal of Transnational Law* 389, 449 (2011).

160 As noted in the introduction to this chapter, a strong form of coordination would have been capable of preserving the safety net and anti-capture benefits of overlapping authority, such as by requiring a consensus or super-majority of all regulators before any one could implement regulatory constraints below an agreed upon baseline.

161 *See* Freeman and Rossi, 1186 (postulating that "it is conceivable that where collective-action problems among the agencies are acute, as when each possesses veto power, capturing even one agency could disable a larger regulatory enterprise"). Professors Freeman and Rossi contend that arbitrage risks stemming from overlapping authority may be controlled through

greater coordination by making it difficult for agencies to act unilaterally without consequences.

CHAPTER 9: VARYING CLIMATE CHANGE GOVERNANCE

1 *See, e.g.*, Joseph P. Tomain, "'Our Generation's Sputnik Moment': Regulating Energy Innovation," 31 *Utah Environmental Law Review* 389, 397 (2011). The nature, timing, and scope of those physical changes and how they will interact with one another remain uncertain. Climate change may generate feedback loops which exacerbate physical changes already occurring. *See* Martin Heimann and Markus Reichstein, "Terrestrial Ecosystem Carbon Dynamics and Climate Feedbacks," 451 *Nature* 451 (January 17, 2008); Robin Kundis Craig, "'Stationarity Is Dead'—Long Live Transformation; Five Principles for Climate Change Adaptation Law," 34 *Harvard Environmental Law Review* 9, 15 (2010).

2 Intergovernmental Panel on Climate Change, "Global Warming of 1.5° C: Summary for Policymakers," 9-13 (2018); Intergovernmental Panel on Climate Change, "Climate Change 2014 Synthesis Report: Summary for Policymakers," 6-8 (2014); US Global Change Research Program, "Global Climate Change Impacts in the United States," 9 (Susan J. Hassol et al. eds., 2009).

3 Alejandro E. Camacho, "Adapting Governance to Climate Change: Managing Uncertainty Through a Learning Infrastructure," 59 *Emory Law Journal* 1, 8 n.23 (2009); Dave Huitema et al., "The Governance of Adaptation: Choices, Reasons, and Effects," 21 *Ecology and Society* 37 (2016).

4 Camacho, "Adapting Governance," 8 n.23; Thomas Peterson et al., "Developing a Comprehensive Approach to Climate Change Mitigation Policy in the United States: Integrating Levels of Government and Economic Sectors," 39 *Environmental Law and Policy Annual Review* 10711 (2009).

5 *See generally Climate Engineering and the Law: Regulation and Liability for Solar Radiation Management and Carbon Dioxide Removal* (Michael B. Gerrard and Tracy Hester eds., 2018); Jay Michaelson, "Geoengineering: A Climate Change Manhattan Project," 17 *Stanford Environmental Law Journal* 73 (1998).

6 EPA, "Endangerment and Cause or Contribute Findings for Greenhouse Gases Under Section 202(a) of the Clean Air Act; Final Rule," 74 Fed. Reg. 66496, 66498, 66524–25, 66531–34 (Dec. 15, 2010); Robin Kundis Craig, "A Public Health Perspective on Sea-Level Rise: Starting Points for Climate Change Adaptation," 15 *Widener Law Review* 521, 522 (2010) (coasts and public health); Jody Freeman and Andrew Guzman, "Climate Change and US Interests," 109 *Columbia Law Review* 1531, 1584–86 (2009) (immigration); Alejandro E. Camacho, "Transforming the Means and Ends of Natural Resources Management," 89 *North Carolina Law Review* 1405, 1434–35 (2011) (ecological resources).

7 Camacho, "Adapting Governance," 25–26; Camacho, "Transforming the Means," 1406–9.

8 Camacho, "Transforming the Means," 1414.

9 *See* P.C.D. Milly et al., "Stationarity Is Dead: Whither Water Management?," 319 *Science* 573 (2008); Craig, "Stationarity," 15.

10 *See, e.g.*, Huitema et al. (focusing on decision process but briefly discussing "level choice"); Stefania Munaretto et al., "Integrating Adaptive Governance and Participatory Multicriteria Methods: A Framework for Climate Adaptation Governance," 19 *Ecology and Society* 74 (2014).

11 Sander Meijerink and Sabina Stiller, "What Kind of Leadership Do We Need for Climate Adaptation? A Framework for Analyzing Leadership Objectives, Functions, and Tasks in Climate Change Adaptation," 31 *Environment and Planning: Government & Policy* 240 (2013).

12 *See, e.g.*, Catrien Termeer et al., "Governance Arrangements for Adaptation to Climate Change," in *Oxford Research Encyclopedia, Climate Science* (Hans Van Storch et al. eds., 2016) (exploring policy instrument design in addition to allocation questions).

13 *See, e.g.*, Daniel A. Farber, "Climate Adaptation and Federalism: Mapping the Issues," 1 *San Diego Journal of Climate and Energy Law* 259, 269–74 (2009).

14 *See generally* Lukas Hakelberg, "Governance by Diffusion: Transnational Municipal Networks and the Spread of Local Climate Strategies in Europe," 14 *Global Environmental Politics* 107 (2014); Martinus Vink et al., "The Role of Knowledge and Power in Climate Change Adaptation Governance: A Systematic Literature Review," 18 *Ecology and Society* 46 (2013).

15 *See, e.g.*, Olivia Green et al., "E.U. Water Governance: Striking the Right Balance Between Regulatory Flexibility and Enforcement?," 18 *Ecology and Society* 10 (2013) (describing "multiple overlapping layers of control or coordination"); Anja Bauer, Judith Feichtinger and Reinhard Steurer, "The Governance of Climate Change Adaptation in 10 OECD Countries: Challenges and Approaches," 14 *Journal of Environmental Policy and Planning* 279, 282, 289 (2012).

16 We do not seek here to systematically evaluate appropriate governance frameworks for all agencies likely connected to climate governance. Many agencies that routinely take actions that compound the threats to natural resources or make adaptation more difficult have not yet been the focus of legislative attention. FEMA, for example, operates the federal flood insurance program, which influences the extent to which floodplains can be developed. *See* National Flood Insurance Program, https://www.fema.gov (accessed December 18, 2018); Matthew D. Zinn, "Adapting to Climate Change: Environmental Law in a Warmer World," 34 *Ecology Law Quarterly* 61, 72 (2007). Policymakers should consider integrating such agencies into adaptation governance frameworks.

17 Robert Glicksman, "Climate Change Adaptation: A Collective Action Perspective on Federalism Considerations," 40 *Environmental Law* 1159 (2010); Alice Kaswan, "Climate Adaption and Land Use Governance: The Vertical Axis," 39 *Columbia Journal of Environmental Law* 390 (2014); Thomas M. Gremillion, "Setting the Foundation: Climate Change Adaptation at the Local Level," 41 *Environmental Law* 1221 (2011); Robin Kundis Craig, "Adapting Water Federalism to Climate

Change Impacts: Energy Policy, Food Security, and the Allocation of Water Resources," 5 *Environmental and Energy Law and Policy Journal* 183, 211 (2010).

18 *See, e.g.,* Jan Corfee-Morlot et al., "Multilevel Risk Governance and Urban Adaptation Policy," 104 *Climatic Change* 169 (2011); Jan Corfee-Morlot et al., "Cities, Climate Change and Multilevel Governance" (OECD Environment Working Paper No. 14, 2009); Brian C. Chaffin, Hannah Gosnell and Barbara A. Cosens, "A Decade of Adaptive Governance Scholarship: Synthesis and Future Directions," 19 *Ecology and Society* 56 (2016); Arun Agarwal et al., "Climate Policy Processes, Local Institutions, and Adaptation Actions: Mechanisms of Translation and Influence," 3 *Wiley Interdisciplinary Reviews: Climate Change* 565, 566 (2012).

19 J.B. Ruhl, "Climate Change Adaptation and the Structural Transformation of Environmental Law," 40 *Environmental Law* 363, 423 (2009).

20 Camacho, "Adapting Governance," 7, 12.

21 Numerous reports conclude that US governmental institutions remain ill-equipped for adaptation. *See, e.g.,* US Gov't Accountability Off., GAO-18-206, "DOD Needs to Better Incorporate Adaptation into Planning and Collaboration at Overseas Installations" (2017); US Gov't Accountability Off., GAO-17-720, "Information on Potential Economic Effects Could Help Guide Federal Efforts to Reduce Fiscal Exposure" (2017) (documenting the federal government's failure to undertake strategic government-wide planning to manage climate risks); US Global Change Research Program, Climate Change Adaptation in United States Federal Natural Resource Science and Management Agencies: A Synthesis, at vi (Jessica E. Halofsky et al. eds, 2015).

22 The US Congress has yet to establish a regulatory program directed at climate adaptation. Many agency activities continue to ignore adaptation, while most that address it are limited to research and information gathering. Some managers still routinely develop strategies based on historically normal conditions, despite recognition that they are likely inapposite under projected climate change scenarios. *See* Alejandro E. Camacho and Robert L. Glicksman, "Legal Adaptive Capacity: How Program Goals and Processes Shape Federal Land Adaptation to Climate Change," 87 *University of Colorado Law Review* 711, 743–806 (2016) (describing range of federal adaptation activities); Alejandro E. Camacho, "Managing ecosystem effects in an era of rapid climate change," in *Climate Change Law* 555, 558–63 (Daniel Farber and Marjan Peeters eds., 2016) (describing adaptation challenge of US and European Union natural resources laws' focus on historical fidelity and nonintervention).

23 *E.g.,* Termeer et al., 12.

24 *See, e.g.,* Corfee-Morlot et al., "Cities," 30–31; Ruhl, "Climate Change Adaptation," 423.

25 *See, e.g.,* Bauer, 6; Eric Massey and Dave Huitema, "The Emergence of Climate Change Adaptation as a Policy Field: The Case of England," 13 *Regional Environmental Change* 341, 348–50 (2013).

26 *See, e.g.,* Gremillion, 1235; Ruhl, "Climate Change Adaptation," 423; Corfee-Morlot et al., "Cities," 30–31.

27 *See* Ruhl, "Climate Change Adaptation," 423; Glicksman, "Climate Change Adaptation," 1190–92.

28 *See* Alejandro E. Camacho, "Assisted Migration: Redefining Nature and Natural Resource Law Under Climate Change," 27 *Yale Journal on Regulation* 171, 208–10 (2010); Camacho, "Transforming the Means," 1424 n.85.

29 Glicksman, "Climate Change Adaptation," 1175; Ruhl, "Climate Change Adaptation," 423. Accordingly, some scholars support a central federal role in addressing spillover effects, providing public goods, and promoting long-term planning. Huitema et al.; Kaswan, 393–95; Blake Hudson, "Fail-Safe Federalism and Climate Change: The Case of US and Canadian Forest Policy," 44 *Connecticut Law Review* 925, 936 (2012).

30 ACES, H.R. 2454, 111th Cong. (2009). *See also* Alejandro E. Camacho, "Managing Adaptation: Developing a Learning Infrastructure in the United States' Federal System," *in Implementing Adaptation Strategies by Legal, Economic, and Planning of Instruments on Climate Change* 44 (Eike Albrecht et al. eds., 2014).

31 *Id.* § 476.

32 *Id.* § 478.

33 *Id.* § 479.

34 *Id.* § 478(d).

35 *Id.* §§ 452, 451, 477.

36 *See* Camacho, "Adapting Governance," 27–28; Glicksman, "Climate Change Adaptation," 1175, 1193.

37 *Cf.* Gremillion, 1248–49; Kaswan, 437. As illustrated by these sources, however, analysts often do not distinguish clearly among the different information-related functions.

38 ACES § 479. Though states would have done much of the natural resource adaptation work, the big-picture decision making would have been primarily federal.

39 *See, e.g.,* Farber, 465; Kaswan, 437, 461; Gremillion, 1248–49.

40 *See, e.g.,* J.B. Ruhl, "General Design Principles for Resilience and Adaptive Capacity in Legal Systems–with Applications to Climate Change Adaptation," 89 *North Carolina Law Review* 1373 (2011); James E. Parker-Flynn, "The Intersection of Mitigation and Adaptation in Climate Law and Policy," *Environs Environmental Law and Policy Journal* 1 (2014).

41 *See, e.g.,* Huitema et al.; Farber, 465.

42 *See, e.g.,* Ruhl, "Climate Change Adaptation," 363. Similarly, social scientific literature discusses assigning authority to the appropriate "fit," "bioregional scale," or "problemsheds." Chaffin et al.

43 *See* Jody Freeman and Jim Rossi, "Agency Coordination in Shared Regulatory Space," 125 *Harvard Law Review* 1131, 1135, 1146 (2012); Kirsten H. Engel, "Harnessing the Benefits of Dynamic Federalism in Environmental Law," 56 *Emory Law Journal* 159, 165 (2006).

44 *See* Camacho, "Assisted Migration," 208–9.

45 Chaffin et al.; Jared Snyder and Jonathan Binder, "The Changing Climate of Cooperative Federalism: The Dynamic Role of the States in a National Strategy to Combat Climate Change," 27 *UCLA Journal of Environmental Law and Policy* 231, 252 (2009).

46 *See, e.g.,* Camacho, "Adapting Governance," 67; Ruhl, "Climate Change Adaptation," 363; Ruhl, "General Design Principles"; Robert L. Glicksman, "From Cooperative to Inoperative Federalism: The Perverse Mutation of Environmental Law and Policy," 41 *Wake Forest Law Review* 719, 801 (2006).

47 Ruhl, "Climate Change Adaptation," 425.

48 *See* Engel, 179.

49 *See* Camacho, "Adapting Governance," 19.

50 *Cf.* Kaswan, 439 (discussing minimizing inefficiency by granting authority to federal and sub-national actors over different functions).

51 *See, e.g.,* William W. Buzbee, "Recognizing the Regulatory Commons: A Theory of Regulatory Gaps," 89 *Iowa Law Review* 1, 23 (2003).

52 *See* David E. Adelman and Kirsten H. Engel, "Adaptive Environmental Federalism," in *Preemption Choice: The Theory, Law and Reality of Federalism's Core Question* 277, 285 (William W. Buzbee ed., 2009).

53 *See, e.g.*, Kresge Found., Rising to the Challenge Together: A Review and Critical Assessment of the State of the US Climate Adaptation Field (2017), https://kresge.org.

54 White House Council on Environmental Quality, "Progress Report of the Interagency Climate Change Adaptation Task Force: Recommended Actions in Support of a National Climate Change Adaptation Strategy" (October 5, 2010); Ryan Plummer, "Can Adaptive Comanagement Help to Address the Challenges of Climate Change Adaptation?," 18.4 *Ecology & Society* 1 (2013); Kaswan, 437, 461.

55 Global Change Research Act of 1990, 15 U.S.C. § 2921 et seq. (2018); US Climate Change Sci. Program & Subcomm. on Global Change Research, The US Climate Change Science Program: Vision for the Program and Highlights of the Scientific Strategic Plan 29 (2003).

56 White House Council on Environmental Quality, "Progress Report," 20 (October 5, 2010).

57 *See, e.g.*, White House Council on Environmental Quality, "Progress Report," 7–8, 18–19, 50.

58 *See* Camacho, "Adapting Governance," 54.

59 ACES §§ 478, 479.

60 *Id.* §§ 451–52, 477.

61 *Cf.* Termeer et al., 13 ("Policymakers must not try to connect everything to everything.").

62 ACES § 478(d).

63 *See* Joseph A. Siegel, "Collaborative Decision Making on Climate Change in the Federal Government," 27 *Pace Environmental Law Review* 257, 259 (2010);

Robert N. Stavins, "A Meaningful US Cap-and-Trade System to Address Climate Change," 32 *Harvard Environmental Law Review* 293, 371 (2008) (discussing "the global commons nature of climate change").

64 *See* William L. Andreen, "Federal Climate Change Legislation and Preemption," 3 *Environmental and Energy Law and Policy Journal 261, 288* (2008) ("Due to the long atmospheric life of GHGs and the way in which they mix, atmospheric concentrations of GHGs are basically uniform across the earth.").

65 *See generally* J.B. Ruhl, "The Political Economy of Climate Change Winners," 97 *Minnesota Law Review* 206 (2012).

66 *See* Hari M. Osofsky and Hannah J. Wiseman, "Hybrid Energy Governance," 2014 *University of Illinois Law Review* 1, 7 and n.25 (2014); Sandeep Vaheesan, "Preempting Parochialism and Protectionism in Power," 49 *Harvard Journal on Legislation* 87, 133–34 (2012) (referring to "the 'tyranny of small decisions'").

67 Kirsten H. Engel and Barak Y. Orbach, "Micro-Motives and State and Local Climate Change Initiatives," 2 *Harvard Law and Policy Review* 119, 120 (2008).

68 *See* Robert W. Hahn, "Climate Policy: Separating Fact from Fantasy," 33 *Harvard Environmental Law Review* 557, 588 (2009) (discussing the free-rider problem); R.T. Pierrehumbert, "Climate Change: A Catastrophe in Slow Motion," 6 *Chicago Journal of International Law* 573, 580 (2006).

69 *See* Michael Mehling and Endre Tvinnereim, "Carbon Pricing and the 1.5 C Target: Near-Term Decarbonisation and the Importance of an Instrument Mix," 12 *Carbon and Climate Law Review* 50, 53 (2018); William W. Buzbee, "Asymmetrical Regulation: Risk, Preemption, and the Floor/Ceiling Distinction," 82 *New York University Law Review* 1547, 1594–95 (2007).

70 David E. Adelman and Kirsten H. Engel, "Adaptive Federalism: The Case against Reallocating Environmental Regulatory Authority," 92 *Minnesota Law Review* 1796, 1848 (2008).

71 United Nations Framework Convention on Climate Change, May 9, 1992, 1771 U.N.T.S. 107.

72 Kyoto Protocol to the United Nations Framework Convention on Climate Change, Dec. 10, 1997, 2303 U.N.T.S. 148.

73 Paris Agreement, Dec. 12, 2015, 55 I.L.M. 743, Art. 4(2)-(3).

74 Steven Ferrey, "Torquing the Levers of International Power," 15 *Washington University Global Studies Law Review* 255, 262 (2016).

75 Daniel A. Farber and Cinnamon P. Carlarne, *Climate Change Law* 16 (2018).

76 549 U.S. 497 (2007).

77 EPA, "Endangerment and Cause."

78 *E.g.*, "Light-Duty Vehicle Greenhouse Gas Emission Standards and Corporate Average Fuel Economy Standards; Final Rule," 75 Fed. Reg. 25324 (May 7, 2010).

79 42 U.S.C. §§ 7507, 7543(b) (2012).

80 Utility Air Regulatory Group v. EPA, 573 U.S. 302 (2014).

81 42 U.S.C. § 7411(a)-(b).

82 "Carbon Pollution Emission Guidelines for Existing Stationary Sources: Electric Utility Generating Units; Final Rule," 80 Fed. Reg. 64662 (Oct. 23, 2015).

83 Basin Elec. Power Corp. v. EPA, 136 S. Ct. 998 (2016). *See* Lisa Heinzerling, "The Supreme Court's Clean-Power Power Grab," 28 *Georgetown Environmental Law Review* 425 (2016).

84 "Standards of Performance for Greenhouse Gas Emissions from New, Modi-fied, and Reconstructed Stationary Sources; Electric Utility Generating Units," 80 Fed. Reg. 64510 (Oct. 23, 2015), "Petition for Reconsideration Denied," 81 Fed. Reg. 27442 (May 6, 2016). In 2018, EPA proposed a substantial weakening of those standards based on its contention that carbon capture and storage is not an adequately demonstrated technology. "Review of Standards of Performance for Greenhouse Gas Emissions from New, Modified, and Reconstructed Stationary Sources: Electricity Generating Units," 83 Fed. Reg. 65424 (Dec. 20, 2018).

85 "Repeal of Carbon Pollution Emission Guidelines for Existing Stationary Sources: Electric Utility Generating Units; Proposed Rule," 82 Fed. Reg. 48035 (Oct. 16, 2017). EPA's proposed replacement for the CPP is the so-called Affordable Clean Energy Rule. "Emission Guidelines for Greenhouse Gas Emissions from Existing Electric Utility Generating Units; Revisions to Emission Guideline Implementing Regulations; Revisions to New Source Review Program; Proposed Rule," 83 Fed. Reg. 44476 (Aug. 31, 2018).

86 "The Safer Affordable Fuel-Efficient (SAFE) Vehicles Rule for Model Years 2021–2026 Passenger Cars and Light Trucks; Notice of Proposed Rulemaking," 83 Fed. Reg. 42986, 42999, 43232-53 (Aug. 24, 2018).

87 42 U.S.C. § 7416 (2012).

88 *See, e.g.*, California Global Warming Solutions Act of 2006, Cal. Health & Safety Code §§ 38500–38599.

89 *See* Michael R. Bloomberg and Jerry Brown, "The US Is Tackling Global Warm-ing, Even if Trump Isn't," *New York Times*, November 14, 2017, www.nytimes.com.

90 Bonnie A. Malloy, "Testing Cooperative Federalism: Water Quality Standards Under the Clean Water Act," 6 *Environmental and Energy Law & Policy Journal* 63, 86–87 (2011).

91 ACES would have created a potentially valuable centralized information genera-tion and dissemination registry to support GHG emission reporting and reduc-tion policies by states and Indian tribes. ACES § 713(a)(1).

92 *See* Coral Davenport, "How Much Has 'Climate Change' Been Scrubbed from Federal Websites? A Lot," *New York Times*, January 10, 2018, www.nytimes.com.

93 *See, e.g.*, US Global Change Research Program, "The National Global Change Research Plan 2012–2021: A Triennial Update" (2017), www.globalchange.gov.

94 *See* Adelman and Engel, "Adaptive Federalism," 1831; *see also* Michael C. Dorf and Charles F. Sabel, "A Constitution of Democratic Experimentalism," 98 *Columbia Law Review* 267, 338 (1998); Charles F. Sabel and William H. Simon, "Minimalism and Ex-perimentalism in the Administrative State," 100 *Georgetown Law Journal* 53, 55 (2011).

95 *See* Alejandro E. Camacho and Robert L. Glicksman, "Functional Government in 3-D: A Framework for Evaluating Allocations of Government Authority," 51 *Harvard Journal on Legislation* 19, 84 (2014).

96 *See* Robert L. Glicksman and Richard E. Levy, "A Collective Action Perspective on Ceiling Preemption by Federal Environmental Regulation: The Case of Global Climate Change," 102 *Northwestern University Law Review* 579, 616–17 (2008).

97 William W. Buzbee, "Contextual Environmental Federalism," 14 *New York University Environmental Law Journal* 108, 126 (2005).

98 *See* Glicksman and Levy, 624–26.

99 *See* Paul S. Weiland, "Federal and State Preemption of Environmental Law: A Critical Analysis," 24 *Harvard Environmental Law Review* 237, 245–46 (2000) (using California's regulation of motor vehicle emissions as an example of decentralized innovation).

100 *See* CPP, 80 Fed. Reg. at 64664; William W. Buzbee, "Federalism-Facilitated Regulatory Innovation and Regression in a Time of Environmental Legislative Gridlock," 28 *Georgetown Environmental Law Review* 451, 470 (2016).

101 *See* Nathan Richardson, "Trading Unmoored: The Uncertain Legal Foundation for Emissions Trading Under § 111 of the Clean Air Act," 120 *Penn State Law Review* 181, 203 (2015).

102 *See* Glicksman and Levy, 596–97.

103 *See* City of Chicago, Climate Change, http://climatechange.cityofchicago.org/ (accessed December 18, 2018).

104 *See* John Cushman, "State of the Union: Trump Glorifies Coal, Shuts Eyes to Climate Risks," *Inside Climate News*, January 21, 2018, https://insideclimatenews.org (noting influence of the fossil fuel industry on federal climate policies).

105 42 U.S.C. § 7416 (2012).

106 As explained in chap. 4, § C.3, the economies of scale and uniformity advantages of centralized regulation of mobile-source emissions may outweigh the perceived diversity, experimentation, expertise, and democratic accountability benefits of decentralized governance.

107 S. Rep. No. 89-192, at 6 (1965).

108 *See* Glicksman and Levy, 632 and n.255.

109 *See* National Research Council of the National Academies, State and Federal Standards for Mobile-Source Emissions 264–65 (2006); Ann Carlson, "Iterative Federalism and Climate Change," 103 *Northwestern University Law Review* 1097, 1134 (2009).

110 The Trump administration's 2018 proposal to essentially preclude California from regulating GHGs from motor vehicles would undercut the experimentation benefits of decentralized standard setting that Congress endorsed when it adopted the preemption waiver provision in the CAA. Trump's EPA contends that a waiver for GHG emissions is barred by the Energy Policy and Conservation Act, which prohibits the states from adopting or enforcing an average fuel economy standard if a federal standard has been adopted pursuant to that Act. 49 U.S.C. § 32919 (2012).

At least one court has apparently rejected EPA's preemption analysis. *See* Cent. Valley Chrysler-Jeep, Inc. v. Goldstene, 529 F. Supp. 2d 1151, 1176 (E.D. Cal. 2007) ("State laws that are granted waiver of preemption under the Clean Air Act that have the effect of requiring even substantial increases in average fuel economy performance are not preempted [by § 32919] where the required increase in fuel economy is incidental to the state law's purpose of assuring protection of public health and welfare under the Clean Air Act."). If EPA's preemption analysis is correct, however, Congress should consider restoring California's regulatory authority (for example, by amending the Energy Policy and Conservation Act to conform to the CAA's allocation of standard-setting authority between EPA and the states for other automotive air pollutants).

111 "The Safer Affordable Fuel-Efficient (SAFE) Vehicles Rule," 83 Fed. Reg. 42986.

112 "Montreal Protocol on Substances that Deplete the Ozone Layer," Sept. 16, 1987, S. Treaty Doc. No. 100-10, 1522 U.N.T.S. 29.

113 US Dep't of State, "The Montreal Protocol on Substances that Deplete the Ozone Layer," www.state.gov/.

114 42 U.S.C. § 7671m(b) (2012); *see* also Steven J. Shimberg, "Stratospheric Ozone and Climate Protection: Domestic Legislation and the International Process," 21 *Environmental Law* 2175, 2176 (1991).

115 42 U.S.C. §§ 7671–7671q.

116 *Id.* § 7671m(a); see Nancy D. Adams, Comment, "Title VI of the 1990 Clean Air Act Amendments and State and Local Initiatives to Reverse the Stratospheric Ozone Crisis: An Analysis of Preemption," 19 *Boston College Environmental Affairs Law Review* 173, 193 (1991).

117 *Cf.* William W. Buzbee, "State Greenhouse Gas Regulation, Federal Climate Change Legislation, and the Preemption Sword," 1 *San Diego Journal of Climate and Energy Law* 23, 61 (2009) (discussing the relationship between the adequacy of international treaty commitments and the need to preserve state authority to foster climate mitigation).

118 42 U.S.C. § 7410.

119 Under the CAA, EPA reviews state plans and may adopt plans for delinquent states. *Id.* § 7410(c). Federal and state agencies are thus engaged in overlapping and hierarchically coordinated planning and implementation.

120 *Cf. id.* §§ 7411(a)-(b) (standards of performance for new stationary sources), 7413(a)(3) (exclusive authority to enforce those standards in EPA).

121 *Id.* § 7413(a)(1), (b)(1).

122 As noted in chap. 4, § C.3, some state officials have explained that overlapping enforcement authority helps promote compliance by providing them a federal "bad cop" foil when federal officials are committed to vigorous enforcement.

123 42 U.S.C. § 7410(c), (k) (2012).

124 *Id.* § 7413(a)(1).

125 33 U.S.C. § 1319(a)(1) (2012).

126 *See, e.g.*, United States v. Murphy Oil USA, Inc., 143 F. Supp. 3d 1054, 1092 (W.D. Wis. 2001); United States v. LTV Steel Co., Inc., 118 F. Supp. 2d 827 (N.D. Ohio 2000).

127 *See* United States v. Power Eng'g Co., 303 F.3d 1232 (10th Cir. 2002) (construing the Resource Conservation and Recovery Act); *but cf.* Harmon Indus., Inc. v. Browner, 191 F.3d 894 (8th Cir. 1999) (precluding federal over-filing on res judicata grounds).

128 *See, e.g.*, Elizabeth Shogren, "8 ways EPA Administrator Scott Pruitt suppressed science," *Grist*, July 7, 2018, https.//grist.org.

129 It is even possible that states seek to claim the mantle of policy leadership on climate mitigation efforts, much as California has done, through the exercise of independent standard setting. *See* Barry G. Rabe, Michael Román and Arthus Dobelis, "State Competition as a Source Driving Climate Change Mitigation," 14 *New York University Environmental Law Journal* 1, 8 (2005); William W. Buzbee, "Clean Air Act Dynamism and Disappointments: Lessons for Climate Legislation to Prompt Innovation and Discourage Inertia," 32 *Washington University Journal of Law and Policy* 33, 68 (2010).

130 The duplicative administrative costs that coordination has the potential to reduce seem underwhelming (especially if functions such as dissemination of information relevant to standard setting are coordinated, as described above) in comparison to the potential costs of responding to the climate-related damage that inadequate regulation is likely to produce. Concomitant independent state functions to effectuate state standards (including planning, permitting and enforcement) may also be appropriate.

131 42 U.S.C. § 7543(b) (2012) provides the standards governing California's waiver requests.

132 The Royal Society, Geoengineering the Climate: Science, Governance, and Uncertainty 11 (2009), https://royalsociety.org. Some prefer the term "climate remediation." Bipartisan Policy Center, "Geoengineering: A National Strategic Plan for Research on the Potential Effectiveness, Feasibility, and Consequences of Climate Remediation Technologies," 3, 6 (2011), http://bipartisanpolicy.org.

133 William C.G. Burns, "Human Rights Dimensions of Bioenergy with Carbon Capture and Storage: A Framework for Climate Justice in the Realm of Geoengineering," in *Climate Justice: Case Studies in Global and Regional Governance Challenges* 149, 154 (Randall Abate ed., 2016); Ulrike Niemier and Simone Tilmes, "Sulfur injections for a cooler planet," 357 *Science* 246 (July 21, 2017), DOI: 10.1126/science.aan331.

134 *See* Kelsi Bracmort and Richard K. Lattanazio, Congressional Research Serv. Report R41371, Governance and Technology Policy 16–19 (2013); Tracy Hester and Michael B. Gerrard, "Going Negative: The Next Horizon in Climate Engineering Law," 32 *Natural Resources and Environment* 4 (Spring 2018).

135 *See* Eli Kintisch, "Technologies," in *Climate Engineering and the Law: Regulation and Liability for Solar Radiation Management and Carbon Dioxide Removal* 41–51 (Michael B. Gerrard and Tracy Hester eds., 2018); Burns, 151; Albert C. Lin, "Carbon Dioxide Removal After Paris," 45 *Ecology Law Quarterly* 533 (2018).

136 Michael B. Gerrard, "Introduction and Overview," in Gerrard and Hester, 22 (noting limited exceptions).

137 Lin, "Carbon Dioxide Removal," 543–44; Burns, 156.

138 Gerrard, 3, 11; Christopher H. Trisos et al., "Potentially dangerous consequences for biodiversity of solar geoengineering implementation and termination," 2 *Nature Ecology and Evolution* 475 (2018).

139 Gerrard, 3; Burns, 156.

140 *See* John Virgoe, "International governance of a possible geoengineering intervention to combat climate change," 95 *Climatic Change* 103, 107 (2009), doi. org/10.1007/s10584-008-9523-9 (describing geoengineering as "local action with a global impact").

141 Gerrard, 2, 4; David W. Keith et al., "Research in Global Sun Block Needed Now," 463 *Nature* 426, 427 (January 28, 2010); David G. Victor, "On the Regulation of Geoengineering," 24 *Oxford Review of Economic Policy* 322, 328 (2008).

142 Albert C. Lin, "Does Geoengineering Present a Moral Hazard?," 40 *Ecology Law Quarterly* 673, 697 (2013).

143 *See* Lin, "Carbon Dioxide Removal," 546; Ralph S. Bodle et al., Options and Proposals for the International Governance of Geoengineering 18 (2014), www .ecologic.eu/.

144 *See* Hester and Gerrard, 3.

145 *See, e.g.,* Carol Rose, *Commons, Cognition, and Climate Change,* 32 *Journal of Land Use and Environmental Law* 296, 324 (2017) (referring to "the sci-fi-like character of geoengineering").

146 *See* Hester and Gerrard, 3–5; Rose, 325; David A. Dana, "Geoengineering and the Question of Weakened Resolve," https://papers.ssrn.com (accessed December 18, 2018).

147 *See* Joshua B. Horton, Andrew Parker and David Keith, "Liability for Solar Geo-engineering: Historical Precedents, Contemporary Innovations, and Governance Possibilities," 22 *New York University Environmental Law Journal* 225, 225 (2015); Albert C. Lin, "The Missing Pieces of Geoengineering Research Governance," 100 *Minnesota Law Review* 2509, 2513 (2016).

148 Jane C.S. Long, "A Prognosis, and Perhaps a Plan, for Geoengineering Governance," 3 *Carbon and Climate Law Review* 177, 177 (2013).

149 *See* Solar Radiation Management Governance Initiative, "Solar Radiation Management: The Governance of Research" (2010), https://royalsociety.org.

150 Dr. David R. Morrow, Forum for Climate Engineering Assessment, International Governance of Climate Engineering 3 (June 2017), ceassessment.org. For discussion of the applicability of existing international law mechanisms to geoengineering, *see* John G. Shepherd et al., The Royal Society, Geoengineering the Climate: Science, Governance, and Uncertainty 40 (2009), https://royalso ciety.org.

151 Analysts seem mostly to focus on the centralization dimension. *See, e.g.,* Morrow, 10–11.

152 *But cf.* Bracmort and Lattanazio, 22 (recognizing the need to create flexible regulatory frameworks for an array of functions); Lin, "The Missing Pieces," 2516 (discussing potential overlap of research and deployment).

153 Kirsten H. Engel, "State Environmental Standard-Setting: Is There a 'Race' and Is It 'To the Bottom'?," 48 *Hastings Law Journal* 271, 285 (1997).

154 For a list of possible standards to constrain geoengineering, see Karen N. Scott, "International Law in the Anthropocene: Responding to the Geoengineering Challenge," 34 *Michigan Journal of International Law* 309 (2013).

155 *See* Robert L. Olson, Geoengineering for Decision Makers: Science and Technology 39 (2011), www.wilsoncenter.org; Long, 181.

156 *See* chap. 9, § C.3 (discussing whether overlapping horizontal or vertical authority is justified).

157 Bodle et al., 139.

158 The tradeoffs may cut in different directions for CDR techniques, whose impacts are more likely to be regional or local in character, so that a more decentralized international structure for both standard setting and implementation may be appropriate. *See* Bracmort and Lattanazio, 22; Bodle et al., 126.

159 Bipartisan Policy Center, "Geoengineering," 13, 20; *cf.* Geoengineering Research Evaluation Act of 2017, H.R. 4586, 115th Cong. (2017) (bill that would have required the National Academy of Sciences to establish a research agenda and report on geoengineering governance mechanisms).

160 Lin, "The Missing Pieces," 2562.

161 Indeed, not everyone agrees that government intervention in or oversight of geoengineering research is required at all. *See* Lin, "The Missing Pieces," 2532.

162 *See* chap. 9, § C.4 (exploring the advantages of coordinated research authorization).

163 *See* Victor, 325. Decentralizing research authority may increase the risk of leaks of information about geoengineering technologies to those with incentives to deploy them in ways that may harm some or all ecosystems. There seems to be broad consensus, however, that geoengineering research should be transparent. *See, e.g.*, Michael Burger and Justin Gundlach, "Research Governance," in Gerrard and Hester, 269, 283.

164 *See* Solar Radiation Management Governance Initiative, "Solar Radiation Management," 29; Bodle et al., 141 (finding the distinction between research and deployment to be "increasingly artificial").

165 *See* Victor, 330.

166 Olson, 44.

167 Universally applicable minimum standards mitigate the risk, discussed in chap. 2, that overlapping authority will create a "regulatory commons" producing under-regulation.

168 *See* 42 U.S.C. §§ 2011(b), 2021(k) (2012).

169 *Cf.* H 6011, The Geoengineering Act of 2017 (proposed Rhode Island statute to create a licensing program for geoengineering activities).

170 *See* Vishal Garg, Note, "Engineering a Solution to Climate Change: Suggestions for an International Treaty Regime Governing Geoengineering," 2014 *University of Illinois Journal of Technology and Policy* 197 (2014).

171 *See* Long, 180; Bipartisan Policy Center, "Geoengineering," 29; David W. Keith, "Geoengineering and the Climate: History and Prospect," 25 *Annual Review of Energy and Environment* 245, 275–76 (2000).

172 Rose, 323–24.

173 *See* Adam D.K. Abelkop and Jonathan C. Carlson, "Reining in Phaeton's Chariot: Principles for the Governance of Geoengineering," 21 *Transnational Law and Contemporary Problems* 763, 797–98 (2013); Morrow, 8.

174 Wilfried Rickels et al., Large-Scale Intentional Interventions into the Climate System? Assessing the Climate Engineering Debate 116 (2011).

175 *See* John H. Barton, "Nuclear Power: The Politics of Security and Development," 25 *Stanford Law Review* 622, 635 (1973).

176 Bodle et al., 128.

177 *See* Lin, "The Missing Pieces," 2534–35; Bipartisan Policy Center, "Geoengineering," 14; Shepherd et al., xii, 52.

178 *See* Nat'l Research Council, "Climate Intervention: Reflecting Sunlight to Cool Earth," 122 (2015), www.alachuacounty.us; Bodle et al., 128, 140.

179 *See* Rickels et al., 106.

180 1996 "Protocol to the Convention on the Prevention of Marine Pollution by Dumping of Wastes and Other Matter," November 7, 1996, 36 I.L.M. 7.

181 Bracmort and Lattanazio, 33–34.

182 "Montreal Protocol on Substances that Deplete the Ozone Layer," Sept. 16, 1987, S. Treaty Doc. No. 100-10, 1522 U.N.T.S. 29.

183 *Id.* Art. 2.

184 Bodle et al., 21.

185 *See* Garg, 216.

186 Concurrent SRM experiments may make it difficult to isolate the impacts each has. Bodle et al., 128.

187 *Cf.* Evan R. Seamone, "The Precautionary Principle as the Law of Planetary Defense: Achieving the Mandate to Defend the Earth against Asteroid and Comet Impacts While There Is Still Time," 17 *Georgetown International Environmental Law Review* 1, 10 (2004) (calling for similar coordination to protect against astronomical objects colliding with the Earth).

188 *See* Barbara A. Finamore, "Regulating Hazardous and Mixed Waste at Department of Energy Nuclear Weapons Facilities: Reversing Decades of Environmental Neglect," 9 *Harvard Environmental Law Review* 83, 90 (1985).

189 *See* Chelsea Harvey, "Can we refreeze the Artic? Scientists are beginning to ask," *ClimateWire*, March 6, 2018; Virgoe, 114.

190 For discussion of the weaknesses of international enforcement mechanisms, however, see Bracmort and Lattanazio, 29.

191 *See* Bodle et al., 140.
192 Keith et al., "Research in Global Sun Block," 427; Lin, "Carbon Dioxide Removal," 567–69 (recommending a cautious "learning-by-doing approach"); Gerrard, 24 (supporting "an evolutionary approach").

CONCLUSION

1 Donald P. Moynihan, "Protection versus Flexibility: The Civil Service Reform Act, Competing Administrative Doctrines, and the Roots of Contemporary Public Management Debate," 16 *Journal of Policy History* 1, 3 (2004).
2 Woodrow Wilson, "The Study of Administration," 2 *Political Science Quarterly* 197 (1887). *See also* Owen E. Hughes, *Public Management and Administration: An Introduction* 26–27 (3d ed. 2003) (describing integration of scientific management theory into public administration).
3 Exec. Office of the President, "Delivering Government Solutions in the 21ˢᵗ Century: Reform Plan and Reorganization Recommendations," 118 (2018).
4 Alejandro E. Camacho, "Can Regulation Evolve? Lessons from a Study in Maladaptive Management," 55 *UCLA Law Review* 293 (2007); Alejandro E. Camacho, "Adapting Governance to Climate Change: Managing Uncertainty Through a Learning Infrastructure," 59 *Emory Law Journal* 1 (2009).
5 Exec. Office of the President, 118.
6 *See* Camacho, "Adapting Governance," 49–50 (discussing a "learning infrastructure" that emphasized "regular monitoring, assessment, and adjustment of all agency decision making as judged against stated statutory goals"); *cf.* Raymond H. Brescia, "Understanding Institutions: A Multi-Dimensional Approach," 17 *University of New Hampshire Law Review* (2018) (noting that institutional characteristics and needs "can shift, change, and transform over time").
7 *See* Camacho, "Adapting Governance," 23–25 (discussing procedural strategies such as adaptive management for climate change adaptation); Robin Kundis Craig and J.B. Ruhl, "Designing Administrative Law for Adaptive Management," 67 *Vanderbilt Law Review* 1 (2014); David L. Markell, "Emerging Legal and Institutional Responses to Sea-Level Rise in Florida and Beyond," 42 *Columbia Journal of Environmental Law* 1, 3 (2016); Craig Anthony (Tony) Arnold and Lance H. Gunderson, "Adaptive Law and Resilience," 43 *Environmental Law Reporter News and Analysis* 10426 (2013).
8 5 U.S.C. §§ 551–559, 701–706 (2012). *See* Kathryn E. Kovacs, "Superstatute Theory and Administrative Common Law," 90 *Indiana Law Journal* 1207, 1223–37 (2015).
9 *See* Alejandro E. Camacho and Robert L. Glicksman, "Legal Adaptive Capacity: How Program Goals and Processes Shape Federal Land Adaptation to Climate Change," 87 *University of Colorado Law Review* 711, 720–39 (2016) (distinguishing between procedural and substantive legal adaptive capacity).
10 *See* J.B. Ruhl, "General Design Principles for Resilience and Adaptive Capacity in Legal Systems—with Applications to Climate Change Adaptation," 89 *North Carolina Law Review* 1373, 1379 (2010) (discussing the structural and procedural

components of a legal system); Barbara A. Cosens et al., "The role of law in adaptive governance," 22 *Ecology and Society* 30 (2017).

11 *Cf.* Exec. Office of the President, 118 (bemoaning that "building evaluation into program design so that we can learn and improve is currently the exception rather than the rule").

12 *See* William N. Eskridge, Jr. and John Ferejohn, "Super-Statutes," 50 *Duke Law Journal* 1215, 1216 (2000) ("A super-statute is a law or series of laws that (1) seeks to establish a new normative or institutional framework for state policy and (2) over time does 'stick' in the public culture such that (3) the super-statute and its institutional or normative principles have a broad effect on the law—including an effect beyond the four corners of the statute.").

13 *See* Kovacs, 1223–37 (asserting that the APA is a super-statute).

14 US Comm'n on the Organization of the Executive Branch of the Government, "The Hoover Commission on Organization of the Executive Branch of the Government" (1949).

15 Exec. Order No. 13781, "Comprehensive Plan for Reorganizing the Executive Branch," § 1, 82 Fed. Reg. 13959 (Mar. 16, 2017); Exec. Office of the President.

16 Exec. Order No. 13871, § 2(c); Memorandum from Mick Mulvaney for Heads of Executive Departments and Agencies, "Comprehensive Plan for Reforming the Federal Government and Reducing the Federal Civilian Workforce," 1 (April 12, 2017), www.whitehouse.gov.

17 *See* Exec. Office of the President, 13.

18 *See, e.g.,* Exec. Order No. 13781 (requiring the OMB Director, in developing a plan to reorganize the executive branch, to consider "whether some or all of the functions of an agency, a component, or a program are appropriate for the Federal Government or would be better left to State or local governments or to the private sector through free enterprise"); Exec. Office of the President, 17 (identifying devolution of the activities of the federal government as one of the plan's mission alignment imperatives).

19 *Cf.* Cary Coglianese, Heather Kilmartin and Evan Mendelson, "Transparency and Public Participation in the Federal Rulemaking Process: Recommendations for the New Administration," 77 *George Washington Law Review* 924, 961 (2009) (calling for administrative reforms "that facilitate, to the greatest extent possible, empirical evaluation of their impacts").

20 Richard Elmore, "Graduate Education in Public Management: Working the Seams of Government," 6 *Journal of Policy Analysis and Management* 69 (1986) (describing move to teach students "how to make public decisions rigorously and analytically on the basis of systematic quantitative evidence").

21 Exec. Order No. 12866, "Regulatory Planning and Review," § 2(b), 58 Fed. Reg. 51735 (Oct. 4, 1993). As a former OIRA Administrator has put it, "OIRA helps to collect widely dispersed information—information that is held throughout the executive branch and by the public as a whole. OIRA is largely in the business of helping to identify and aggregate views and perspectives of a wide range of

sources both inside and outside the federal government." Cass R. Sunstein, "The Office of Information and Regulatory Affairs: Myths and Realities," 126 *Harvard Law Review* 1838, 1840 (2013).

22 Anthony M. Bertelli and Lawrence E. Lynn, Jr., "A Precept of Managerial Responsibility: Securing Collective Justice in Institutional Reform Litigation," 29 *Fordham Urban Law Journal* 317, 351–52 (2001) ("A merit system shifted the emphasis in public administration from popular representation to neutral competence in the performance of official duties.").

23 *See, e.g.*, Peter L. Strauss and Cass R. Sunstein, "The Role of the President and the OMB in Informal Rulemaking," 38 *Administrative Law Review* 181, 185–86 (1986); Christopher C. DeMuth and Douglas H. Ginsburg, "White House Review of Agency Rulemaking," 99 *Harvard Law Review* 1075, 1081 (1986).

24 *See, e.g.*, Nicholas Bagley and Richard L. Revesz, "Centralized Oversight of the Regulatory State," 106 *Columbia Law Review* 1260, 1262 (2006) (referring to the "profound institutional bias against regulation" reflected in the OIRA review process); Sidney A. Shapiro, "OMB and the Politicization of Risk Assessment," 37 *Environmental Law* 1083 (2007) (criticizing OIRA's politicization of the science used in agency risk assessments); Wendy E. Wagner, "A Place for Agency Expertise: Reconciling Agency Expertise with Presidential Power," 115 *Columbia Law Review* 1001 (2015); *but cf.* Sunstein, 1874–75 ("Federal officials, most of them nonpolitical, know a great deal, and the OIRA process helps to ensure that what they know is incorporated in agency rulemakings.").

25 *See, e.g.*, US Gov't Accountability Office, "Improvements Needed to Monitoring and Evaluation of Rules Development as Well as to the Transparency of OMB Regulatory Reviews," GAO–09–205 (April 2009).

26 So do public policy and public administration professionals. *See, e.g.*, Network of Schools of Public Policy, Affairs, and Administration, "NASPAA Standards: Commission on Peer Review and Accreditation," 2,4 (2014).

27 *See, e.g.*, Yariv Pierce, "Put the Town on Notice: School District Liability and LGBT Bullying Notification Laws," 46 *University of Michigan Journal of Law Reform* 303, 339 (2012) (describing CRS as "an apolitical research agency within the Library of Congress"). Others have concurred with this characterization. *See, e.g.*, Catherine L. Fisk and Deborah C. Malamud, "The NLRB in Administrative Law Exile: Problems with Its Structure and Function and Suggestions for Reform," 58 *Duke Law Journal* 2013, 2081 (2009); Wendy E. Wagner, "Learning from Brownfields," 13 *Journal of Natural Resources and Environmental Law* 217, 241 (1998).

28 2 U.S.C. § 166(d)(5) (2012).

29 CRS describes its mission as "serv[ing] the Congress [. . .] by providing comprehensive and reliable legislative research and analysis that are timely, *objective*, authoritative and confidential." Library of Congress, "History and Mission," www .loc.gov (emphasis added). *See also* Keeffe v. Library of Congress, 777 F.2d 1573, 1580 (D.C. Cir. 1985) (quoting CRS manual stating that legislators and their staffs

"must have confidence that when you assist them, you do so with your knowledge of your field, not from your convictions of 'what ought to be done'").

30 2 U.S.C. § 166(d)(1), (5).

31 US Gov't Accountability Office, "About GAO," www.gao.gov.

32 *Id.*

33 Stephen Breyer, *Breaking the Vicious Circle: Toward Effective Risk Regulation* 59–63 (1993).

34 *See* chap. 3, § D.3, chap. 4, § C.3, chap. 8, § E.2.

35 For example, coordination or centralization may be more appropriate for the distribution of information but less so for information analysis. *See* chap. 7, § D.

36 *Cf.* Judith Resnik, "Accommodations, Discounts, and Displacement: The Variability of Rights as a Norm of Federalism(s)," 17 *Jus Politicum, Revue de droit politique* (2017) (critiquing in the context of federalism attempts to essentialize arguments for allocations of authority based on subject-matter competency, and maintaining that courts serve as mediating mechanisms to accommodate normative conflicts between central governments, subunits, individuals, and organizations); Judith Resnik, "Federalism(s)'s Forms and Norms: Contesting Rights, De-Essentializing Jurisdictional Divides, and Temporizing Accommodations," in *Nomos LV: Federalism and Subsidiarity* (James Fleming ed., 2014).

37 *See, e.g.,* Harvey Brooks, "The Resolution of Technically Intensive Public Policy Disputes," 9 *Science, Technology and Human Values* 39, 46 (Winter 1984) ("Public participation [. . .] confers political legitimacy on the policy choices that are made and secures public acceptance and cooperation in the actual implementation of these choices.").

38 *See, e.g.,* Sidney A. Shapiro and Richard E. Levy, "Heightened Scrutiny of the Fourth Branch: Separation of Powers and the Requirement of Adequate Reasons for Agency Decisions," 1987 *Duke Law Journal* 387.

39 *See, e.g.,* "Report of the Commission on Evidence-Based Policymaking, The Promise of Evidence-Based Policymaking," 1 (2017) (calling for "a future in which rigorous evidence is created efficiently, as a routine part of government operations, and used to construct effective public policy), https://ourpublicservice.org; Glen Staszewski, "Reason-Giving and Accountability," 93 *Minnesota Law Review* 1253 (2009); Mathilde Cohen, "When Judges Have Reasons Not to Give Reasons: A Comparative Law Approach," 72 *Washington and Lee Law Review* 483, 507 (2015) ("Reason-giving also promotes accountability toward the general public [. . .] in a variety of ways, ranging from public debate to legislative action.").

40 *See* Bernard W. Bell, "Legislative History Without Legislative Intent: The Public Justification Approach to Statutory Interpretation," 60 *Ohio State Law Journal* 1, 29–30 (1999).

41 *See* Evan J. Criddle, "When Delegation Begets Domination: Due Process of Administrative Lawmaking," 46 *Georgia Law Review* 117, 134 (2011); Lisa Schultz Bressman, "Accommodation and Equal Liberty," 42 *William and Mary Law Review* 1007, 1037 (2001).

42 NAPSAA, 7.

43 *Cf.* Rena Steinzor and Sidney Shapiro, *The People's Agents and the Battle to Protect the American Public* 54–71 (2010) (documenting how congressional conservatives, in their zeal for shrinking government, have relied on tax and budget cuts to "hollow out" five federal agencies responsible for protecting the public health and safety).

44 *Cf.* David L. Markell and Robert L. Glicksman, "Dynamic Governance in Theory and Application, Part I," 58 *Arizona Law Review* 563, 578 (2016) (arguing that "improved capacity, through advances in technology and otherwise, may create significant opportunities for the government to improve its practices").

45 *See* Thomas M. Nichols, *The Death of Expertise: The Campaign against Established Knowledge and Why it Matters* (2017); Naomi Oreskes and Erik M. Conway, *Merchants of Doubt* (2011).

Treasury Department. *See* Department of the Treasury
Trump, Donald, 3–4
Trump administration, 63–64, 107, 216, 246–47; on California, 324n110; on climate change mitigation, 209; on EPA, 86, 208; Reform Plan, of 2018, 1–4, 55, 58, 234, 253n29; removing website climate change information, 209–10

United Nations Framework Convention on Climate Change (UNFCCC), 206–7
USDA. *See* Department of Agriculture

values tradeoffs, 66–72
Volcker, Paul, 179–80
Volcker Alliance, 181, 186
Volcker rule, 185

Wall Street Reform and Consumer Protection Act. *See* Dodd-Frank Act
water quality standards (WQS), 84
Weisbach, David A., 115–16
Wilmarth, Arthur, 185
Wilson, James Q., 2
Wilson, Woodrow, 234
WQS. *See* water quality standards

ABOUT THE AUTHORS

Alejandro E. Camacho is Professor of Law and Director of the Center for Land, Environment, and Natural Resources at the University of California, Irvine School of Law. He has contributed dozens of articles to leading legal and scientific journals including *Proceedings of the National Academy of Sciences, Yale Journal on Regulation*, and *Harvard Journal on Legislation*.

Robert L. Glicksman is J.B. and Maurice C. Shapiro Professor of Environmental Law at The George Washington University Law School. He is the author of several books on administrative law, environmental law, and natural resources law, and of many articles on these topics that have been published in leading legal journals.